Courts and LGBTQ+ Rights in an Age of Judicial Retrenchment

OXFORD COMPARATIVE CONSTITUTIONALISM

Ex-Ministers as Constitutional Judges

Comparative constitutional law has a long and distinguished history in intellectual thought and in the construction of public law. As political actors and the people who create or modify their constitutional orders, they often wish to learn from the experience and learning of others. This cross-fertilization and mutual interaction has only accelerated with the onset of globalization, which has transformed the world into an interconnected web that facilitates dialogue and linkages across international and regional structures. Oxford Comparative Constitutionalism seeks to publish scholarship of the highest quality in constitutional law that deepens our knowledge of local, national, regional, and global phenomena through the lens of comparative public law.

ALSO PUBLISHED IN THIS SERIES

Ex-Ministers as Constitutional Judges
Mathias Möschel

Redefining Comparative Constitutional Law
Essays for Mark Tushnet
Edited by Madhav Khosla and Vicki C. Jackson

Foreign Relations Federalism
The EU in Comparative Perspective
Thomas Verellen

Responsive Judicial Review
Democracy and Dysfunction in the Modern Age
Rosalind Dixon

Outsourcing Rulemaking Powers
Constitutional Limits and National Safeguards
Cedric Jenart

Abusive Constitutional Borrowing
Legal Globalization and the Subversion of Liberal Democracy
Rosalind Dixon and David Landau

Courts and LGBTQ+ Rights in an Age of Judicial Retrenchment

REHAN ABEYRATNE
Professor and Associate Dean, Western Sydney University School of Law, Australia

OXFORD
UNIVERSITY PRESS

OXFORD
UNIVERSITY PRESS

Great Clarendon Street, Oxford, OX2 6DP,
United Kingdom

Oxford University Press is a department of the University of Oxford.
It furthers the University's objective of excellence in research, scholarship,
and education by publishing worldwide. Oxford is a registered trade mark of
Oxford University Press in the UK and in certain other countries

Published in the United States of America by Oxford University Press
198 Madison Avenue, New York, NY 10016, United States of America

British Library Cataloguing in Publication Data

Data available

Library of Congress Control Number: 2024952137

ISBN 9780198888277

DOI: 10.1093/9780191995040.001.0001

For Eila and Ahana

Acknowledgements

This book project began in 2020 and has benefitted from the generosity of many friends, colleagues, and institutions along the way. The idea for the book emerged from my teaching constitutional law at The Chinese University of Hong Kong (CUHK) and from conversations with students and colleagues in Hong Kong on the resilience of LGBTQ+ rights. I thank the many interlocutors who shaped my early thinking on these issues, including Ngoc Son Bui, Surabhi Chopra, Stuart Hargreaves, David Law, Mara Malagodi, Ryan Mitchell, Chris Roberts, Samuli Seppänen, Marco Wan, and Po Jen Yap. I also thank the CUHK law faculty's research committee, led by then-Associate Dean (now Dean) Xi Chao for supporting the initial research for this project through the GRF Proposal Early Submission Incentive Scheme.

The book received strong early support from Richard Albert and Robert Schütze, coeditors of the Oxford University Press Series on Comparative Constitutionalism. I am grateful to them for believing in this project and for their support throughout.

At OUP, I thank Brian Stone for shepherding my proposal through the review process and Charlotte Kershaw for all the editorial help. I also appreciate the constructive feedback I received from peer reviewers.

I benefited from workshops at CUHK, the Hebrew University of Jerusalem, the UNSW Gilbert + Tobin Centre of Public Law, and the International Society of Public Law (ICON-S) Annual Conference. Special thanks to colleagues who kindly invited me to present my work at these fora including Margit Cohn, Rosalind Dixon, and Asif Hameed. And thanks also to participants at these events for their valuable feedback.

I am deeply grateful to colleagues who read and provided feedback on various parts of the manuscript including Gautam Bhatia, Melissa Crouch, Erin Delaney, Rosalind Dixon, Stuart Hargreaves, Surbhi Karwa, Kelley Loper, Mara Malagodi, Douglas McDonald-Norman, Stefano Osella, Iddo Porat, Jemimah Roberts, Theunis Roux, and Po Jen Yap.

I was blessed with excellent research assistants to whom I am indebted for their hard work at various stages of the project: Shamik Datta, Samantha Lloyd, and Tang Tsz Fei Faye.

I moved to Australia in 2023 and spent the final year writing this book at Western Sydney University (WSU) School of Law. I am grateful to Dean Catherine Renshaw and my colleagues at WSU for their warmth and support that enabled me to complete this project.

Parts of Chapter 4 draw from my prior works, including *Enforcing Socioeconomic Rights in Neoliberal India*, 29 MINN. J. INT'L L. 1 (2020) and *South Asia, in* CAMBRIDGE HANDBOOK OF COMPARATIVE LAW (Mathias Siems & Po Jen Yap eds., 2024). Parts of Chapter 5 also build on previous works, including *More Structure, More Deference: Proportionality in Hong Kong, in* PROPORTIONALITY IN ASIA (Po Jen Yap ed., 2020) and *Judicial Review in Hong Kong, in* ROUTLEDGE HANDBOOK OF CONSTITUTIONAL LAW IN GREATER CHINA (Ngoc Son Bui, Stuart Hargreaves, & Ryan Mitchell eds., 2023).

Finally, a word for my family who have kept me sane throughout this long journey. My parents were always encouraging and provided helpful suggestions on the cover design. My children, Eila and Ahana, bring me endless joy and make this all worthwhile. Finally, my better half, Anna, was the first person to whom I pitched the project and the last person to read each draft. This book would not exist without her support and guidance.

Contents

List of Abbreviations xv

1. Introduction 1
2. Theoretical Framework and Methodology 9
3. LGBTQ+ Rights, Culture Wars, and Polarization in the United States 27
4. LGBTQ+ Rights Amid Institutional Crises and Rising Ethnonationalism in India 99
5. LGBTQ+ Rights, Economic Freedom, and the Remaining Fragments of Liberal Constitutionalism in Hong Kong 171
6. Conclusion 233

Selected Bibliography 243
Index 259

Detailed Contents

List of Abbreviations xv

1. Introduction 1
 I. Setting the Scene 1
 II. Structure of the Book 4

2. Theoretical Framework and Methodology 9
 I. Background 9
 II. Scholarly Contribution 15
 III. Case Selection and Methodology 22
 IV. Scope and Limitations 25

3. LGBTQ+ Rights, Culture Wars, and Polarization in the United States 27
 I. Introduction 27
  A. Background 27
  B. Chapter Overview 31
 II. The Gradual Recognition of LGBTQ+ Rights (1986–2015) 33
  A. The Rise of Federal Judicial Supremacy 33
  B. LGBTQ+ Rights—The Early Years 36
  C. *Bowers* and the Advent of "Cultural War" 38
  D. A Divided Legal and Cultural Landscape 40
  E. Toward Legalization and Same-Sex Marriage 42
 III. LGBTQ+ Rights in the Context of Two Culture Wars 49
  A. From *Bowers* to *Lawrence* 49
  B. The Judicial, Scholarly, and Political Divide 51
  C. A Shift in Engagement with Foreign Materials 56
  D. Originalism's Triumph 59
  E. Winning One Culture War and Losing Another 61
  F. *Obergefell's* Exceptionalism 63
 IV. Polarization, Trump, and the Makings of Partisan Supreme Court 65
  A. The Rise of Political Polarization 66
  B. Judicial Polarization 69
  C. A Partisan Supreme Court 72
  D. Institutional and Reputational Self-Preservation 76
 V. LGBTQ+ Rights in the Second Roberts Court (2018–23) 81
  A. Expanding Federal Statutory Protection for LGBTQ+ Persons 83
  B. Privileging the First Amendment 85
  C. Incrementally Broadening Exemptions 91

VI. Conclusion: *Institutional Self-Preservation v. Partisan Decision-Making* 96

4. LGBTQ+ Rights Amid Institutional Crises and Rising Ethnonationalism in India 99
I. Introduction 99
A. Background 99
B. Chapter Overview 101
II. LGBTQ+ Rights in an Era of Transition (2001–14) 104
A. Neoliberalism and the Overflowing Docket 104
B. Oscillating Between Judicial Poles 108
III. The Shift in Indian Constitutionalism under Modi (2014–19) 117
A. A New Political, Social, and Economic Order 117
B. Caution in the SCI's Constitutional Jurisprudence 120
1. Money Bills and Ordinances 120
2. Fundamental Rights 122
IV. Privacy and the Decriminalization of Same-Sex Relations 126
A. The Constitutional Right to Privacy 128
B. Reading Down Section 377 130
V. An Institution in Crisis and a Shift on LGBTQ+ Rights (2019–23) 135
A. Institutional Strife at the SCI 136
1. Master of Roster 136
2. Judicial Appointments 138
B. Undue Influence on the SCI 141
C. Transgender Rights under Modi 144
1. Subverting the *NALSA* Judgment 144
2. The Transgender Rights Act 2019 147
D. The Elusive Promise of Same-Sex Marriage 150
1. The Politics of Same-Sex Marriage 150
2. The *Supriyo* Judgment 154
3. Echoes of *Koushal* 161
VI. Conclusion: Institutional and Reputational Self-Preservation 164

5. LGBTQ+ Rights, Economic Freedom, and the Remaining Fragments of Liberal Constitutionalism in Hong Kong 171
I. Introduction 171
A. Background 171
B. Chapter Overview 174
II. Constitutional Adjudication under "One Country, Two Systems" (1997–2019) 176
A. The Sino-British Joint Declaration and the Basic Law 176
B. Judicial Deference to the NPCSC 179
C. Judicial Deference to the HKSAR Government 182
III. Developing a Progressive LGBTQ+ Rights Jurisprudence (2006–19) 187
A. Same-Sex Conduct and "Intense" Scrutiny 188
B. Status Discrimination Cases 191

IV. From Hybrid to Authoritarian (2019–21) 197
A. The National Security Law 198
B. Electoral Changes 201
V. LGBTQ+ Rights in Authoritarian Hong Kong 203
A. Changing Official Gender Markers 204
B. Housing and Estate Benefits for Same-Sex Couples 207
C. Same-Sex Unions 211
D. Moving Toward Judicial Self-Preservation 214
E. The Government's Fine Line on Judicial Independence 222
VI. Conclusion—An Uneasy Truce 226

6. Conclusion 233
I. The Exceptionalism of LGBTQ+ Rights 233
II. From Progressive to Self-Preserving 233
III. The Changing Audiences for LGBTQ+ Rights Judgments 235
IV. Pinkwashing or Necessary Adaptation? 239
V. The Future of LGBTQ+ Rights and Liberal Constitutionalism 241

Selected Bibliography 243
Index 259

Abbreviations

ACLU	American Civil Liberties Union
ALJ	Administrative Law Judge
BJP	Bharatiya Janata Party
BLAG	Bipartisan Legal Advisory Group
BORO	Bill of Rights Ordinance
CA	Constituent Assembly
CAA	Citizenship Amendment Act 2019
CADA	Colorado Anti-Discrimination Act
CCRC	Colorado Civil Rights Commission
CE	Chief Executive
CEDAW	Convention on the Elimination of All Forms of Discrimination Against Women
CFA	Court of Final Appeal
CFI	Court of First Instance
CJI	Chief Justice of India
CSS	Catholic Social Services
DOJ	Department of Justice
DOMA	Defense of Marriage Act
ECHR	European Convention of Human Rights
ECtHR	European Court of Human Rights
FCC	Federal Communications Commission
FMA	Foreign Marriage Act
HA	Hong Kong Housing Authority
HKID	Hong Kong Identity Card
HKSAR	Hong Kong Special Administrative Region
HKU	The University of Hong Kong
HOS	Home Ownership Scheme
ICCPR	International Covenant on Civil and Political Rights
INC	Indian National Congress
IWG	Inter-departmental Working Group
LegCo	Legislative Council
LGBTQ+	Lesbian, Gay, Bisexual, Transgender, and Queer (and other gender and sexual diverse-identified people)
MSM	Men Who Have Sex with Men
NALSA	National Legal Services Authority
NGO	Non-Governmental Organization
NJAC	National Judicial Appointments Commission
NPC	National People's Congress
NPCSC	National People's Congress Standing Committee

NRC	National Register of Citizens
NSL	National Security Law
OCI	Overseas Citizen of India
OCTS	One Country, Two Systems
PIL	Public Interest Litigation
PRC	People's Republic of China
PRH	Public Rental Housing
RSS	Rashtriya Swayamsevak Sangh
SAR	Special Administrative Region
SCI	Supreme Court of India
SLP	Special Leave Petition
SMA	Special Marriage Act
SRS	Sexual Reassignment Surgery

1
Introduction

I. Setting the Scene

Imagine an associate named Sharon at an elite Washington D.C. law firm. She has just been appointed to the firm's fundraising committee. Every year, the committee chooses a non-profit organization to support through the firm's annual fundraiser. The committee is meeting to discuss which organization to select for the upcoming year. Sharon raises her hand. Climate change is the defining issue of our times, she says, and proposes that the firm supports a non-profit organization advocating for a zero-carbon world.

A senior partner intervenes. What a wonderful suggestion, he says. But there's a problem: some of the firm's most valued clients are oil and gas companies. Let's avoid this issue, just to be safe.

No problem, thinks Sharon, and she raises her hand again. How about voting rights? Democracy in the United States is on the brink. The Supreme Court has gutted the Voting Rights Act, permitted partisan gerrymandering, and enabled unlimited political campaign spending. She suggests the firm could support one of many possible non-profits fighting against these regressive developments.

The same partner again raises an objection—the firm represents major Republican Party donors. Let's avoid this issue too, he says, so we don't appear partisan or to be taking political sides.

Another associate then suggests selecting a group that works on lesbian, gay, bisexual, transgender, and queer (LGBTQ+) rights. He names an organization involved in organizing pride events across the United States as the possible benefactor. This is greeted with appreciative nods and smiles across the room, including from Sharon, who, of course, supports LGBTQ+ rights and is glad to have at least one avenue to advance a progressive cause without pushback from her employer.

This fictional exchange is familiar to those in corporate multinational offices around the world. One could imagine a similar scenario playing out in New Delhi, with firms unlikely to sponsor organizations resisting environmentally harmful infrastructure projects or those advocating for fundamental rights in Kashmir. In Hong Kong—the world's most neoliberal polity—any proposal to help poor or vulnerable communities affected by global capitalism would be dead on arrival. And with the recent crackdown on protests and dissenting voices, so would any suggestion to support organizations that promote universal suffrage or liberal political reform.

Courts and LGBTQ+ Rights in an Age of Judicial Retrenchment. Rehan Abeyratne, Oxford University Press.
 DOI: 10.1093/9780191995040.003.0001

I suspect that, as in Washington D.C., a proposal to support LGBTQ+ rights would receive a comparatively warm reception in these corporate venues. The takeaway here is not that LGBTQ+ rights are solely the province of urban elites—to the contrary, queer individuals in less affluent and liberal parts of the world are most in need of legal protection.[1] Rather, it is that LGBTQ+ rights have been enthusiastically adopted by liberal elites to signal that they endorse cosmopolitan values like equality and human dignity, while incurring little by way of political and economic costs in doing so.

This book argues that courts in Washington D.C., New Delhi, and Hong Kong are similarly situated to the firm in my hypothetical, with judges in much the same predicament as Sharon and her counterparts. Judges on these courts tend to hail from the economically moderate and socially progressive milieu that dominate law firms. They too want to advance—and want to be seen to advance—the rights of disadvantaged groups but have to be cautious in doing so within the turbulent political environment they now inhabit. LGBTQ+ rights have become a judicial safe space: an arena for judges to showcase their commitment to liberal values and to incrementally advance the rights of historically marginalized groups in societies where, for various reasons, liberal constitutionalism is under threat.

The book explores the evolution of LGBTQ+ jurisprudence in the United States, India, and Hong Kong, focusing on their apex courts—the U.S. Supreme Court, the Supreme Court of India (SCI), and the Hong Kong Court of Final Appeal (CFA), respectively. Judges on these courts, until recently, were educated and socialized into the legal profession during the height of global constitutionalism (1980s to early 2000s). In that era, courts took on a leading role in advancing constitutional rights within their jurisdictions. Apex court judges also saw themselves as engaged in a transnational cosmopolitan project, of which LGBTQ+ rights were an integral part. Progressive judicial decisions decriminalizing same-sex relations and recognizing same-sex marriage after the turn of the millennium—judgments that were unthinkable only a decade earlier—demonstrated the promise of global constitutionalism.

Now, midway through the 2020s, it is clear that those heights are behind us. As reactionary forces took hold in each of these societies, their apex courts, too, turned conservative. While all three courts were earlier praised for their progressive recognition and protection of constitutional rights, they each have overturned, cut back, or avoided ruling on most salient constitutional rights issues in recent years. In doing so, each court—for different reasons and in response to distinct pressures—has enabled the rise of illiberal and authoritarian political forces in its respective jurisdiction.

[1] *See, e.g.*, Supriyo @ Supriya Chakraborty v. Union of India, 2023 I.N.S.C. 920 (India), paras. 85–94 (per Chandrachud, C.J.); MAYA SHARMA, LOVING WOMEN: BEING LESBIAN IN UNPRIVILEGED INDIA (2006).

LGBTQ+ rights, as I will show, are both an exception to and a window into understanding this judicial regression. LGBTQ+ rights are exceptional because they long remained a bastion for progressive, judge-led constitutionalism even as other rights were brought low. However, even LGBTQ+ rights judgments in all three jurisdictions have become less progressive and increasingly cautious in their rulings and remedies. I argue that recent judgments in this area exemplify a broader shift in judicial approach away from global constitutionalism and toward institutional self-preservation. I explain the various factors that courts in each jurisdiction must contend with in these fraught times and use LGBTQ+ judgments to show how these factors are strategically balanced. In doing so, I distinguish between cases where a cautious, strategic approach is warranted and others where it appears to be a pretext toward some other end, such as maintaining the appearance of judicial independence.

* * *

I will be critical of these courts and of some LGBTQ+ rights judgments in the pages that follow. To be clear: the LGBTQ+ rights revolution has been transformative and reaches far beyond courts.[2] It is rightly celebrated. Like Sharon in the opening hypothetical, I am an ally of the LGBTQ+ community and am delighted by the advances, judicial or otherwise, in their societal acceptance and the recognition of their rights. The book seeks to critique what I see as shallow, inconsistent, and sometimes insincere judicial commitments to LGBTQ+ rights and the problematic downstream effects thereof.

At an institutional level, one's view of LGBTQ+ rights adjudication depends on underlying commitments to liberal constitutionalism and to the role of courts therein. I am broadly committed to liberal constitutionalism insofar as it entails a commitment to individual rights, especially those of unpopular and minority groups, within a broadly majoritarian democratic political system. I am not committed to—and in fact, strongly oppose—neoliberal, oligarchic, or other forms of elite-led liberal constitutionalism that became predominant in the United States, India, and Hong Kong by the early twenty-first century. And like most liberal constitutionalists, I worry about the rise of illiberal, authoritarian, and ethnonationalistic political forces that undermine constitutional systems of societies already strained by the depredations of economic elites.

As for the role of courts, I follow Rosalind Dixon in adopting a "sometimes" view of judicial capacity and the promise of judicial review.[3] I am not a proponent

[2] *See LGBT: Moving Toward Equality*, Human Rights Watch (Jan. 23, 2015), https://www.hrw.org/news/2015/01/23/lgbt-moving-towards-equality.

[3] Rosalind Dixon, Responsive Judicial Review: Democracy and Dysfunction in the Modern Age 13–16 (2023).

of the heroic conception of judges,[4] which was ascendant during the height of global constitutionalism, but has led to backlash and fallen into disfavor over the past decade or so.[5] I am also not in the camp of those who see little to no redeeming value in judicial review or wish to abandon the practice altogether.[6] The value of judicial review is contingent, varying not just across legal systems and cultures but also, as I will argue, within individual societies as political dynamics evolve and judges adapt accordingly.

II. Structure of the Book

The book is divided into six chapters. Chapter 2 sets out the historical and institutional context for this research, describes the book's contribution to the existing literature, and explains the case selection and methodology. In short, it lays the foundation for the three case study chapters to follow.

Chapters 3, 4, and 5 present detailed case studies of the United States, India, and Hong Kong, respectively. Each chapter sets out the relevant history and political context, including the judicial role in advancing (and in recent years, retrenching) liberal constitutionalism. Courts in each society have used LGBTQ+ rights strategically to navigate turbulent political waters over the past two decades. These chapters show how those strategic considerations shifted over time as the politics (and, in some cases, the courts too) moved in a conservative direction.

Chapter 3 discusses LGBTQ+ rights at the U.S. Supreme Court in the context of intensifying political and judicial polarization. The Supreme Court's earlier decisions such as *Romer v. Evans* (1996),[7] *Lawrence v. Texas* (2003),[8] *United States v. Windsor* (2013),[9] and *Obergefell v. Hodges* (2015)[10] progressively broadened the scope of LGBTQ+ rights protection as a majority of the American public came around to support anti-discrimination laws for sexual minorities, decriminalizing gay sex, and same-sex marriage. Justice Anthony Kennedy and his liberal colleagues used some of these cases to engage in the project of liberal (and global) constitutionalism even as the Court moved in a conservative direction on many other issues, including voting rights and the right to bear arms.

[4] Ronald Dworkin, Law's Empire (1986).

[5] Ran Hirschl, *Opting out of "Global Constitutionalism,"* 12(1) L. & Ethics Hum. Rts. 1 (2018).

[6] *See, e.g.*, Ryan Doerfler & Samuel Moyn, *The Ghost of John Hart Ely*, 75 Vand. L. Rev. 769 (2022).

[7] Romer v. Evans, 517 U.S. 620 (1996) (striking down a Colorado state constitutional amendment that prevented any local government from recognizing gay, lesbian, and bisexual people as a protected class).

[8] Lawrence v. Texas, 539 U.S. 558 (2003) (ruling that criminal bans on sodomy were unconstitutional).

[9] United States v. Windsor, 133 S. Ct. 2675 (2013) (striking down federal law that defined marriage exclusively as between men and women).

[10] Obergefell v. Hodges, 135 S. Ct. 2584 (2015) (recognizing a constitutional right to same-sex marriage).

The year after *Obergefell* was decided, Donald Trump was elected President. Trump accelerated political polarization with his divisive rhetoric and discriminatory policies. Yet, perhaps the most consequential legacy of his first term was the appointment of three Supreme Court justices. The Supreme Court took a sharp rightward turn with the appointments of Justices Kavanaugh (2018) and Barrett (2020), replacing Justices Kennedy and Ginsburg, respectively. With a 6–3 conservative supermajority, the Court overturned significant precedents on issues like abortion and affirmative action that had protected vulnerable and minority groups.

Yet, today's partisan and polarized Court does not seem interested in overruling *Lawrence* or *Obergefell*.[11] And its LGBTQ+ decisions of this decade—including *Fulton v. City of Philadelphia* (2021),[12] *303 Creative LLC v. Elenis* (2023),[13] and *Bostock v. Clayton County* (2020)[14]—are not uniformly conservative or reactionary. To be sure, they do not seek to advance the projects of liberal or global constitutionalism. These cases serve a different strategic purpose: enabling the conservatives justices to counter the narrative that they have turned the Court into a partisan institution. *Fulton* and *303 Creative LLC* help show that the Court does not disdain precedent or dismiss the concerns of minority groups. The opinions of conservative justices in these cases showed rhetorical sympathy for the LGBTQ+ community, while reaching outcomes that followed precedent and comported with mainstream public opinion. *Bostock*, meanwhile, usefully demonstrates that both in its methods (textualism) and its outcomes (expanded statutory protection for sexual and gender minorities), the current Supreme Court does not invariably rule in line with Republican Party prerogatives.

Chapter 4 explores the Supreme Court of India's LGBTQ+ rights jurisprudence. As the SCI has issued groundbreaking, progressive judgments on these issues, it has also faced a legitimacy crisis along several dimensions. First, the Court's heavy workload and polyvocal structure[15] have resulted in convoluted, non-linear case law that its own justices have trouble following.[16] Second, the SCI has failed to uphold core civil and political rights against multipronged efforts to subvert liberal constitutionalism by the Hindu nationalist Bharatiya Janata Party (BJP) led

[11] *See* Dobbs v. Jackson Women's Health Organization, 142 S. Ct. 2228, 2280 (2022) (emphasizing that *Lawrence* and *Obergefell* are not affected by the Court's ruling that there is no constitutional right to abortion).

[12] Fulton v. City of Philadelphia, 141 S. Ct. 1868 (2021).

[13] 303 Creative LLC v. Elenis, 143 S. Ct. 2298 (2023).

[14] Bostock v. Clayton County, 140 S. Ct. 1731 (2020).

[15] *See* Nick Robinson, *Structure Matters: The Impact of Court Structure on the Indian and U.S. Supreme Courts*, 61 Am. J. Comp. L. 173, 184 (2013); Nick Robinson, *A Quantitative Analysis of the Indian Supreme Court's Workload*, 10 J. Empirical L. Stud. 570 (2013).

[16] Tarunabh Khaitan, Koushal v Naz: *Judges Vote to Recriminalise Homosexuality*, 78 Modern L. Rev. 672, 679 (2015) ("The fragmentation of the Court into small benches deciding thousands of cases every year had led to a situation where even a conscientious judge would find it next to impossible to respect stare decisis").

by Prime Minister Narendra Modi.[17] Third, the SCI's institutional legitimacy and independence have been undermined by the conduct of recent Chief Justices, including credible allegations of sexual harassment and misuse of the "master of roster" power.[18]

The SCI's major judgments on LGBTQ+ rights provide insights into the Court's operation in this fraught constitutional context. Its early cases reflected the workload dimension of the crisis, with inconsistent judgments emerging from fragmented judicial benches. In *Koushal v. Naz Foundation* (2013), the Court upheld Section 377 of the Indian Penal Code, which criminalized homosexual intercourse.[19] A few months later, in *National Legal Services Authority (NALSA) v. Union of India* (2014),[20] the Supreme Court gave constitutional recognition to a third gender and allowed people to self-identify in their chosen gender. In *Puttuswamy v. Union of India* (2017), the SCI recognized a broad right to privacy.[21] Justice Chandrachud's plurality opinion explicitly criticized *Koushal*, saying, "[Its] rationale that prosecution of a few is not an index of violation is flawed and cannot be accepted . . . we disagree with the manner in which *Koushal* has dealt with the privacy-dignity-based claims of LGBTQ+ persons on this aspect."[22] One year later, in *Navtej Johar v. Union of India* (2018), the Court struck down Section 377 to the extent that it banned consensual, private acts among adults.[23]

The latter two judgments, particularly the opinions by then-Justice (later Chief Justice) Chandrachud, engaged extensively with foreign materials and are framed by universal values.[24] But Chandrachud along with a few other justices also appear to be using such language and references strategically. They helped demonstrate that the SCI remained committed to liberal constitutionalism even as it remained silent as the Modi government violated other fundamental rights, and its justices came under suspicion for various abuses of power.

The gap between rhetoric and action is most evident in *Supriyo @ Supriya Chakraborty v. Union of India* (2023). The SCI in that case declined to recognize same-sex marriage or even to require the government to legalize same-sex

[17] *See generally*, Tarunabh Khaitan, *Killing a Constitution with a Thousand Cuts: Executive Aggrandizement and Party-State Fusion in India*, 14 L. & ETHICS HUM. RTS. 49 (2020); Anuj Bhuwania, *The Indian Supreme Court in the Modi Era*, IACL GLOBAL ROUNDTABLE 2020 BLOG (Nov. 23, 2020), https://www.iacl-democracy-2020.org/blog/2016/3/23/blog-post-sample-9wntn-6ye75-hwawc-xx9lz-p6k2z-85m67-nkxzl-m76y3-gmmc6.

[18] APARNA CHANDA ET AL., COURT ON TRIAL: A DATA DRIVEN ACCOUNT OF THE SUPREME COURT OF INDIA 70–85 (2023); GAUTAM BHATIA, UNSEALED COVERS: A DECADE OF THE CONSTITUTION, THE COURTS AND THE STATE 310–29 (2023).

[19] *See* Koushal v. Naz Foundation (2014) 1 S.C.C. 1 (India).

[20] National Legal Services Authority (NALSA) v. Union of India (2014) 5 S.C.C. 438 (India).

[21] Puttuswamy v. Union of India (2017) 10 S.C.C. 1 (India).

[22] *Id.* at para. 128.

[23] Navtej Johar v. Union of India, 2018 I.N.S.C. 790 (India).

[24] *See* Sujit Choudhry, *Postcolonial Proportionality: Johar, Transformative Constitutionalism and Same-Sex Rights in India*, *in* THE GLOBAL SOUTH AND COMPARATIVE CONSTITUTIONAL LAW (Philip Dann et al. eds., 2020).

unions. The four separate judicial opinions therein detail the multiple forms and long history of discrimination endured by the LGBTQ+ community. Chief Justice Chandrachud's minority judgment discusses these issues in the most depth but concluded by recording only "the assurance of the Solicitor General that the Union Government will constitute a Committee . . . for the purpose of defining and elucidating the scope of the entitlements of queer couples who are in unions."[25] As the SCI's independence is increasingly threatened, and its rights-projective jurisprudence is mostly in the rear-view mirror, such non-binding directions provide a means through which to preserve what is left of the institution's (and its justices') reputation.

Chapter 5 examines LGBTQ+ rights judgments in Hong Kong. Liberal constitutionalism in this context is characterized by Hong Kong's radically free market economic system, hybrid political system, and its status as a Special Administrative Region (SAR) of the People's Republic of China. The Court of Final Appeal, more than the U.S. and Indian Supreme Courts, writes for an international audience.[26] It consistently cites foreign materials in fundamental rights judgments, particularly from common law jurisdictions such as Canada and the United Kingdom, as well as from the European Court of Human Rights.[27] However, Hong Kong courts have become increasingly reluctant to rule against the government.[28] The Beijing-imposed National Security Law (NSL) in 2020,[29] followed by major electoral changes in 2021 that converted Hong Kong from a hybrid polity to an authoritarian one,[30] has constrained judicial review to an unprecedented degree.

Yet even in the post-NSL environment, the CFA has advanced transgender rights,[31] provided housing and estate benefits to same-sex couples,[32] and ruled that the government must create a legal framework to recognize same-sex unions.[33] LGBTQ+ rights is, therefore, perhaps the only remaining site for liberal

[25] *Supriyo*, 2023 I.N.S.C. 920 at para. 340 (per Chandrachud, C.J.).

[26] This is driven, in part, by Hong Kong's status as a global financial center and the only common law jurisdiction in Greater China. The United Kingdom entered Hong Kong as a party to the International Covenant on Civil and Political Rights in 1991 largely in response to concerns voiced by the business community that liberal institutions might not survive beyond the handover of sovereignty to China in 1997. *See* Richard Swede, *One Territory—Three Systems? The Hong Kong Bill of Rights*, 44 I.C.L.Q. 358, 359–60 (1995).

[27] *See* David S. Law, *Judicial Comparativism and Judicial Diplomacy*, 163 U. Penn. L. Rev. 927, 986–90 (2015).

[28] *See generally*, Rehan Abeyratne, *More Structure, More Deference: Proportionality in Hong Kong*, *in* Proportionality in Asia 25 (Po Jen Yap ed., 2020). *See also*, Po Jen Yap, Courts and Democracies in Asia 45 (2017) (arguing that courts must weigh fundamental rights protection against the "political sensitivities of the central government in Beijing").

[29] Law of the People's Republic of China on Safeguarding National Security in the Hong Kong Special Administrative Region, GN (E) 72 of 2020 (H.K.).

[30] Basic Law, Annexes I–II (as amended in 2021).

[31] Q v. Commissioner of Registration, [2023] H.K.C.F.A 4 (ruling that transgender persons can have their gender identity officially changed without having to undergo full sexual reassignment surgery).

[32] Infinger v. Hong Kong Housing Authority, [2024] H.K.C.F.A. 29; Ng Hon Lam Edgar v. Secretary for Justice, [2024] H.K.C.F.A. 30.

[33] Sham Tsz Kit v. Secretary for Justice, [2023] H.K.C.F.A. 28.

constitutional judgments and to signal that the Court retains some independence. The CFA has also avoided political blowback by proceeding incrementally and providing remedial flexibility. In *Sham Tsz Kit v. Secretary for Justice* (2023), the Court did not recognize a constitutional right to same-sex marriage and even declined to legalize same-sex unions. It ruled that the government was "in violation of its positive obligation . . . to establish an alternative framework for legal recognition of same-sex partnerships" and directed that the declaration of invalidity be suspended for two years to "afford the Government time to comply with its aforesaid obligation."[34] Given the political environment in Hong Kong today, and the precarious position in which the judiciary finds itself, the judgment and remedy in *Sham Tsz Kit* were likely driven by concerns of institutional self-preservation.

The SAR government, for its part, is keen to attract international capital and businesses back to Hong Kong following years of negative press. Chapter 5 concludes by showing how the CFA's LGBTQ+ rights jurisprudence helps to legitimate both the government's authoritarian and neoliberal policies. High-profile judgments on LGBTQ+ rights usefully counter the narrative of liberal constitutional decline by showing that minority groups can still prevail (and that the government can still lose) on constitutional rights matters. The CFA has also made Hong Kong a more attractive destination for multinational companies and their LGBTQ+ employees to reside and do business by ensuring that same-sex married couples are granted the same privileges that opposite-sex couples receive.

Chapter 6 compares the three case studies along several dimensions. It discusses the courts' respective uses of LGBTQ+ rights, the audiences for whom judges write, and the normative implications of these developments. It concludes that an elite, judge-led approach to these rights, especially one that is most concerned with preserving appearances, is neither desirable nor likely to persist for long. Whether a more substantive and sustainable model of LGBTQ+ rights (and of liberal constitutionalism) emerges remains to be seen. It seems unlikely in the present moment.

[34] *Id.* at para. 260(b).

2

Theoretical Framework and Methodology

I. Background

Consider two major trends in global constitutionalism since the turn of the millennium. Both have been the subject of extensive scholarly and media attention. The first is the populist backlash against liberal (and global) constitutionalism; the second is a concurrent rise of liberal constitutional recognition and protection of LGBTQ+ rights.

In 2005, both the incidence of and confidence in liberal constitutional democracy were at an all-time high.[1] References to an "almost irresistible tide"[2] of constitutional democracy or the "end of history"[3] captured the prevailing, triumphant zeitgeist.[4] Similarly, the comparative constitutional law literature was replete with studies on the "global community of courts,"[5] the rise of "juristocracy,"[6] and the "global expansion of judicial power."[7]

It seemed to many observers that global constitutionalism would rise inexorably. By "global constitutionalism"[8] I mean: (1) the notion of constitutionalism

[1] Yana Gorokhovskaia et al., Freedom in the World 2023: Marking 50 Years in the Struggle for Democracy (2023) (showing seventeen straight years of democratic decline since the high point in 2005); V-Dem Institute, Defiance in the Face of Autocratization (2023) (showing that the "level of democracy enjoyed by the average global citizen in 2022 is down to 1986 levels" and that the percentage of the world's population living in autocratic states was 72 percent in 2022, compared to 46 percent in 2012).

[2] Samuel P. Huntington, The Third Wave: Democratization in the Late Twentieth Century 20 (1991).

[3] Francis Fukuyama, *The End of History?*, 16 Nat'l Interest 3, 4 (Summer 1989) (arguing that the world was not only witnessing the end of the Cold War "but the end of history as such: that is, the end point of mankind's ideological evolution and the universalization of Western liberal democracy as the final form of human government").

[4] Yascha Mounk, The People vs. Democracy: Why Our Freedom Is in Danger & How to Save It 4 (2018) ("Despite vociferous criticism, Fukuyama's core assumption [about the end of history] . . . proved highly influential").

[5] Anne-Marie Slaughter, *A Global Community of Courts*, 44 Harv. Int'l L.J. 191 (2003).

[6] Ran Hirschl, Towards Juristocracy: The Origins and Consequences of the New Constitutionalism (2004).

[7] The Global Expansion of Judicial Power (C. Neal Tate & Torbjorn Vallinder eds., 1997).

[8] For varying accounts of global constitutionalism, *see* Michel Rosenfeld, *Is Global Constitutionalism Meaningful or Desirable?*, 25 Eur. J. Int'l L. 177 (2014); Antje Wiener et al., *Global Constitutionalism: Human Rights, Democracy and the Rule of Law*, 1 Global Constitutionalism 1 (2012); Peer Zumbansen, *Comparative, Global and Transnational Constitutionalism: The Emergence of a Transnational Legal-Pluralist Order*, 1 Global Constitutionalism 16 (2012).

Courts and LGBTQ+ Rights in an Age of Judicial Retrenchment. Rehan Abeyratne, Oxford University Press.
 DOI: 10.1093/9780191995040.003.0002

and constitutional rights as a shared project across political boundaries, based on a theoretical foundation of liberal cosmopolitanism;[9] (2) the cross-jurisdictional interactions of constitutional courts and judges around this notion; and (3) the period in which this concept came to the fore and dominated global politics. That period extended from the end of World War II to the early 2000s. It was characterized by the growth of liberal democracy—first in post-war Europe, then through decolonization in the Global South, and finally with the fall of the Eastern bloc—along with a rise in the number of written constitutions with justiciable bills of rights.[10] Constitutional courts assumed greater importance in this period, combining the solemnity of their depoliticized decision-making process with the gravitas of having the final word on an increasingly wide range of matters.[11]

From the 1980s especially, constitutional judges became central players in the entrenchment and spread of liberal, cosmopolitan values. By the turn of the century, some judges had radically altered their constitutional systems through broad, cosmopolitan readings of fundamental rights provisions.[12] Such judges not only cited each other[13] but also gathered in elite forums to discuss their accomplishments and compare tactics.[14] Scholars in that era saw constitutional courts as essential institutions in the development of liberal democracy[15] and emphasized their role in upholding fundamental rights.[16] Academic work from the 1990s and 2000s advanced notions of a "global community of judges" engaged in "judicial dialogue."[17] During this period, in line with these

[9] Cosmopolitanism has a long history originating in Ancient Greece, where Diogenes the Cynic remarked "I am a citizen of the world" when asked where he was from. Its modern origins can be traced to the work of Immanuel Kant. Cosmopolitanism, as used in this book, is not universalism. The term as conceived here is grounded in domestic law but recognizes the reality of global legal pluralism. It sees liberal constitutional democracies as engaged in a shared project to recognize that conception in law and to learn from the experiences of other jurisdictions. *See generally*, Garrett Wallace Brown, Grounding Cosmopolitanism: From Kant to the Idea of a Cosmopolitan Constitution (2009); Vlad Perju, *Cosmopolitanism and Constitutional Self-Government*, 8 Int'l J. Const. L. 326 (2010).

[10] Samuel Issacharoff, Democracy Unmoored: Populism and the Corruption of Popular Sovereignty 16 (2023).

[11] *See* David S. Law & Mila Versteeg, *The Evolution and Ideology of Global Constitutionalism*, 99 Cal. L. Rev. 1163, 1194–99 (2011); Alec Stone Sweet, *Constitutional Courts*, *in* Oxford Handbook of Comparative Constitutional Law 816 (Michel Rosenfeld & Andras Sajo eds., 2012).

[12] *See generally*, Towering Judges: A Comparative Study of Constitutional Judges (Rehan Abeyratne & Iddo Porat eds., 2021).

[13] *See* Anne-Marie Slaughter, *A Typology of Transjudicial Communication*, 29 U. Richmond L. Rev. 99 (1994).

[14] *See* Iddo Porat, *Towering Judges and Global Constitutionalism*, *in* Towering Judges: A Comparative Study of Constitutional Judges 21 (Rehan Abeyratne & Iddo Porat eds., 2021) (describing the annual Yale Law School Global Constitutional Seminar, which was created to provide "a forum for those judges engaged in the practice of democratic constitutionalism to learn from one another") (internal quotation marks omitted).

[15] *See, e.g.*, Stone Sweet, *supra* note 11.

[16] *See, e.g.*, Charles R. Epp, The Rights Revolution: Lawyers, Activists, and Supreme Courts in Comparative Perspective (1998).

[17] *See, e.g.*, Anne-Marie Slaughter, *A Global Community of Courts*, 44 Harv. Int'l L.J. 191 (2003); Claire L'Heureux-Dubé, *The Importance of Dialogue: Globalization and the International Impact of the Rehnquist Court*, 34 Tulsa L.J. 15 (1998).

developments, Ronald Dworkin's work imbued judges with a heroic, universal morality.[18]

This era now seems like a distant memory.[19] Liberal constitutionalism has been under siege. The United States, India, Hungary, Brazil, Turkey, and Indonesia—to cite a few notable examples—have elected or are currently led by political leaders with illiberal, authoritarian tendencies.[20] Scholars have shown that while many of these countries remain ostensibly democratic,[21] they have suffered from "backsliding,"[22] "erosion,"[23] or "rot."[24] While scholars disagree as to the relative weight of the causal factors for this decline, most point to growing economic inequality,[25] cultural backlash,[26] and the governance failures of neoliberal, technocratic elites[27] to explain crisis in liberal constitutionalism. The severity of the current predicament is also contested.[28] Is this a "crisis"[29] or merely a cyclical "market correction"?[30] Whatever the degree and time horizon, the effects appear to be clear and relatively consistent across jurisdictions. Authoritarians use

[18] *See generally*, RONALD DWORKIN, LAW'S EMPIRE (1986). *See also*, Ken I. Kersch, *The New Legal Transnationalism, the Globalized Judiciary, and the Rule of Law*, 4 WASH. U. GLOBAL STUD. L. REV. 345, 351 (2005) ("The rise of Kantian legal theory in the American legal academy in the 1970s . . . promulgated a picture of a judge (famously dubbed 'Hercules') as the heroic tribune of universal morality").

[19] ISSACHAROFF, *supra* note 10, at 16 (noting that it is "difficult to recapture the optimism that filled the democratic world only a quarter century ago . . . For many observers, myself included, the question of the day was how quickly these newly liberated parts of the world would achieve the levels of prosperity and liberty associated with advanced democratic countries").

[20] TOM GINSBURG & AZIZ Z. HUQ, HOW TO SAVE A CONSTITUTIONAL DEMOCRACY 26–30, 46–47 (2018).

[21] That is, they have not succumbed to military coups or other sudden ends. *See* STEVEN LEVITSKY & DANIEL ZIBLATT, HOW DEMOCRACIES DIE: WHAT HISTORY REVEALS ABOUT OUR FUTURE 3 (2018) (noting that during the Cold War "three out of every four democratic breakdowns" occurred in "spectacular fashion" through coups d'état); Tom Ginsburg et al., *The Coming Demise of Liberal Constitutionalism?*, 85 U. CHI. L. REV. 239, 244 (2019) (discussing the decline in military coups in recent years and the higher incidence of "democratic backsliding").

[22] *See* Nancy Bermeo, *On Democratic Backsliding*, 27 J. DEMOCRACY 5 (2016) (unpacking the concept of backsliding and illustrating its different types); WOJCIECH SADURSKI, POLAND'S CONSTITUTIONAL BREAKDOWN 14–29 (2019) (arguing that developments in Poland were best described as "anti-constitutional populist backsliding").

[23] *See generally*, LEVITSKY & ZIBLATT, *supra* note 21.

[24] *See* SANFORD LEVINSON & JACK M. BALKIN, DEMOCRACY AND DYSFUNCTION 105–38 (2019).

[25] *See* Rosalind Dixon & Julie Suk, *Liberal Constitutionalism and Economic Inequality*, 85 U. CHI. L. REV. 369 (2018); GANESH SITARAMAN, THE CRISIS OF THE MIDDLE-CLASS CONSTITUTION: WHY ECONOMIC INEQUALITY THREATENS OUR REPUBLIC (2017).

[26] *See* PIPPA NORRIS & RONALD INGLEHART, CULTURAL BACKLASH: TRUMP, BREXIT, AND AUTHORITARIAN POPULISM (2019).

[27] *See* MOUNK, *supra* note 4 (noting the growing importance of central banks and how "many institutions that were under the effective control of elected legislators fifty years ago are now ruled by unelected technocrats who are free from political accountability").

[28] Tushnet and Bugarič, for instance, argue that populism *per se* is not necessarily problematic or incompatible with constitutionalism. *See* MARK TUSHNET & BOJAN BUGARIČ, POWER TO THE PEOPLE: CONSTITUTIONALISM IN THE AGE OF POPULISM (2022).

[29] Jack M. Balkin, *Constitutional Crisis and Constitutional Rot*, *in* CONSTITUTIONAL DEMOCRACY IN CRISIS? 13 (Mark A. Graber et al. eds., 2018).

[30] Zachary Elkins, *Is the Sky Falling? Constitutional Crises in Historical Perspective*, *in* CONSTITUTIONAL DEMOCRACY IN CRISIS? 49, 65 (Mark A. Graber et al. eds., 2018).

a similar playbook to undermine liberal constitutional institutions in piecemeal and incremental ways,[31] while often pretending to be ordinary, democratically elected leaders.[32] Executive power has been aggrandized, with fewer checks and balances and less accountability than in prior years.[33] Mechanisms for constitutional change—such as the amendment and replacement procedures—have been used toward "abusive" ends.[34] Some constitutional courts have been captured or sidelined, reducing their authority and potential to exercise meaningful judicial review.[35] More broadly, public and scholarly confidence in courts has declined,[36] and the notion of "global judicial dialogue" seems passé.[37]

Constitutional scholars in recent years have also shown the limitations of courts as democracy-builders,[38] questioned the degree to which they can protect constitutional rights,[39] and cast doubt on the empirical basis of judicial dialogue.[40] Postcolonial critics and others on the political left have pointed out the Western, imperialist connotations of cosmopolitanism, which has been used, among other things, to justify neoliberal globalization and cultural hegemony at the expense of the countries and peoples of the Global South.[41]

Meanwhile, LGBTQ+ rights have been on the opposite trajectory in roughly the same time span. Take same-sex marriage. The Netherlands became the first country to permit same-sex marriage in 2001; today, more than thirty other countries have followed suit.[42] A similar story unfolds on the decriminalization of

[31] LEVITSKY & ZIBLATT, *supra* note 21, at 3; ISSACHAROFF, *supra* note 10, at 10–11 (noting that institutional failure is a common factor across jurisdictions facing democratic challenges). *See also*, LARRY DIAMOND, ILL WINDS: SAVING DEMOCRACY FROM RUSSIAN RAGE, CHINESE AMBITION, AND AMERICAN COMPLACENCY (2019) (describing a "generic playbook" and the "autocrats' twelve-step program").

[32] *See* ROSALIND DIXON & DAVID LANDAU, ABUSIVE CONSTITUTIONAL BORROWING AND THE SUBVERSION OF LIBERAL DEMOCRACY (2021).

[33] *See* Tarunabh Khaitan, *Executive Aggrandizement in Established Democracies: A Crisis of Liberal Democratic Constitutionalism*, 17(1) INT'L J. CONST. L. 342 (2019).

[34] David Landau, *Abusive Constitutionalism*, 47 U.C. DAVIS L. REV. 189 (2013).

[35] *See* Bojan Bugarič & Tom Ginsburg, *The Assault on Postcommunist Courts*, 27 J. DEMOCRACY 69 (2016); David Landau & Rosalind Dixon, *Abusive Judicial Review: Courts Against Democracy*, 53 U.C. DAVIS L. REV. 1313 (2020).

[36] *See, e.g.*, Michael J. Nelson & Alicia Uribe-McGuire, *Confidence in the US Supreme Court Is Declining, and That Puts Its Decisions at Risk from Congress*, LSE US CENTRE BLOG (July 24, 2018), https://blogs.lse.ac.uk/usappblog/2018/07/24/confidence-in-the-us-supreme-court-is-declining-and-that-puts-its-decisions-at-risk-from-congress/.

[37] David S. Law & Wen-Chen Chang, *The Limits of Global Judicial Dialogue*, 86 WASH. L. REV. 523 (2011).

[38] *See, e.g.*, TOM DALY, THE ALCHEMISTS: QUESTIONING OUR FAITH IN COURTS AS DEMOCRACY-BUILDERS (2017).

[39] *See generally*, ADAM S. CHILTON & MILA VERSTEEG, HOW CONSTITUTIONAL RIGHTS MATTER (2020) (concluding on the basis of a broad empirical study that constitutional rights, aside from "organizational rights," are not consistently upheld in the face of government repression).

[40] *See generally*, Law & Chang, *supra* note 37.

[41] *See, e.g.*, AFTER COSMOPOLITANISM (Rosi Braidotti et al. eds., 2012); LAW & GLOBALIZATION FROM BELOW: TOWARDS A COSMOPOLITAN LEGALITY (Bonaventura de Sousa Santos & Cesar A. Rodrigo-Garavito eds., 2009); JAMES TULLY, STRANGE MULTIPLICITY: CONSTITUTIONALISM IN AN AGE OF DIVERSITY (1995).

[42] *Marriage Equality Around the World*, HUMAN RIGHTS CAMPAIGN, https://www.hrc.org/resources/marriage-equality-around-the-world.

homosexuality and same-sex relations. A status and practice that, a generation or two ago, were socially taboo and prohibited in criminal codes around the world are now legal in most countries, across every continent.[43] A newer development is the constitutional recognition of a third-gender or non-binary status, which has been recognized in approximately ten countries over the past decade or so.[44]

These trends appear to be at odds: How can liberal constitutionalism be in decline while the constitutional rights of historically marginalized LGBTQ+ groups are expanding? This book provides a limited answer to this question in the context of judicial decision-making within the apex courts of three societies. It explores how and why the U.S. Supreme Court, the Supreme Court of India (SCI), and the Hong Kong Court of Final Appeal (CFA) have progressively realized LGBTQ+ rights as they have simultaneously regressed on other constitutional rights,[45] and as their societies have witnessed a decline in liberal constitutionalism.[46]

These three apex courts have led the way in advancing LGBTQ+ rights in their respective jurisdictions. But a subtle shift occurred in the judicial approach to these rights as liberal constitutionalism both at home and abroad came under threat. Around the turn of the millennium, when liberal constitutionalism was the dominant paradigm, judges on these courts were engaged—and saw themselves to be engaged—in a transnational liberal project, of which LGBTQ+ rights were an integral part.

Early progressive judgments on LGBTQ+ issues were central to the liberal (and global) constitutional projects. Take the landmark progressive judgments from each jurisdiction. The U.S. Supreme Court struck down a Colorado ban

[43] *See* Jean-François Mignot, *Decriminalizing Homosexuality: A Global Overview Since the 18th Century*, ANNALES DE DÉMOGRAPHIE HISTORIQUE (2022); Holning Lau, *Decriminalizing Same-Sex Activity: Jurisprudence from the Global South*, 22 INT'L J. CONST. L. __ (forthcoming).

[44] *See* Stefano Osella & Ruth Rubio-Marin, *Gender Recognition at the Crossroads: Four Models and the Compass of Comparative Law*, 21(2) INT'L J. CONST. L. 574 (2023).

[45] *See generally*, Michael J. Klarman, *Foreword: The Degradation of American Democracy—and the Court*, 134 HARV. L. REV. 1, 178–231 (2020) (documenting how the Roberts Court has failed to uphold rights related to the democratic process); APARNA CHANDRA ET AL., COURT ON TRIAL: A DATA DRIVEN ACCOUNT OF THE SUPREME COURT OF INDIA (2023) (documenting the multiple institutional crises facing the SCI and the resulting decline in, among other things, its ability to uphold the rights of underprivileged groups); Johannes Chan, *A Storm of Unprecedented Ferocity: The Shrinking Space of the Right to Political Participation, Peaceful Demonstration, and Judicial Independence in Hong Kong*, 16 INT'L J. CONST. L. 373 (2018) (describing rising threats to judicial independence and constitutional rights protection in Hong Kong).

[46] *See generally*, Josh Chafetz & David Pozen, *How Constitutional Norms Break Down*, 65 U.C.L.A. L. REV. 1430 (2018) (analyzing the breakdown of constitutional norms under President Trump alongside the long-running deterioration of other institutions); Tarunabh Khaitan, *Killing a Constitution with a Thousand Cuts: Executive Aggrandizement and Party-State Fusion in India*, 14 L. & ETHICS HUM. RTS. 49 (2020) (cataloguing the means through which the Modi government has imperiled liberal constitutionalism in India since 2014); Cora Chan, *Thirty Years from Tiananmen: China, Hong Kong, and the Ongoing Experiment to Preserve Liberal Values in an Authoritarian State*, 17 INT'L J. CONST. L. 439, 450 (2017) (describing the "emerging authoritarian ascendance" in Hong Kong). *See also*, SARAH REPUCCI & AMY SLIPOWITZ, FREEDOM IN THE WORLD 2021: DEMOCRACY UNDER SIEGE (2021) (measuring democratic decline around the world, including in the United States, India, and Hong Kong).

on laws preventing sexual orientation-based discrimination,[47] a Texas statute criminalizing intimate sexual conduct between same-sex persons,[48] and provisions of the Defense of Marriage Act that denied federal benefits to same-sex married couples.[49] In 2015, the Court held that same-sex couples had a constitutional right to marry, thereby legalizing same-sex marriage throughout the United States.[50] In India, the SCI gave legal recognition to a third gender,[51] and, after establishing an expansive fundamental right to privacy,[52] struck down a law that, *inter alia*, criminalized same-sex intercourse.[53] The Hong Kong CFA, meanwhile, invalidated a ban on public "homosexual buggery,"[54] permitted a postoperative transgender person to marry her male partner,[55] ruled that same-sex spouses of expatriates were entitled to dependent visas,[56] and held that a gay civil servant (lawfully married in New Zealand) was entitled to spousal benefits.[57]

But since 2020, these courts have become increasingly cautious. Their recent LGBTQ+ rights jurisprudence reflects the fragmentary remnants of liberal constitutionalism as reactionary forces took hold in all three societies. Consider, in this context, the post-2020 LGBTQ+ judgments issued by each court. In 2021 and 2023, the U.S. Supreme Court issued judgments that provided limited exemptions to anti-discrimination laws aimed at combatting sexual orientation-based discrimination. These exemptions were based on First Amendment rights to free speech and the free exercise of religion.[58] In 2023, a five-judge bench of the SCI unanimously declined to recognize a constitutional right to marriage in India or to strike down the Special Marriage Act and Foreign Marriage Act that confine marriage to opposite-sex couples.[59] By a 3-2 margin, the Court declined to hold that the state had a positive obligation to provide legal recognition for same-sex unions, and held that same-sex couples were not eligible to adopt children.[60] In 2023, the CFA, like the SCI, declined to extend the constitutional right to marriage to same-sex couples.[61] But the Court held that the Hong Kong government was in violation of its constitutional obligations by failing to create a legal framework that

[47] Romer v. Evans, 517 U.S. 620 (1996).
[48] Lawrence v. Texas, 539 U.S. 558 (2003).
[49] United States v. Windsor, 133 S. Ct. 2675 (2013).
[50] Obergefell v. Hodges, 135 S. Ct. 2584 (2015).
[51] National Legal Services Authority (NALSA) v. Union of India, (2014) 5 S.C.C. 438 (India).
[52] Puttuswamy v. Union of India, (2017) 10 S.C.C. 1 (India).
[53] Navtej Johar v. Union of India, 2018 I.N.S.C. 790 (India).
[54] Secretary of Justice v. Yau Yuk Lung, [2006] 4 H.K.L.R.D. 19 (C.F.A.).
[55] W v. Registrar of Marriages, [2013] 3 H.K.L.R.D. 90 (C.F.A).
[56] QT v. Director of Immigration, [2018] H.K.C.F.A. 28.
[57] Leung Chun Kwong v. Secretary for the Civil Service, [2019] H.K.C.F.A. 19.
[58] Fulton v. City of Philadelphia, 141 S. Ct. 1868 (2021); 303 Creative LLC v. Elenis, 143 S. Ct. 2298 (2023).
[59] Supriyo @ Supriya Chakraborty v. Union of India, 2023 I.N.S.C. 920 (India) (per Chandrachud, C.J.), para. 340 (holding also that transgender people have the right to marry opposite sex partners).
[60] *Id.* (per Bhat, J.), paras. 67, 120.
[61] Sham Tsz Kit v. Secretary for Justice, [2023] H.K.C.F.A. 28, 97.

recognized same-sex unions. The CFA gave the government two years to devise a remedy.[62]

I will show that the judicial approach to LGBTQ+ rights in these courts evolved from one committed to liberal constitutionalism to one concerned primarily with self-preservation. I argue that LGBTQ+ rights have become a means for judges on increasingly constrained and regressive courts to preserve their reputations and, in some cases, to uphold what is left of liberal—and global—constitutionalism.

II. Scholarly Contribution

This book advances scholarship in two main ways. First, it describes how courts have advanced LGBTQ+ rights protection while they have overturned, pared back, or avoided ruling on other rights. In doing so, it contributes to the growing literature on LGBTQ+ rights. Scholarship on the United States, India, and Hong Kong has documented the expansion and limits of LGBTQ+ rights from doctrinal,[63] socio-legal,[64] and historical perspectives.[65] There are wide-ranging, global studies of these developments in the field of comparative politics,[66] as well as comparative legal accounts of the interpretive moves and remedial strategies employed in LGBTQ+ rights judgments.[67] There is also rich, interdisciplinary scholarship that foregrounds the role of social movements and politics, with courts playing a secondary role. In the three selected jurisdictions, where much progressive change has been court-led, scholars have documented how LGBTQ+ activists, in the face of public and political opposition, have channeled their energies to the judiciary.[68]

[62] *Sham Tsz Kit*, [2023] H.K.C.F.A. 31 (Judgment on Relief and Costs).

[63] *See, e.g.*, What *Obergefell v. Hodges* Should Have Said: The Nation's Top Legal Experts Rewrite America's Same-Sex Marriage Decision (Jack M. Balkin ed., 2020); Robert Wintemute, *Lesbian, Gay, Bisexual and Transgender Human Rights in India: From Naz Foundation to Navtej Singh Johar and Beyond*, *in* Human Rights in India 152 (Satvinder Juss ed., 2019); Michael Ramsden & Luke Marsh, *Same-Sex Marriage in Hong Kong: The Case for a Constitutional Right*, 19 Int'l J. Hum. Rts. 90 (2015).

[64] *See, e.g.*, Kenji Yoshino, Speak Now: Marriage Equality on Trial, The Story of Hollingsworth v. Perry (2015); Dipika Jain, Impact of the Naz Foundation Judgment on the Gay, Bisexual and Transgender People in Delhi: An Empirical Investigation (2012); Kelley Loper, *The Courts, Public Opinion and the Rights of Lesbian, Gay, Bisexual and Transgender Persons: A Hong Kong Study*, 20 Australian J. Asian L. 4(1) (2019).

[65] *See, e.g.*, William N. Eskridge Jr. & Christopher R. Riano, Marriage Equality: From Outlaws to In-Laws (2020); Queering India: Same-Sex Love and Eroticism in Indian Culture and Society (Ruth Vanita ed., 2001); Marco Wan, *The Invention of Tradition; Same-Sex Marriage and Its Discontents in Hong Kong*, 18 Int'l J. Comp. L. 539 (2020).

[66] *See, e.g.*, Global Perspectives on Same-Sex Marriage: A Neo-Institutional Approach (Bronwyn Winter et al. eds., 2018); The Lesbian and Gay Movement and the State: Comparative Insights into a Transformed Relationship (David Paternotte & Manon Tremblay eds., 2011).

[67] *See* Stewart Chang, *Made in Taiwan: Alternative Global Models for Marriage Equality*, 34 Conn. J. Int'l L. 143 (2019); Holning Lau, *Comparative Perspectives on Strategic Remedial Delays*, 91 Tul. L. Rev. 259 (2016); Holning Lau, Sexual Orientation and Gender Identity Discrimination (2018).

[68] *See* Arvind Narrain, *Vacillating between Empathy and Contempt: The Indian Judiciary and LGBT Rights*, *in* Envisioning Global LGBT Human Rights: (Neo)colonialism, Neoliberalism,

A related and more U.S.-centric narrative describes the cycle of backlash and counter-backlash that takes place when courts issue progressive judgments on divisive social issues.[69]

This book breaks new ground by exploring LGBTQ+ rights adjudication within the broader context of declining liberal constitutionalism and judicial retrenchment within the three societies. It shows how LGBTQ+ rights adjudication is distinctive—a site of progressive (or at least less regressive) judicial decision-making as courts have retreated elsewhere.

Second, this book provides a framework for understanding this phenomenon. It argues that LGBTQ+ rights decisions enable courts to strategically advance the following objectives: (1) to sustain a progressive rights agenda with minimal political backlash and (2) preserve (what is left of) the judicial reputation for independence and commitment to constitutional rights in response to charges of partisan decision-making, political capture, or government silencing. In fleshing out the first objective, I build on the literature on strategic judicial decision-making, which pays careful attention to the institutional context in which courts operates.[70] The framework assumes that judges anticipate and react to the political preferences of other branches of government.[71] It assumes that the effectiveness of constitutional judicial review is contingent on the compliance (or at least acquiescence) of political actors.[72] A large body of scholarship in the United States has shown that Supreme Court constitutional decisions broadly correlate with public opinion.[73] Thus, Supreme Court justices are influenced not only by political actors but also by broader societal attitudes. The literature on strategic judicial decision-making generally is U.S.-centric,[74] focusing on how judges advance their policy preferences within the two-party political framework in the United States. The influence of public opinion on judicial decision-making

Resistance and Hope (Nancy Nicol et al. eds., 2018); Amy Barrow, *Sexual Orientation, Gender Identity, and Equality in Hong Kong: Rights, Resistance, and Possibilities for Reform*, 15 Asian J. Comp. L. 126 (2020).

[69] *See* Michael Klarman, From the Closet to the Altar: Courts, Backlash, and the Struggle for Same-Sex Marriage (2014); Gerald N. Rosenberg, The Hollow Hope: Can Courts Bring About Social Change? (2d ed. 2008).

[70] Lee Epstein et al., *The Supreme Court as a Strategic National Policymaker*, 50 Emory L.J. 583, 585 (2001).

[71] *Id.* at 585; Lee Epstein & Jack Knight, The Choices Justices Make (1998).

[72] Eric C. Ip, Hybrid Constitutionalism: The Politics of Constitutional Review in the Chinese Special Administrative Regions 21 (2019).

[73] *See generally*, Barry Friedman, The Will of the People: How Public Opinion Has Influenced the Supreme Court and Shaped the Meaning of the Constitution (2009); Lee Epstein & Andrew D. Martin, *Does Public Opinion Influence the Supreme Court? Possibly Yes (But We're Not Sure Why)*, 13(2) J. Const. L. 263 (2010); Robert A. Dahl, *Decision-Making in a Democracy: The Supreme Court as a National Policymaker*, 6 J. Pub. L. 279 (1957).

[74] *See* Theunis Roux, *American Ideas Abroad: Comparative Implications of US Supreme Court Decision-Making Models*, 13 Int'l J. Const. L. 90, 91–92 (2015).

has not received nearly as much scholarly attention in the Indian[75] or Hong Kong[76] contexts. This book broadens the strategic inquiry by looking at apex courts in India and Hong Kong, which must contend with serious threats to their independence and to the survival of liberal constitutionalism in their jurisdictions.

The degree of backlash to progressive LGBTQ+ judgments has been relatively low because these issues are not the primary political concern for reactionary political forces in these three societies. While the Republican Party in the United States, the ruling Bharatiya Janata Party (BJP) in India, and the pro-Beijing government in Hong Kong formally oppose LGBTQ+ rights (or a subset thereof), they have their main sights set elsewhere: on abortion,[77] religious minorities,[78] and "national security,"[79] respectively. In part, this is because public support for LGBTQ+ rights has increased substantially over the past decades, which limited the political fallout from recent, progressive judicial decisions.[80]

Moreover, social movements have been effective in raising the profile of LGBTQ+ issues through political activism and channeling resources toward strategic litigation.[81] Consider the change in social attitudes in Hong Kong over the

[75] While no comprehensive study has been conducted measuring the Indian public's influence on its Supreme Court, recent scholarship has shown that landmark judgments on the basic structure doctrine and public interest litigation sought to align the Court with popular opinion, the dominant regime, or both. *See* Anuj Bhuwania, Courting the People: Public Interest Litigation in Post-Emergency India 21–35 (2017) (arguing at the Supreme Court chose to "imitate [Prime Minister] Indira Gandhi's populism to survive her political onslaught"); Theunis Roux, The Politico-Legal Dynamics of Judicial Review: A Comparative Analysis 147–48 (2018) (arguing that the SCI transformed from a legalist to an instrumentalist Court and that "[b]y positioning itself, first as an institutional voice for the vulnerable and the marginalized, and then as a more middle-class friendly enforcer of good-governance standards, the Court has become the most trusted public institution in India").

[76] In Hong Kong, the literature on strategic judicial decision-making has focused on how courts balance liberal constitutionalism against the prerogatives of the local and PRC governments. Public opinion has been largely neglected. *See, e.g.*, Po Jen Yap & Julius Yam, *Legalism and Strategic Judicial Decision-Making in Hong Kong*, 53 Hong Kong L.J. 207 (2023); Julius Yam, *Approaching the Legitimacy Paradox in Hong Kong: Lessons for Hybrid Regime Courts*, 46 L. & Soc. Inquiry 153 (2021).

[77] Neil S. Siegel, *The Wages of Crying Roe: Some Realism About Dobbs v. Jackson Women's Health Organization*, 2 J. Am. Const. Hist. 101 (2024).

[78] Sumit Ganguly, *Modi's Undeclared Emergency*, 34(3) J. Democracy 144 (2023); Hartosh Singh Bal, *The Broken Compact: Modi's India Replaces Constitutional Values with Those of the RSS*, Caravan (Oct. 20, 2023), https://caravanmagazine.in/politics/modi-india-constitutional-values-rss.

[79] Surabhi Chopra & Eva Pils, *The Hong Kong National Security Law and the Struggle over Rule of Law and Democracy in Hong Kong*, 50(3) Fed. L. Rev. 292 (2022); Cora Chan, *From Legal Pluralism to Dual State: Evolution of the Relationship Between the Chinese and Hong Kong Legal Orders*, 16(1) L. & Ethics Hum. Rts. 99 (2022).

[80] Klarman, *supra* note 69, at 196–203; Holning Lau et al., Support in Hong Kong for Same-Sex Couples' Rights Grew Over Four Years (2013–2017): Over Half of People in Hong Kong Now Support Same-Sex Marriage (2017); Rukmini S., *Homosexuality in India: What the Data Shows*, LiveMint (Sept. 14, 2018), https://www.livemint.com/Politics/nLQiPpl5UICajLDXETJ3EO/Homosexuality-in-India-What-data-shows.html ("Between 1990 and 2014, the share of Indian respondents in the [World Values Survey] WVS who believed 'homosexuality is never justifiable' fell from 89% to 24%—from an overwhelming majority to a clear minority").

[81] *See generally*, Klarman, *supra* note 69; Yeshwant Naik, Homosexuality in the Jurisprudence of the Supreme Court of India (2017); Carole J. Petersen, *Values in Transition: The Development of the Gay and Lesbian Rights Movement in Hong Kong*, 19 Loy. L.A. Int'l & Comp. L. Rev. 337 (1997).

past decade. The Centre for Comparative and Public Law at the University of Hong Kong conducted surveys on public attitudes toward the rights of same-sex couples in 2013 and in 2023. Here is what the authors concluded in 2023:

> Over the past ten years, the share of Hong Kong people who favour protecting gay and lesbian rights has grown markedly. In 2013, only a minority of Hong Kong people surveyed said that same-sex couples should be permitted to marry (38%). Just over half of people expressed agreement with same-sex marriage (50.4%) in 2017. By 2023, 60% agreed with same-sex marriage; only 17% said they did not support same-sex marriage, and 23% were neutral.[82]

Thus, reactionary political movements do not gain as much traction from railing against advances on LGBTQ+ rights as they do on other, more divisive—and therefore politically salient—issues.

In some cases, progressive LGBTQ+ rights judgments are co-opted within reactionary political narratives. For instance, following the SCI's 2014 *NALSA* judgment that constitutionally protected transgender and third-gender status in India, the BJP-led Parliament enacted the Transgender Persons (Protections of Rights) Act in 2019. Critical scholarship has shown how transgender rights have been subsumed within the Hindu nationalist project and have served the BJP's political ends.[83]

Permitting some progressive judicial-making may also work to mask the illiberal, authoritarian turn in these societies. The Hong Kong government, for example, bristles at accusations that the rule of law and judicial independence have been undermined since the passage of a draconian National Security Law (NSL) in 2020.[84] By not publicly condemning or criticizing the CFA's ruling on same-sex marriage—which requires the government to legalize some form of same-sex unions—the government can claim that it remains committed to the rule of law and judicial independence while undermining those principles through other means.

Courts have more room to operate in some areas of the law than others. Challenges to prohibitions on same-sex conduct, for instance, tend to produce categorical judgments in which the impugned provisions were struck down or read down with immediate effect. These provisions, like the Texas sodomy ban, Section 377 of the Indian Penal Code, and Section 188(c) of the Hong Kong Crimes Ordinance, were outdated remnants of premodern or colonial times and had fallen out of public favor. As such, the three apex courts were able to recognize privacy

[82] Holning Lau et al., Support in Hong Kong for Same-sex Couples' Rights Grew Over Ten Years (2013–2023): 60 Percent Now Support Same-Sex Marriage (2023).

[83] Ila Nagar & Debanuj DasGupta, *Transgender Rights and Religiosities in India: NALSA Judgment and Beyond*, 29(3) GLQ: J. Lesbian & Gay Stud. 329 (2023); Jennifer Ung Loh, *Transgender Identity, Sexual versus Gender "Rights" and the Tools of the Indian State*, 119 Feminist Rev. 39 (2018).

[84] *See, e.g.*, *HKSAR Government's Response to 2023 World Justice Project Rule of Law Index*, Gov't of the HKSAR (Oct. 25, 2023), https://www.info.gov.hk/gia/general/202310/25/P2023102500827.htm.

and dignity-based rights of sexual minorities with little backlash. By contrast, in cases in which the positive recognition of same-sex marriage was sought, these courts had to tread more carefully, especially in India and Hong Kong, where government opposition to such recognition was fierce. Both the SCI and CFA declined to recognize the right of same-sex couples to marry. Each court instead left the ultimate solution to their respective legislature.

The second objective—to preserve judicial reputations—focuses less on the incentives of political leaders and more on the interests of courts (and judges therein). Judges write for multiple audiences, both at home and abroad.[85] Domestic audiences include the general public, the bar, and political leaders. Foreign audiences include fellow judges on apex or constitutional courts in other countries and, especially in the case of Hong Kong, intergovernmental organizations and transnational business interests.[86] Judges care about their reputations,[87] especially among the elite circles in which most of them were socialized and that they professionally inhabit.[88] These circles lean progressive on social issues like LGBTQ+ rights,[89] which help to explain why judicial opinions in this area consistently and empathetically reference the discrimination suffered by the affected communities regardless of the outcome in particular cases. These judges also care about maintaining the sociological legitimacy of their respective apex courts,[90] particularly when those courts are accused of toeing the government line or pursuing illiberal ends.

Each apex court faces distinct challenges in maintaining its reputation for structural independence and impartial decision-making. The U.S. Supreme Court in recent years has grown weary of academic and media commentary that depicts the institution as partisan and ruling in line with the prerogatives of the Republican Party. Consider, in this context, the U.S. Supreme Court's judgment in *Bostock v. Clayton County*.[91] The majority opinion, authored by the conservative Justice Gorsuch, ruled that the term "sex" in Title VII of the Civil Rights Act applied to sexual and gender diverse persons, protecting them from discrimination.[92]

[85] *See* LAWRENCE BAUM, JUDGES AND THEIR AUDIENCES: A PERSPECTIVE ON JUDICIAL BEHAVIOR (2006).

[86] Julius Yam & Cora Chan, *Oratory Leadership of Chief Justices in Post-Handover Hong Kong*, INT'L J. CONST. L. (forthcoming).

[87] *See* Nuno Garoupa & Tom Ginsburg, *Judicial Audiences and Reputation: Perspectives from Comparative Law*, 47 COLUM. J. TRANSNAT'L L. 452 (2009).

[88] *See* NEAL DEVINS & LAWRENCE BAUM, THE COMPANY THEY KEEP: HOW PARTISAN DIVISIONS CAME TO THE SUPREME COURT (2019). One especially important audience in the U.S. context is the Federalist Society. *See* AMANDA HOLLIS-BRUSKY, IDEAS WITH CONSEQUENCES: THE FEDERALIST SOCIETY AND THE CONSERVATIVE COUNTERREVOLUTION (2014).

[89] DEVINS & BAUM, *supra* note 88, at 112–14.

[90] Richard H. Fallon Jr., *Legitimacy and the Constitution*, 118 HARV. L. REV. 1789, 1795 (2005) (defining sociological legitimacy as existing in a "strong sense" when the "relevant public" regards the institution as "justified, appropriate or otherwise deserving of support for reasons beyond fear of sanctions or mere hope for personal reward").

[91] Bostock v. Clayton County, 140 S. Ct. 1731, 1754 (2020).

[92] *Id.*

The judgment provides a useful counterpoint to the partisan narrative, signaling that the Court remains independent despite controversial recent appointments that have shifted constitutional case law in other areas strongly toward the political right.

In India and Hong Kong, the apex courts do not face a legitimacy crisis borne out of partisan judicial decision-making. Rather, they face grave threats to their institutional independence. The SCI's reputation has suffered over the past decade from multiple scandals, from corruption to sexual harassment, that have plagued its justices.[93] These internal crises, combined with the Modi government's strategy to control judicial appointments and provide post-retirement opportunities for SCI justices, have left the Court institutionally weak and largely silent in the face of major constitutional rights violations.[94] Though the Court did not evade the same-sex marriage issue—as it has with respect to many other important constitutional matters[95]—its judgment in *Supriyo* was poorly reasoned, inconsistent with precedent, and ultimately at odds with its own rhetoric recognizing the discrimination faced by same-sex couples and India's LGBTQ+ communities more broadly.[96]

In Hong Kong, meanwhile, the CFA saw its constitutional jurisdiction shrink with the passage of the NSL in 2020. The CFA's personnel has not markedly changed like the U.S. Supreme Court, nor has it faced the internal crises of the SCI. Rather, the environment in which the CFA operates has changed significantly. The reputational challenge for the CFA is to show that it can still function independently in this new, illiberal era. Progressive LGBTQ+ rights judgments issued after the passage of the NSL help protect the Court's reputation.[97] Lower profile judgments recognized the rights of transgender persons to change their gender identity without undergoing full sexual reassignment surgery,[98] and permitted same-sex couples to live in public housing as a family unit.[99] The landmark post-NSL judgment in *Sham Tsz Kit* held that by failing to provide legal recognition to same-sex couples, the Hong Kong government was in violation of its positive obligations under Article 14 of the Bill of Rights Ordinance.[100] The CFA suspended its declaration of invalidity for two years to allow the government to establish a legal framework to recognize same-sex unions.

[93] Gautam Bhatia, Unsealed Covers: A Decade of the Constitution, the Courts, and the State (2023), Part III.

[94] Rehan Abeyratne & Surbhi Karwa, *The Institutional Failings of India's Chief Justice in the Age of Modi*, Int'l J. Const. L. (forthcoming).

[95] Bhatia, *supra* note 93, at 301–09, 423–25.

[96] Kartik Kalra, *The Supreme Court's Marriage Equality Judgment—I: On the Right to Marry and a Case of Abstention Through Delegitimisation*, Indian Const. L. & Phil. Blog (Oct. 21, 2023), https://indconlawphil.wordpress.com/2023/10/21/the-supreme-courts-marriage-equality-judgment-i-on-the-right-to-marry-and-a-case-of-abstention-through-delegitimisation-guest-post/.

[97] *See* Yam, *supra* note 76.

[98] Q v. Commissioner of Registration, [2023] H.K.C.F.A 4.

[99] Infinger v. Hong Kong Housing Authority, [2024] H.K.C.F.A. 29.

[100] *Sham Tsz Kit*, [2023] H.K.C.F.A. 28.

Amidst this variance among cases and across jurisdictions, two broad patterns emerge. The first is that courts have gradually shifted from a positive to a defensive posture in LGBTQ+ rights judgments. Earlier cases, like *Lawrence*, *Navtej Johar*, and *W v. Registrar of Marriages* had a strong cosmopolitan valence: They expanded the sphere of LGBTQ+ rights and fit squarely within the paradigm of global constitutionalism. Later cases, like *Fulton*, *Supriyo*, and *Sham Tsz Kit*, are more circumspect and self-preservationist in nature. They advanced the law on LGBTQ+ rights incrementally (if at all) and not always in a progressive direction.

The second pattern is that, despite the change in substance, the idealistic language of global constitutionalism remains largely in place. This reveals the continuing hegemony of that discourse despite the illiberal turn in these societies. It also demonstrates how courts have used LGBTQ+ rights decisions to display a rhetorical commitment to liberal constitutional values even as their judgments may fall short of, or even undermine, those ideals.

In *Fulton*, for instance, Chief Justice Roberts' opinion for the Court ruled that City of Philadelphia could not stop referring children to a Catholic foster care agency on the grounds that the agency would not certify same-sex couples for adoption. Excluding the agency on that basis, the Court held, violated its right to the free exercise of religion.[101] The Court's three liberal justices joined the opinion, which followed a line of precedent that had prioritized the First Amendment rights to free expression and religious freedom over the rights of LGBTQ+ persons.[102] Roberts made clear in *Fulton* that he recognized the importance of "equal treatment" and that "gay persons and gay couples cannot be treated as social outcasts or as inferior in dignity or worth," even as the Court ruled against those interests and against same-sex couples.[103]

In *Supriyo*, Justice Ravindra Bhat's principal judgment on behalf of himself and Justice Kohli (and endorsed in full by Justice Narsimha) ruled not only against the recognition of same-sex marriage but also that the SCI could not require the government to provide legal recognition to same-sex unions or to enable same-sex couples to adopt children. Still, the judgment made clear that the "felt indignities of persons belonging to the LGBTQIA+ community need no proof" and that "the court is alive to the feelings of being left out, experienced by the queer community."[104] This language creates the impression, as Saptarshi Mandal put it, that "the judgment bears ample evidence of the judges' empathy for the petitioners," which should not be dismissed as "mere platitudes."[105] Perhaps. But it also serves

[101] *Fulton*, 141 S. Ct. at 1882.

[102] Boy Scouts of America v. Dale, 530 U.S. 640 (2000); Masterpiece Cakeshop, Ltd. v. Colo. Civil Rights Comm'n, 138 S. Ct. 1719 (2018).

[103] *Fulton*, 141 S. Ct. at 1882 (citing *Masterpiece Cakeshop*, 138 S. Ct. at 1727).

[104] *Supriyo*, 2023 I.N.S.C. 920 at paras. 112, 149 (per Bhat, J.).

[105] Saptarshi Mandal, *The Supreme Court's Marriage Equality Verdict*, 43 Econ. & Pol. Wkly. 8, 8–9 (Oct. 28, 2023).

a reputational purpose for judges to show fidelity to liberal values while their judgments substantively undermine those values.

By focusing on judicial decision-making in these increasingly challenging political and institutional contexts, the book aims to enrich our understanding of how courts have responded to these challenges across the three jurisdictions and to draw comparative insights from their strategic use of LGBTQ+ rights jurisprudence.

III. Case Selection and Methodology

The three jurisdictions selected for this study—the United States, India, and Hong Kong—are sufficiently similar across significant institutional and political dimensions to enable meaningful comparative analysis. Yet, they represent distinct regions, cultures, and threats to liberal constitutionalism, which adds richness and complexity to the analysis. The book therefore adopts a methodology that Ran Hirschl calls "concept formation through multiple description."[106] This approach seeks to generate "analytical frameworks for thinking critically about constitutional norms and practices . . . [by focusing] on a single practice . . . as carried out or encountered by different jurisdictions."[107] Within the broader discipline of comparative law, this methodology falls within the mainstream "functional" approach, which identifies legal rules that perform a similar function across case studies and compares how those rules operate or fulfill that role in each context.[108]

In the period under study (roughly 2000–2023), these jurisdictions share three important institutional and political characteristics: (1) common law legal systems, (2) courts empowered with strong-form judicial review, and (3) a threshold-level commitment to liberal constitutionalism. There is no necessary relationship among these factors. For one thing, judicial review exists and serves useful functions in non-liberal states.[109] For another, liberal constitutional states like New Zealand may only exercise weak-form judicial review[110] or, like France

[106] RAN HIRSCHL, COMPARATIVE MATTERS: THE RENAISSANCE OF COMPARATIVE CONSTITUTIONAL LAW 238 (2014).

[107] *Id.*; Ran Hirschl, *The Question of Case Selection in Comparative Constitutional Law*, 53 AM. J. COMP. L. 125, 129 (2005).

[108] *See* KONRAD ZWEIGERT & HEIN KÖTZ, INTRODUCTION TO COMPARATIVE LAW 34–35 (Tony Weir trans., 3d ed. 1998) ("The basic methodological principle of all comparative law is that of functionality . . . in law the only things which are comparable are those which fulfil the same function"); MATHIAS SIEMS, COMPARATIVE LAW 32 (3d ed. 2022) ("The main advantage of the functional method is that it provides the necessary link between the different rules that legal systems employ. Thus, the shared purpose of these rules is the common denominator . . . which allows comparability of these legal systems").

[109] Tamir Moustafa & Tom Ginsburg, *Introduction: The Functions of Courts in Authoritarian Politics*, *in* RULE BY LAW: THE POLITICS OF COURTS IN AUTHORITARIAN REGIMES 1 (Tom Ginsburg & Tamir Moustafa eds., 2012).

[110] *See* MARK TUSHNET, WEAK COURTS, STRONG RIGHTS: JUDICIAL REVIEW AND SOCIAL WELFARE RIGHTS IN COMPARATIVE CONSTITUTIONAL LAW (2009).

prior to 2010, may only permit judicial review of legislation in the abstract.[111] But, as I will explain, each of these characteristics is essential for this study.

First, all three jurisdictions have common law legal systems. Though common law and civil law jurisdictions have largely converged in their exercise of constitutional judicial review,[112] there remain important differences between them that are pertinent here. In the three apex courts examined herein, judicial opinions are usually authored by a single judge, whose judicial philosophy and methods can be gleaned through a careful reading of their judgments. There is also—at least formally—a reliance on precedent and adherence to *stare decisis*. This enables comparative doctrinal analysis among the three jurisdictions that would not be possible otherwise. For instance, opinions are unsigned in many civil law jurisdictions. This is the case in Taiwan, where the Constitutional Court's judgments, including its landmark decision on same-sex marriage, are not attributed to specific judges.[113]

Second, the three judiciaries, including apex courts, have the power of strong-form judicial review and a range of remedial tools at their disposal. They are empowered to strike down laws that are constitutionally suspect. But, though they have this great power, these courts need not—and often do not—exercise it to the full extent. In some cases, they elect to read down impugned provisions, to employ creative remedies like suspended declarations of invalidity, or to evade matters altogether (due to the discretionary nature of their jurisdiction). This wide range of review and remedial options is on display in the LGBTQ+ rights jurisprudence of the United States, India, and Hong Kong. Partly because of the prominent judicial role in these jurisdictions, they have all experienced predominantly court-led advances on LGBTQ+ rights. In this respect, they are distinct from most other liberal constitutional jurisdictions that have seen similar progress on LGBTQ+ rights. Countries like Canada, the United Kingdom, Spain, France, and Germany have primarily recognized the rights of their LGBTQ+ communities through legislation. In other countries, major social questions such as whether to adopt a legal framework for same-sex marriage were put through public referenda and only entrenched in legislation after a majority voted in favor of such changes. This is what happened in Australia and Switzerland. While these developments are hugely consequential for LGBTQ+ rights, they are not covered in this book as they do not reveal much about the judicial dynamics underlying the recognition of these rights.

Third, the cases studies share a legal and political culture characterized (at least in principle) by liberal constitutionalism. To wit, these jurisdictions possess written constitutions with fundamental rights and maintain a liberal conception of

[111] *See* Alec Stone Sweet, *Why Europe Rejected American Judicial Review—And Why It May Not Matter*, 101 MICH. L. REV. 2744 (2003).

[112] *See* David S. Law, *Generic Constitutional Law*, 89 MINN. L. REV. 652 (2005); Mark Tushnet, *The Inevitable Globalization of Constitutional Law*, 49 VA. J. INT'L L. 985 (2009); Vicki C. Jackson, *Constitutional Law in an Age of Proportionality*, 124 YALE L.J. 3094, 3096 (2015).

[113] J.Y. Interpretation No. 748 (2017) (English Translation) (Taiwan). *See also*, Chang, *supra* note 67.

those rights in which individual citizens can have their rights enforced against the state.[114] This is essential because the judicial recognition of LGBTQ+ rights relies on broad interpretations of, among others, the rights to equality, dignity, and privacy. Further, liberal constitutionalism has been eroded in all three jurisdictions even as LGBTQ+ rights have been progressively realized, enabling a side-by-side analysis of these two contrasting trends within each jurisdiction.[115]

Each of the case studies also has distinctive characteristics. The United States, India, and Hong Kong are located in separate geographic regions (North America, South Asia, and East Asia, respectively) and have distinct judicial cultures (attitudinal, instrumental, and collegial, respectively).[116] They are also at different points in their struggle for LGBTQ+ rights. The United States has a longer history of social activism and judicial decisions on these issues. As a result, the book adopts a wider lens for the United States, recounting events from the 1980s to the present day, with a focus on post-2000 developments. The Indian and Hong Kong case studies cover events from approximately 2000 to 2024, which is when much of the social mobilization and judicial activity on LGBTQ+ rights took place in those societies.

Perhaps most importantly, the three jurisdictions face distinct challenges to liberal constitutionalism. In the United States, extreme political and social polarization has resulted not only in bitter political contests but also in the radicalization of the Republican Party. In India, the Modi government has undermined the country's pluralistic, liberal constitutional order and seems intent on replacing it with one that is distinctly illiberal and ethnonationalistic. Hong Kong's hybrid "one country, two systems" model remains standing in name only. The region is now ruled by an authoritarian government though strands of liberal constitutionalism have survived, including a degree of judicial independence and unfettered economic freedom.

Selecting case studies that have experienced a similar phenomenon—court-led advancement of LGBTQ+ rights in otherwise perilous times for liberal constitutionalism—in distinct political and cultural environments, enables the book to develop a single analytical framework that can be used to generate

[114] Note that it is possible for liberal constitutionalism to be sustained by a political culture that respects individual rights with minimal judicial involvement, as is the case in Australia whose constitution has no bill of rights.

[115] Careful readers will notice that I do not mention democracy here. This is because liberal constitutionalism, especially of the court-led form, can be exercised even in hybrid or non-democratic societies. Indeed, Hong Kong has never been a democratic polity. The United States and India hold regular elections, but their institutions of democratic governance are under severe strain. They are, at best, flawed or dysfunctional democracies today.

[116] *See* BENJAMIN ALARIE & ANDREW J. GREEN, COMMITMENT AND COOPERATION ON HIGH COURTS: A CROSS-COUNTRY EXAMINATION OF INSTITUTIONAL CONSTRAINTS ON JUDGES 2–8 (2017); ROUX, *supra* note 75, at ch. 2; Simon N.M. Young & Antonio Da Roza, *The Judges*, *in* HONG KONG'S COURT OF FINAL APPEAL: THE DEVELOPMENT OF THE LAW IN CHINA'S HONG KONG (Simon N.M. Young and Yash Ghai eds., 2013).

nuanced, critical analysis of LGBTQ+ rights jurisprudence in each jurisdiction. It also eliminates potential case studies where the two developments were not broadly coterminous. In South Africa, for instance, the Constitutional Court had issued its landmark progressive LGBTQ+ judgments by 2005,[117] prior to the country (and the world) turning markedly in an illiberal direction.[118]

IV. Scope and Limitations

A few notes before we proceed. First, I do not claim that the advancement of LGBTQ+ rights in the past two decades is a universal trend. As of February 2025, only thirty-eight countries recognized same-sex marriage, and these countries are largely clustered in the Americas and Europe.[119] In Asia, only three jurisdictions permit same-sex marriage (Nepal, Taiwan, and Thailand), and many countries still criminalize same-sex intercourse.[120] Some countries, meanwhile, have moved in a regressive direction. Brunei modified its criminal laws in 2019 to make anal sex punishable by stoning to death, while Indonesia adopted a new Criminal Code in December 2022 that criminalized all extramarital sex, including same-sex relations.[121] Moreover, illiberal and authoritarian-leaning governments in recent years have advanced regressive, patriarchal narratives that are misogynistic and often hostile to LGBTQ+ groups.[122] The transgender community has become a prominent target for reactionary politics, particularly in the United States and Europe.[123]

[117] *See* National Coalition for Gay and Lesbian Equality v. Minister of Justice, 1999 (1) SA 6 (CC) (S. Afr.) (decriminalizing same-sex relations); Minister of Home Affairs v. Fourie, 2006 (1) SA 524 (CC) (S. Afr.) (ruling that same-sex couples have a constitutional right to marry).

[118] Jacob Zuma's election as President in 2009 is widely viewed as a turning point toward illiberal rule in South Africa. *See, e.g.*, Raymond Suttner, Recovering Democracy in South Africa (2015); Daniel Silander, *Contemporary Challenges to South African Democracy*, *in* South Africa's Democracy at the Crossroads 187 (Daniel Silander et al. eds., 2022).

[119] Prominent exceptions include South Africa. In the past five years, several countries in Central and South America have recognized same-sex marriage including Costa Rica, Cuba, Chile, Ecuador, and Mexico. Argentina and Brazil were ahead of much of the Global North in this regard, legalizing same-sex marriage in 2010 and 2013, respectively.

[120] Elaine Jeffreys & Pan Wang, *Pathways to Legalizing Same-Sex Marriage in China and Taiwan: Globalization and "Chinese Values"*, *in* Global Perspectives on Same-Sex Marriage: A Neo-Institutional Approach 198 (Bronwyn et al. eds., 2018).

[121] Martin Banks, *Brunei Under Fire for Draconian Anti-Homosexuality Laws*, Parliament Magazine (Apr. 26, 2019), https://www.theparliamentmagazine.eu/articles/news/brunei-under-fire-draconian-anti-homosexuality-laws; *Indonesia: New Criminal Code Disastrous for Rights*, Human Rights Watch, https://www.hrw.org/news/2022/12/08/indonesia-new-criminal-code-disastrous-rights.

[122] *See* Agnieszka Graff et al., *Introduction: Gender and the Rise of the Global Right*, 44 Signs: J. Women in Culture & Soc. 541 (2019); Erica Chenoweth & Zoe Marks, *Revenge of the Patriarchs: Why Autocrats Fear Women*, 101 Foreign Aff. 103 (2022); Elin Bjarnegård & Daniela Donno *Window-Dressing or Window of Opportunity? Assessing the Advancement of Gender Equality in Autocracies*, 20(1) Pol. & Gender 229 (2023); Emanuela Lombardo et al., *De-Democratization and Opposition to Gender Equality Politics in Europe*, 28(3) Soc. Pol. 521 (2021).

[123] *See* Ari Ezra Waldman, *Policing Queer Sexuality*, 121 Mich. L. Rev. 985 (2023); Osella & Rubic-Marin, *supra* note 44.

The story told in this book is one of judicial advancement of LGBTQ+ rights in three jurisdictions, where significant progressive strides have been made, but much work remains to be done and the institutional and doctrinal foundations of past LGBTQ+ judicial victories are potentially fragile.

Second, by focusing on LGBTQ+ rights, I do not mean to imply that progressive decision-making is absent in other areas of these courts' dockets. In India, for instance, the Supreme Court has advanced gender rights generally in recent years by, *inter alia*, permitting menstruating women to enter a Hindu temple,[124] and decriminalizing adultery.[125] The book will briefly touch upon these related areas, but the focus remains on LGBTQ+ rights as it is the common denominator for progressive constitutional adjudication across the case studies.

Third, many other literatures have important things to say about the politics and legal recognition of LGBTQ+ rights, including feminist, queer, postcolonial, and critical international legal scholarship.[126] As this is a book primarily concerned with judicial adjudication and liberal constitutionalism, it will not engage directly with this critical scholarship, but will draw insights from it.

Finally, a word about strategic judicial decision-making and the objectives of this book. Many factors—legal, institutional, and political—are at play in constitutional rights judgments, especially in the fraught environments in which these courts operate. Professional norms militate against judges sharing their internal deliberations with the public. And, even if these deliberations were fully transparent, we could never fully grasp the subconscious elements underlying each judge's philosophy and outlook on particular issues. Legal researchers must therefore work with imperfect and incomplete information to construct an account of what courts (and judges therein) are seeking to achieve in each judgment and across lines of precedent.

My hope is that this book will help make sense of this jurisprudence in the context of liberal constitutional decline in these societies, even if reasonable minds may disagree as to the considerations at play in a particular case and regardless of whether present judicial (and constitutional) trends continue.

[124] Indian Young Lawyers Association v. State of Kerala, (2019) 11 S.C.C. 1 (India).

[125] Joseph Shine v. Union of India, (2018) S.C.C. 1676 (India).

[126] *See, e.g.*, Shreya Atrey, *Feminist Constitutionalism: Mapping a Discourse in Contestation*, 20(2) INT'L J. CONST. L. 611 (2022); Lisa Duggan, *The New Homonormativity: The Sexual Politics of Neoliberalism*, *in* MATERIALIZING DEMOCRACY: TOWARD A REVITALIZED CULTURAL POLITICS 175 (Russ Castronovo & Dana D. Nelson eds., 2002); RAHUL RAO, OUT OF TIME: THE QUEER POLITICS OF POSTCOLONIALITY (2020); Ratna Kapur, *The (Im)possibility of Queering International Human Rights Law*, *in* QUEERING INTERNATIONAL LAW 131 (Diane Otto ed., 2018); Aeyal Gross, *The Politics of LGBT Rights in Israel and Beyond: Nationality, Normativity, and Queer Politics*, 46 COLUM. HUM. RTS. L. REV. 81 (2015).

3

LGBTQ+ Rights, Culture Wars, and Polarization in the United States

I. Introduction

A. Background

On June 24, 2022, the U.S. Supreme Court issued its long-awaited judgment in *Dobbs v. Jackson Women's Health Organization*.[1] It ruled that the U.S. Constitution does not protect a right to abortion, overturning *Roe v. Wade* (1973) and *Planned Parenthood v. Casey* (1992).[2] *Dobbs* has been criticized along several lines. It showed contempt toward *Roe* and *Casey* in setting aside half a century of precedent.[3] It adopted a narrow reading of "history and tradition" to determine what rights are implicitly protected (or not) under the Due Process Clause of the Fourteenth Amendment.[4] It enabled states to restrict abortion access in ways that jeopardized the reproductive health and, in some cases, the lives of pregnant women.[5] And *Dobbs* both highlights and exacerbates democratic dysfunction in the United States today.[6]

A less remarked upon feature of *Dobbs* is the way that conservative justices sought to distinguish abortion access from LGBTQ+ rights. Justice Alito's majority opinion repeatedly drew a distinction between the right to abortion and other substantive due process rights including the right to sexual privacy (including gay sex) and the right to same-sex marriage, which were recognized by the Supreme Court in *Lawrence v. Texas* (2003)[7] and *Obergefell v. Hodges* (2015),[8] respectively.[9]

[1] Dobbs v. Jackson Women's Health Organization, 142 S. Ct. 2228 (2022).

[2] *Id.* at 2242 (overruling Roe v. Wade, 410 U.S. 113 (1973) and Planned Parenthood v. Casey, 505 U.S. 833 (1992)).

[3] *See* Reva B. Siegel, *Memory Games:* Dobbs's *Originalism as Anti-Democratic Living Constitutionalism—and Some Pathways for Resistance*, 101 Tex. L. Rev. 1127, 1135 (2023); Mary Ziegler, Dobbs *and the Jurisprudence of Exclusion*, 55 Polity 419, 419–20 (2023).

[4] *Dobbs*, 142 S. Ct. at 2242 (citing Washington v. Glucksberg, 521 U.S. 702, 721 (1997)); Darryl Lenard Hutchinson, *Thinly Rooted: Tradition, and Reproductive Justice*, 65 Ariz. L. Rev. 385 (2023).

[5] *See generally*, Reva Siegel et al., *Equal Protection in Dobbs and Beyond: How States Protect Life Inside and Outside the Abortion Context*, 43 Colum. J. Gender & L. 67 (2023).

[6] *See generally*, David Landau & Rosalind Dixon, Dobbs, *Democracy, and Dysfunction*, 2023 Wis. L. Rev. 1569 (2023); Melissa Murray & Kate Shaw, Dobbs *and Democracy*, 137 Harv. L. Rev. 728 (2024).

[7] Lawrence v. Texas, 539 U.S. 558 (2003).

[8] Obergefell v. Hodges, 135 S. Ct. 2584 (2015).

[9] *Dobbs*, 142 S. Ct. at 2261, 2277–78, 2280.

Courts and LGBTQ+ Rights in an Age of Judicial Retrenchment. Rehan Abeyratne, Oxford University Press.
 DOI: 10.1093/9780191995040.003.0003

Justice Kavanaugh's concurring opinion similarly sought to assuage concerns that precedents like *Lawrence* and *Obergefell* might be overturned next. He said, "I emphasize what the Court today states: Overruling *Roe* does *not* mean the overruling of those precedents, and does *not* threaten or cast doubt on those precedents."[10] Kavanaugh might have felt compelled to write this in response to Justice Thomas who, in a separate concurrence, declared that the Court should reconsider all its substantive due process precedents, including those on LGBTQ+ rights.[11]

As a doctrinal matter, if the Court were to apply the "history and tradition" test consistently, Justice Thomas has a point. If the right to abortion was not sufficiently "deeply rooted" to warrant constitutional protection, why would LGBTQ+ rights be any different? Justice Alito's *Dobbs* majority opinion sought to distinguish them by pointing out that the recognition of substantive due process rights, including the LGBTQ+ rights, did not engage the competing interest of "potential life."[12] While this is true, it neglects the inconvenient fact that both *Roe* and *Casey* sought to balance competing interests and did not protect a right to abortion toward the latter stages of pregnancy.[13] More importantly, Justice Alito said nothing about the entrenchment of sexual privacy and same-sex marriage in America's constitutional history. Same-sex marriage, for instance, was first recognized in Massachusetts in 2003. Thus, it is a less deeply rooted right in the United States than abortion, which should make *Obergefell* more (not less) likely to be overturned than *Roe*.

Doctrinal accounts, then, fail to explain why Supreme Court's LGBTQ+ rights and abortion jurisprudence have taken such divergent paths. This is no surprise in the American context. The law and political science literature in the United States largely rejects the traditional, "legal" model of adjudication in which judges base their decisions solely on the facts and relevant legal materials before them in a given case.[14] An alternative explanation, advanced by Neil Siegel, is that *Lawrence* and *Obergefell* enjoy greater public support than the abortion precedents and "most of the justices cannot help being affected by sea changes in American culture and popular beliefs about gay rights."[15]

There is solid empirical evidence to suggest that the Supreme Court tends to track popular opinion in its constitutional decision-making. Several generations of scholarship, starting with Robert Dahl's seminal 1957 paper,[16] have shown that the

[10] *Id.* at 2309 (Kavanaugh, J., concurring).

[11] *Id.* at 2301 (Thomas, J., concurring) ("[I]n future cases, we should reconsider all of this Court's substantive due process precedents, including *Griswold*, *Lawrence*, and *Obergefell*. Because any substantive due process decision is demonstrably erroneous . . . we have a duty to correct the error established in those precedents") (internal quotes omitted).

[12] *Id.* at 2261, 2280.

[13] *Roe*, 410 U.S. at 164–66; *Casey*, 505 U.S. at 874–77, 879.

[14] Benjamin Alarie & Andrew J. Green, Commitment and Cooperation on High Courts: A Cross-Country Examination of Institutional Constraints on Judges 3 (2017).

[15] Neil S. Siegel, *The Wages of Crying Roe: Some Realism About* Dobbs v. Jackson Women's Health Organization, 2 J. Am. Const. Hist. 101, 117 (2024).

[16] Robert A. Dahl, *Decision-Making in a Democracy: The Supreme Court as a National Policymaker*, 6 J. Pub. L. 279 (1957).

Supreme Court is responsive to, and largely falls in line with, popular opinion and the policy preferences of legislative majorities.[17]

The leading theory for this correlation between judicial decision-making and public/political preferences is that the Court behaves strategically. Put simply, in the long-term, judges are more likely to adapt their decisions to conform to the other branches, for judicial review depends on the compliance (or at least acquiescence) of political actors and enforcement by the executive branch.[18] Thus, as Epstein, Knight, and Martin put it, judges "have a strategic incentive to anticipate and then react to the preferences of elected officials."[19] Other studies have shown that judges may act strategically when writing majority opinions,[20] separate opinions,[21] and in setting agendas.[22]

The main competitor to the strategic model is the "attitudinal model," which posits that judges make decisions based on their individual ideology and political preferences.[23] While the debate among models of judicial decision-making is beyond the scope of this chapter, I adopt the view that judicial attitudes and ideology have a significant impact on (but do not fully account for) how the Supreme Court decides constitutional cases.[24] Today's Supreme Court justices are clearly motivated by personal ideology and political preferences, but there is room for other strategic considerations.[25]

One of those considerations is public opinion. As Siegel notes, same-sex marriage is supported by approximately 70 percent of the public according to Gallup,[26]

[17] *See* Barry Friedman, The Will of the People: How Public Opinion Has Influenced the Supreme Court and Shaped the Meaning of the Constitution (2009); Lee Epstein & Andrew D. Martin, *Does Public Opinion Influence the Supreme Court? Possibly Yes (But We're Not Sure Why)*, 13(2) J. Const. L. 263 (2010); Kevin T. McGuire & James A. Stimson, *The Least Dangerous Branch Revisited: New Evidence on Supreme Court Responsiveness to Public Preferences*, 66 J. Pol. 1018 (2004).

[18] *See* Lee Epstein & Jack Knight, The Choices Justices Make (1998); Mario Bergara et al., *Modeling Supreme Court Strategic Decision Making: The Congressional Constraint*, 28 Legis. Stud. Q. 247 (2003).

[19] Lee Epstein et al., *The Supreme Court as a Strategic National Policymaker*, 50 Emory L.J. 583, 585 (2001).

[20] *See* Forrest Maltzman et al., Crafting Law on the Supreme Court: The Collegial Game (2000).

[21] *See* Melinda Gann Hall & Paul Brace, *State Supreme Courts and Their Environments: Avenues to General Theories of Judicial Choice*, *in* Supreme Court Decision-Making: New Institutionalist Perspectives 281 (Cornell Clayton & Howard Gillman eds., 1999). The attitudinal model may, however, better explain a judge's decision to dissent. *See* Virginia A. Hettinger et al., *Comparing Attitudinal and Strategic Accounts of Dissenting Behavior on the U.S. Courts of Appeals*, 48 Am. J. Pol. Sci. 123 (2004).

[22] *See* Gregory A. Caldeira et al., *Sophisticated Voting and Gate-Keeping in the Supreme Court*, 15 J. L. Econ. & Org. 549 (1999).

[23] *See generally*, Jeffrey A. Segal & Harold J. Spaeth, The Supreme Court and the Attitudinal Model Revisited (2002).

[24] *See* Donald R. Songer, *The Dog That Did Not Bark: Debunking the Myths Surrounding the Attitudinal Model of Supreme Court Decision Making*, 33 Just. Sys. J. 340, 356–57 (2012).

[25] *See* Hettinger et al., *supra* note 21, at 123; Epstein et al., *supra* note 19, at 585.

[26] Siegel, *supra* note 15, at 117; Megan Brenan, *Same-Sex Relations, Marriage Still Supported by Most in U.S.*, Gallup (June 24, 2024), https://news.gallup.com/poll/646202/sex-relations-marriage-supported.aspx (reporting that 69 percent of Americans supported same-sex marriage in 2024).

which appears to make *Obergefell* less vulnerable to judicial overruling than *Roe* and *Casey*. But this is an incomplete explanation. While same-sex marriage enjoys comparatively higher public approval than abortion, it is a close call. In 2024, Gallup found that 50 percent of Americans believed that abortion should be legal in certain circumstances, while 35 percent believed that abortion should be permitted in all circumstances, and 12 percent thought it should be illegal.[27]

Moreover, following *Dobbs*, states across the country—including conservative states like Kentucky, Montana, and Kansas—have voted against abortion-restrictive measures in statewide referendums. Other states, including closely divided ones like Michigan, have amended their constitutions to enshrine a right to abortion.[28]

Among Republicans, robust majorities have supported abortion in certain circumstances over the past three decades, with 64 percent in favor in 2024.[29] 12 percent of Republicans said it should be legal under all circumstances, while 23 percent said it should be banned outright.[30] This partisan divide on abortion may seem to explain the conservative justices' willingness to overturn *Roe* and *Casey*. Yet, as Siegel concedes, a majority of Republicans remain opposed to same-sex marriage— in 2024, only 46 percent supported it.[31]

Other strategic considerations, then, must also factor into the calculus for the conservative justices (other than Justice Thomas) who wish to preserve certain LGBTQ+ rights like same-sex marriage but have not been so charitable to other constitutional rights. Indeed, *Dobbs* was just one of many Supreme Court decisions over the past decade that have pared back or overturned bedrock liberal precedents.[32]

What are the strategic considerations at play in the LGBTQ+ rights context? And what do they reveal about the trajectory of liberal constitutionalism in the United States? To address these questions, this chapter examines LGBTQ+ rights in the Supreme Court within the broader context of growing political and judicial polarization. It explains how and why certain LGBTQ+ rights became well entrenched and have survived the conservative judicial assault on other constitutional rights, especially those of minority groups and women.

[27] *Where Do Americans Stand on Abortion?*, GALLUP (June 17, 2024), https://news.gallup.com/poll/321143/americans-stand-abortion.aspx.

[28] Amanda Terkel & Jiachuan Wu, *Abortion Rights Have Won in Every Election Since Roe v. Wade Was Overturned*, NBC NEWS (Aug. 10, 2023), https://www.nbcnews.com/politics/elections/abortion-rights-won-every-election-roe-v-wade-overturned-rcna99031.

[29] *Abortion Trends by Party Identification*, GALLUP, https://news.gallup.com/poll/246278/abortion-trends-party.aspx (last visited Sept. 21, 2024).

[30] *Id.*

[31] Siegel, *supra* note 15, at 117; Brenan, *supra* note 26.

[32] *See, e.g.*, Students for Fair Admissions v. Harvard, 600 U.S. 181 (2023); Kennedy v. Bremerton School District, 597 U.S. 507 (2022).

B. Chapter Overview

Part II briefly discusses the rise of federal judicial power, before surveying developments on LGBTQ+ rights from the 1980s to 2015. Rejected until the 1990s, rights to sexual privacy and same-sex marriage won gradual public and judicial acceptance in the first two decades of the twenty-first century. The Court's landmark LGBTQ+ decisions, *Lawrence*, *United States v. Windsor*,[33] and *Obergefell* served a distinct strategic purpose. They provided an avenue through which Justice Kennedy and the liberal justices could engage in the project of liberal (and global) constitutionalism even as the Court moved in a conservative direction on most other constitutional rights.

The story of the gradual, progressive recognition of LGBTQ+ rights, marked by periods of progressive change followed by conservative backlash is well known, as is the liberal victory in the culture wars on major issues like same-sex marriage. What is less well known, as Part III explains, is how *Obergefell* reflects a conservative victory in a higher-level culture war. As political polarization intensified in the early 2000s, the Supreme Court shifted in its reference to, and public engagement with, foreign materials. The Rehnquist Court (1986–2005), especially in its early years, was not averse to citing foreign materials in constitutional cases. Its liberal members were no more likely to cite foreign sources than its conservative members.[34]

But following a judicial, scholarly, and political backlash, the Roberts Court (2005–present)—including its liberal members—stopped citing foreign materials.[35] Compare the citation of foreign sources in *Lawrence* (2003) and *Obergefell* (2015). Justice Kennedy authored the majority opinion in both cases. While he cites and engages with several foreign sources in *Lawrence*, he abstains from this practice in *Obergefell*.[36] Kennedy's cosmopolitanism is well documented, both in his jurisprudence and in his non-judicial pursuits.[37] But it appears that he avoided foreign citation in *Obergefell* to avoid the sort of backlash that the Court encountered after *Lawrence* and other culturally salient constitutional judgments of the early 2000s.

The disavowal of comparative engagement was part of a broader conservative victory in which originalism became the prevailing mode of constitutional interpretation. The Roberts Court in the 2000s turned away from looking for an

[33] United States v. Windsor, 133 S. Ct. 2675 (2013).

[34] *See* Ryan C. Black et al., *We Are the World: The U.S. Supreme Court's Use of Foreign Sources of Law*, 46 British J. Pol. Sci. 891–92 (2014).

[35] *See* Angioletta Sperti, *United States of America: First Cautious Attempts of Judicial Use of Foreign Precedents in the Supreme Court's Jurisprudence*, *in* The Use of Foreign Precedents by Constitutional Judges 406 (Tania Groppi & Marie-Claire Ponthoreau eds., 2013).

[36] *Compare Lawrence*, 539 U.S. at 574–77, *with Obergefell*, 135 S. Ct. at 2593–2608.

[37] *See* Stephen C. McCaffrey, *There's a Whole Word Out There: Justice Kennedy's Use of International Sources*, 44 McGeorge L. Rev. 201 (2013).

emerging consensus around the world (or even within the United States) to determine the existence and scope of implicit rights under the Fourteenth Amendment. In this context, *Obergefell* is especially remarkable—it advanced the rights of a historically marginalized group in an otherwise dark time for liberal constitutional rights adjudication.

Part IV discusses how, following Donald Trump's election as President in 2016, both American politics and the Supreme Court became more sharply polarized. Trump's greatest institutional legacy was to appoint three conservative Supreme Court justices to replace a conservative (Antonin Scalia), a moderate (Anthony Kennedy), and a liberal justice (Ruth Bader Ginsburg). Because these appointments so radically altered the Supreme Court, I refer to the period since 2018 as the Second Roberts Court. Part IV explains how this new Court is fundamentally different from the First Roberts Court (2005–17), both in its jurisprudence and in the backlash it drew from liberal commentators and politicians, who advocated for reforms to rein in the Court.

Part V engages with the Second Roberts Court's LGBTQ+ jurisprudence. While transgender rights remain largely unrecognized and subject to fierce cultural (and legal) contestation, the rights to engage in private homosexual conduct and marry a partner of the same sex are well entrenched. The Second Roberts Court has shifted sharply to the right on most constitutional rights issues but has restrained itself on LGBTQ+ rights. Past progressive landmarks like *Lawrence* and *Obergefell* appear to be safe.[38] And post–2018 LGBTQ rights cases—*Bostock v. Clayton County*(2020),[39] *Fulton v. Philadelphia* (2021),[40] and *303 Creative LLC v. Elenis* (2023)[41]—enabled the Court to push back against its critics.

Fulton and *303 Creative* required the Court to determine whether conservative applicants could invoke their First Amendment rights to free speech and the free exercise of religion to obtain exemptions from anti-LGBTQ+ discrimination laws. In both cases, the Court upheld the exemptions, but these rulings were not radical departures from precedent. Justice Kennedy—who cast the deciding vote on previous progressive LGBTQ+ rulings like *Lawrence* and *Obergefell*—had authored majority opinions in *Dale v. Boy Scouts of America* (2000)[42] and *Masterpiece Cakeshop, Ltd. v. Colo. Civil Rights Comm'n* (2018)[43] that similarly privileged the First Amendment over competing LGBTQ+ rights claims. *Fulton* and *303 Creative*, moreover, are filled with rhetoric—even from Republican-appointed justices—that show compassion for the LGBTQ+ community even as they reached conservative rulings.

[38] *See Dobbs*, 142 S. Ct. at 2261 (2022) (distinguishing *Lawrence* and *Obergefell*).
[39] Bostock v. Clayton County, 140 S. Ct. 1731 (2020).
[40] Fulton v. Philadelphia, 141 S. Ct. 1868 (2021).
[41] 303 Creative LLC v. Elenis, 143 S. Ct. 2298 (2023).
[42] Dale v. Boy Scouts of America, 530 U.S. 640 (2000).
[43] Masterpiece Cakeshop, Ltd. v. Colo. Civil Rights Comm'n, 138 S. Ct. 1719 (2018).

In *Bostock*, two conservative justices joined their liberal colleagues to hold that Title VII of the Civil Rights Act 1964, which prohibits workplace discrimination on the basis of sex, applies to discrimination on sexual orientation and gender identity grounds.[44] More remarkably still, the Trump-appointed Justice Neil Gorsuch authored the majority opinion. This opinion usefully demonstrated that conservative justices, relying on textualist interpretive methods, can still arrive at outcomes favored by the political left.

Part VI concludes by assessing the apparent shift in the Supreme Court's strategic priorities. In short, LGBTQ+ rights initially served, among other things, to advance a progressive rights agenda with minimal political backlash. But in recent years, with its 6–3 conservative supermajority, that interest is no longer served. LGBTQ+ rights now play a legitimating role for an institution whose "sociological legitimacy"[45] among audiences beyond conservative legal and political circles has deteriorated. The post-2018 cases usefully counter the dominant narrative that the Court is a partisan and reactionary institution.

II. The Gradual Recognition of LGBTQ+ Rights (1986–2015)

A. The Rise of Federal Judicial Supremacy

The United States has the world's longest-surviving Constitution. Adopted in 1788 in the aftermath of revolution, the Constitution famously vested sovereignty in "We the People" and broke the shackles of monarchic, British rule.[46] It was—and remains—a liberal Constitution, in which power is divided not only among Congress, the executive, and the judiciary, but also between the federal and state governments. This design was intended to prevent tyranny and protect individual liberties. But the Constitution also limited the exercise of democracy in many ways.[47] The political community to which the U.S. Constitution initially applied was exclusionary. Women and Native Americans had no political or electoral voice. And African Americans were mentioned only obliquely through provisions that (1) counted "three-fifths of all other persons" toward the calculation of congressional and electoral college seats,[48] (2) required that fugitive slaves who escaped to

[44] Justice Ginsburg was still on the Court when *Bostock* was decided, but the 6–3 margin suggests that the decision would have come down the same way (probably by a 5–4 majority) even if it were decided after her death.

[45] Richard H. Fallon Jr., *Legitimacy and the Constitution*, 118 Harv. L. Rev. 1789, 1795 (2005).

[46] U.S. Const. pmbl.

[47] On the undemocratic origins of the U.S. Constitution, see Michael J. Klarman, The Framers' Coup: The Making of the United States Constitution (2016). On undemocratic continuities in the Constitution today, see Maggie Blackhawk, *The Supreme Court, 2022 Term—Foreword: The Constitution of American Colonialism*, 137 Harv. L. Rev. 1 (2023); Nikolas Bowie, *Antidemocracy*, 135 Harv. L. Rev. 160 (2021).

[48] U.S. Const. art. I, § 2, cl. 3.

free states "be delivered" back to their owners,[49] and (3) established that Congress could not end the Atlantic slave trade prior to 1808.[50]

The Bill of Rights (1791)—the first ten amendments to the Constitution—was similarly limited in its scope and application. Owing to its vintage, the Bill of Rights only protects a narrow range of civil and political rights, including the freedom of speech and assembly, the right to a jury trial, and the right against self-incrimination.[51] It bars unreasonable searches and seizures as well as cruel and unusual punishment.[52] Some rights are peculiar to the American context—such as the right to bear arms—while others, like the prohibition on forcing homeowners to quarter soldiers, have fallen into desuetude.[53] Perhaps most importantly, the Bill of Rights initially applied only to the federal government, with states subject only to the rights limitations found in their own constitutions.[54]

Thus, the federal judiciary in its early years had limited authority. Article III of the Constitution vests judicial power "in one supreme Court, and in such Inferior Courts" as Congress might establish.[55] *Marbury v. Madison* (1803)[56] famously established judicial supremacy over the Constitution and is widely regarded as inaugurating what we call today "strong-form judicial review."[57]

The U.S. Civil War (1861–65) finally ended slavery and led to constitutional amendments that fundamentally altered the country's constitutional framework. Of those, the Fourteenth Amendment (1868) has been especially transformative. In addition to conferring citizenship on all persons born within the United States (including former slaves) the Fourteenth Amendment enshrined rights such as "due process" and the "equal protection of laws" that applied to the states.[58] It has been the primary vehicle through which minority groups—notably African Americans, women, and the LGBTQ+ community—have been able to advance their claims for equality in court.[59]

[49] *Id.* art. IV, § 2, cl. 3.

[50] *Id.* art. I, § 9, cl. 1.

[51] *Id.* at amends. I, V, VI, VII.

[52] *Id.* at amends. IV and VIII.

[53] *Id.* at amends. II and III.

[54] *See* Jamal Greene, How Rights Went Wrong: Why Our Obsession with Rights Is Tearing America Apart 7–31 (2021) (showing how the Bill of Rights was understood in the early republic to constitute part of self-government and was enforced more by juries and legislatures than by courts).

[55] U.S. Const, art. III, § 1.

[56] Marbury v. Madison, 5 U.S. (1 Cranch) 137 (1803).

[57] On the difference between "strong-form" and "weak-form" review, see Mark Tushnet, Weak Courts, Strong Rights: Judicial Review and Social Welfare Rights in Comparative Constitutional Law (2009).

[58] U.S. Const., amend. XIV.

[59] The Supreme Court's use of the Fourteenth Amendment to assist minority groups that are disadvantaged in the political process originated in United States v. Carolene Products, 304 U.S. 144, 152 n.4 (1938) (providing that "prejudice against discrete and insular minorities may be a special condition, which tends seriously to curtail the operation of those political processes ordinarily to be relied upon to protect minorities, and which may call for a correspondingly more searching judicial inquiry"). For an overview of the Fourteenth Amendment equality jurisprudence, see Julie Novkov, *Equality*, *in* Oxford Handbook of the U.S. Constitution 455 (Mark Tushnet et al. eds., 2015).

The judicial reception to such claims, at least at the Supreme Court, has varied significantly over time. The high watermark from a progressive standpoint was the Warren Court (1953–69), which ended school segregation in *Brown v. Board of Education* (1954)[60] and advanced civil and political rights in several areas including criminal justice,[61] free speech,[62] voting rights,[63] and the right to use contraception.[64] The Burger Court (1973–86), though more conservative than its predecessor, also advanced the rights of minority groups in important ways, by recognizing, *inter alia*, abortion rights in *Roe v. Wade* (1973),[65] affirmative action for racial minorities in college admissions,[66] and equal rights for women in both domestic and work-related contexts.[67]

The spate of high-profile progressive victories in the Supreme Court had important political consequences. On the liberal side, advocacy groups came to view the judiciary, and the Supreme Court in particular, as the primary protector of liberty and fundamental rights, especially for "discrete and insular minorities" who lack political power.[68] This expanded judicial role was most famously defended by John Hart Ely in his landmark book DEMOCRACY AND DISTRUST (1980). Ely argued that judicial interventions were most beneficial—and most normatively desirable—when they protected or improved the democratic process, *inter alia*, by ensuring minority representation and keeping open the "channels" of political change.[69]

As it turned out, the judicial takeover encompassed substantive political and social issues—including access to contraception, abortion, and gun rights—as well as procedural ones. This shift had several consequences. Courts are institutionally conservative both procedurally and culturally. They reach decisions by looking to the past, both in interpreting established legal texts and in extracting rules from past cases. And they comprise judges who mostly hail from elite backgrounds and hold establishmentarian political views. Thus, when often radical and countercultural claims for equality and other rights are moved from the political to the judicial realm, they are sanitized and brought into the mainstream.[70] Moreover, by taking these issues out of the ordinary political process, Congress

[60] Brown v. Board of Education, 347 U.S. 483 (1954).

[61] *See, e.g.*, Miranda v. Arizona, 384 U.S. 436 (1966); Brady v. Maryland, 373 U.S. 83 (1963).

[62] *See, e.g.*, New York Times Co. v. Sullivan, 376 U.S. 254 (1964); Brandenburg v. Ohio, 395 U.S. 444 (1969).

[63] *See, e.g.*, Baker v. Carr, 369 U.S. 186 (1962); Reynolds v. Sims, 377 U.S. 533 (1964).

[64] *See* Griswold v. Connecticut, 381 U.S. 479 (1965).

[65] *Roe*, 410 U.S. 113.

[66] *See* Regents of the University of California v. Bakke, 438 U.S. 265 (1978).

[67] *See, e.g.*, Frontiero v. Richardson, 411 U.S. 677 (1973); Weinberger v. Wiesenfeld, 420 U.S. 636 (1975).

[68] *Carolene Products*, 304 U.S. at 152 n.4.

[69] *See* JOHN HART ELY, DEMOCRACY AND DISTRUST: A THEORY OF JUDICIAL REVIEW 101–03 (1980).

[70] For a detailed historical account of how the First Amendment was defanged in this way, see LAURA WEINRIB, THE TAMING OF FREE SPEECH (2016).

and other elected officials were disempowered.[71] This is a two-way process: the Supreme Court especially gained power and public adulation, while politicians on both sides of the aisle were happy to defer to the judiciary on thorny questions of public policy.[72]

Some structural features of the American constitutional system have contributed to the Supreme Court being especially powerful and unaccountable. The U.S. Constitution is framed in broad terms, with many provisions requiring judicial interpretation. It is arguably the world's most difficult constitution to amend,[73] which gives the Supreme Court the final word on constitutional disputes. The Supreme Court also has discretion over most of its docket, enabling it to choose which cases to hear. Moreover, judges are appointed to the federal bench for life. Unlike every other major democracy, there is no term limit or retirement age for federal judges, including those on the Supreme Court.[74] It is also extraordinarily difficult for Congress to remove sitting judges, who may only be removed by impeachment by a majority of the House of Representatives followed by a conviction by two-thirds of the Senate. All told, the U.S. Supreme Court has broad discretion to operate on its own terms and decide cases independently. There is a dark side to this extraordinary judicial supremacy that we will explore in Part IV. Suffice it to say here that by insulating the Supreme Court (and its justices) so fully from political oversight, the American constitutional system leaves lawmakers few options to rein in a Court that is untethered to precedent and rules in line with the prerogatives of one political party.

B. LGBTQ+ Rights—The Early Years

The battle for LGBTQ+ rights is distinct from the civil rights and women's rights movements of the mid-twentieth century. Though the gay liberation movement started in the 1960s,[75] the major advancements on LGBTQ+ rights took place between the 1990s and 2010s. By this time, "juristocracy" was well entrenched in the

[71] *See* Ryan D. Doerfler & Samuel Moyn, *The Ghost of John Hart Ely*, 75 VAND. L. REV. 769 (2022) (showing that the Supreme Court has failed to protect minorities and to improve the political process as Ely had envisioned and empowered judges at the expense of elected representatives).

[72] On the American history and politics of this development, see KEITH WHITTINGTON, POLITICAL FOUNDATIONS OF JUDICIAL SUPREMACY (2009). For a comparative account, see RAN HIRSCHL, TOWARDS JURISTOCRACY: THE ORIGINS AND CONSEQUENCES OF THE NEW CONSTITUTIONALISM (2004) (arguing that political and economic elites enabled judicial supremacy to insulate their policies even if they lost at the ballot box).

[73] U.S. CONST., art. V; Richard Albert, *The World's Most Difficult Constitution to Amend?*, 110 CAL. L. REV. 2005 (2022).

[74] *See* Stephen Gardbaum, *Courts and Democratic Backsliding: A Comparative Perspective on the United States*, 2024 L. & POL'Y 1, 2–3 (2024).

[75] For an account of LGBTQ+ encounters with the state prior to the 1960s, see ANNA LVOVSKY, VICE PATROL: COPS, COURTS, AND THE STRUGGLE FOR URBAN GAY LIFE BEFORE STONEWALL (2021).

United States, and much of the advocacy was directed toward judicial fora, seeking constitutional redress.[76]

Social mobilization for LGBTQ+ rights on a national scale began in 1969.[77] In the 1960s, gay rights organizations were few, and public mobilization was minimal. The turmoil surrounding race relations, the Vietnam War, and high-profile assassinations made LGBTQ+ issues "at most a minor distraction for most Americans."[78] The police raid of the Stonewall Bar in downtown Manhattan in June 1969 and the subsequent demonstrations in New York City and other cities around the country mobilized the gay liberation movement.[79] The early 1970s witnessed the formation of Lambda Legal, the National Gay Task Force, and Gay Rights Advocates, among other leading advocacy groups. These organizations fought to publicize LGBTQ+ rights issues in the media and to educate the general public on the discrimination and stigma faced by gays and lesbians in particular. In the context of this increased activism, and the landmark Supreme Court judgment in *Loving v. Virginia* (1967),[80] some same-sex couples applied for marriage licenses. When they were denied by state authorities, they commenced litigation, which was not only "decisively rejected" but also met "with derision."[81] Given the prevailing societal norms, which strongly disfavored LGBTQ+ rights, this judicial posture is hardly surprising. Indeed, when the first public opinion poll on same-sex marriage was conducted in 1988—more than a decade later—only 12 percent of respondents said that homosexual couples should have the right to marry.[82]

But same-sex marriage was not the activists' main concern in the 1970s and 80s.[83] Smaller, incremental goals, such as protection from employment discrimination and repealing anti-sodomy laws, were prioritized. These initiatives had notable successes, including, a proliferation of local and state-level anti-discrimination ordinances, the elimination of the U.S. Civil Service Commission's blanket bar on employing homosexuals, and the repeal of anti-sodomy laws in almost half the states. The American Civil Liberties Union's National Gay Rights Project was

[76] *See* HIRSCHL, *supra* note 72 (defining "juristocracy" as rule by judges arising out of the constitutionalization of rights and exercise of judicial review); Leonore F. Carpenter, *The Next Phase: Positioning the Post-*Obergefell *LGBT Rights Movement to Bridge the Gap Between Formal and Lived Equality*, 13 STAN. J. C.R. & C.L. 255, 256–57 (2017).

[77] On the radical and multifaceted history of queer activism, see MARC STEIN, RETHINKING THE GAY AND LESBIAN MOVEMENT (2nd ed., 2023).

[78] MICHAEL J. KLARMAN, FROM THE CLOSET TO THE ALTAR: COURTS, BACKLASH, AND THE STRUGGLE FOR SAME-SEX MARRIAGE 15 (2014).

[79] *Id.* at 17.

[80] Loving v. Virginia, 388 U.S. 1 (1967) (striking down anti-miscegenation laws and declaring that marriage is a fundamental right under the U.S. Constitution).

[81] KLARMAN, *supra* note 78, at 19.

[82] GERALD N. ROSENBERG, THE HOLLOW HOPE: CAN COURTS BRING ABOUT SOCIAL CHANGE? 400–01 (2d ed. 2008).

[83] Indeed, many activists and thinkers opposed the normalization of plural LGBTQ+ identities by domesticating them within mainstream institutions. For a critical account along these lines against same-sex marriage, see MICHAEL WARNER, THE TROUBLE WITH NORMAL: SEX, POLITICS, AND THE ETHICS OF QUEER LIFE (2000).

launched in 1979 and had several victories in court, including in First Amendment cases establishing the right of gay students to form university student unions. LGBTQ+ visibility also improved in this period. Gay and lesbian politicians successfully ran for public office, and President Jimmy Carter appointed openly gay individuals to presidential commissions.[84]

These progressive developments, however, would lead to a backlash. Ronald Reagan's election as President in 1980 was achieved, in part, by gaining the support of Christian evangelicals. While a majority of evangelicals supported Jimmy Carter—a born-again Christian himself—in 1976, religious conservatives, led by Reverend Jerry Falwell's Moral Majority, mobilized to shift evangelical support to Reagan. Nearly two-thirds of evangelicals voted for Reagan in 1980, following a marked shift in Republican Party policy positions and tactics. The Republican Party platform in 1980 included for the first time a plank, supported by Falwell, to defend "the traditional American family."[85] The presidential campaign later included attack ads against President Carter for his support of gay rights. Reagan also reversed his own position on abortion to take a hardline pro-life position and reversed the Republican Party's stance in favor of the Equal Rights Amendment. Once in power, the Reagan administration ended gay organizations' access to federal agencies and appointed religious conservatives with openly anti-gay views to prominent federal posts. More broadly, Reagan's Justice Department (DOJ) asserted a conservative vision of the Constitution, which was opposed to the expansion of rights in several areas including LGBTQ+ issues.[86] The AIDS epidemic in this period only worsened the situation. It led to an increase in discrimination against gay men especially, as well as in public support for anti-sodomy statutes, which could now be defended on public health grounds.[87]

C. *Bowers* and the Advent of "Cultural War"

Thus, when the U.S. Supreme Court decided *Bowers v. Hardwick* (1986),[88] the national landscape was not favorable for LGBTQ+ rights. As noted, in 1988, only 12 percent of poll respondents said that same-sex couples should have the right to marry.[89]

84 Klarman, *supra* note 78, at 23–25.
85 *Id.* at 32.
86 Thomas M. Keck, *The Reagan Revolution to the Present*, *in* Oxford Handbook of the U.S. Constitution 113, 115–16 (Mark Tushnet et al. eds., 2015) (discussing the significance of a 1988 DOJ Office of Legal Policy Report titled "The Constitution in the Year 2000: Choices Ahead in Constitutional Interpretation").
87 Klarman, *supra* note 78, at 34–36.
88 Bowers v. Hardwick, 478 U.S. 186 (1986).
89 Rosenberg, *supra* note 82, at 400–01.

Against this backdrop, the Supreme Court's decision in *Bowers* was not surprising. At issue was a Georgia statute that criminalized sodomy generally—not simply among homosexuals.[90] The respondent was charged with violating the statute after committing "that act with another adult male" in the respondent's bedroom.[91] The Eleventh Circuit held in the respondent's favor, ruling that the statute violated his constitutional rights under the Ninth Amendment and the Due Process Clause of the Fourteenth Amendment, as his conduct was private, intimate and, therefore, beyond the reach of the law.[92] The Eleventh Circuit here relied, *inter alia*, on the Supreme Court's judgments in *Griswold v. Connecticut* and *Roe v. Wade*, which had established a fundamental right to privacy, including with respect to intimate relations.[93]

The Supreme Court reversed by a 5–4 margin. The majority opinion, authored by Justice White, framed the case narrowly. Rather than casting the question presented as one involving the rights to privacy and due process, Justice White, described it as follows:

> The issue presented is whether the Federal Constitution confers a fundamental right upon homosexuals to engage in sodomy and hence invalidates the laws of the many States that still make such conduct illegal and have done so for a very long time.[94]

This framing telegraphed both the reasoning and outcome in this case. Justice White went on to explain how the precedents relied upon by the Eleventh Circuit pertained to "whether or not to beget or bear a child,"[95] which bore no resemblance "to the claimed constitutional right of homosexuals to engage in acts of sodomy."[96] He further stressed that, until 1961, all fifty states criminalized sodomy and that in 1986, twenty-four states continued to do so.[97] Rather than highlight the progressive decriminalization of sodomy, Justice White cited these facts to show that a right to sodomy had not been historically recognized. He concluded by warning that a ruling in favor of the respondent would lead to the floodgates opening to legal challenges against "adultery, incest, and other sexual crimes," as well as against laws based on "notions of morality."[98] For these reasons, the Court ruled against the respondent and upheld the Georgia anti-sodomy statute.[99]

90 *Bowers*, 478 U.S. at 188 (quoting Georgia Code Ann. ß 16-6-2 (1984)).
91 *Id.*
92 *Id.* at 188–89.
93 *Id.* at 189.
94 *Id.* at 190.
95 *Id.*
96 *Id.* at 190–91.
97 *Id.* at 193–94.
98 *Id.* at 196.
99 *Id.*

While the *Bowers* judgment was decried by LGBTQ+ organizations, it galvanized their fundraising and activism. The 1987 National March on Washington for Lesbian and Gay Rights drew between 200,000 and 300,000 people, and the AIDS epidemic forced thousands out of the closet, leading to increased visibility for the LGBTQ+ community. By 1992, presidential candidates for the Democratic Party were actively courting LGBTQ+ voters. Bill Clinton promised on the campaign trail to repeal the ban on sexually diverse people serving in the military and to appoint gay cabinet members. His campaign received substantial funding from LGBTQ+ groups, and 72 percent of self-identified gay voters cast a ballot for Clinton in the general election.[100]

Once in office, however, President Clinton was unable to follow through on his campaign promises. Pat Buchanan, who ran unsuccessfully for the Republican nomination in 1992, proclaimed a "cultural war" at the Republican National Convention and made clear his party's opposition to the "amoral idea" that same-sex couples have the same legal rights as heterosexual couples.[101] Thus began in earnest the rise of political polarization in the United States.[102]

D. A Divided Legal and Cultural Landscape

The story of LGBTQ+ rights since the 1990s is marked by cycles of progressive developments followed by conservative backlash as the two sides hardened their positions and fought pitched battles over LGBTQ+ rights in various forums and at different levels of government.[103] Within this divisive political climate, President Clinton abandoned his plan to open the military to those with sexually diverse identities. The Clinton administration instead adopted the "Don't Ask, Don't Tell" policy that allowed sexually diverse individuals to serve but only if they kept their sexuality closeted.[104] In September 1996, just prior to his reelection, Clinton signed the Defense of Marriage Act (DOMA), which was supported by veto-proof majorities in Congress.[105]

[100] Klarman, *supra* note 78, at 38–44.

[101] Patrick Joseph Buchanan, *Culture War Speech: Address to the Republican National Convention* (Aug. 17, 1992), https://voicesofdemocracy.umd.edu/buchanan-culture-war-speech-speech-text. On the origins of the culture wars, see James Davison Hunter, Culture Wars: The Struggle to Define America (1991).

[102] *See* Jack M. Balkin, The Cycles of Constitutional Time 31, 44 (2020); David Pozen et al., *A Computational Analysis of Constitutional Polarization*, 105 Cornell L. Rev. 1 (2019) (showing that constitutional discourse has become more polarized over the past four decades).

[103] For a comprehensive account of LGBTQ+ rights developments in this period, see William N. Eskridge Jr. & Christopher R. Riano, Marriage Equality: From Outlaws to In-Laws 81–270 (2020).

[104] *See* National Defense Research Institute, Sexual Orientation and U.S. Military Personnel Policy: An Update of RAND's 1993 Study 39–68 (2010).

[105] Pub. L. No. 10–199, 110 Stat. 2419 (1996) (codified at 1 U.S.C. § 7 (2006) and 28 U.S.C. § 1738C (2006)).

DOMA, which defined marriage under federal law as between one man and one woman, was part of a broader backlash against the Supreme Court of Hawaii's decision in *Baehr v. Lewin* (1993).[106] *Baehr* held that the state's denial of marriage licenses to same-sex couples constituted discrimination on the basis of sex, which triggered strict scrutiny review under the Hawaiian Constitution.[107] The Hawaiian Supreme Court then remanded the case to the District Court to determine whether the state could show that its policy to deny same-sex couples marriage licenses "furthers compelling state interests and is narrowly drawn to avoid unnecessary abridgments of constitutional rights."[108] This judgment led to a swift backlash in Hawaii. In early 1994, the state legislature enacted a law defining marriage as between one man and one woman. Republicans then mobilized conservative and swing voters across the country, raising the specter of a Hawaii-led domino effect on same-sex marriage in other states. By 1997, more than half the states had enacted so-called defense of marriage legislation. While Democrats in California and a few other states were able to block such laws, they were unable to prevent popular initiatives from amending those state constitutions to prohibit same-sex marriage.[109]

Meanwhile, in Colorado, conservative activists prevailed in a statewide referendum to enact a constitutional amendment titled "No Protected Status based on Homosexual, Lesbian, or Bisexual Orientation."[110] This amendment, known as "Amendment 2,"[111] prevented the state of Colorado, or any authority within it, from enacting any law or policy providing special protection to gay, lesbian, or bisexual people. Its principal effect was to overturn several city ordinances that prohibited sexual orientation-based discrimination.

Legal challenges against Amendment 2 eventually reached the U.S. Supreme Court in *Romer v. Evans* (1996). Justice Kennedy, writing for a 6–3 majority, held that Amendment 2 conflicted with the Fourteenth Amendment's Equal Protection Clause.[112] He explained that Amendment 2 lacked a rational basis and that "its sheer breadth . . . seems inexplicable by anything but animus towards the class it affects."[113] In dissent, Justice Scalia took the majority to task for "imposing upon all Americans the resolution favored by the elite class from which the Members of this institution are selected."[114] This charge of elitism, along with references to "Kulturkampf" and a "cultural debate" between those who sought to preserve "traditional sexual mores against the efforts of a politically powerful minority,"[115]

[106] Baehr v. Lewin, 74 Haw. 530 (1993).
[107] *Id.* at 582.
[108] *Id.*
[109] Klarman, *supra* note 78, at 56–60.
[110] Colo. Const., Art. II (as amended by Amendment 2).
[111] *Romer v. Evans*, 517 U.S. 620, 623 (1996).
[112] *Id.* at 632.
[113] *Id.* at 635.
[114] *Id.* at 636 (Scalia, J., dissenting).
[115] *Id.*

captured the increasing polarization and brewing culture wars of the period. This charged language also previewed Scalia's dissents in subsequent LGBTQ+ rights cases, which became increasingly vitriolic and dovetailed with his criticism of judicial cosmopolitanism, which he viewed as similarly elitist and undemocratic.[116]

While *Romer* was a significant victory, national public sentiment, as Scalia suggested in his *Romer* dissent, remained divided on LGBTQ+ rights. In a 1999 Gallup poll, 50 percent of respondents said they considered homosexuality "an acceptable alternative lifestyle"; another Gallup poll that year showed that 50 percent also supported legalizing gay sex.[117]

In the 2000s, cultural acceptance, or at least tolerance, of non-heterosexual conduct and lifestyles increased dramatically. By 2003, Gallup reported that 60 percent of respondents supported legalizing gay sex. In response to another Gallup question that year, 32 percent said they had become more accepting of gays and lesbians, compared to only 8 percent who said they had grown less accepting.[118] This greater societal acceptance correlated with a rise in the number of gay characters and gay issues discussed in the popular media, and a concomitant rise in the number of gays and lesbians coming out. By 2000, 74 percent of Americans said that they knew a gay person compared to only 25 percent in 1985.[119] And, by 2005, almost 3,000 private employers, governments, and universities across the country included "sexual orientation" as a prohibited ground in their anti-discrimination laws or policies.[120]

E. Toward Legalization and Same-Sex Marriage

Within this more hospitable climate, the Supreme Court decided *Lawrence v. Texas*(2003). This case concerned the constitutionality of a Texas statute that criminalized sexual relations between two persons of the same sex.[121] The named petitioner was arrested by police in his residence along with another man, with whom he was engaged in same-sex intercourse. They were both charged and convicted under this statute.[122] The Supreme Court granted certiorari to consider three questions. First, the Court considered whether the statute violated the Equal Protection Clause of the Fourteenth Amendment by criminalizing only homosexual conduct and excluding identical heterosexual conduct.[123]

[116] *See, e.g., Lawrence*, 539 U.S. at 598 (Scalia, J., dissenting); Norman Dorsen, *The Relevance of Foreign Legal Materials in U.S. Constitutional Cases: A Conversation between Justice Antonin Scalia and Justice Stephen Breyer*, 3 Int'l J. Const. L. 519, 521, 526 (2005).

[117] Rosenberg, *supra* note 82, at 409.

[118] *Id.*

[119] Klarman, *supra* note 78, at 73.

[120] Rosenberg, *supra* note 82, at 413.

[121] *Lawrence*, 539 U.S. at 562.

[122] *Id.* at 562–63.

[123] *Id.* at 564.

Second, it examined whether petitioners' criminal convictions violated "their interests in liberty and privacy" under the Due Process Clause of the Fourteenth Amendment.[124] Finally, given the factual similarity of this case to *Bowers*, which a Texas Court of Appeals had relied upon to rule against petitioners, the Court asked whether *Bowers* should be overruled.[125]

Justice Kennedy's opinion, on behalf of a five-justice majority, determined that this case should be decided on Due Process grounds, just as *Bowers* was.[126] He proceeded to examine that judgment in detail. The *Bowers* Court, according to Kennedy, framed the case incorrectly—"it failed to appreciate the extent of the liberties at stake."[127] *Bowers*, like *Lawrence*, did not simply concern whether the Constitution "confers a fundamental rights upon homosexuals to engage in sodomy."[128] Rather, the statutes at issue touched upon "the most private human conduct . . . and in the most private of places, the home."[129] Justice Kennedy remarkably went on to declare not just that *Bowers* was overruled, but that it "was not correct when it was decided."[130]

In reaching that conclusion, his analysis had two main sections. The first section, which I will address in Part III, engaged in a wide-ranging comparative analysis to weaken the historical foundation on which *Bowers* relied. The second section focused on two landmark cases in the 1990s that undermined *Bowers*' doctrinal foundations: *Casey* (1992) and *Romer* (1996). *Planned Parenthood v. Casey* (1992) upheld a woman's right to choose in the abortion context.[131] It also reiterated the "substantive force of liberty" in the Due Process Clause, which extended to private, personal decisions relating to the family.[132] *Romer*, as discussed earlier, held that laws targeting sexual minorities as a class for unfavorable treatment lacked a rational basis and violated the Equal Protection Clause.[133] Given the principles expressed in these cases, as well as the judicial[134] and academic opprobrium that

[124] *Id.*
[125] *Id.*
[126] *Id.* at 564–66 (noting that the Georgia statute at issue in *Bowers* prohibited "the conduct whether or not the participants were of the same sex," while the Texas statute only criminalized same-sex conduct).
[127] *Id.* at 567.
[128] *Id.*
[129] *Id.*
[130] *Id.* at 578.
[131] *Casey*, 505 U.S. at 901.
[132] *See id.* at 851; *Lawrence*, 539 U.S. at 573–74.
[133] *Romer*, 517 U.S. at 632; *Lawrence*, 539 U.S. at 574–75. Justice Kennedy concluded that the equal protection analysis was not apposite in the *Lawrence* context, as it might have left the impression that broader prohibitions—such as the Georgia statute at issue in *Bowers*—may have been constitutionally permissible. However, Justice O'Connor's concurring opinion relied on the Equal Protection Clause and distinguished *Lawrence* from *Bowers* (where she voted to uphold the Georgia statute) on the grounds that the Texas statute in *Lawrence* singled out homosexual conduct. *See Lawrence*, 539 U.S. at 579 (O'Connor, J., concurring).
[134] *Lawrence*, 539 U.S. at 576 (noting that five state courts declined to follow *Bowers* in interpreting provisions of their state constitutions that were comparable to the Due Process Clause of the Fourteenth Amendment).

Bowers had generated,[135] Justice Kennedy stated that petitioners were "entitled to respect for their private lives," which the Due Process Clause protected from government interference.[136] The Court therefore held that the Texas statute criminalizing same-sex intercourse was unconstitutional.

Lawrence, though groundbreaking, was hardly unexpected. National polls showed majority support for legalization in 2003. And only thirteen states still maintained laws criminalizing sodomy, compared to twenty-five when *Bowers* was decided in 1986.[137] Thus, while some conservative commentators decried the *Lawrence* judgment, there was no widespread move to re-criminalize gay sex.[138]

By contrast, support for same-sex marriage remained stubbornly low in this period. Toward the end of the 1990s, polls revealed that approximately a third of Americans supported same-sex marriage—about 10 to 20 percent higher than in the 1980s, but still well short of a majority.[139] Similarly, a Gallup poll from January 2000 showed that 40 percent of respondents favored civil unions for same-sex couples, while 55 percent of respondents opposed.[140] From 1996 to 2006, both Pew Research Center and Gallup polls showed that support for same-sex marriage remained below 40 percent.[141]

Thus, when the Massachusetts Supreme Judicial Court ruled in November 2003 that the state's constitution required the government to recognize same-sex marriage,[142] the backlash was swift and sweeping. Thirteen states enacted constitutional amendments in 2004 prohibiting same-sex marriage.[143] The congressional and presidential elections that year mobilized conservative support to help reelect George W. Bush and to shore up Republican majorities in the House and Senate.[144] Inspired by the Massachusetts example, and reflecting the increasing geographic polarization in the country, liberal enclaves began to recognize same-sex marriage, only to be reversed at the state level. In San Francisco, then-Mayor Gavin Newsom ordered local officials to issue marriage licenses to same-sex couples in February 2004. The California Supreme Court ordered the city to cease and desist one month later, after more than 4,000 such licenses had been issued. Trial judges in Baltimore, Seattle, and New York, among other cities, held that their state constitutions protected a right to same-sex marriage. They were all reversed by their respective state supreme courts in 2006–07.

[135] *Id.* (citing CHARLES FRIED, ORDER AND LAW: ARGUING THE REGAN REVOLUTION—A FIRSTHAND ACCOUNT 81–84 (1991); RICHARD POSNER, SEX AND REASON 341–350 (1992)).

[136] *Id.* at 578–79.

[137] *Lawrence*, 539 U.S. at 573 (adding that among those thirteen states, four "enforce their laws only against homosexual conduct").

[138] KLARMAN, *supra* note 78, at 86–88.

[139] *Id.* at 74.

[140] ROSENBERG, *supra* note 82, at 406.

[141] *Id.* at 403.

[142] Goodridge v. Dept. of Public Health, 798 N.E.2d (Mass. 2003).

[143] *See* ESKRIDGE & RIANO, *supra* note 103, at 270–81.

[144] *See* KLARMAN, *supra* note 78, at 108–13.

The legal tide began to turn in 2008. The California and Connecticut Supreme Courts ruled that same-sex marriage was protected under their respective state constitutions, which triggered yet another backlash. Proposition 8—a proposed amendment to the Californian Constitution to eliminate the right of same-sex couples to marry—was the clearest manifestation of this countermovement. Though Proposition 8 succeeded, it also spurred gay rights activism in California and around the country toward securing the right to same-sex marriage.[145]

By 2009, polls showed majority support for same-sex marriage in several states. Reflecting this growing public support, Vermont, New Hampshire, and Maine passed marriage equality legislation that year, while Wisconsin, Washington, and Nevada enacted laws providing same-sex couples many of the benefits enjoyed by married couples.[146] The Iowa Supreme Court in 2009 recognized a right to same-sex marriage in its state constitution.[147] In addition, Barack Obama assumed the presidency in January 2009 with the support of 70 percent of self-identified gays and lesbians.[148] Obama's victory in the 2008 presidential election, with Democratic majorities in the House and Senate, appeared to bode well for LGBTQ+ rights at the federal level.

However, while President Obama pledged to repeal "don't ask, don't tell" on the campaign trail—a promise he fulfilled in 2011—he initially stopped short of supporting marriage equality or repealing DOMA.[149] Obama's dithering on same-sex marriage illustrated the increasingly divided cultural landscape over which he presided. As a candidate for the Illinois State Senate in 1996, he declared his "unequivocal support for gay marriage."[150] Later, when pursuing federal office, he stepped back from this position, stating "I'm a Christian . . . I believe . . . that marriage is something sanctified between a man and a woman."[151]

As President, he continued to tread cautiously[152] as the country became more divided politically and culturally. In November 2009, Maine voters enacted a constitutional amendment reversing the law that had legalized same-sex marriage. One year later, in Iowa, voters recalled three of the state Supreme Court justices who had recognized a right to same-sex marriage in the state's constitution.[153]

[145] *See id.* at 124–42 (describing the new advocacy organizations, boycotts, and protests that arose in California after Proposition 8, followed by a wave of activism across the country).

[146] *See* Eskridge & Riano, *supra* note 103, at 349–67.

[147] *See* Varnum v. Brien, 763 N.W.2d 862 (Iowa 2009).

[148] Klarman, *supra* note 78, at 139.

[149] *Id.* at 140–42; Elisabeth Bumiller, *Obama Ends "Don't Ask, Don't Tell" Policy*, N.Y. Times (July 22, 2011), https://www.nytimes.com/2011/07/23/us/23military.html.

[150] Randall Kennedy, The Persistence of the Color Line: Racial Politics and the Obama Presidency 23 (2011).

[151] *Id.*

[152] *See* Brian Montopoli, *Obama Stands by Opposition to Same-Sex Marriage—But Feelings "Evolving"*, CBS News (22 Dec. 2010), https://www.cbsnews.com/news/obama-stands-by-opposition-to-same-sex-marriage-but-feelings-evolving/ (quoting President Obama at a 2010 press conference saying that his views on same-sex marriage were "evolving" and that he supported "strong civil union[s]").

[153] Klarman, *supra* note 78, at 153.

North Carolina in 2012 joined all the other southern states in constitutionally barring same-sex marriage.[154] Meanwhile, also in 2012, Washington, Maryland, and New Jersey enacted legislation to enable same-sex marriage.[155] Given the salience of this issue, and the impending presidential election in 2012, Obama finally got off the fence.[156]

In May 2012, in the midst of the reelection campaign, then-Vice President Joe Biden remarked on Meet the Press that he was "absolutely comfortable" with same-sex marriage.[157] Three days later, President Obama declared that he, too, now supported marriage equality.[158] The Obama administration, in its second term, demonstrated this support in its federal court filings. In *Hollingsworth v. Perry*(2013), the U.S. Supreme Court was asked to determine the constitutionality of California's Proposition 8 ballot initiative, which amended the state's constitution to bar same-sex marriage.[159] A federal district court held that Proposition 8 violated the Equal Protection Clause of the Fourteenth Amendment.[160] Thereafter, the state of California refused to defend the law, which led to the initiative's official proponents intervening to defend it instead.[161] The Obama administration submitted a brief urging the Supreme Court to hold Proposition 8 unconstitutional.[162] But the Court declined to reach a judgment on the merits. It held that the official proponents, as ordinary citizens, lacked Article III standing in this case, which led to same-sex marriage resuming in California under the District Court's judgment.[163]

On the same day—June 26, 2013—the Supreme Court also issued its judgment in *United States v. Windsor*.[164] The case concerned the constitutionality of the DOMA.[165] The Obama administration, like the state of California in *Hollingsworth*, refused to defend DOMA before the Supreme Court,[166] leading the Bipartisan Legal Advisory Group (BLAG) of the Republican-controlled U.S. House of Representatives to step

[154] Campbell Richardson, *North Carolina Voters Pass Same-Sex Marriage* Ban, N.Y. Times (May 8, 2012), https://www.nytimes.com/2012/05/09/us/north-carolina-voters-pass-same-sex-marriage-ban.html.

[155] Klarman, *supra* note 78, at 194–95.

[156] On the "evolution" of Obama's views on same-sex marriage, see Eskridge & Riano, *supra* note 103, at 454–81.

[157] Corbett Daly, *Obama Backs Same-Sex Marriage*, CBS News (May 9, 2012), https://www.cbsnews.com/news/obama-backs-same-sex-marriage/.

[158] *Id.*

[159] Hollingsworth v. Perry, 133 S. Ct. 2652 (2013).

[160] *See* Perry v. Schwarzenegger, 704 F. Supp. 2d 921, 1004 (N.D. Cal. 2010).

[161] *Hollingsworth*, 133 S. Ct. at 2660–61.

[162] *See* Brief for the United States as Amicus Curiae Supporting Petitioners, Hollingsworth v. Perry, 133 S. Ct. 2652, No. 12-144 (2013).

[163] *Hollingsworth*, 133 S. Ct. at 2668.

[164] *Windsor*, 133 S. Ct. 2675.

[165] *Id.* at 2682.

[166] The Solicitor General's brief argued that DOMA "violates the fundamental constitutional guarantee of equal protection." Brief for the United States on the Merits Question, *Windsor*, 133 S. Ct. 2675 (No. 12-307).

in.[167] Unlike in *Perry*, the Court ruled that BLAG had standing to defend DOMA.[168] Justice Kennedy, writing on behalf of five justices, ruled that DOMA was unconstitutional as it deprived "the liberty of the person protected by the Fifth Amendment."[169] He added, echoing *Romer*, that DOMA "singles out" and "imposes a disability" on a class of persons, whose marriages are deemed "less worthy than the marriages of others."[170] Thus, Justice Kennedy concluded, whatever legitimate purpose DOMA may have sought to achieve, "no legitimate purpose overcomes the purpose and effect to disparage and to injure those whom the State, by its marriage laws, sought to protect in personhood and dignity."[171]

Windsor set the stage for the Supreme Court to consider whether the fundamental right to marry in the U.S. Constitution extended to same-sex couples. The Court finally heard this issue in *Obergefell v. Hodges* (2015).[172] The petitioners were fourteen same-sex couples who challenged laws or constitutional amendments in Michigan, Kentucky, Ohio, and Tennessee that defined marriage as between one man and one woman.[173] When this case reached the Supreme Court, the legal landscape had swung decisively in favor of marriage equality. Thirty-six states and the District of Columbia recognized same-sex marriage by 2015. And all but two federal courts of appeal that had ruled on this issue held that same-sex marriage bans were unconstitutional.[174]

Justice Kennedy again authored the principal opinion for a Court that was divided 5–4, with the liberal justices (Ginsburg, Breyer, Sotomayor, and Kagan) joining the majority. He acknowledged that the right to marry is rooted in "history and tradition" but insisted that rights "come not from ancient sources alone."[175] Rather, rights also emerge from "a better informed understanding of how constitutional imperatives define a liberty that remains urgent in our own era."[176] Justice Kennedy declared that the choice of whom to marry is "inherent in the concept of individual autonomy," that marriage "safeguards children and families," and that "marriage is a keystone of our social order."[177]

The majority opinion built on *Windsor* and *Lawrence* in treating equal protection and due process as "interlocking . . . constitutional safeguards in the context of the legal treatment of gays and lesbians."[178] *Lawrence*, as Justice Kennedy pointed

[167] *Id.* at 2684. *Cf. Hollingsworth*, 133 S. Ct. at 2660.
[168] *Windsor*, 133 S. Ct. at 2688–89.
[169] *Id.* at 2695. *See also*, Heather K. Gerken, *Windsor's Mad Genius: The Interlocking Gears of Rights and Structure*, 95 B.U. L. Rev. 587, 589 (2015).
[170] *Windsor*, 133 S. Ct. at 2695–96; *Romer*, 517 U.S. at 632.
[171] *Windsor*, 133 S. Ct. at 2696.
[172] *Obergefell*, 135 S. Ct. 2584.
[173] *Id.* at 2593.
[174] *Id.* at 2597.
[175] *Id.* at 2602.
[176] *Id.*
[177] *Id.* at 2599–601.
[178] *Id.* at 2604.

out, was decided under the Due Process Clause but also drew upon principles of equality to hold that states "cannot demean . . . or control" the lives of LGBTQ+ persons "by making their private sexual conduct a crime."[179] Same-sex couples were excluded from the institution of marriage and the benefits thereof. As such, they were denied equal treatment under the law and were deprived of the liberty to marry the partner of their choice. As Kennedy put it, "The imposition of this disability on gays and lesbians serves to disrespect and subordinate them."[180] The Court concluded that this "disability" violated both the Due Process and Equal Protection Clauses of the Fourteenth Amendment and thus held that the right to marriage extends to same-sex couples.[181]

Obergefell, then, represented a landmark victory for the LGBTQ+ community. It built on past judgments, like *Romer*, *Windsor*, and *Lawrence*, to guarantee marriage equality throughout the United States. Two aspects of Justice Kennedy's majority opinion in *Obergefell* would also prove significant in less obvious ways. First, this opinion built on his jurisprudence from those prior cases to fully embrace a blended approach that combines equal protection and due process into a single analysis.[182] While this was rhetorically powerful move, it also reflected Kennedy's libertarian impulse to frame these issues in individual rather than group-based terms.[183] Indeed, in *Obergefell* and this entire line of precedent, Kennedy and the liberal justices never recognized same-sex couples, or LGBTQ+ persons generally, as a protected class. Laws that discriminate on the basis of sexual orientation or gender identity are subject only to "rational basis review" while classifications based on, *inter alia*, race, sex, and national origin are accorded heightened scrutiny.[184] We will return to this critique of *Obergefell* in Part V.

Second, in a departure from his cosmopolitan approach in *Lawrence*, Justice Kennedy abstained from foreign citations or comparative analysis in *Obergefell*. As the next Part shows, this appears to have been a strategic choice to minimize backlash, borne out of the conservative blowback—judicial, scholarly, and political—that arose in response to *Lawrence* and other cases in the early 2000s whose rulings engaged with foreign sources. And it formed part of a larger conservative victory on how to interpret the Constitution.

[179] *Id.* (citing *Lawrence*, 539 U.S. at 578).

[180] *Id.*

[181] *Id.* at 2604–05, 2608.

[182] On this blended approach, see Laurence H. Tribe, Lawrence v. Texas: *The "Fundamental Right" That Dare Not Speak Its Name*, 117 HARV. L. REV. 1893 (2004); Rebecca L. Brown, *Liberty, the New Equality*, 77 N.Y.U. L. REV. 1491 (2002); Kenneth L. Karst, *The Liberties of Equal Citizens: Groups and the Due Process Clause*, 55 UCLA L. REV. 99 (2007).

[183] *See* Kenji Yoshino, *The New Equal Protection*, 124 HARV. L. REV. 747, 749 (2011).

[184] Race-based classifications are subject to "strict scrutiny," while those based on sex are accorded "intermediate scrutiny." In practice, most classifications are struck down under either tier of scrutiny. *See id.* at 755–57.

III. LGBTQ+ Rights in the Context of Two Culture Wars

This Part explores a shift in the Supreme Court's interpretive approach between *Lawrence* (2003) and *Obergefell* (2015) in the context of two related culture wars. Liberals scored substantive victories on decriminalizing gay sex and on same-sex marriage, but conservatives prevailed in the high-level clash on how the Supreme Court should (or should not) engage with foreign materials. The conservative triumph on the latter reflected a broader shift in the Court's method of constitutional interpretation wherein originalism trumped living constitutionalism.

The Supreme Court's engagement with foreign materials in *Lawrence* (2003), and in other high-profile cases around the turn of the millennium, proved to be a flashpoint of controversy. Yet, citing foreign materials *per se* was hardly new or revolutionary. From its founding years, Americans courts have taken notice of international and foreign law.[185] What changed in the 2000s was the politics around references to foreign sources.[186] Conservative judges, politicians, and scholars argued that the Court's comparative inquiry in select cases served to align American constitutional law with an emerging transnational consensus—an enterprise they deemed elitist and undemocratic.

A. From *Bowers* to *Lawrence*

Perhaps surprisingly, the first references to foreign sources in the LGBTQ+ rights are found in Chief Justice Burger's concurring opinion *Bowers v. Hardwick* (1986). Recall that *Bowers* upheld a Georgia ban on consensual sodomy.[187] Burger wrote separately to "underscore [his] . . . view that in constitutional terms there is no such thing as a fundamental right to commit homosexual sodomy."[188] To lend support to this view, he declared that individual decisions "relating to homosexual conduct have been subject to state intervention throughout the history of Western civilization. Condemnation of those practices is firmly rooted in Judeao-Christian moral and ethical standards."[189] He went on to describe how homosexual sodomy was a "capital crime under Roman Law" and, more pointedly, how its prohibition was firmly rooted in the English common law that was later transplanted to Georgia.[190]

[185] *See* Harold Hongju Koh, *International Law as Part of Our Law*, 98 AM. J. INT'L L. 43, 45 (2004); David Zaring, *The Use of Foreign Decisions by Federal Courts: An Empirical Analysis*, 3 J. EMPIRICAL L. STUD. 297, 301 (2006) (showing that from 1945 to 2005, federal courts maintained a consistent rate of foreign citations).

[186] *See, e.g.*, *Lawrence*, 539 U.S. 558; Atkins v. Virginia, 536 U.S. 304 (2002) (holding that the execution of mentally disabled persons violated the Eighth Amendment to the Constitution); Roper v. Simmons, 543 U.S. 551 (2005) (ruling that it was unconstitutional to impose the death penalty on minors).

[187] *Bowers*, 478 U.S. at 196.

[188] *Id.* (Burger C.J., concurring).

[189] *Id.*

[190] *Id.* at 196–97.

Jump ahead seventeen years to *Lawrence*. Justice Kennedy's majority opinion, which overruled *Bowers*, used foreign sources largely in response to the "sweeping nature" of Chief Justice Burger's pronouncements on the condemnation of homosexual sodomy in "Western civilization."[191] Burger's opinion, according to Justice Kennedy, failed to consider "other authorities pointing in an opposite direction."[192] Among other things, Justice Kennedy pointed to the Wolfenden Report, which recommended in 1957 that the British Parliament repeal laws criminalizing private homosexual conduct. Such laws were eventually repealed in the United Kingdom in 1967, almost two decades before *Bowers* was decided.[193] Justice Kennedy further referred to the landmark European Court of Human Rights judgment in *Dudgeon v. United Kingdom* (1981), which held that laws prohibiting consensual homosexual conduct in Northern Ireland violated the European Convention of Human Rights.[194]

In dissent, Justice Scalia, joined by Chief Justice Rehnquist and Justice Thomas, criticized the majority for believing that rights "spring into existence" because "*foreign nations* decriminalize conduct."[195] He contrasted this use of foreign citations with that in *Bowers*, noting that the majority opinion in the latter "*never* relied on 'values we share with a wider civilization.'"[196]

As a formal legal matter, Justice Scalia is correct. The references to Roman and English law are found in Chief Justice Burger's concurrence, rather than in Justice White's majority opinion in *Bowers*. But Scalia went on to describe the *Lawrence* majority's discussion of foreign materials as "meaningless dicta."[197] If so, why is it more problematic than Burger's references to foreign sources in *Bowers*? The remainder of Scalia's dissent revealed the broader legal and cultural fault lines at play here.

Scalia referred to Kennedy's use of foreign materials as "dangerous."[198] And, quoting Justice Thomas from a prior case, he declared that the Court "should not impose foreign moods, fads, or fashions on Americans."[199] This critique combines Scalia's distaste for living constitutionalism with his view that cosmopolitan judging is elitist and antithetical to democratic rule.[200] These threads recur in Scalia's jurisprudence and in conservative legal scholarship in the 2000s. Both

[191] *Lawrence*, 539 U.S. at 571.
[192] *Id.* at 572.
[193] *Id.* at 572–73 (citing The Wolfenden Report: Report of the Committee on Homosexual Offenses and Prostitution (1963)).
[194] *Id.* at 573 (citing Dudgeon v. United Kingdom, 45 Eur. Ct. H.R. (1981)).
[195] *Id.* at 598 (Scalia J., dissenting) (emphasis in original).
[196] *Id.* (emphasis in original).
[197] *Id.*
[198] *Id.*
[199] *Id.* (quoting Foster v. Florida, 537 U.S. 990 n. _ (2002) (Thomas, J., concurring in denial of certiorari)).
[200] *See* Dorsen, *supra* note 116, at 526 (criticizing the cosmopolitan view of judging as "arrogant" and enabling judges to "make up what the moral values of America should be on all sorts of issues").

emerged in response to a perceived elite, liberal movement to impose progressive values through the courts.

B. The Judicial, Scholarly, and Political Divide

At a formal level, the divide over foreign citations is puzzling. U.S. federal courts have cited foreign sources at a roughly consistent rate from the mid-twentieth century to the early twenty-first century.[201] Moreover, the Supreme Court's use of foreign law does not appear to have had a partisan tilt in earlier generations. While ideologically similar coalitions of judges were most likely to cite foreign law, liberal justices were no more likely than their conservative counterparts to do so.[202] To the contrary, one study of the Rehnquist Court (1986–2005) found that conservative justices cited foreign law in majority opinions more often than liberal justices did.[203] Other studies have shown that, through 2008, Justice Scalia relied on foreign law more frequently than Justice Breyer, and that Scalia was among the justices who travelled abroad the most.[204] And perhaps most significantly, the Supreme Court in that period rarely cited foreign judgments in constitutional cases.[205] From 1986 to 2010, less than 0.3 percent of all opinions (majority, concurrences, and dissents) in constitutional cases cited foreign case law.[206]

Given both the low incidence and consistent use of foreign references over time and among liberal and conservative justices, it is not citation to foreign materials *per se* that drew so much attention in the 2000s. Rather, it was their use in constitutional cases on culturally divisive issues that raised conservative hackles. Take, for instance, *Atkins v. Virginia* (2002). Justice Stevens, writing for a six-justice majority, held that the practice of executing mentally retarded defendants violated the Eighth Amendment.[207] In support of this conclusion, Justice Stevens noted, "[W]ithin the world community, the imposition of the death penalty for crimes committed by mentally retarded offenders is overwhelmingly disapproved."[208] In separate dissents, Chief Justice Rehnquist and Justice Scalia criticized this statement. Rehnquist noted that he "fail[s] to see . . . how the views of other countries"

[201] Zaring, *supra* note 185, at 301.
[202] Black et al., *supra* note 34, at 892.
[203] *See* David M. O'Brien, *More Smoke than Fire: The Rehnquist Court's Use of Comparative Judicial Opinions and Law in the Construction of Constitutional Rights*, 22 J. L. & POL. 83 (2006).
[204] David S. Law, *Judicial Comparativism and Judicial Diplomacy*, 163 U. PENN. L. REV. 927, 937–38 (2015); Ryan C. Black et al., *Upending Global Debate: An Empirical Analysis of the U.S. Supreme Court's Use of Transnational Law to Interpret Domestic Doctrine*, 103 GEO. L.J. 1, 32 (2014).
[205] Law, *supra* note 204, at 932 ("It is difficult to identify a national high court that pays less attention to foreign constitutional jurisprudence than the U.S. Supreme Court").
[206] Sperti, *supra* note 35, at 405.
[207] *Atkins*, 536 U.S. at 321.
[208] *Id.* at 316 (n 21).

support the Court's decision.[209] Scalia, more acerbically, called the Court's reference to "the views of . . . members of the so-called 'world community'" its "Most Feeble Effort to fabricate 'national consensus.'"[210]

A similar dynamic emerged in *Roper v. Simmons* (2005), an Eighth Amendment case in which Justice Kennedy authored a five-justice majority opinion holding juvenile capital punishment unconstitutional.[211] His opinion contained an entire section on foreign practices.[212] The comparative analysis, therefore, played a larger role in this case than in *Lawrence* or *Atkins*, but it only appeared after the principal holding had been reached solely with reference to U.S. sources.[213] Justice Kennedy further noted that while the United States is the only country in the world that executes juveniles, this global "reality" was not "controlling."[214]

Nonetheless, Justice Scalia, in dissent, tore into the majority stating, "[T]he basic premise of the Court's argument—that American law should conform to the laws of the rest of the world—ought to be rejected out of hand."[215] Of course, the majority opinion never claimed that American law should so conform, but Scalia was skeptical of its intentions. In a revealing passage, he made clear his belief that the majority was hiding its true colors:

> The Court's parting attempt to downplay the significance of its extensive discussion of foreign law is unconvincing. "Acknowledgment" of foreign approval has no place in the legal opinion of this Court *unless it is part of the basis for the Court's judgment*—which is surely what it parades as today.[216]

What particularly rankled Scalia in *Roper* was the majority's reference to *Trop v. Dulles* (1958).[217] Chief Justice Warren, writing for a plurality in that case, took account of "the evolving standards of decency that mark the progress of a maturing society" to determine whether a particular punishment qualified as "cruel and unusual" under the Eighth Amendment.[218] Speaking at an event with Justice Breyer at American University, Scalia stated plainly, "I detest that phrase, because I'm afraid that societies don't always mature. Sometimes they rot."[219]

However, Scalia's main criticisms were not rooted in the empirical basis for such evolving standards but in the elite pretentions of this enterprise. A few

[209] *Id.* at 324–25 (Rehnquist J., dissenting).
[210] *Id.* at 347 (Scalia, J., dissenting).
[211] *Roper*, 543 U.S. at 578.
[212] *Id.* at 575–78.
[213] *Id.* at 564–68. *Cf. Lawrence*, 539 U.S. at 572–73; *Atkins*, 536 U.S. at 316 (n 21).
[214] *Roper*, 543 U.S. at 575.
[215] *Id.* at 624 (Scalia, J., dissenting).
[216] *Id.* at 628.
[217] *Id.* at 561 (quoting Trop v. Dulles, 356 U.S. 86 (1958)).
[218] *Trop*, 356 U.S. at 100–01 (plurality opinion).
[219] Dorsen, *supra* note 116, at 525.

cherry-picked examples from left-leaning countries, in his view, should not displace the views of a majority of Americans. He noted in his remarks at American University that justices cite foreign law "[w]hen it agrees with what . . . [they] would like the case to say, and when it doesn't agree we don't use it."[220] He went on to ask the students in attendance:

> Do you think you're representative of American society? Do you not realize you are a small layer of cream at the top of the educational system, and that your views on innumerable things are not the views of America at large? And doesn't it seem somewhat arrogant for you to say, when you later become judges, I can make up what the moral values of America should be . . . Yet that's the only context in which the use of foreign law makes sense.[221]

Both *Roper* and *Lawrence* also overruled precedents that were fewer than twenty years old, which fueled the charges that these were radically different and destabilizing decisions. Scalia made this point in his *Lawrence* dissent, drawing a distinction between the LGBTQ+ rights and abortion contexts. As he pointed out, the majority in *Casey* (1992) declared, "Liberty finds no refuge in a jurisprudence of doubt," when faced with calls to overturn *Roe* (1973).[222] He added, "The Court's response today, to those who have engaged in a 17-year crusade to overrule *Bowers* . . . is very different. The need for stability and certainty presents no barrier."[223]

Atkins, *Lawrence*, and *Roper* also drew the ire of conservative lawmakers in Congress and in state legislatures. From 2003 to 2005, Republicans in the U.S. House of Representatives introduced several bills and resolutions targeting the Supreme Court's use of foreign law.[224] One resolution specifically criticized opinions by Justices Stevens, Breyer, Kennedy, and Ginsburg that cited foreign sources.[225] It further "remind[ed]" these justices "of the judicial oath they took as a precondition to assuming their responsibilities," and that "the executive and legislative branches . . . are the only branches whose officers are elected by the people."[226] A subsequent resolution, called the "Reaffirming American Independence Resolution," cautioned against the "inappropriate judicial reliance on foreign judgments, laws, or pronouncements," which "threate[n] the sovereignty of the United States, the separation of powers, and the President's and the Senate's treaty-making authority."[227] Sponsors of this resolution even threatened

220 *Id.* at 521.
221 *Id.* at 526.
222 *Lawrence*, 539 U.S. at 586 (Scalia, J., dissenting) (citing *Casey*, 505 U.S. at 844).
223 *Id.*
224 *See* David S. Law, *Generic Constitutional Law*, 89 MINN. L. REV. 652, 657 (2005).
225 *See* H.R. Res. 468, 108th Cong. (2003).
226 *Id.*
227 H.R. Res. 568, 108th Cong. (2004).

to impeach justices who relied on foreign law, leading Democratic congressional leaders to accuse them of "judicial intimidation."[228]

At the state level, legislators in more than thirty states proposed resolutions or laws to limit the use of foreign law.[229] Several states, including Kansas, Oklahoma, Arizona, Louisiana, and Tennessee, successfully enacted legislation or constitutional amendments banning or curtailing the reliance on foreign law, suggesting that they shared the democracy and sovereignty-based concerns expressed by Justice Scalia and Republican lawmakers in Congress.[230]

Conservative-leaning scholarship in the 2000s added more weight to these critiques.[231] Roger P. Alford wrote several articles in this period criticizing the liberal justices' use of comparative law in constitutional adjudication as, among other things, "haphazard."[232] Alford also made the case that foreign sources are "misuse[d]" if they are deployed to "thwart the domestic opinions of Americans."[233] Referring to this as the "international countermajoritarian difficulty," Alford argued that relying on "international majoritarian values . . . dramatically undermines sovereignty . . . [and] trump[s] the democratic will reflected in state and federal [law]."[234]

Scalia's elite-centric criticism of foreign citations was most powerfully articulated and elaborated upon by Ken Kersch. In a 2005 article, he tied the use of foreign judicial citations to broader developments in that period.[235] The "new legal transnationalism," according to Kersch, formed "part of an elite-driven, politically-motivate worldwide trend toward judicial governance, which is antithetical to democratic self-rule, if not to the rule of law itself."[236] Though this framing exaggerates the degree to which justices engaged in comparative analysis and the threat posed

[228] Law, *supra* note 224, at 657; *Hearing on H. Res. 568 Before the Subcomm. on the Const. of the House Comm. on the Judiciary*, 108th Cong., 2d Sess. 1, 42–43 (2004) (statement of Rep. Jerrold Nadler, Ranking Member of the Subcommittee on the Constitution).

[229] *See* Law, *supra* note 204, at 939.

[230] *Id.*; FAIZA PATEL ET AL., FOREIGN LAW BANS: LEGAL UNCERTAINTIES AND PRACTICAL PROBLEMS 1-4 (2013) (arguing that fears of Sharia Law infiltrating domestic law motivated some of these bans).

[231] *See, e.g.*, Eric Posner, *Transnational Legal Process and the Supreme Court's 2003–2004 Term: Some Skeptical Observations*, 12 TULSA J. COMP. & INT'L L. 23, 36 (2004); Roger P. Alford, *In Search of a Theory for Constitutional Comparativism*, 52 U.C.L.A. L. REV. 639 (2005). Conservative judges on the U.S. Courts of Appeals also argued against using foreign law. *See, e.g.*, Richard Posner, *No Thanks, We Already Have Our Own Laws*, LEGAL AFF., July–Aug. 2004; Diarmuid F. O'Scannlain, *What Role Should Foreign Practice and Precedent Play in the Interpretation of Domestic Law?*, 80 NOTRE DAME L. REV. 1893 (2005); J. Harvie Wilkinson III, *The Use of International Law in Judicial Decisions*, 27 HARV. J.L. & PUB. POL'Y 423 (2004).

[232] *See* Roger P. Alford, *Lower Courts and Constitutional Comparativism*, 77 FORDHAM L. REV. 647, 662 (2008) (arguing that "the quixotic and haphazard approach . . . that the Supreme Court adopted in *Lawrence* and *Roper*" may account for the lower courts' reluctance to engage in comparative analysis).

[233] Roger P. Alford, *Misusing International Sources to Interpret the Constitution*, 98 AM. J. INT'L L. 57, 58 (2004).

[234] *Id.* at 58–61.

[235] *See* Ken I. Kersch, *The New Legal Transnationalism, the Globalized Judiciary, and the Rule of Law*, 4 WASH. U. GLOBAL STUD. L. REV. 345 (2005).

[236] *Id.* at 346.

to American sovereignty,[237] it correctly identified two trends that peaked in the mid-2000s: cosmopolitan legal scholarship and global constitutionalism.

In the 1990s and 2000s, there was an explosion in legal scholarship that sought to theorize and, in some cases, encourage judicial engagement with foreign sources.[238] The global influence of American constitutionalism was strong in those years, even if it has since declined.[239] In this period, Anne-Marie Slaughter chronicled the rise of "judicial dialogue"[240] and a "global community of courts."[241] She documented, among other things, the increasing frequency of both formal and informal "transjudicial communication."[242] Judges around the turn of the millennium, as Slaughter showed, were "coming together in all sorts of ways" from "seminars to training sessions and judicial organizations."[243]

One such event was the Yale Law School Global Constitutional Seminar, which brought leading judges from around the world together to learn from each other's experiences. Participants included constitutional court justices including Aharon Barak (Israel), Pedro Cruz Villalón (Spain), Lech Garlicki (Poland), Dieter Grimm (Germany), Frank Iacobucci (Canada), and László Sólyom (Hungary).[244] Inaugurated in 1996, the Seminar exemplified the height of global constitutionalism, when judges were seen as integral players in the seemingly inevitable spread of constitutional democracy. As Owen Fiss remarked on the Seminar's twentieth anniversary:

> This seminar was a product of its time—a triumphant moment in the history of democratic constitutionalism viewed on a world scale... The aim was to create a forum for those judges engaged in the practice of democratic constitutionalism to learn from one another. We assumed that by sharing their knowledge and experience the values then being applauded ["liberal democracy, constitutionalism, and cosmopolitanism"]... would be deepened and extended.[245]

[237] *See* Mark Tushnet, *Transnational/Domestic Constitutional Law*, 37 Loy. L.A. L. Rev. 239, 248 (2003) (referring to the controversy over the use of foreign law as a "tempest in a teapot") (internal quotation marks omitted).

[238] *See, e.g.*, Harold Hongju Koh, *Transnational Legal Process*, 75 Neb. L. Rev. 181 (1996); Vicki Jackson, *Constitutional Comparison: Convergence, Resistance, Engagement*, 119 Harv. L. Rev. 109 (2005); Sarah H. Cleveland, *Our International Constitution*, 31 Yale J. Int'l L. 1 (2006).

[239] Heinz Klug, *Model and Anti-Model: The United States Constitution and the "Rise of World Constitutionalism"*, 2000 Wis. L. Rev. 597 (2000); David S. Law & Mila Versteeg, *The Declining Influence of the United States Constitution*, 87 N.Y.U. L. Rev. 762 (2012).

[240] *See* Anne-Marie Slaughter, *A Typology of Transjudicial Communication*, 29 U. Richmond L. Rev. 99 (1994).

[241] Anne-Marie Slaughter, *A Global Community of Courts*, 44 Harv. Int'l L.J. 191 (2003).

[242] *See* Slaughter, supra note 240.

[243] Slaughter, *supra* note 241, at 192.

[244] *See* Global Reconfigurations, Constitutional Obligations, and Everyday Life ii (Judith Resnik & Clare Ryan eds., 2018), https://documents.law.yale.edu/sites/default/files/gcs2018.pdf.

[245] *See* Owen Fiss, *Remarks on the 20th Anniversary of the Global Constitutional Seminar 1996–2016* (Sept. 21, 2016), https://law.yale.edu/centers-workshops/gruber-program-global-justice-and-womens-rights/global-constitutionalism-seminar/global-constitutionalism-20th-anniversary/remarks-20th-anniversary.

Through these interactions, and aided by the rise of the internet, judges became more aware of each other's opinions. This led to what Slaughter called "constitutional cross-fertilization," in which courts cited each other's precedents on a range of constitutional issues.[246] She argued that these courts engaged in an "active and ongoing dialogue" because they recognized, *inter alia*, the value of learning from each other's "experience and reasoning."[247] David Law and Wen-Chen Chang have subsequently shown that the U.S. Supreme Court has been, at most, a marginal player in such "dialogue."[248] Law and Chang also argue that "dialogue" does not capture how judges work with foreign materials or the mechanisms through which norms migrate across borders. Among other critiques, Law and Chang point out that dialogue implies a two-way conversation, when in fact norms tend to travel in one direction: from a few "highly prestigious courts" (like the U.S. Supreme Court) to less prominent courts.[249]

C. A Shift in Engagement with Foreign Materials

Though "judicial dialogue" may not fully or accurately describe the Supreme Court's engagement with foreign materials, it captured the cosmopolitan spirit of the 1990s and early 2000s. Several justices in this period expressed support for, and believed they were engaged in, this sort of collaborative exercise with courts around the world. Justice Breyer, who was the leading proponent of such engagement, expressed excitement that "the global legal enterprise is upon us,"[250] and encouraged legal "cross-fertilization" between the United States and European Union.[251] Breyer also defended his citations to foreign law as efforts to "learn" and stressed the importance of showing other countries' courts that "we read, and are interested in [their opinions]."[252] Channeling the ethos of this period, Justice Breyer further stated his belief in the eventual triumph of judicial cosmopolitanism. In an address to the American Society of International Law, he said, "Ultimately, I believe the 'comparativist' view that several of us have enunciated will carry the day . . . because of the enormous value . . . of trying to learn from the similar experience of others."[253]

[246] Slaughter, *supra* note 241, at 193.
[247] *Id. See also*, Sujit Choudhry, *Globalization in Search of Justification: Toward a Theory of Comparative Constitutional Interpretation* 74 Ind. L.J. 819 (1999).
[248] David S. Law & Wen-Chen Chang, *The Limits of Global Judicial Dialogue*, 86 Wash. L. Rev. 523, 568–69, 575 (2011) .
[249] *Id.* at 523.
[250] Stephen Breyer, *The Supreme Court and the New International Law, Address to the 97th Annual Meeting of the American Society of International Law* (Apr. 4, 2003), http://www.supremecourtus.gov/publicinfo/speeches/sp_04-04-03.html.
[251] Elizabeth Greathouse, *Justices See Joint Issues with the EU*, Wash. Post, July 9, 1998, at A24.
[252] Dorsen, *supra* note 116, at 522–23.
[253] Breyer, *supra* note 250.

Justice Kennedy also expressed the idea of "mutuality" between the United States and other countries. He said, "If we are asking the rest of the world to adopt our idea of freedom . . . other nations and other peoples can define and interpret freedom in a way that's at least instructive to us."[254] Kennedy benefitted more directly than most from exposure to foreign legal systems. For more than twenty years, he taught a summer course at the University of Salzburg in Austria.[255] His co-instructor, Professor Sionaidh Douglas-Scott, focused on human rights in Europe, while Kennedy taught students about the U.S. Bill of Rights. The course, titled Fundamental Rights, was effectively a comparative human rights course.[256] This experience likely played a significant role in enhancing Justice Kennedy's understanding of the European jurisprudence and his citation thereof.

Other justices made similar statements in the 1990s and 2000s, both in print and in speeches. Justice Ginsburg published law review articles on the value of comparative inquiry and how, in several contexts, it "could prove enlightening or valuable."[257] Two justices appointed by Republican presidents, Chief Justice Rehnquist and Justice O'Connor, also weighed in on this issue. O'Connor, a centrist and pragmatic jurist who longed played the role of "median" or "swing" justice,[258] urged the Court to be more flexible and "borrow ideas from other legal systems . . . to remain progressive."[259] Like Justice Breyer, she expressed confidence that, over time, the Court would "rely increasingly, or take notice at least increasingly, on international and foreign courts in examining domestic issues."[260]

Rehnquist, though a conservative jurist, also encouraged greater comparative judicial engagement. Writing in 1993, with a nod to global constitutionalism, he said, "[N]ow that constitutional law is solidly grounded in so many countries, it is time that the United States courts begin looking to the decisions of other constitutional courts to aid in their own deliberative process."[261] Rehnquist would go on to cite foreign law in his partial concurrence/dissent in *Casey* (1992), which

[254] Jeffrey Toobin, *Swing Shift: How Anthony Kennedy's Passion for Foreign Law Could Change the Supreme Court*, New Yorker, Sept. 12, 2005, at 42, 50.

[255] McCaffrey, *supra* note 37, at 210.

[256] *Id.*

[257] Ruth Bader Ginsburg, *"A Decent Respect to the Opinions of [Human]Kind": The Value of a Comparative Perspective in Constitutional Adjudication*, 64 Cambridge L.J. 575, 584 (2005). *See also*, Ruth Bader Ginsburg, *Looking Beyond Our Borders: The Value of a Comparative Perspective in Constitutional Adjudication*, 22 Yale L. & Pol'y Rev. 329 (2004).

[258] *See* Andrew D. Martin et al., *The Median Justice on the United States Supreme Court*, 83 N.C. L. Rev. 1275 (2005); Neal Devins, *Explaining* Grutter v. Bollinger, 152 U. Pa. L. Rev. 347, 349–50 (2003).

[259] *See* Sandra Day O'Connor, *Broadening Our Horizons: Why American Lawyers Must Learn About Foreign Law*, 45 Fed. Law. 20, 20-21 (1998).

[260] Bill Rankin, *U.S. Justice Is Honored: O'Connor Says Court Has Its Ear to the World*, Atlanta J.-Const., Oct. 29, 2003, at A3.

[261] William Rehnquist, *Constitutional Courts—Comparative Remarks*, *in* Germany and Its Basic Law: Past, Present and Future—A German–American Symposium 411, 412 (Paul Kirchhof & Donald P. Kommers eds., 1993). Rehnquist further noted that American judges and scholars were "laggard[s] in relying on comparative law and decisions of other countries."

was joined by Justices Scalia and Thomas,[262] as well as the majority opinion in *Washington v. Glucksberg* (1997).[263]

Amid this ethos of cosmopolitanism and dialogue with courts around the world, it is not surprising that the Rehnquist Court engaged with comparative materials in constitutional cases, and that both liberal and conservative justices in this period cited foreign materials.[264]

Rehnquist's death in 2005, followed by O'Connor's retirement a few months later, altered the judicial politics on foreign citations. Until the mid-2000s, the divide between "liberal" and "conservative" justices was not as pronounced.[265] Justices appointed by Republican presidents, like Chief Justice Rehnquist, Justice O'Connor, and Justice Kennedy, engaged with and cited foreign legal developments. The latter two, along with fellow Republican appointees Justices Stevens and Souter, also joined or wrote separately in favor of progressive judgments, including *Lawrence*.[266] By 2006, following the appointments of Chief Justice Roberts and Justice Alito, the battle lines were drawn between liberal and conservative justices on the issue of foreign citations.

During the judicial confirmation hearings for Roberts and Alito, the backlash to the Supreme Court's use of foreign law was apparent. Both nominees made clear their aversion to relying on foreign sources. Roberts echoed Scalia's selection-based criticism, declaring, "Foreign law, you can find anything you want. If you don't find it in the decisions of France or Italy, it's in the decisions of Somalia or Japan or Indonesia or wherever."[267] Alito, meanwhile, leaned on American exceptionalism to say, "I don't think that foreign law is helpful in interpreting the Constitution … We have our own law, we have our own traditions, we have our own precedents, and we should look to that in interpreting our Constitution."[268]

Indeed, 2005 marked a turning point in the Supreme Court's approach to foreign law. In the first six years of the Roberts Court (2005–10), there were zero references to foreign precedents.[269] Erstwhile proponents of foreign engagement, like Justice O'Connor (shortly before her retirement) and Justice Stevens, acknowledged that

[262] *Casey*, 505 U.S. at 833, 945 n.1 (1992) (Rehnquist, C.J., concurring in part and dissenting in part) (positively citing abortion decisions from German and Canadian courts).

[263] *Glucksberg*, 521 U.S. 702 at 718, n.16 (1997) (citing laws in Canada, Britain, New Zealand, Australia, and Colombia).

[264] Black et al., *supra* note 34, at 892.

[265] *See* Pamela S. Karlan, *The Supreme Court, 2011 Term—Foreword: Democracy and Disdain*, 126 HARV. L. REV. 1, 6 & n.33 (2012).

[266] *See, e.g., Atkins*, 536 U.S. at 305.

[267] Confirmation Hearing on the Nomination of John G. Roberts Jr. to be Chief Justice of the United States: Hearing Before the S. Comm. on the Judiciary, 109th Cong. 200–01 (2005) (Statement of John G. Roberts Jr., Supreme Court Nominee).

[268] Confirmation Hearing on the Nomination of Samuel A. Alito, Jr. to be an Associate Justice of the Supreme Court of the United States: Hearing Before the S. Comm. on the Judiciary, 109th Cong. 471 (2006) (Statement of Samuel A. Alito, Jr., Supreme Court Nominee).

[269] Sperti, *supra* note 35, at 406.

it had "gotten us into a lot of trouble,"[270] and that "it is not popular."[271] It appears, therefore, that the Court internalized the criticism it received from, among others, Justice Scalia.[272]

D. Originalism's Triumph

Zooming out from the specific battle over foreign citations, the First Roberts Court also saw conservatives score a broader cultural victory in making originalism the dominant mode of constitutional interpretation. I refer to originalism's triumph as a cultural rather than legal development because the Supreme Court does not (and has never) consistently adopted an originalist approach in constitutional cases.[273] Moreover, when justices with distinctly different judicial philosophies—from Ruth Bader Ginsburg to Clarence Thomas—all claim to be originalists, the term loses meaning.[274] But originalism has become the most prominent *purported* method of interpretation, even if the interpretive terrain remains more contested in practice.

While originalism today takes many forms, the underlying premise is that the Constitution's meaning is fixed at the time of adoption and should be interpreted by reference to the text alongside historical sources that shed light on its original meaning.[275] Originalism's main competitor is living constitutionalism,[276] which also takes various forms. This mode of interpretation posits that constitutional meaning changes over time through, *inter alia*, common law incrementalism or judicial responses to social movements.[277]

Justice Scalia led the charge for originalist supremacy.[278] He had limited success in converting his colleagues on the Rehnquist Court to originalism. Aside from

[270] Roger Alford, *Quotable Quotes from the Fordham Law Review Symposium*, Opinio Juris (Oct. 8, 2007), http://opiniojuris.org/2007/10/08/quotable-quotes-from-the-fordham-law-review-symposium/.

[271] Alford, *supra* note 231, at 649 (citing Transcript of Oral Argument at 41, Kennedy v. Louisiana, 128 S. Ct. 2641 (2008) (No. 07–343)).

[272] *See* Austin Parrish, *Storm in a Teacup: The U.S. Supreme Court's Use of Foreign Law*, 2007 Ill. L. Rev. 637, 641 n.19 (2007).

[273] *See* Eric J. Segall, Originalism as Faith (2018); Richard H. Fallon Jr., *Selective Originalism and Judicial Role Morality*, 102 Tex. L. Rev. 221 (2023); Jack M. Balkin, *We are All Cafeteria Originalists Now (and We Always Have Been)*, Wm. & Mary Bill Rts. J. (forthcoming).

[274] *See* Conor Casey & Adrian Vermeule, *If Every Judge Is an Originalist, Originalism Is Meaningless*, Wash. Post (Mar. 25, 2022), https://www.washingtonpost.com/outlook/2022/03/25/if-every-judge-is-an-originalist-originalism-is-meaningless/.

[275] *See* Lawrence B. Solum, *What Is Originalism? The Evolution of Contemporary Originalist Theory*, *in* The Challenge of Originalism: Theories of Constitutional Interpretation 12 (Grant Huscroft & Bradley W. Miller eds., 2011).

[276] *See* Lawrence B. Solum, *Originalism v. Living Constitutionalism: The Conceptual Structure of the Great Debate*, 113 Nw. U. L. Rev.1243 (2019).

[277] *See* David A. Strauss, The Living Constitution (2010); Robert Post & Reva Siegel, *Roe Rage: Democratic Constitutionalism and Backlash*, 42 Harv. C.R.-C.L. L. Rev. 373 (2007).

[278] *See, e.g.*, Antonin Scalia, *Originalism: The Lesser Evil*, 57 U. Cin. L. Rev. 849, 855 (1988–89) (describing the "frailty of . . . [the] theoretical underpinnings" and lack of consistent methodology in non-originalist approaches to constitutional interpretation.)

his fellow originalist Justice Thomas, the other justices, including those appointed by Republican presidents, like Justices O'Connor and Souter, had no interest in that mode of interpretation. But his persistence paid off in the First Roberts Court. As with the fight over foreign citations, Scalia's advocacy for originalism won adherents first among the law professoriate and then among his colleagues on the Court. For instance, four of today's leading originalist scholars—Lawrence Solum, Randy Barnett, John McGinnis, and Michael Rappaport—began writing extensively on this topic in the 2000s.[279]

As for Scalia's colleagues, there is evidence of a shift in their practice and in their rhetoric around originalism during the First Roberts Court. Consider, first, the practice of originalism. Justice Scalia authored possibly the most significant majority opinion of his career in *District of Columbia v. Heller* (2008).[280] The case concerned whether the Second Amendment protected an individual right to bear arms. The Court split 5–4, with Justice Kennedy siding with the four conservative justices. Scalia's majority opinion relied on historical evidence to substantiate the majority's ruling that individuals had a constitutional right to bear arms.[281] That Scalia was able to command a majority (including non-originalists like Chief Justice Roberts and Justice Kennedy) behind a full-throated originalist opinion was remarkable and, at the time, unprecedented in a case of such magnitude. What is perhaps even more telling, however, is that Justice Stevens' dissent for the liberal justices also adopted an originalist approach. He relied on historical sources to reach the opposite conclusion.[282] While historians tend to think Stevens got the better of the argument,[283] Scalia won the substantive battle on the Second Amendment and got the liberal justices to play by his rules.

The rhetorical predominance of originalism also became apparent toward the end of the 2000s and early 2010s. The First Roberts Court witnessed a consolidation of liberal and conservative blocs following the replacement of liberal-leaning Republican appointees in 2009 (David Souter) and 2010 (John Paul Stevens) with President Obama's selections of Sonia Sotomayor and Elena Kagan, respectively. Following Kagan's appointment, the Court was divided between four liberal justices appointed by Democratic presidents, and four conservative justices appointed by Republican presidents.[284] The "swing" justice (until 2018) was Justice

[279] *See e.g.*, Lawrence B. Solum, *Incorporation and Originalist Theory*, 18 J. CONTEMP. L. ISSUES 409 (2009); Randy E. Barnett, *Scalia's Infidelity: A Critique of "Faint-Hearted" Originalism*, 75 U. CIN. L. REV. 7 (2006); John O. McGinnis & Michael B. Rappaport, *A Pragmatic Defense of Originalism*, 100 NW. U. L. REV. 383 (2006).

[280] District of Columbia v. Heller, 554 U.S. 570 (2008).

[281] *Id.* at 576–603, 636.

[282] *Id.* at 642–80 (Stevens, J., dissenting).

[283] *See, e.g.*, Robert Churchill, *A Plague on All Our Houses: The Uses and Abuses of History in D.C. v. Heller*, PANORAMA, https://thepanorama.shear.org/2023/10/30/a-plague-on-all-our-houses-the-uses-and-abuses-of-history-in-d-c-v-heller/ (last visited, Sept. 22, 2024).

[284] *See id*; NEAL DEVINS & LAWRENCE BAUM, THE COMPANY THEY KEEP: HOW PARTISAN DIVISIONS CAME TO THE SUPREME COURT 149–52 (2019).

Kennedy, who was appointed by President Reagan, but voted with the liberal bloc in several landmark cases, including the major LGBTQ+ rights decisions.

During Justice Kagan's confirmation hearing in 2010, she memorably said, "[W]e are all originalists."[285] Justice Ginsburg made a similar statement a year later, saying, "I count myself as an originalist too."[286] Both justices added context to their answers to make clear that they did not subscribe to a purely historicist method of interpretation. But the fact that they called themselves originalists is revealing—it demonstrated that the interpretive zeitgeist had fundamentally shifted.

E. Winning One Culture War and Losing Another

Let us return to *Obergefell* in light of the foregoing discussion. With this context, we can better understand why Justice Kennedy's majority opinion makes no specific mention of foreign law and why he emphasized marriage's historical roots.[287] His only references in *Obergefell* to developments outside the United States were by way of background. He said, "Until the mid-20th century, same-sex intimacy long had been condemned as immoral by the state itself *in most Western nations*, a belief often embodied in the criminal law."[288] He also noted the historical significance of marriage and that "institution has existed for millennia and across civilizations."[289] However, unlike in *Lawrence*, where Justice Kennedy discussed how the United Kingdom and members of the Council of Europe no longer criminalized sodomy,[290] his *Obergefell* opinion did not mention recent international developments on same-sex marriage.

It is unlikely that Justice Kennedy and the majority were unaware or insufficiently briefed on foreign law in *Obergefell*. As discussed, Justice Kennedy has spent significant time in Europe and at least two other members of the majority, Justices Breyer and Ginsburg, were also cosmopolitan in their outlook. Moreover, an amicus brief for "Foreign and Comparative Law Experts" including Harold Koh, was filed in this case, detailing global developments on same-sex marriage.[291] As Law and Chang have demonstrated, judicial citations are not a reliable indicator of whether justices actually consider foreign law in their decision-making.[292]

[285] Confirmation Hearing on the Nomination of Elena Kagan to be an Associate Justice of the Supreme Court of the United States: Hearing Before the S. Comm. on the Judiciary, 111th Cong. 1044 (2010) at 62 [hereinafter Kagan Confirmation Hearing].

[286] Ariane de Vogue, *Justice Ginsburg Speaks About Gender Equality*, ABC NEWS (Nov. 18, 2011), https://abcnews.go.com/blogs/politics/2011/11/justice-ginsburg-speaks-about-gender-equality/.

[287] *Obergefell*, 135 S. Ct. at 2593–2608.

[288] *Id.* at 2596 (emphasis added).

[289] *Id.* at 2594.

[290] *Cf. Lawrence*, 539 U.S. at 2481.

[291] Brief of Foreign and Comparative Law Experts Harold Hongju Koh, Thomas Buergenthal, Sarah H. Cleveland, Laurence R. Helfer, Ryan Goodman, and Sujit Choudhry as Amici Curiae in Support of Petitioners, *Obergefell*, 135 S. Ct. 2584 (Nos. 14-556, 14-562, 14-571, 14-574).

[292] Law & Chang, *supra* note 248, at 559–62.

To the contrary, justices may be well versed and up to date with foreign developments without publicly signaling that knowledge through citations.[293]

A more likely explanation, therefore, is that Justice Kennedy was familiar with developments on same-sex marriage around the world but chose not to cite them. This decision served two strategic purposes. First, as persuasive authority, foreign citations were not helpful in this case.[294] Though there was a global trend toward legalizing same-sex marriage, only twenty countries permitted same-sex couples to marry in 2015. This does not qualify as an international "consensus" of the sort claimed, for instance, in the context of the juvenile death penalty.[295]

Second, by 2015, the politics surrounding foreign citations had changed. The *Obergefell* majority opinion fits within the broader retrenchment from global constitutionalism following the backlash to the Court's heightened—or at least more visible—reliance on foreign legal developments in the early 2000s. Justice Kennedy might have wished to avoid the additional controversy that might have followed from citing foreign sources, particularly in the highly polarized political climate in which *Obergefell* was decided.[296]

This apparently strategic choice was a wise one. *Obergefell* avoided an uproar over foreign citations and faced minimal backlash in domestic politics. Though the decision was met with pockets of resistance from a few counties and marriage registrars, it was broadly accepted.[297] As with much of the Supreme Court's rights jurisprudence, the judgment accorded with majority public sentiment. By 2014, Pew and Gallup polls found that 52 and 55 percent of Americans, respectively, approved of same-sex marriage. By May 2015, Pew reported 55 percent approved of marriage equality, with 39 percent opposed, while Gallup showed 60 percent approval compared to only 37 percent opposed. Polls indicate that support for marriage equality has retained majority support ever since, with Gallup reporting 60 percent or greater support since 2015.[298] By 2017, a majority or plurality of

[293] *See id.*

[294] The dissenting justices, meanwhile, found it useful to stress how recently and in how few foreign jurisdictions same-sex marriage had been recognized. *See Obergefell*, 135 S. Ct. at 2640 (Alito, J., dissenting); 135 S. Ct. at 2612 (Roberts C.J., dissenting). Thus, their foreign citations served a strategic purpose too, albeit an aversive or negative one. *See* Kim Lane Scheppele, *Aspirational and Aversive Constitutionalism: The Case for Studying Cross-Constitutional Influence Through Negative Models*, 1 INT'L J. CONST. L. 296 (2003).

[295] *Cf. Roper*, 543 U.S. at 575–78.

[296] *See* DEVINS & BAUM, *supra* note 284, at 113 (showing that approximately 72 percent of Democrats held views in line with the outcome in *Obergefell*, compared to only 35 percent of Republicans).

[297] *See* Jack M. Balkin, *The Long and Winding Road to Marriage Equality*, *in* WHAT OBERGEFELL V. HODGES SHOULD HAVE SAID 3, 47–54 (Jack M. Balkin ed., 2020). *See also*, MARK TUSHNET, TAKING BACK THE CONSTITUTION: ACTIVIST JUDGES AND THE NEXT AGE OF AMERICAN LAW 101 (2020) (referring to *Obergefell* as the "last real battle" for LGBTQ+ rights).

[298] *Attitudes on Same-Sex Marriage*, PEW RSCH. CTR. (May 14, 2019), https://www.pewforum.org/fact-sheet/changing-attitudes-on-gay-marriage/; Justin McCarthy, *U.S. Support for Gay Marriage Stable, at 63%*, GALLUP (May 22, 2019), https://news.gallup.com/poll/257705/support-gay-marriage-stable.aspx.

the population in all but two states (Alabama and Mississippi) favored same-sex marriage.[299]

Obergefell was decided at an opportune moment, as the judgment enjoyed broad popular support. President Obama called the decision a "victory for America," and his administration covered one side of the White House in rainbow-colored light on the day *Obergefell* was decided.[300] By 2015, the Court could deflect countermajoritarian criticisms by pointing to the increasing acceptance of same-sex marriage in "central institutions of American life" as well as numerous state judicial decisions and laws validating the practice.[301] And by eschewing foreign citations, Justice Kennedy could keep the Court—and the country—in line with Western Europe and Canada, without generating the sort of backlash that accompanied *Lawrence* and other hot-button cosmopolitan judgments in the 2000s.[302]

While Justice Kennedy previously deployed foreign citations to support progressive judgments, *Obergefell* was decided in a different time. Not only was the Supreme Court more conservative and the country more polarized in 2015, but the enthusiasm for judicial dialogue and cosmopolitanism had faded.[303] In this new world, the project of global constitutionalism, which Justice Kennedy had championed, was advanced in *Obergefell*, ironically, by declining to engage with foreign materials.

The upshot was that the conservative bloc on the Supreme Court prevailed on the foreign citations culture war, while losing the substantive battle on same-sex marriage. And, as we have seen, the move away from engaging foreign materials constituted part of a larger conservative victory on constitutional interpretation.

F. *Obergefell's* Exceptionalism

To appreciate the significance of the liberal victory on same-sex marriage, consider how the First Roberts Court moved the country to the right on several planks of liberal constitutionalism, even if not as dramatically as its successor.[304] Following the appointment of Justice Alito in 2006, the Court issued several landmark judgments that favored business interests and the wealthy at the expense of ordinary citizens and labor unions. It held in *Citizen's United v. Federal Election*

[299] *See The American Values Atlas*, PRRI, http://ava.prri.org/#lgbt/2017/States/lgbt_ssm/2,3,9 (last visited Apr. 13, 2021).

[300] Adam B. Lerner, *White House Set Aglow with Rainbow Pride*, POLITICO (June 26, 2015), https://www.politico.com/story/2015/06/white-house-set-aglow-with-rainbow-pride-119490.

[301] *Obergefell*, 135 S. Ct. at 2605, 2611.

[302] *Lawrence*, 539 U.S. at 558; *Roper*, 543 U.S. at 551; *Atkins*, 536 U.S. at 304.

[303] *See* David S. Law, *Alternatives to Liberal Constitutional Democracy*, 77 MD. L. REV. 223, 224 (2017).

[304] *See* Adam Liptak, *Court Under Roberts Is Most Conservative in Decades*, N.Y. TIMES (July 24, 2010), https://www.nytimes.com/2010/07/25/us/25roberts.html.

Commission (2008) that the First Amendment right to free expression included the right to spend money on political campaigns.[305] By invalidating laws that restricted independent political spending, the Court unleashed a torrent of dark money (particularly from conservative groups) into federal and state elections.[306] In *Janus v. AFSCME* (2018), the Supreme Court weakened labor unions by ruling that they could not charge fees to non-members.[307]

The Supreme Court in this era also cut back on the rights of racial minorities. In *Shelby County v. Holder* (2013), the Court struck down two provisions of the Voting Rights Act, which enabled states to redraw district lines and engage in voter suppression to minimize the political voice of African Americans in particular.[308] A few years earlier, in *Parents Involved in Community School v. Seattle School District 1* (2007), the Court ruled that it was unconstitutional for a school district to consider race in determining the composition of schools.[309] Justice Breyer's long dissent in that case reflected the liberal justices' frustration with the conservative retrenchment on core pillars of the constitutional order. He wrote:

> [The Court] distorts precedent, it misapplies the relevant constitutional principles, it announces legal rules that will obstruct efforts by state and local governments to deal effectively with the growing resegregation of public schools, it threatens to substitute for present calm a disruptive round of race-related litigation, and it undermines *Brown*'s promise of integrated primary and secondary education that local communities have sought to make a reality.[310]

In this context, the Court's progressive judgments on same-sex marriage in *Windsor*(2013) and especially *Obergefell* (2015) appear all the more remarkable.

Obergefell also proved to an exception to the test that rights recognized within the Due Process Clause of the Fourteenth Amendment must be "deeply rooted in this Nation's history and tradition" and "implicit in the concept of ordered liberty."[311] Justice Kennedy had joined Chief Justice Rehnquist's majority opinion in *Glucksberg*, which announced this test. In *Obergefell*, Kennedy sidestepped *Glucksberg* by showing that marriage itself was deeply rooted in the nation's history. He declared that rights "come not from ancient sources alone" but also arise

[305] Citizen's United v. Federal Election Commission, 558 U.S. 310 (2010).

[306] *See* Jane Meyer, Dark Money: The Hidden History of the Billionaires Behind the Rise of the Radical Right (2017).

[307] Janus v. AFSCME, 138 S. Ct. 2448 (2018).

[308] Shelby County v. Holder, 570 U.S. 529 (2013); For an exhaustive account of the Roberts Court's voting and democratic-process related jurisprudence, see Michael J. Klarman, *The Supreme Court, 2019 Term—Foreword: The Degradation of American Democracy—And the Court*, 134 Harv. L. Rev. 1, 178–231 (2020).

[309] Parents Involved in Community School v. Seattle School District 1, 127 S. Ct 2738 (2007).

[310] *Id.* at 2800–01 (Breyer, J., dissenting).

[311] *Glucksberg*, 521 U.S. at 721.

from "a better informed understanding of how constitutional imperatives define a liberty that remains urgent in our own era."[312]

This living constitutionalism gloss on *Glucksberg* has not extended beyond same-sex marriage. Indeed, the Second Roberts Court in *Dobbs* reverted to a much narrower reading of *Glucksberg*—based on ancient sources alone—to conclude that there was no constitutional right to abortion.[313] The Court no longer relies on "evolving standards of decency"[314] or an emerging consensus in the United States (much less around the world) to determine the existence and scope of substantive due process rights.

Obergefell thus exemplifies the exceptionalism accorded by the Supreme Court to certain LGBTQ+ rights, like same-sex marriage. Its progressive ruling and doctrinal maneuvering to reach the preferred result stand apart from the otherwise conservative rights jurisprudence of the First Roberts Court. *Obergefell* along with *Lawrence* and *Windsor* not only accorded with Justice Kennedy's libertarian philosophy but also served to maintain a progressive rights agenda on U.S. Supreme Court and played well to international audiences. As we turn to the Second Roberts Court, LGBTQ+ continue to be exceptional, but as we shall see, they serve a different strategic purpose: institutional self-preservation.

IV. Polarization, Trump, and the Makings of Partisan Supreme Court

Originalism's triumph in elite legal circles was confirmed when then-nominee Elena Kagan declared in 2010, "[W]e are all originalists."[315] A few years later, Republican Senate Majority Leader Mitch McConnell proudly trumpeted Kagan's statement, along with similar remarks from Justice Ginsburg, on his official website.[316] McConnell, a former judge, placed enormous value on judicial appointments and led the Republicans in Congress toward securing a conservative supermajority on the Supreme Court.

In February 2016, Justice Scalia unexpectedly passed away. President Obama, who had less than a year remaining in his second term, nominated Merrick Garland to fill Scalia's seat. A moderate judge respected by the Republican leadership, Garland was supposed to have bipartisan appeal with the potential to be confirmed by a Republican-controlled Senate. But McConnell had other ideas. He stalled Garland's nomination, arguing that the next presidential election was

[312] *Obergefell*, 135 S. Ct. at 2602.
[313] *Dobbs*, 142 S. Ct. at 2242.
[314] *Trop*, 356 U.S. at 100–01.
[315] Kagan Confirmation Hearing, *supra* note 285.
[316] *"We Are All Originalists"*, Mitch McConnell: Republican Leader (Oct. 13, 2020), https://www.republicanleader.senate.gov/newsroom/research/we-are-all-originalists-barrett.

approaching, and that the new president should select Scalia's replacement. There was no precedent for such a long delay, but because Hillary Clinton was widely expected to win the 2016 election, Obama and the Democrats in Congress did not fight McConnell too strongly. As it turned out, of course, Donald Trump would upset Clinton in the presidential election, and McConnell's gamble paid off spectacularly for those yearning for a long-term conservative majority on the Court.

The Supreme Court today has a 6–3 conservative supermajority, with the six conservative justices appointed by Republican presidents and the three liberal justices appointed by Democratic presidents. The Court—like the country—is deeply divided along partisan lines. The gap between justices appointed by Democratic and Republican presidents has widened, just as a yawning political divide has emerged between the two parties. The Court retains little, if any, institutional credibility, with many observers now treating it as a partisan institution.[317]

This Part examines how we arrived at this dysfunctional state of affairs and discusses the Court's attempts to salvage its reputation against charges of partisan decision-making and corruption.

A. The Rise of Political Polarization

When Ronald Reagan became President in 1980, the Supreme Court was seen as an institution that, by and large, favored the policy prerogatives of the Democratic Party. Since conservatives were not winning on the merits of their legal arguments, they decided to change the composition of the Court and the entire federal judiciary. The Reagan administration prioritized judicial appointments like no previous presidential administration and made them distinctly partisan. The Federalist Society—launched by students at Yale and Chicago law schools in the early 1980s, under the supervision of then-Professor Antonin Scalia—would become a key player in shaping potential conservative judicial nominees and maintaining a pool of suitable candidates for conservative administrations to draw from.[318] Commitment to certain interpretive philosophies (like textualism and originalism), alongside apparent political leanings on major social issues like abortion, became the most important factors in determining who would be appointed to the bench.[319]

The present wave of political polarization can be traced back to the 1990s. Bill Clinton's election as President in 1992 (ending twelve years of Republican rule)

[317] *See, e.g.*, Richard L. Hasen, *The Supreme Court's Pro-Partisanship Turn*, 51 Geo. L.J. Online 108 (2020); Mathew Levendusky et al., *Has the Supreme Court Become Just Another Political Branch? Public Perceptions of Approval and Legitimacy in a Post-*Dobbs *World*, 10(10) Sci. Advances eadk9590 (2024).

[318] On the origins and impact of the Federalist Society, see Amanda Hollis-Brusky, Ideas with Consequences: The Federalist Society and the Conservative Counterrevolution (2014).

[319] *See id.* at ch. 6.

led to a fierce conservative backlash. Newt Gingrich's "Contract with America," the Republican legislative agenda for the 1994 congressional elections, coupled with his five-year reign as Speaker of the House (1994–99), was the most concrete early manifestation of this polarization.[320] Gingrich's political strategy—to cast Democrats as unpatriotic and dangerous—flipped more than fifty seats in 1994 and gave Republicans their first majority in the House of Representatives since 1952. It marked an epochal shift toward hardline political stances that has metastasized into the alarming level of political dysfunction that we witness today.[321] As Jack Balkin put it, the country is in a state of constitutional "rot."[322]

A significant feature of American political polarization is its asymmetry. Republicans have moved substantially further to the political right than Democrats have moved to the left.[323] Republicans in Congress have, with more force and regularity than their colleagues across the bench, adopted strong ideological positions and played constitutional "hardball"—tactics that are within constitutional bounds but are in tension with democratic, bipartisan norms.[324]

Gingrich's cynical electoral strategy gradually became the ordinary course of politics, especially for Republicans. Several factors contributed to this asymmetric polarization. At a structural level, the Senate and Electoral College—which were designed to be countermajoritarian institutions—became increasingly undemocratic.[325] Both institutions favor smaller states. In the Senate, every state is represented by two senators regardless of their size. California, which has more than seventy times the population of Wyoming, thus receives no more representation in this powerful body. Similarly, no state is awarded fewer than three electoral votes in the Electoral College, which determines the presidential election every four years.

Due to demographic shifts in recent years, liberal voters who largely favor the Democratic Party disproportionately live in big cities and along the coasts. The vast interior of the United States, which is predominantly Republican, contains a majority of the smaller states that are overrepresented in both the Senate and Electoral College.[326] As a result, Republicans commanded Senate majorities in

[320] *See* Thomas E. Mann & Norman J. Ornstein, It's Even Worse Than It Looks: How the American Constitutional System Collided with the New Politics of Extremism 31–43 (2012).

[321] *See id.* at 50 (arguing that since the early 1990s, the "rules, practices, and norms designed to ensure a reasonable level of deliberation and fair play [in Congress were] . . . often sacrificed for political expediency").

[322] Balkin, *supra* note 102, at 44–46.

[323] *Id.* at 31.

[324] *See* Mark Tushnet, *Constitutional Hardball*, 37 J. Marshall. L. Rev. 523 (2004); Joseph Fishkin & David Pozen, *Asymmetric Constitutional Hardball*, 118 Colum. L. Rev. 915 (2018) (explaining how Republicans resort to hardball tactics more frequently and with more force than Democrats).

[325] *See* Sanford Levinson, Our Undemocratic Constitution 49–62, 81–101 (2006); Steven Levitsky & Daniel Ziblatt, Tyranny of the Minority: Why American Democracy Reached the Breaking Point (2023), at ch. 6.

[326] *See* Dante J. Scala & Kenneth M. Johnson, *Political Polarization along the Rural-Urban Continuum? The Geography of the Presidential Vote, 2000–2016*, 672 Annals Am. Acad. Pol. & Soc. Sci. 162 (2017).

2016 and 2018 despite receiving only 45 and 48 percent, respectively, of the national popular vote.[327] Meanwhile, Democratic presidential candidates won more votes nationally than their Republican counterparts in every election but one from 1992 to 2020, but Republicans prevailed in three of those elections due to their Electoral College advantage.[328] This imbalance has been hugely significant, among other things, for federal judicial nominations. Donald Trump, despite winning only 46 percent of the national vote in 2016, was elected President and appointed three Supreme Court justices in four years.

Republicans have capitalized on these advantages through various undemocratic means. In many cases, such tactics were first adopted by Republican leaders at the state level and later successfully replicated in national politics.[329] Following the 2010 census, the Republican Party engaged in an unprecedented level of partisan gerrymandering in which they redrew the boundaries of congressional districts to maximize the value of their voters and diminish those of Democratic voters.[330] This cynical strategy worked. In the 2012 election, for example, Republicans won a 33-seat majority in the House of Representatives despite winning fewer votes than Democrats nationally, and less than 48 percent of the total vote. Republicans also led voter suppression efforts by enacting voter-ID laws in several states that disproportionately harmed lower income and minority groups who favor the Democratic Party.[331]

Various economic and cultural factors have also contributed to political polarization. The Supreme Court's decision in *Citizen's United* (2010) unleashed unlimited spending on elections, allowing a few wealthy individuals and entities to have an outsized effects on the candidates chosen to contest political office and their policy platforms.[332] Billionaire donors, including the Koch brothers, have had an especially pernicious effect on the Republican Party, leading it to adopt extreme political positions that are out of line with the mainstream of American public opinion.[333] Meanwhile, broad shifts in the national economy have seen manufacturing jobs move overseas or lost to automation.[334] Coupled with the rise of immigration—and the right-wing political rhetoric that falsely blames immigrants for the loss of these jobs—vast swathes of the country feel alienated or

[327] LEVITSKY & ZIBLATT, *supra* note 325, at ch. 6.

[328] *Id.* (the exception was 2004, when George W. Bush won a majority of the popular vote).

[329] *See* JACOB M. GRUMBACH, LABORATORIES AGAINST DEMOCRACY: HOW NATIONAL PARTIES TRANSFORMED STATE POLITICS 151–75 (2022).

[330] Klarman, *supra* note 308, at 46–47.

[331] *Id.* at 48–51; LEVITSKY & ZIBLATT, *supra* note 325, at ch. 4.

[332] *Citizen's United*, 558 U.S. 310; MEYER, *supra* note 306.

[333] *See, e.g.*, Michael Beckel, *GOP's Senate Hopes Energized by Koch Network Ad Blitz*, CTR. PUB. INTEGRITY (Sept. 4, 2014), https://publicintegrity.org/politics/gops-senate-hopes-energized-by-koch-network-ad-blitz/.

[334] *See* Abu Bakar Siddique, *Job Market Polarization and American Poverty*, 57(30) J. LAB. MKT. RSCH. (2023).

like "strangers in their own land."[335] There is deep resentment toward Washington and toward the "Blue" coastal states in which education levels and median incomes are substantially higher than in the "Red" states of the interior.[336]

This resentment is amplified by a polarized media landscape led by right-wing media channels like Fox News and, to a lesser extent, left-leaning channels like MSNBC. American news media used to be required to present matters of public importance fairly, reflecting different points of view.[337] The Federal Communications Commission (FCC) abolished this "Fairness Doctrine" in 1987 under the Reagan administration, which along with the rise of national cable TV, enabled the likes of Fox News and MSNBC to emerge. Republicans and Democrats thus receive political news from diametrically opposed sources and have their partisan views reinforced within their respective media bubbles.[338] Social media in recent years has also become polarized, with online users sorting themselves into separate "online echo chambers,"[339] and reacting much more positively to posts from like-minded users than those holding different political views.[340]

B. Judicial Polarization

As politics became polarized, so too did the judiciary.[341] Partisan responses to culturally salient Supreme Court decisions were once more pronounced between elites and non-elites, with Democratic and Republican elites sharing similar views. But today, we see elite polarization: the most conservative Americans today are highly educated and wealthy Republicans; the most liberal Americans are highly educated and wealthy Democrats.[342] Thus, the Supreme Court itself—comprised of nine legal elites—has become especially polarized in recent years, mirroring the shift in elite culture.

[335] *See generally*, ARLIE RUSSELL HOCHSCHILD, STRANGERS IN THEIR OWN LAND: ANGER AND MOURNING ON THE AMERICAN RIGHT (2016).

[336] *See generally*, Andrew Gelman, RED STATE, BLUE STATE, RICH STATE, POOR STATE: WHY AMERICANS VOTE THE WAY THEY DO (2010); PIPPA NORRIS & RONALD INGLEHART, TRUMP, BREXIT, AND AUTHORITARIAN POPULISM (2019).

[337] *See* Filipe Campante & Daniel Hojman, *Media and Polarization: Evidence from the Introduction of Broadcast TV in the United States*, 100 J. PUB. ECON. 79 (2013).

[338] *See* John V. Duca & Jason L. Saving, *Income Inequality, Media Fragmentation, and Increased Political Polarization*, 35 CONTEMP. ECON. POL'Y 392 (2016).

[339] Matteo Cinelli et al., *The Echo Chamber Effect on Social Media*, PROC. NATL ACAD. SCI. 118, e2023301118 (2021).

[340] Kristina Lerman et al., *Affective Polarization and Dynamics of Information Spread in Online Networks*, 1(8) NPJ COMPLEXITY (2024).

[341] On judicial polarization, see Iddo Porat, *Court Polarization: A Comparative Perspective*, 46 HASTINGS INT'L & COMP. L. REV. 1 (2023); Richard L. Hasen, *Polarization and the Judiciary*, 22 ANN. REV. POL. SCI. 261 (2019); Neal Devins & Lawrence Baum, *Split Definitive: How Party Polarization Turned the Supreme Court into a Partisan* Court, 2016 SUP. CT. REV. 301 (2016).

[342] *See* DEVINS & BAUM, *supra* note 284, 112–14.

From the early 1990s until 2018, the Court was roughly balanced between liberal and conservative justices, and the justices' interpretive philosophies did not necessarily correlate with a political party. Judicial appointments became noticeably more politicized and divisive under President George W. Bush (2000–08). And as with political polarization, judicial polarization is asymmetric. Those in conservative legal circles were disappointed by Republican-appointed moderate and liberal-leaning justices like Anthony Kennedy and David Souter. They believed that these appointees were not only insufficiently vetted but also affected by the so-called Greenhouse Effect. Named after veteran *New York Times* reporter Linda Greenhouse, who covered the Supreme Court from 1978 to 2008, the Greenhouse Effect refers to the phenomenon of conservative judges, especially those on the Supreme Court, moderating their views to receive more favorable coverage in the *Times* and other mainstream news sources. Lawrence Baum has shown that while some justices (like Scalia and Thomas) are sufficiently anchored in conservative legal values to avoid this effect, others, like Justices Kennedy and Souter, moved substantially to the left in their voting patterns on civil liberties cases as their tenures on the Court progressed.[343] When George W. Bush became President, conservative legal elites, led by the Federalist Society, ensured that judicial nominees from the district courts up to the Supreme Court were bona fide conservatives.[344] While nominees were ostensibly chosen for their judicial philosophy, the Federalist Society almost always supported candidates who had clear right-leaning, Republican political values as well.[345]

If we look at Republican Supreme Court nominees over the past twenty years, it becomes clear that they fit a certain judicial (and political) profile. Chief Justice Roberts and Justice Alito both worked in Republican administrations, with Alito authoring a concurring/dissenting opinion in *Casey* when he was a judge on the Third Circuit Court of Appeals that would have upheld burdensome requirements for women seeking an abortion.[346] Justice Kavanaugh similarly worked in a Republican administration and helped draft Independent Counsel Ken Starr's report recommending the impeachment of President Bill Clinton.

Justice Gorsuch worked in the Bush administration's justice department. Prior to that, he completed a doctorate on assisted suicide under the supervisor of John Finnis, a leading proponent of natural law. Gorsuch is an avowed originalist, which was clear from his jurisprudence on the Tenth Circuit Court

[343] *See* Lawrence Baum, Judges and Their Audiences: A Perspective on Judicial Behavior 139–50 (2006).
[344] *See* Hollis-Brusky, *supra* note 318, at ch. 6.
[345] *Id.*
[346] Planned Parenthood v. Casey, 947 F. 2d 682 (3rd Cir. 1991) (Alito, J., concurring in part and dissenting in part).

of Appeals prior to his elevation to the Supreme Court. Justice Barrett, meanwhile, clerked for Justice Scalia, and then worked as a law professor, writing several journal articles that laid out her conservative judicial philosophy.[347] Along with Kavanaugh and Roberts, she also worked for George W. Bush's legal team that worked to stop the recount in Florida following the closely contested 2000 presidential election. All of these justices (and Clarence Thomas, who was nominated by President George H.W. Bush in 1991) were members of the Federalist Society.[348]

By contrast, if we examine the recent nominees of Democratic presidents, none of them has clearly left-leaning views. To the contrary, they were selected for their moderate and small-c conservative judicial philosophies. Justice Sotomayor, for instance, was first appointed to the federal bench by a Republican President: George H.W. Bush. Justice Kagan, while having worked in the Clinton and Obama administrations, was known as a moderate and someone who effectively reached out to conservatives. Judge Merrick Garland—who was nominated by President Obama to replace Justice Scalia but was not confirmed—also had a reputation for moderation and bipartisanship. Justice Ketanji Brown Jackson has some hallmarks of a left-leaning jurist, including her stint as a public defender and her role on the U.S. Sentencing Commission in reducing sentences for crack cocaine offenders. Still, Jackson made clear in her confirmation hearing that while she did not have a strong judicial philosophy, she saw value in originalism and believed that constitutional meaning was fixed at the time of its enactment.[349] She also disavowed living constitutionalism.[350]

Overall, while political and judicial polarization predated Donald Trump's political rise, but both were turbocharged during his presidency (2016–20).[351] As the most demagogic, illiberal, and divisive President of the modern age, Trump inspires fierce confidence and devotion from his political base, and a combination of disbelief and horror from his opponents, including members of the Republican establishment and the Democrats. Despite all of Trump's norm-breaking (and often law-breaking) behavior and rhetoric, his most enduring legacy was the appointment of three Supreme Court justices within just one presidential term. These justices, all drawn from the Federalist Society pool, have fundamentally reshaped the Court.

[347] *See, e.g.*, Amy Coney Barrett, *Originalism and Stare Decisis*, 92 NOTRE DAME L. REV. 1921 (2017); Amy Coney Barrett & John Copeland Nagle, *Congressional Originalism*, 19 J. CONST. L. 1 (2016).

[348] *See* HOLLIS-BRUSKY, *supra* note 318, at ch. 6.

[349] *See* James Hohmann, *Justice Jackson and the Power of Originalism*, WASH. POST (Apr. 7, 2022), https://www.washingtonpost.com/opinions/2022/04/07/justice-jackson-power-originalism/.

[350] *Id.*

[351] *See* BALKIN, *supra* note 102, at 55–62.

C. A Partisan Supreme Court

On January 6, 2021, outgoing President Donald Trump organized a rally to support his unsubstantiated claim that the 2020 presidential election had been stolen. Thousands of Trump's supporters gathered at the "Save America" rally and, shortly thereafter, some of them stormed the U.S. Capitol building. The ensuing riots left seven people dead, more than one hundred others injured, and the Capitol severely damaged.[352]

One week later, the House of Representatives—controlled by the Democratic Party—impeached Trump for "incitement to insurrection."[353] The U.S. Constitution requires two-thirds of the Senate (67 of its 100 members) to vote in favor of conviction. As it turned out, only fifty-seven senators voted to convict: all fifty Democrats and seven Republicans. Forty-three Republican Senators voted to acquit Trump despite the clear evidence that he had incited the mob to attack their place of work. It is worth recalling that this was Trump's second impeachment and acquittal. In December 2019, the House of Representatives impeached him on two counts (abuse of power and obstruction of Congress), before all but one of the Senate Republicans voted to acquit him.[354]

Fast-forward to 2024. Donald Trump is the Republican nominee for President. Because Congress failed to bar him from office through the impeachment process, legislators and voters in several states tried to keep Trump off the ballot using a constitutional provision that had not been invoked since the Civil War (1861–65).[355] That provision, Section Three of the Fourteenth Amendment, prevents individuals who have "previously taken an oath . . . to support the Constitution" and have "engaged in insurrection or rebellion" against the United States from holding federal office.[356]

In December 2023, the Colorado Supreme Court ruled that Trump was disqualified from the primary ballot in that state due to his role in the insurrection on January 6, 2021.[357] Trump appealed, and the case came before the U.S. Supreme Court. A few months prior to the Supreme Court's decision in this case, the eminent conservative legal scholars William Baude and Michael Stokes Paulsen meticulously set forth the originalist case for (1) Section Three remaining in force after

[352] *See* UNITED STATES SENATE, EXAMINING THE U.S. CAPITAL ATTACK: A REVIEW OF THE SECURITY, PLANNING, AND RESPONSE FAILURES ON JANUARY 6 (2022), at 1–2.

[353] Nicholas Fandos, *Trump Impeached for Inciting Insurrection*, N.Y. TIMES (Jan. 13, 2021), https://www.nytimes.com/2021/01/13/us/politics/trump-impeached.html.

[354] Nicholas Fandos & Michael D. Shear, *Trump Impeached for Abuse of Power and Obstruction of Congress*, N.Y. TIMES (Dec. 18, 2019), https://www.nytimes.com/2019/12/18/us/politics/trump-impeached.html.

[355] *See* Edward Helmore, *US Supreme Court Under Pressure to Rule Swiftly on States' Trump Ballot Bans*, GUARDIAN (Dec. 30, 2023), https://www.theguardian.com/us-news/2023/dec/29/maine-trump-ballot-us-supreme-court.

[356] U.S. CONST., amend. XIV, § 3.

[357] *See* Anderson v. Griswold, No. 23SA300 (Colo. Dec. 19, 2023).

the Civil War; (2) its application to all federal offices, including the presidency; and (3) its operation as a self-executing provision that automatically disqualifies candidates from office without congressional action.[358] A leading constitutional historian, Mark Graber, further established that the events of January 6 would have been understood by the framers of the Fourteenth Amendment as an "insurrection" and that Trump "engaged" in it.[359]

As a result of this scholarship, and because of Trump's egregious conduct, the American law professoriate widely believed the Supreme Court would uphold the Colorado judgment.[360] However, in an unsigned, *per curiam* opinion, the Court ruled that states could not bar Trump from the ballot.[361] The Court expressed concerns about the practical consequences of states disqualifying candidates on a piecemeal basis, as it could potentially disenfranchise voters and generally cause election-related chaos.[362]

More surprisingly, the Court ruled that Congress has the exclusive power to enforce Section Three. Courts and individual states thus lack the authority to declare a candidate ineligible for office unless explicitly authorized by an Act of Congress.[363] The *per curiam* opinion—which the three liberal justices did not join—was the product of five conservative justices, all appointed by Republican presidents.[364] At least three of these justices are purported originalists. They not only disregarded the historical evidence that Section Three was self-enforcing but also relied on consequentialist, pragmatic election-related concerns that are anathema to the originalist mode of interpretation.

These events highlight the extreme levels of political and judicial polarization in the United States today. Both Republicans in Congress and their appointees on the Supreme Court demonstrably put their party interests and policy prerogatives ahead of their self-professed principles and certainly ahead of the public interest.

The 6–3 conservative supermajority on the Supreme Court has issued several other rulings that align a little too neatly with the increasingly right-wing positions of the Republican Party. While the First Roberts Court moved in a conservative direction on issues ranging from voting rights to the Second Amendment,

[358] *See* William Baude & Michael Stokes Paulsen, *The Sweep and Force of Section Three*, 172 U. PENN. L. REV. 605 (2024).
[359] *See* Mark Graber, *Section Three of the Fourteenth Amendment: Insurrection*, WM. & MARY BILL RTS. J. (forthcoming).
[360] *See* Samuel Moyn, *"Liberal Originalism" Rest in Peace*, BALKINIZATION (Feb. 12, 2024), https:// balkin.blogspot.com/2024/02/liberal-originalism-rest-in-peace.html.
[361] *See* Trump v. Anderson, 601 U.S. 100, 117 (2024).
[362] *Id.* at 115–17.
[363] *Id.* at 114–16.
[364] Justice Barrett wrote a separate opinion as did Justices Sotomayor, Kagan, and Jackson, jointly. Both opinions agreed that states lack the power to enforce Section 3 against a presidential candidate, but thought it was unnecessary for the Court to rule that Congress must declare a candidate ineligible. *See id.* at 117–18 (Barrett, J., concurring in part and concurring in the judgment), 118–23 (Sotomayor, J., Kagan, J., and Jackson, J., concurring in the judgment).

the Second Roberts Court has turned the country more sharply to the right by overruling well-entrenched constitutional precedents. *Dobbs* (2022), as discussed, overturned fifty years of precedent that recognized a constitutional right to abortion.[365] The decision has had catastrophic effects on reproductive health, especially for women from minority and disadvantaged communities.[366] Because the decision deviated so far from mainstream public opinion, it has galvanized women and other pro-choice groups to make their voices heard through the political process. For instance, Democrats scored victories in several statewide referendums on abortion and performed better than expected in the 2022 midterm elections.[367]

That year, the Court also issued a landmark judgment in *Kennedy v. Bremerton School District* ruling that a high school football coach's postgame Christian prayer was constitutionally protected.[368] *Kennedy* effectively overruled a 1971 precedent, which set forth the judicial test for whether government action violated the Establishment Clause of the First Amendment.[369] One year later, in *Students for Fair Admissions v. Harvard* (2023), the Supreme Court overturned another half-century old precedent by ruling that race could not be used as a factor in the university admissions process.[370] All these cases were decided 6–3, with the liberal justices in dissent.

Aside from their disregard for *stare decisis*, these rulings also demonstrate how the Second Roberts Court favors traditionally powerful and privileged segments of society—namely, White, male Christians—over historically disadvantaged groups like women, people of color, and religious minorities. These cases also fit within a broader pattern in which the conservative supermajority entrenches the Republican Party's political agenda through judicial means, since these policies are too divisive and politically unpopular among the American public to enact through legislation.

The Second Roberts Court has also enacted into law key structural components of the Republican agenda. Two rulings from the Court's 2024 term are illustrative. In *Trump v. United States*, the six conservative justices, led by Chief Justice Roberts, ruled that former President Trump is entitled to broad immunity from criminal prosecution arising out of his actions around the 2020 election.[371] The Court ruled that presidents have absolute immunity in exercising "core constitutional powers" and are entitled to presumptive immunity for other official acts including those

365 *Dobbs*, 142 S. Ct. at 2242. While all six conservative justices upheld the impugned Mississippi abortion law, Chief Justice Roberts would not have overruled *Roe* and *Casey*. *See id.* at 2311 (Roberts, C.J., concurring in the judgment).

366 Siegel et al., *supra* note 5, at 81–90.

367 *Id.* at 96–97.

368 *Kennedy*, 597 U.S. 507 (2022).

369 *Id.* (effectively overruling Lemon v. Kurtzman, 403 U.S. 602 (1971)).

370 *Students for Fair Admissions*, 600 U.S. 181 (2023) (overturning Regents of the University of California v. Bakke, 438 U.S. 265 (1978) and Grutter v. Bollinger, 539 U.S. 306 (2003), which had permitted universities to use race as a factor in the admissions process).

371 Trump v. United States, 144 S. Ct. 2312, 2347 (2024).

that fall within the "outer perimeter" of their powers.[372] Chief Justice Roberts' majority opinion then spelled out which charges against Trump fell into each category and granted presumptive immunity even to some acts that Trump's counsel had conceded were not official acts.[373]

At one level, this ruling appears clearly partisan: it handed a clear victory to a Republican former President who was running again for the same office. But it also harkened back to an older strain of conservative legal thought. Developed during the Nixon administration (1969–74), and predominant in the George W. Bush years (2001–08), it advocates for presidential supremacy and the removal of constraints or accountability on executive power.[374] With *Trump*, the Supreme Court was able to achieve the most significant victory to date for this aspect of the conservative legal movement.

Another longstanding goal of the conservative legal movement has been to dismantle the administrative state that emerged in the 1930s New Deal era and has expended ever since.[375] While the Supreme Court has issued several decisions to undermine the administrative state over the past decade,[376] it issued the coup de grâce in *Loper Bright Enterprises v. Raimondo*.[377] By a 6–3 majority, the Court overruled its decision in *Chevron, U.S.A. Inc. v. National Resources Defense Council Inc.* (1984).[378] It thereby invalidated the principle of *Chevron* deference, which had served for forty years as the lodestone of federal administrative law. *Chevron* required courts to defer to reasonable agency interpretations of congressional statutes. As long as their policies fell within the spectrum of reasonableness, administrative agencies were free to operate without express legislative authorization from Congress. And given the dysfunction in Congress, this leeway was crucial to the continuing operation of government. *Chevron* also enabled presidential administrations to change policies on key issues like environmental regulation and immigration without undue judicial interference. While the effects of *Loper Bright* will take a few years to manifest, the administrative state will be subject to more

[372] *Id.* at 2330–32.

[373] *Id.* at 2333–40. In a separate opinion, Justice Barrett registered her disagreement on this point. She said the majority's ruling "limits the introduction of protected conduct as *evidence* in a criminal prosecution of a President, beyond the limits afforded by executive privilege." *Id.* at 2354 (Barrett, J., concurring in part).

[374] *See* Julian E. Zelizer, *The Conservative Embrace of Presidential Power*, 88 B.U. L. Rev. 499 (2008); Jack Goldsmith, The Terror Presidency: Law and Judgment Inside the Bush Administration (2007); John Yoo, Defender in Chief: Donald Trump's Fight for Presidential Power (2020).

[375] *See, e.g.*, Philip Hamburger, The Administrative Threat (2017); Steven G. Calabresi & Gary Lawson, *The Depravity of the 1930s and the Modern Administrative State*, 94 Notre Dame L. Rev. 821 (2019). *See also*, Adam B. Cox & Emma Kauffman, *The Adjudicative State*, 132 Yale L.J. 1769, 1722–23 (2023) (arguing that while the Roberts Court is "antibureaucracy" in some areas, in other areas—such as immigration—it favors agency adjudication to keep less privileged groups out of federal court).

[376] *See* Gillian E. Metzger, *The Supreme Court, 2016 Term—Foreword: 1930s Redux: The Administrative State Under Siege*, 131 Harv. L. Rev. 1, 34–35 (2017).

[377] Loper Bright Enterprises v. Raimondo, 144 S. Ct. 2244 (2024).

[378] Chevron, U.S.A. Inc. v. National Resources Defense Council Inc., 467 U.S. 837 (1984).

onerous judicial oversight, and the federal government will probably function less effectively.

The Second Roberts Court is, therefore, more reactionary and brazenly partisan than its predecessors,[379] and it has contributed to democratic backsliding in the United States.[380] But the justices still wish to appear impartial and preserve a minimal degree of sociological legitimacy. As we shall see, this desire to maintain appearances is fueled not only by a concern for their reputations but also to fend off potential reforms that could limit the Court's power and make it more accountable.

D. Institutional and Reputational Self-Preservation

Since 2016, the Supreme Court has faced heightened institutional scrutiny. Justice Scalia's death in February that year seemed to be an opportunity for Democrats to obtain a liberal majority on the Court for the first time in half a century. But President Obama's nominee, Judge Merrick Garland, was stonewalled by Senate Majority Leader Mitch McConnell. The hardball strategy to postpone Judge Merrick Garland's hearing until a new president was elected paid off with Donald Trump's unexpected victory.

The balance between liberal and conservative justices fundamentally changed during the Trump administration (2017–20). In 2018, the moderate Anthony Kennedy retired was replaced by the more conservative Brett Kavanaugh. In September 2020, Ruth Bader Ginsburg, the leader of Court's liberal wing, passed away. Though she died only two months before the presidential election, President Trump and a Republican-led Senate were nonetheless able to confirm her replacement—the conservative Amy Coney Barrett—prior to Trump's election loss.

These appointments emerged after pitched partisan battles in the Senate. Kavanaugh faced heated questioning from Democratic senators following testimony of credible sexual assault allegations against him as well as evidence of his support for racial profiling.[381] On Barrett's nomination, Senate Democrats boycotted the Judiciary Committee vote in protest over the expedited scheduling

[379] *See* Lee Epstein, *Partisanship "All the Way Down" on the U.S. Supreme Court*, 51 PEPP. L. REV. 489 (2024); Stephen Jessee et al., *A Decade-Long Longitudinal Survey Shows That the Supreme Court Is Now Much More Conservative than the Public*, 119 PROC. NATL ACAD. SCI. e2120284119 (2022).

[380] *See* Aziz Z. Huq, *The Supreme Court and the Dynamics of Democratic Backsliding*, 699 ANNALS AM. ACAD. POL. & SOC. SCI. 50 (2024).

[381] *See* Rebecca Shabad, *An Angry Emotional Kavanaugh Accused Democrats of "Search and Destroy"*, NBC NEWS (Sept. 27, 2018), https://www.nbcnews.com/politics/congress/christine-blasey-ford-tells-senate-memories-brett-kavanaugh-assault-have-n913531; Stephanie Ebbs et al., *Sen. Cory Booker Releases 'Confidential Kavanaugh Emails in Combative Supreme Court Confirmation Hearing*, ABC NEWS (Sept. 7, 2018), https://abcnews.go.com/Politics/democrats-threaten-release-confidential-kavanaugh-documents/story?id=57643589.

of her hearing. Many pointed to the double standards of McConnell and the Republican leadership, who refused to hold a hearing for Garland under similar circumstances in 2016.[382] Considering their resort to hardball in other domains, the Republican tactics on these nominations were no surprise. But because the Supreme Court wields so much power in American society, and the justices are given lifetime appointments, the political stakes were especially high.

Once Democrats regained a majority in the Senate, they put forward bills to expand the Supreme Court.[383] The U.S. Constitution is notoriously difficult to amend, but Congress has the authority to alter the bench size. Indeed, legislation more than 150 years ago fixed the current number of Supreme Court justices at nine—it was six at the Court's founding.[384]

Another bill would have imposed term limits on the justices.[385] The Constitution specifies that federal judges "shall hold their Offices during good Behaviour,"[386] which has been widely understood to mean that they have life tenure.[387] The bill aimed to get around this issue by instituting eighteen-year term limits but allowing justices to serve in a limited capacity thereafter. Unlike the plan to expand the Court—which would escalate the tit-for-tat partisan battle—this plan had the potential to lower the political stakes of Supreme Court nominations. The eighteen-year terms would be staggered so that every presidential administration would be able to nominate at least one Supreme Court justice, and the Court's composition would not hinge on individual retirement decisions.[388]

Legal scholars also proposed various reforms to balance or defang the Court. Daniel Epps and Ganesh Sitaraman, for instance, proposed a lottery—in which the Supreme Court would sit in panels comprised of judges drawn at random from the Courts of Appeal—as well as a "Balanced Bench" reform. The latter envisions a Court comprising an equal number of Republican and Democratic-appointed justices, along with additional justices drawn from the federal bench who received unanimous support from the political nominees.[389] Ryan Doerfler and Samuel

[382] *See* Marianne Levine, *Senate Democrats to Boycott Barrett's Judiciary Committee Vote Thursday*, POLITICO (Oct. 21, 2020), https://www.politico.com/news/2020/10/21/senate-democrats-to-boycott-barretts-judiciary-committee-vote-thursday-430945.

[383] *See Expand the Supreme Court: Senator Markey and Reps. Nadler, Johnson, and Jones Introduce Legislation to Restore Justice and Democracy to Judicial System*, ED MARKEY (Apr. 15, 2021), https://www.markey.senate.gov/news/press-releases/expand-the-supreme-court-senator-markey-and-reps-nadler-johnson-and-jones-introduce-legislation-to-restore-justice-and-democracy-to-judicial-system.

[384] *See "Court Packing": Legislative Control over the Size of the Supreme Court*, CONG. RSCH. SERV. (Dec. 14, 2020), https://crsreports.congress.gov/product/pdf/LSB/LSB10562.

[385] *Whitehouse, Booker, Blumenthal, Padilla Introduce New Supreme Court Term Limits Bill*, SHELDON WHITEHOUSE (Oct. 19, 2023), https://www.whitehouse.senate.gov/news/release/whitehouse-booker-blumenthal-padilla-introduce-new-supreme-court-term-limits-bill/.

[386] U.S. CONST, art. III, § 1.

[387] *See* Steven G. Calabresi & James Lindgren, *Term Limits for the Supreme Court: Life Tenure Reconsidered*, 29 HARV. J. L. & PUB. POL'Y 769, 824 (2006).

[388] *See* Diane P. Wood, *Why Term Limits for Supreme Court Justices Makes Sense*, BRENNAN CTR. (Aug. 19, 2024), https://www.brennancenter.org/our-work/analysis-opinion/why-term-limits-supreme-court-justices-make-sense.

[389] *See* Daniel Epps & Ganesh Sitaraman, *How to Save the Supreme Court*, 129 YALE L.J. 148 (2019).

Moyn, meanwhile, proposed more radical reforms that would disempower the Court by stripping it of jurisdiction or by requiring a supermajority of justices to invalidate legislation.[390]

The political and scholarly interest in reform was strong enough that, in 2021, a few months after President Biden assumed office, he formed a Commission to consider such reforms.[391] The bipartisan Commission included leading scholars and jurists of various political orientations. Perhaps because of the wide range of views among its members, the Commission did not propose any reforms. Its report instead provided an overview of current debates, historical background, and arguments for and against reform proposals.[392] Though the Commission ultimately failed to bring about any change to the status quo, it signaled to the Court that it was under public and political scrutiny. And for the first time in living memory, the Court faced the possibility of having Congress alter its size or operations.

While the calls for structural reforms have ebbed, the Court has remained in the public spotlight for the unethical conduct of some justices and its partisan decision-making. On ethics, investigative reporting in 2023 revealed close ties between sitting justices and Republican donors. Justice Thomas accepted lavish gifts and school tuition payments from right-wing billionaire Harlan Crowe, while Justice Alito took luxury fishing vacations with the billionaire Paul Singer, who had cases before the Supreme Court.[393] Both Thomas and Alito denied any wrongdoing,[394] but such revelations damaged the Court's reputation for ethical conduct and integrity.

The Supreme Court is not bound by the judicial code of ethics that applies to other federal judges. Rather, the justices had abided by an unwritten convention that they should recuse themselves in cases where there is a real or perceived conflict of interest. These recent disclosures demonstrated that the conventional

[390] *See* Ryan Doerfler & Samuel Moyn, *Democratizing the Supreme Court*, 109 CAL. L. REV. 1703 (2021).

[391] *President Biden to Sign Executive Order Creating the Presidential Commission on the Supreme Court of the United States*, White House (Apr. 9, 2021), https://www.whitehouse.gov/briefing-room/statements-releases/2021/04/09/president-biden-to-sign-executive-order-creating-the-presidential-commission-on-the-supreme-court-of-the-united-states/.

[392] *See* PRESIDENTIAL COMMISSION ON THE SUPREME COURT OF THE UNITED STATES: FINAL REPORT (2021).

[393] *See* Joshua Kaplan et al., *Clarence Thomas Had a Child in Private School. Harlan Crow Paid the Tuition*, PROPUBLICA (May 4, 2023), https://www.propublica.org/article/clarence-thomas-harlan-crow-private-school-tuition-scotus; Justin Elliot et al., *Justice Samuel Alito Took Luxury Fishing Vacation with GOP Billionaire Who Later Had Cases Before the Court*, PROPUBLICA (June 20, 2023), https://www.propublica.org/article/samuel-alito-luxury-fishing-trip-paul-singer-scotus-supreme-court.

[394] They also cast themselves as victims of a partisan witch hunt. *See* Samuel A. Alito Jr., *ProPublica Misleads Its Readers*, WALL ST. J. (June 20, 2023), https://www.wsj.com/articles/propublica-misleads-its-readers-alito-gifts-disclosure-alaska-singer-23b51eda; Steve Benen, *The Biggest Flaw in Justice Clarence Thomas' Newest Complaints*, MSNBC (May 13, 2024), https://www.msnbc.com/rachel-maddow-show/maddowblog/biggest-flaw-justice-clarence-thomas-newest-complaints-rcna151935.

approach was inadequate. Faced with a media storm and calls for an ethics code from Democrats in Congress,[395] the Court finally adopted a written code of conduct in November 2023.[396]

The code is not legally binding and is unlikely to have much practical effect on the justices' conduct.[397] Indeed, its adoption did little to diminish the calls for ethics reform. In July 2024, President Biden proposed that Congress adopted legislation to impose mandatory ethics rules on the Supreme Court.[398] While Biden's proposal failed in Congress, it is notable that this issue garnered enough salience to be placed on the national political agenda. Notably, around the same time, Justice Kagan proposed that the Chief Justice appoint a panel of federal judges to enforce the Court's new code of conduct.[399]

The Court also appears concerned that the media and public view it in partisan political terms. Such perceptions increased after *Dobbs*,[400] but, on this front too, Justices Alito and Thomas acted in ways that damaged the Court's credibility. Justice Alito flew an upside-down American flag—a symbol of support for the January 6, 2021 Capitol attack—at his house a few days after that incident.[401] It was later reported that he hoisted another right-wing protest flag at his vacation homes.[402] Alito denied any connection to these symbols, claiming that his wife displayed the flag during a political altercation with some neighbors.[403] Meanwhile, Justice Thomas's wife, Ginni, worked to keep Trump in power after his election loss in 2020 and promoted the January 6 rally. An April 2022 poll found that 52 percent of respondents believed that, due to her involvement in these events, Justice Thomas should recuse himself from cases involving the 2020 election and Trump.[404] He, of course, did not do so.

[395] Andrew Chung & John Kruzel, *Under Fire, US Supreme Court Unveils Ethics Code for Justices*, REUTERS (Nov. 14, 2023), https://www.reuters.com/legal/us-supreme-court-announces-formal-ethics-code-justices-2023-11-13/.

[396] *Statement of the Court Regarding the Code of Conduct*, SUPREME COURT OF THE UNITED STATES, https://www.supremecourt.gov/about/Code-of-Conduct-for-Justices_November_13_2023.pdf.

[397] *See* Michael Waldman, *New Supreme Court Ethics Code Is Designed to Fail*, BRENNAN CTR. (Nov. 14, 2023), https://www.brennancenter.org/our-work/analysis-opinion/new-supreme-court-ethics-code-designed-fail.

[398] *See Fact Sheet: President Biden Announces Bold Plan to Reform the Supreme Court and Ensure No President Is Above the Law*, WHITE HOUSE (July 29, 2024), https://www.whitehouse.gov/briefing-room/statements-releases/2024/07/29/fact-sheet-president-biden-announces-bold-plan-to-reform-the-supreme-court-and-ensure-no-president-is-above-the-law/.

[399] Suzanne Monyak & Lydia Wheeler, *Elena Kagan Endorses High Court Ethics Enforcement Mechanism*, BLOOMBERG L. (July 26, 2024), https://news.bloomberglaw.com/us-law-week/elena-kagan-endorses-supreme-court-ethics-enforcement-mechanism.

[400] *See* Levendusky et al., *supra* note 317.

[401] *See* Ankush Khardori, *The Alito Scandal Is Worse Than It Seems*, POLITICO (May 30, 2024), https://www.politico.com/news/magazine/2024/05/30/alito-scotus-flag-00160450.

[402] *See* Jodi Kantor et al., *Another Provocative Flag Was Flown at Another Alito Home*, N.Y. TIMES (May 22, 2024), https://www.nytimes.com/2024/05/22/us/justice-alito-flag-appeal-to-heaven.html.

[403] *Id.*

[404] *52% Say Justice Thomas Should Sit Out Election Cases, Quinnipiac University National Poll Finds*, QUINNIPIAC (Apr. 6, 2022), https://poll.qu.edu/poll-release?releaseid=3842.

The Court's more institutionally minded members, like Justices Kavanaugh and Barrett, have made a concerted effort in recent years to speak publicly about the Court's role in idealistic, non-partisan terms, and to explicitly reject any suggestion that they favor certain causes or litigants over others.[405] Chief Justice Roberts famously declared at his confirmation hearing that his job as a judge would be "to call balls and strikes, and not to pitch or bat."[406] In 2018, he made unusually pointed public comments in response to President Trump's remarks that judges appointed by Democratic presidents were hostile to his political agenda. Roberts said, "We do not have Obama judges or Trump judges, Bush judges or Clinton judges."[407] These comments underscore his concern for the Court's institutional reputation. But this concern should not be conflated with judicial moderation.[408] Roberts has played a major role in turning American constitutional law in a sharply rightward direction. In 2024 alone, he wrote the majority opinion in *Trump v. Anderson* (granting broad immunity to former President Trump) and in *Loper Bright*, which overruled *Chevron*.

Justice Gorsuch wrote separately in *Loper Bright*, in part, to counter the narrative that this Court is especially hostile to precedent. Gorsuch noted that while the Warren and Burger courts overruled approximately three cases per term, the current Court only overrules an average of one or two cases per term.[409] This fact illuminates little—it does not tell us about the relative importance of those cases or their political valence. But the fact that Gorsuch dug out these statistics fits within a broader pattern in the current Court.

While the conservative supermajority has been radically transforming constitutional law along partisan lines, it knows that it must maintain at least a modicum of sociological legitimacy to remain clear of structural or ethical reforms. Gallup's public approval rating of the Supreme Court dropped to a record low of 40 percent in 2021 and has remained steady since then, with 41 percent approving of the Court's work in 2023. The rating dropped from 49 percent in 2015 to 42 percent in

[405] *See, e.g.*, Steve Karnowski, *Justice Kavanaugh Seeks to Dispel the Notion That the Supreme Court Is Partisan*, AP News (July 14, 2023), https://apnews.com/article/supreme-court-brett-kavanaugh; Chandelis Duster, *Justice Amy Coney Barrett Says Supreme Court Is "Not a Bunch of Partisan Hacks"*, CNN (Sept. 13, 2021), https://edition.cnn.com/2021/09/13/politics/amy-coney-barrett-supreme-court-not-partisan/index.html.

[406] *Chief Justice Roberts Statement—Nomination Process*, U.S. Courts., https://www.uscourts.gov/educational-resources/educational-activities/chief-justice-roberts-statement-nomination-process (last visited Sept. 24, 2024); Robert Barndes & Michael Karlik, *Roberts Says Supreme Court Will Reopen to Public and Defends Legitimacy*, Wash. Post (Sept. 10, 2022), https://www.washingtonpost.com/politics/2022/09/10/supreme-court-roberts-legitimacy/.

[407] *Chief Justice Roberts Rebukes Trump's "Obama Judge" Gibe*, BBC (Nov. 22, 2018), https://www.bbc.com/news/world-us-canada-46294734.

[408] *See* Eric Segall, *The Rule Maker-In-Chief: John Roberts and the Myth of the Umpire Judge*, Dorf on Law (Aug. 5, 2024), https://www.dorfonlaw.org/2024/08/the-rule-maker-in-chief-john-roberts.html; James D. Zirin, *The Supremely Partisan Court of Chief Justice Roberts*, The Hill (Sept. 20, 2024), https://thehill.com/opinion/judiciary/4889319-the-supremely-partisan-court-of-chief-justice-roberts/.

[409] *See* Loper Bright, 144 S. Ct. at 2279–80 (Gorsuch, J., concurring).

2016, which coincides with the stalled nomination of Merrick Garland. Similarly, the rating fell from 58 percent in 2020 to 40 percent in 2021 as the Republicans in Congress rushed through Amy Coney Barrett's nomination.[410] The public, in other words, recognizes what has happened to the Supreme Court in recent years. Democratic leaders, like President Biden, tried to capitalize on their discontentment and push for reforms.

The justices' avowals that the Court is not partisan or that it respects precedent have proved insufficient to reverse public and political sentiment. They also needed to demonstrate these values in their jurisprudence. And, as Part V will show, LGBTQ+ rights cases in the early 2020s usefully showed that the Second Roberts Court does not invariably rule along partisan lines on constitutional matters.

V. LGBTQ+ Rights in the Second Roberts Court (2018–23)

This Part discusses LGBTQ+ rights in the Second Roberts Court and the purposes they have served for this unpopular and apparently partisan institution. We begin by assessing the effects of the Supreme Court's landmark decision in *Obergefell* (2015) that legalized same-sex marriage throughout the United States.

While *Obergefell* was a landmark and transformative judgment,[411] we must resist the temptation to view it as the culmination of the LGBTQ+ rights struggle. As an initial matter, *Obergefell* was not even the end of the story on same-sex marriage. The judgment enabled couples to marry across the United States, but it did not guarantee that other rights flowing from marriage would also be recognized. It remains difficult, for instance, for same-sex couples to have their parental rights recognized in some states, especially with respect to non-biological children.[412]

Obergefell is also a classic example of "homonormativity."[413] As Lisa Duggan explained, the term refers to "a politics that does not contest dominant heteronormative assumptions and institutions but upholds and sustains them while promising the possibility of a demobilized gay constituency and a privatized, depoliticized gay culture anchored in domesticity and consumption."[414] By relying so heavily on the traditional values of marriage, *Obergefell* sanitizes and domesticates LGBTQ+ politics into a historically conservative institution.

[410] Megan Brennan, *Views of Supreme Court Remain Near Record Lows*, GALLUP (Sept. 29, 2023), https://news.gallup.com/poll/511820/views-supreme-court-remain-near-record-lows.aspx.

[411] *See* Russell K. Robinson & David M. Frost, *Marriage Equality and Intersectionality*, 23 ANALYSES SOC. ISSUES IN PUB. POL'Y 2019 (2023) (showing how many LGBTQ+ people of color view *Obergefell* as empowering and personally meaningful).

[412] *See* Susan Hazeldean, *Illegitimate Parents*, 55 U.C. DAVIS L. REV. 1583 (2022).

[413] Lisa Duggan, *The New Homonormativity: The Sexual Politics of Neoliberalism*, *in* MATERIALIZING DEMOCRACY: TOWARD A REVITALIZED CULTURAL POLITICS 175 (Russ Castronovo & Dana D. Nelson eds., 2002).

[414] *Id.* at 179; WARNER, *supra* note 83, at ch. 3.

Critical race scholars have noted that progressive Supreme Court decisions like *Obergefell* spotlight the experiences of a small, privileged, and White subsection of the LGBTQ+ community.[415] Plaintiffs like Jim Obergefell and Edith Windsor were strategically selected to put a comforting and familiar face on issues like marriage equality.[416] Intersectional analysis, including as to the specific harms to LGBTQ+ persons who also belong to racial minorities, is absent both in the filings and in the final judgments.[417]

At a doctrinal level, *Obergefell* left at least two gaps. First, the judgment says nothing about LGBTQ+ rights outside the context of same-sex marriage. Justice Kennedy's majority opinion, for instance, repeatedly emphasizes the societal and personal benefits of marriage, which elevates marriage as a normative ideal to the detriment of the dignity and rights of unmarried LGBTQ+ persons.[418] Thus, while same-sex marriage is broadly accepted by the American public, the rights of other sexual and gender minorities, including the transgender community, remain deeply contested and the site of ongoing legal battles and culture wars.[419]

Section A below explains how the Second Roberts Court provided welcome (and unexpected) relief to these minority groups by interpreting a civil rights statute that prohibited sex discrimination to apply to sexual orientation and gender identity-based discrimination too.

Second, the *Obergefell* Court did not provide guidance on how to balance the rights of same-sex couples with competing rights, including First Amendment protections of free speech and the free exercise of religion. Justice Kennedy gestured toward this issue, declaring:

> [I]t must be emphasized that religions, and those who adhere to religious doctrines, may continue to advocate with utmost, sincere conviction that, by divine precepts, same-sex marriage should not be condoned. The First Amendment ensures that religious organizations and persons are given proper protection.[420]

But this statement simply acknowledges the competing interests involved. It remained to be seen how the Court would weigh the rights of LGBTQ+ persons, including same-sex couples, against the rights of those who wished to express their opposition to same-sex marriage.

[415] *See, e.g.*, Russell K. Robinson, *Unequal Protection*, 68 Stan. L. Rev. 151 (2016); Darren Lenard Hutchinson, *Gay Rights for Gay Whites? Race, Sexual Identity, and Equal Protection Discourse*, 85 Cornell L. Rev. 1358 (2000); Devon W. Carbado, *Black Rights, Gay Rights, Civil Rights*, 47 UCLA L. Rev. 1467 (2000).

[416] Robinson, *supra* note 415, at 227.

[417] *Id.* at 228–29.

[418] *See* Melissa Murray, Obergefell v. Hodges *and Nonmarriage Inequality*, 104 Cal. L. Rev. 1207, 1209–11 (2016).

[419] For an overview of recent (and regressive) developments on LGBTQ+ rights, see Ari Ezra Waldman, *Policing Queer Sexuality*, 121 Mich. L. Rev. 985 (2023).

[420] *Obergefell*, 135 S. Ct. at 2607.

Section B demonstrates how the Supreme Court has consistently leaned in favor of the First Amendment, with the Second Roberts Court incrementally building on prior precedents in this area.

A. Expanding Federal Statutory Protection for LGBTQ+ Persons

Title VII of the Civil Rights Act (1964) prohibits workplace discrimination on various grounds including sex. In 2012, the Obama administration determined that this prohibition on sex discrimination encompassed discrimination on the basis of sexual orientation and gender identity.[421] Under President Trump, however, the government changed its stance, concluding that "absurd" or "extreme" results would follow if Title VII were interpreted so broadly.[422] This reversion to a narrow interpretation of "sex" was challenged in three separate cases. In one case, the plaintiff, Gerald Bostock, alleged that he was fired from his position as a child welfare advocate because he was openly gay. The Eleventh Circuit Court of Appeals in that case concluded Title VII did not extend to discrimination on the basis of sexual orientation. In a similar case, Donald Zarda alleged that he was fired from his job as a skydiving instructor because he revealed to the company that he was gay. But in that case, the Second Circuit Court of Appeals ruled that Title VII protected Zarda, as sexual orientation fell within the definition of "sex." Finally, Aimee Stephens, a transgender woman, filed a complaint with the Equal Employment Opportunity Commission, alleging that she was terminated due to her gender identity. The case eventually came before the Sixth Circuit Court of Appeals, which ruled in Stephens' favor on the theory that she had been subject to unlawful sex stereotyping.[423]

The cases were consolidated before the Supreme Court in *Bostock v. Clayton County* (2020). Justice Gorsuch—a Trump-appointee and avowed textualist—authored the majority opinion on behalf of six justices (including Chief Justice Roberts, and Justices Ginsburg, Breyer, Sotomayor, and Kagan). Gorsuch carefully parsed the words and meaning of Title VII. He noted that when the statute was adopted in 1964, the term "Sex . . . referred to status as either male or female [as] determined by reproductive biology."[424] True to his interpretive approach, Justice Gorsuch would not deviate from what he found to be the "ordinary public meaning" of the statute.[425] But, he explained, the definition of sex was only the start of the inquiry as to the statute's meaning. Gorsuch relied heavily on Title VII's

[421] *See* Tara Leigh Grove, *Which Textualism?*, 134 HARV. L. REV. 265, 269 (2020).

[422] *Id.*

[423] *See* Allison Greenberg, *Lessons from* Bostock*: Analysis of the Jurisprudential (Mis)Treatment of "Sex" in Title VII Cases*, 13 U.C. IRVINE L. REV. 317, 319 (2022).

[424] *Bostock*, 140 S. Ct. at 1739.

[425] *Id.* at 1738.

language that prevents employers from acting in certain ways "because of" sex. For Gorsuch, these words established a "but-for test"—in other words, it requires a showing that sex was at least one factor motivating the discriminatory action.[426] If Congress intended for sex to be the sole or major factor, it would have qualified the language in this provision by adding a term like "solely" or "primarily" before "because of."[427]

Thus, Justice Gorsuch established that Title VII only required a showing that sex was a motivating factor in employment discrimination. He then applied this meaning to the cases before the Court. He found that it was "impossible to discriminate against a person for being homosexual or transgender without discriminating against that individual based on sex."[428] Here Gorsuch adopted (without citing) a theory pushed by legal scholars, like Andrew Koppelman, that sexual orientation discrimination is a form of sex discrimination.[429] As Gorsuch explained, if a gay man is fired because he is attracted to men, "[T]he employer discriminates against him for traits or actions that it tolerates in his female colleague."[430] Thus, biological sex is a "but-for cause" of the male employee's discharge.[431] A similar analysis unfolded with respect to the transgender woman who was terminated on account of her gender identity. Gorsuch put it as follows:

> If the employer retains an otherwise identical employee who was identified as female at birth, the employer intentionally penalizes a person identified as male at birth for traits or actions that it tolerates in an employee identified as female at birth. Again, the individual employee's sex plays an unmistakable and impermissible role in the discharge decision.[432]

Bostock was a momentous victory for LGBTQ+ rights. By holding that "sex" in Title VII encompassed sexual orientation and gender identity, the judgment redefined the concept of sex discrimination, which could have implications across both federal and state laws.[433] It was lauded by liberal scholars and journalists, who referred to the judgment as "symbolic and consequential,"[434] "obviously correct,"[435] and a

[426] *Id.* at 1739.
[427] *Id.*
[428] *Id.* at 1741.
[429] *See, e.g.*, Andrew M. Koppelman, *Why Discrimination Against Lesbians and Gay Men Is Sex Discrimination*, 69 N.Y.U. L. Rev. 197 (1994).
[430] *Bostock*, 140 S. Ct. at 1741.
[431] *Id.*
[432] *Id.*
[433] *See* Susannah Cohen, *Redefining What It Means to Discriminate Because of Sex:* Bostock's *Equal Protection Implications*, 122 Colum. L. Rev. 407 (2022); Greenberg, *supra* note 423, at 339–46 (noting the limitations of the decision and how they can be remedied in future cases).
[434] Adam Liptak, *Civil Rights Law Protects Gay and Transgender Workers, Supreme Court Rules*, N.Y. Times (June 16, 2020), https://www.nytimes.com/2020/06/15/us/gay-transgender-workers-supreme-court.html.
[435] Andrew Koppelman, Bostock, *LGBT Discrimination, and the Subtractive Moves*, 105 Minn. L. Rev. Headnotes 1 (2020).

"historic victory for LGBT Americans, for civil rights more broadly, and for the rule of law."[436]

The decision predictably came under fire from conservative justices and scholars. Justice Alito, joined by Justice Thomas, penned an angry and long dissent totaling more than 100 pages, accusing the Court of legislating from the bench.[437] Justice Kavanaugh in a separate dissent echoed that message, invoking the separation of powers to declare, "[W]e are judges, not Members of Congress . . . [O]ur role is not to make or amend the law."[438] Conservative scholars, meanwhile, referred to *Bostock* as "bogus,"[439] "outlandish,"[440] and an exercise in "halfway textualism."[441]

More importantly for our purposes, this judgment was issued by a Supreme Court that had not produced a progressive outcome in a high-stakes constitutional case in years. Given how politicized—and often nakedly partisan—the Court's constitutional decision-making has become, judicial reputation is likely to have factored into the majority opinion and in Chief Justice Roberts' decision to join it. Through his majority opinion, Gorsuch was able to demonstrate not only that a Trump-nominated justice could write a progressive opinion but also that the textualist interpretive approach does not invariably tilt in a partisan direction.

B. Privileging the First Amendment

The U.S. Supreme Court, as a general matter, is averse to accommodating competing rights. As Jamal Greene has demonstrated, the Court has viewed "rights as trumps" for the past century.[442] It recognizes only a few rights as sacrosanct, and then rules in ways that privilege those rights over others.[443] This is distinct—and, I would argue, less normatively desirable—than the competing model of proportionality, which has been adopted in Canada, the United Kingdom, most of continental Europe, Latin America, and even in several Asian jurisdictions.[444] When

[436] Michael C. Dorf, *Does Justice Gorsuch's Magnificent Opinion in the Title VII Sexual Orientation and Gender Identity Cases Redeem Textualism?*, DORF ON LAW (June 16, 2020), http://www.dorfonlaw.org/2020/06/does-justice-gorsuchs-magnificent.html.

[437] *Bostock*, 140 S. Ct. at 1754–56 (Alito, J., dissenting).

[438] *Id.* at 1823 (Kavanaugh, J., dissenting).

[439] Mitchell N. Berman & Guha Krishnamurthi, Bostock *Was Bogus: Textualism, Pluralism, and Title VII*, 97 NOTRE DAME L. REV. 67 (2021).

[440] Nelson Lund, *Unleashed and Unbound: Living Textualism in* Bostock v. Clayton County, 21 FEDERALISM SOC'Y REV. 158 (2020).

[441] Josh Blackman & Randy Barnett, *Justice Gorsuch's Halfway Textualism Surprises and Disappoints in the Title VII Cases*, NAT'L REV. (June 26, 2020), https://www.nationalreview.com/2020/06/justice-gorsuch-title-vii-cases-half-way-textualism-surprises-disappoints/.

[442] *See* Jamal Greene, *The Supreme Court, 2017 Term—Foreword: Rights as Trumps?*, 132 HARV. L. REV. 28 (2018).

[443] *Id.* at 32–34.

[444] *Id.* at 56–59.

it works as intended, proportionality focuses less on the competing rights claims and more on the facts of a particular case.[445] It asks the government to justify its incursions on rights by providing evidence to demonstrate, *inter alia*, that there are legitimate aims behind the impugned law; that the law is rationally connected to those aims; that the law is proportionate to achieve the aims; and that it does not excessively burden the rights of those affected.

By contrast, the U.S. Supreme Court has largely avoided proportionality.[446] It elevates the holders of certain rights over those asserting other (lesser) rights, and in some instances, it allows those privileged few to obtain exemptions from laws of general application. This categorical approach was adopted in *Boy Scouts of America v. Dale* (2000).[447] James Dale, a former Eagle Scout, had his Boy Scouts membership revoked when the organization learned that he was "an avowed homosexual and gay rights activist."[448] Dale lived in New Jersey and filed suit claiming that the Boy Scouts had violated the state's public accommodation law by revoking his membership on the basis of sexual orientation.[449] The case worked its way up the state court system to the New Jersey Supreme Court, which ruled in Dale's favor. It held that the Boy Scouts were a place of public accommodation and its conduct toward Dale thus violated the state's public accommodation law.[450]

The Supreme Court, by a 5–4 margin, disagreed. Chief Justice Rehnquist wrote the majority opinion joined by Justices O'Connor, Scalia, Kennedy, and Thomas. Rehnquist relied on *Roberts v. United States Jaycees* (1984), where the Court recognized an implicit right within the First Amendment to "associate with others in pursuit of a wide variety of political, social, economic, educational, religious, and cultural ends."[451] *Roberts* ultimately upheld the anti-discrimination law at issue in that case, ruling that the state had a compelling interest in prohibiting discrimination that outweighed the group's First Amendment right to exclude certain persons from membership.[452]

In *Dale*, the Court followed *Roberts* in asking: (1) whether the Boy Scouts were engaged in "expressive association" such that the group was protected by the First Amendment; (2) if so, whether the "forced inclusion of Dale" significantly burdened that right; and (3) if that burden overrode the state's competing interest

[445] *Id.* at 63; GREENE, *supra* note 54, at 54–57.

[446] Justice Breyer was a notable exception in this regard—he argued that proportionality should be adopted in several areas of constitutional adjudication. *See* STEPHEN BREYER, ACTIVE LIBERTY: INTERPRETING OUR DEMOCRATIC CONSTITUTION 49 (2006). On the ways in which the U.S. constitutional law employs elements of proportionality, see Vicki C. Jackson, *Constitutional Law in an Age of Proportionality*, 124 YALE L.J. 3094 (2015).

[447] Boy Scouts of America v. Dale, 530 U.S. 640 (2000).

[448] *Id.* at 644.

[449] *See* N.J. Stat. Ann. §§ 10:5–4, 10:5–5 (West Supp. 2000).

[450] *Dale*, 530 U.S. at 644–46.

[451] Roberts v. United States Jaycees, 468 U.S. 609, 622 (1984).

[452] *Id.* at 623–26.

in preventing discrimination.[453] While this structure resembles proportionality, Chief Justice Rehnquist applied it in ways that privileged the First Amendment.

The Court quickly determined, based on the Boy Scouts' widely known and disseminated values, that it was engaged in expressive activity.[454] On the question of whether the Boy Scouts would be significantly burdened in that expressive activity by keeping Dale as a member, the Court declined to undertake the fact-based inquiry that was necessary here. The New Jersey Supreme Court had conducted a careful analysis to conclude that by excluding Dale, the Boy Scouts had failed to comply with its own stated commitments to "a diverse and representative membership" and its broader objective to "reach all eligible youth."[455]

The Supreme Court majority, however, simply accepted that the Boy Scouts "teach[es] that homosexual conduct was not morally straight."[456] It took the belief as sincerely held and did not inquire as to whether the Boy Scouts had expressed a view on homosexuality. In dissent, Justice Stevens, on behalf of himself and the liberal justices (Souter, Ginsburg, and Breyer), showed that the Boy Scouts' Law or Oath referred to principles such as "morally straight" and "clean," but neither document "says the slightest thing about homosexuality."[457] Thus, the majority in *Dale* tipped the scale in favor of the First Amendment and toward a categorical rather than fact-based approach to these matters. Once the Court decided that homosexuality was contrary to the Boy Scouts' values, it followed that the New Jersey law significantly burdened the organization's First Amendment rights.

Finally, as to whether New Jersey's public accommodation law infringed upon the Boy Scouts' expressive associational rights, the Court again favored the First Amendment. As Rehnquist put it, retaining Dale would "significantly burden the organization's right to oppose or disfavor homosexual conduct. The state interests ... do not justify such a severe intrusion on the Boy Scouts' rights to freedom of expressive association."[458]

The Supreme Court's ruling in *Dale* was largely forgotten after the progressive judgments in *Lawrence* (2003), *Windsor* (2013), and *Obergefell* (2015). But *Dale* would form the foundation of a strand of doctrine in which those opposed to same-sex marriage could invoke the First Amendment to exempt themselves from anti-discrimination laws. Justice Kennedy—who wrote the majority opinions in *Lawrence*, *Windsor*, and *Obergefell*—contributed to this line of precedent by joining the lead opinions in *Dale* and in *Masterpiece Cakeshop* (2018). His opinion in the latter case, written on behalf of a 7–2 majority (including liberal Justices

[453] *Dale*, 530 U.S. at 648–53.
[454] *Id.* at 649–50.
[455] *Id.* at 650–651 (citing Dale v. Boy Scouts of America, 160 N.J. 562, 618 (1999)) (internal quotes omitted).
[456] *Id.* at 651.
[457] *Id.* at 668 (Stevens, J., dissenting).
[458] *Id.* at 659.

Breyer and Kagan), showed that even in a post-*Obergefell* world, First Amendment claims would trump anti-discrimination legislation designed to protect LGBTQ+ rights.

The facts of *Masterpiece Cakeshop* are straightforward. A same-sex couple, Charlie Craig and Dave Mullins, walked into a bakery in Lakewood, Colorado. The bakery was known, among other things, to produce elaborate, custom-made wedding cakes. Craig and Mullins told the storeowner, Jack Phillips, that they wanted a cake for their wedding. Phillips declined, saying that he did not make cakes for same-sex weddings due to his religious opposition to same-sex marriage.[459] Craig and Mullins filed a complaint against Phillips under the Colorado Anti-Discrimination Act, which, *inter alia*, prohibits discrimination on sexual orientation grounds in places of public accommodation.[460] Complaints under the Act are initially sent to the Colorado Civil Rights Division, which determines whether there is probably cause that the Act was violated. Here, the Civil Rights Division determined that probable cause existed and sent the case to the Colorado Civil Rights Commission (CCRC), which conducted a formal hearing before a state administrative law judge (ALJ).[461]

The parties agreed as to what Phillips said and that his store clearly fell within the definition of a public accommodation. The parties further agreed that Craig and Mullins had not asked for a specific type of cake or for it to convey a particular message. The couple simply asked for a wedding cake and Phillips refused.

Based on these facts, the ALJ ruled against Phillips, finding that his actions constituted unlawful discrimination on the basis of sexual orientation. Both the CCRC and Court of Appeals affirmed this decision.[462] At the Supreme Court, Phillips rehearsed two constitutional arguments that had failed at the state level. First, he argued that his First Amendment right to free speech would be infringed if he were compelled "to exercise his artistic talents to express a message with which he disagreed."[463] Second, he claimed his First Amendment right to the free exercise of religion would also be violated if he were forced to act contrary to his sincerely held religious beliefs.[464]

As in *Dale*, the Supreme Court took these First Amendment arguments at face value without interrogating their factual basis. Serious constitutional concerns would emerge had Phillips been compelled to create a cake whose message he objected to. But that's not what happened here. Craig and Mullins had not specified what kind of cake they wanted. They may well have selected a generic cake that had no relation to same-sex marriage. They also did not force Phillips to express any

[459] *Masterpiece Cakeshop*, 138 S. Ct. at 1723–24.
[460] *Id.* at 1725; Colo. Rev. Stat. §24-34-601(2)(a) (2017).
[461] *Masterpiece Cakeshop*, 138 S. Ct. at 1726.
[462] *Id.* at 1726–27.
[463] *Id.* at 1726.
[464] *Id.*

message, much less one that he opposed. As Andrew Koppelman has argued, the Court here acted as if it were deciding a similar case that came before the U.K. Supreme Court, in which a Northern Irish bakery refused on religious grounds to make a case with icing that read "Support Gay Marriage in 2014."[465] In that case, the U.K. Supreme Court ruled—quite reasonably, on the specific facts—that the bakery could not be compelled to promote a message with which it fundamentally disagreed.[466]

Justice Kennedy treated Masterpiece Cakeshop like the U.K. bakery. He wrote at length about "Phillips' dilemma," noting that "the baker likely found it difficult to find a line where the customers' rights to good and services became a demand for him to exercise the right of his own personal expression for their message . . . [that] he could not express in a way consistent with his religious beliefs."[467] This remarkable passage shows how Kennedy substituted his own speculative thoughts about what Phillips might have felt in this case for the factual record, which, again, shows no evidence that Phillips faced this dilemma.

As it turned out, Kennedy's imagined facts did not directly impact the outcome in *Masterpiece Cakeshop*. The Supreme Court ruled in favor of Phillips on a different ground. Justice Kennedy's majority opinion focused on the proceedings before the CCRC. While he largely ignored the factual record in this case, Kennedy carefully examined the record of proceedings before the Commission. He found several instances in which the commissioners acted with "clear and impermissible hostility" toward Phillips' "sincere religious beliefs."[468] One commissioner noted that Phillips is free to believe what he chooses but cannot act on those beliefs while engaging in business in Colorado. These comments appear to merely restate what Colorado's anti-discrimination law provides, but Justice Kennedy thought that they "might be seen as inappropriate and dismissive."[469] Another commissioner noted that freedom of religion had been used "to justify all kinds of discrimination throughout history" and added that they thought it "despicable" that "people . . . use their religion to hurt others."[470] These statements, while rhetorically excessive and potentially offensive, do not clearly relate to Phillips or to the case at hand.

Nonetheless, Justice Kennedy was outraged, finding that it was inappropriate for a Commission charged with enforcing the anti-discrimination statute to denigrate religion this way.[471] He concluded that the Commission's treatment of

[465] Andrew Koppelman, Gay Rights vs. Religious Liberty?: The Unnecessary Conflict 67 (2020). On the rhetorical divide between advocates for LGBTQ+ rights and those for religious liberty, see Linda C. McClain, *The Rhetoric of Bigotry and Conscience in Battles over "Religious Liberty v. LGBT Rights"*, *in* Religious Freedom, LGBT Rights, and the Prospects for Common Ground 212 (William N. Eskridge Jr. & Robin Fretwell Wilson eds., 2018).

[466] Lee v. Asher's Baking Company Ltd., [2018] UKSC 49.

[467] *Masterpiece Cakeshop*, 138 S. Ct. at 1728.

[468] *Id.* at 1729.

[469] *Id.* at 13.

[470] *Id.*

[471] *Id.* at 1729–30.

Phillips' case "violated the state's duty under the First Amendment not to base laws or regulations on hostility to a religion or religious viewpoint."[472]

Thus, *Masterpiece Cakeshop* built on *Dale* in two significant ways. First, Justice Kennedy exaggerated the harms that Phillips faced, in terms of both free expression and religious freedom, in arriving at a categorical decision on religious freedom grounds.[473] As in *Dale*, had the case been resolved on its facts, the Court could have ruled on narrower grounds,[474] rather than placing a thumb on the First Amendment side of the scale. Second and relatedly, *Masterpiece Cakeshop* opened the door to future conservative litigants, by indicating (albeit in dicta) that even commercial enterprises like a bakery can claim First Amendment exemptions from anti-LGBTQ+ discrimination laws.

Masterpiece Cakeshop differed from *Dale* in one crucial respect: its tone toward the LGBTQ+ community. When *Dale* was decided, same-sex relations were still banned in many states and same-sex marriage was a distant dream. Chief Justice Rehnquist's opinion thus echoes the homophobic language in *Bowers* (1986) more than the rhetoric of inclusion and dignity that characterizes *Lawrence* (2003) and *Obergefell* (2015). There was no language in Rehnquist's opinion that expressed sympathy or concern for Dale, but there were repeated references to him as an "avowed homosexual."[475] Both Justice Stevens and Justice Souter noted in their *Dale* dissenting opinions that changing public attitudes and a parallel "decline of stereotypical thinking about race and gender" justified the broad application of New Jersey's public accommodation law.[476] Chief Justice Rehnquist simply dismissed this as "scarcely an argument for denying First Amendment protection to those who refuse to accept these views."[477]

Masterpiece Cakeshop was decided almost two decades later and after same-sex marriage was the law of the land. But Justice Kennedy also went out of his way to stress the gains made by the LGBTQ+ community and his support for their cause. He noted, for instance, how society "has come to the recognition that gay persons and gay couples cannot be treated as social outcasts or as inferior in dignity and worth."[478] Of course, Justice Kennedy played a key role in bringing about such recognition through his majority opinions in *Romer*, *Lawrence*, *Windsor*, and *Obergefell*. This statement in *Masterpiece Cakeshop* implicitly nods to his past jurisprudence and serves a clear reputational purpose. Such dicta turn out to be a recurring feature in cases pitting anti-LGBTQ+ discrimination laws against First Amendment claims. The difference, as we will see, is that by the third decade of the twenty-first century, the Supreme Court's reputation had been so damaged that

[472] *Id.* at 1731.
[473] *See* GREENE, *supra* note 54, at 147–52, 159.
[474] *Id.* at 162–63.
[475] *Dale*, 530 U.S. at 646, 652.
[476] *Id.* at 699–700 (Steven, J., dissenting), 700–01 (Souter, J., dissenting).
[477] *Id.* at 660.
[478] *Masterpiece Cakeshop*, 138 S. Ct. at 1727.

the institution itself—not just its individual justices—needed a facelift. And this would be achieved, in part, by saying the right things about LGBTQ+ rights even if judicial outcomes pointed in the opposite direction.

C. Incrementally Broadening Exemptions

Two major LGBTQ+ rights cases from the early 2020s bear the hallmarks of *Dale* and *Masterpiece Cakeshop*. The first case, *Fulton v. Philadelphia* (2021), recognized a religious exemption to anti-discrimination laws. The second case, *303 Creative LLC v. Elenis* (2023), again involved wedding cakes in Colorado. But it went further than *Masterpiece Cakeshop* in ruling that even commercial entities can claim First Amendment protection from laws of general application. These cases broaden the exemptions carved out in previous cases. While they move the law in a conservative direction, they do not subvert or upend precedent in the vein of *Dobbs*, *Students for Fair Admissions*, or *Kennedy*.[479]

Fulton concerned the eligibility of Catholic Social Services (CSS) to contract with the City of Philadelphia. The City enters annual contracts with private foster care agencies to place children into foster care. CSS had contracted with Philadelphia for over fifty years for this purpose.[480] Because of its religious commitment to opposite-sex marriage, CSS did not certify unmarried couples or same-sex couples to adopt children. After an investigation, the City found that this practice violated both a non-discrimination provision in its contract with CSS as well as anti-discrimination provisions in Philadelphia's Fair Practices Ordinance.[481] The City informed CSS that it would not refer children to, or enter into contracts with, the agency going forward unless it agreed to certify same-sex couples as foster parents. CSS filed suit, arguing that the City's actions violated, *inter alia*, the Free Exercise Clause of the First Amendment.

The District Court and Third Circuit Court of Appeals ruled for the City.[482] They both relied on the Supreme Court's decision in *Employment Division v. Smith*(1990), which held that neutral and generally applicable laws do not run afoul of the Free Exercise Clause if they place incidental burdens on religious groups.[483] In *Masterpiece Cakeshop*, CCRC determined that the Colorado's public accommodation law was a neutral and generally applicable law and thus concluded that its application to the baker (Phillips) was permissible.[484] The Supreme Court

[479] *Dobbs*, 142 S. Ct. 2228; *Students for Fair Admissions*, 600 U.S. 181; *Kennedy*, 597 U.S. 507.
[480] *Fulton*, 141 S. Ct. at 1874–75.
[481] *Id.* at 1875–76.
[482] Fulton v. Philadelphia, 320 F. Supp. 661, 680–90 (E.D. Pa. 2018); Fulton v. Philadelphia 922 F. 3d 140, 152–59 (3rd Cir. 2019).
[483] Employment Division v. Smith, 494 U.S. 872 (1990).
[484] *Masterpiece Cakeshop*, 138 S. Ct. at 1726.

in that case did not rule on this issue, but as discussed, Justice Kennedy's majority opinion stressed the importance of protecting religious freedom in the context of opposition to same-sex marriage.

In *Fulton*, the Supreme Court built on the opening left by *Masterpiece Cakeshop*. It overturned the Third Circuit's judgment and unanimously ruled in favor of CSS. Chief Justice Roberts authored the majority opinion, which was joined by all three liberal justices (Breyer, Sotomayor, and Kagan) as well as Justice Barrett. After summarily declaring that the City's actions burdened CSS' religious exercise, the Chief Justice moved on to discussing whether that burden was constitutionally permissible. The lower courts had ruled that the burden was permissible based on the straightforward application of the test in *Smith*. The CSS, however, asked the Supreme Court to overturn *Smith*.[485] Justice Alito and Justice Gorsuch in separate concurrences—both joined by Justice Thomas—agreed with CSS and would have overruled *Smith*.[486] But Chief Justice Roberts avoided the issue, by finding that the foster care services at issue in this case did not constitute a public accommodation. As a result, he and the majority concluded that the City's Fair Practice Ordinance did not apply to CSS.[487]

Had *Smith* applied, the City's actions would not be judged under the demanding strict scrutiny standard. By determining that this case fell outside *Smith*'s scope, Chief Justice Roberts tilted the balance in favor of CSS' religious freedom claim. The City was forced to demonstrate that its anti-discrimination policies served a compelling purpose. While it put forward three interests—maximizing the number of foster parents, protecting itself from liability, and ensuring equal treatment of both parents and children—these were deemed "insufficient."[488] The majority opinion stressed that the City had "a system of exceptions" within its contracts with agencies, which undermined its claim in this case that an exception could not be granted for CSS.[489]

On the goal of providing equal treatment, the Chief Justice made clear "that this interest was a weighty one" and cited Justice Kennedy's passage in *Masterpiece Cakeshop* that acknowledged how society had come to recognize the "dignity and worth" of gay people and gay couples.[490] As in *Masterpiece Cakeshop*, however, this rhetoric belied the outcome—a categorical, if narrow, victory for the free exercise of religion under the First Amendment, and a corresponding defeat for anti-discrimination laws and the LGBTQ+ communities that they are intended to protect.

485 *Fulton*, 141 S. Ct. at 1876–77.
486 *See id.* at 1926 (Alito, J., concurring); 1931 (Gorsuch, J., concurring).
487 *Id.* at 1881–82.
488 *Id.*
489 *Id.* at 1882.
490 *Id.* (citing *Masterpiece Cakeshop*, 138 S. Ct. at 1727).

Two years later, in *303 Creative*, the Supreme Court was asked to further broaden exemptions to anti-LGBTQ+ discrimination laws. The facts of this case were similar to *Masterpiece Cakeshop*. The case was filed by Lorie Smith, a graphic artist, who worked only a few miles away from Jack Phillip's bakery. Her business, 303 Creative LLC, produced websites and other electronic content. She wished to expand her business to offer custom wedding websites, which would include her "original artwork" and be "expressive in nature."[491] Smith opposed same-sex marriage. While she said that she would create websites for anyone, regardless of sexual orientation, she worried that the State of Colorado would "force her to convey messages inconsistent with her belief that marriage should be reserved . . . to one man and one woman."[492]

Before even starting her wedding websites venture, Smith filed suit seeking an injunction against the state. This case thus raised an obvious standing question, as Smith had not been injured or even offered the service that she worried would be subject to the Colorado Anti-Discrimination Act (CADA). Several liberal commentators have criticized this case as "fake" or "hypothetical."[493] But as Richard Re has pointed out, pre-enforcement review has historically been used by left-leaning groups to challenge unjust laws.[494]

Moreover, Smith appears to have met the "credible threat" threshold to establish standing.[495] The Tenth Circuit Court of Appeals ruled that Smith had standing based, *inter alia,* on the fact that Colorado enforced the CADA against Phillips and Masterpiece Cakeshop. The appellate court further noted the state had "declined to disavow future enforcement" proceedings against Smith.[496] The Tenth Circuit found that Smith's wedding websites would constitute "pure speech" and thus received First Amendment protection.[497] Colorado would have to meet the "strict scrutiny" standard to justify enforcing the CADA against her.[498] While this usually tolls the death knell for the state,[499] the Tenth Circuit held that Colorado met this high burden. Specifically, it ruled that the state had a compelling interest in ensuring "equal access to publicly available goods and services" and that there were no available alternatives since Smith claimed to offer unique services that could not be duplicated elsewhere.[500]

491 *303 Creative*, 143 S. Ct. at 2308 (internal quotes omitted).

492 *Id.*

493 Richard M. Re, *Does the Discourse on* 303 Creative *Portend a Standing Realignment?*, 99 Notre Dame L. Rev. Reflection 67, 68–72 (2023).

494 *Id.* at 68.

495 This is a well-established standard under federal law. *See, e.g.*, Susan B. Anthony List v. Driehaus, 573 U.S. 149 (2014); 303 Creative LLC v. Elenis, 6 F. 4th 1160, 1172–75 (10th Cir. 2021).

496 *303 Creative LLC*, 6 F. 4th at 1174.

497 *Id.* at 1176.

498 *Id.* at 1178.

499 *See* Yoshino, *supra* note 183, at 755.

500 *Id.* at 1179–80.

Smith appealed to the Supreme Court, which split 6–3 along partisan lines. Justice Gorsuch authored the majority opinion on behalf of the conservative justices. Gorsuch agreed with much of the Tenth Circuit's analysis, including with respect to standing and that Smith would be engaged in "pure speech" when designing wedding websites.[501] He then followed the path of *Dale* and *Masterpiece Cakeshop* in acknowledging the "vital role public accommodations law play in realizing the civil rights of all Americans."[502] Gorsuch added, citing *Dale*, that such laws had increased in number and scope.[503] And citing *Masterpiece Cakeshop*, he noted that many states, like Colorado now prohibit discrimination on the basis of sexual orientation, which is "unexceptional" in that states "may protect gay persons, just as [they] can protect other classes of individuals."[504]

As in those cases, these gestures toward the importance of public accommodation laws and the protection of LGBTQ+ rights were overshadowed by paeans to the First Amendment. Justice Gorsuch harked back across American history to figures like James Madison and Justice Louis Brandeis to stress the importance of free speech. He referred to "the freedom to think and speak as one of 'our inalienable human rights' ";[505] he declared that free speech is "indispensable to the discovery and spread of political truth";[506] and he invoked the framers, who in his view, "designed the Free Speech Clause . . . to protect the freedom to think as you will and to speak as you think."[507]

There were, of course, repeated references to Smith's right to express herself artistically through her websites, which would be her "original, customized creation."[508] Gorsuch also dramatized Smith's predicament. He said: "If she wishes to speak, she must either speak as the state demands or face sanctions . . . that may include compulsory participation in remedial . . . training, filing periodic compliance reports as officials deem necessary, and paying monetary fines."[509]

This tendentious framing of the case makes it appear that Colorado issues diktats to its citizens and hovers over their every move. In fact, Colorado's brief in this case—as Gorsuch later acknowledged—made clear that it had no interest in interfering with Smith's choice of websites and conceded that it would be constitutionally problematic for the state to dictate how she designed websites for specific clients. What Colorado did say was that websites created for opposite-sex couples must also be available to same-sex couples. On this framing of the case, the effects on speech are incidental and do not warrant an exemption from CADA.[510]

[501] *303 Creative*, 143 S. Ct. at 2312.
[502] *Id.* at 2314.
[503] *Id.* (citing *Dale*, 530 U.S. at 656–57).
[504] *Id.* at 2315(citing *Masterpiece Cakeshop*, 138 S. Ct. at 1728).
[505] *Id.* at 2310–11 (citing James Madison's remarks in Congress from 1794).
[506] *Id.* at 2311 (citing Whitney v. California, 274 U.S. 357, 375 (1927) (Brandeis, J., concurring)).
[507] *Id.* at 2310 (citing *Dale*, 530 U.S. at 660–61).
[508] *Id.* at 2312 (internal quotes omitted).
[509] *Id.* at 2313 (internal quotes omitted).
[510] *Id.* at 2315–16.

Justice Gorsuch rejected the state's framing as insufficiently sensitive to Smith's free speech concerns. The Court, therefore, ruled in her favor. It held that Smith could not be compelled by Colorado to make websites containing messages with which she disagreed, even though it is far from clear that Colorado intended to do any such thing.[511]

In dissent, Justice Sotomayor (joined by Justices Kagan and Jackson) rejected Gorsuch's approach and framing of this case. She agreed with Colorado and stressed that CADA would target Smith's conduct not her speech.[512] As Justice Sotomayor correctly pointed out, the majority here granted a commercial enterprise—not a private organization, as in *Dale*—the right to deny same-sex couples access to wedding websites available to the general public. In this sense, *303 Creative* did not simply follow *Dale* and *Masterpiece Cakeshop*. It expanded the scope of First Amendment-based exemptions to public accommodation laws. Though Smith raised both free speech and free exercise of religion claims, the Court focused only on the former. This is perhaps because the Court sensed that its precedent in *Smith* (1990), which a majority was unwilling to overturn in *Fulton*, limited the scope of exemptions under the Free Exercise Clause.[513] By turning to free speech, the Court was able to circumvent *Smith* and obtain majority support for a wide exemption to public accommodation laws.

Justice Sotomayor wrote movingly about the history of the gay rights movement.[514] She discussed how public accommodation laws helped to end racial segregation during the civil rights movement, and stressed the need for such laws to protect the LGBTQ+ community. She referred to gender and sexual minorities as a "protected class" and took the Court to task for failing to stand up from them in the way that "brave Justices" of the past had stood up against racial and sex discrimination.[515]

It is true that the majority in *303 Creative* failed to stand up for the LGBTQ+ community. But the Supreme Court, from *Dale* onwards, has consistently privileged First Amendment claims over laws that sought to guard against LGBTQ+ discrimination. It also bears emphasis that while state-level public accommodation laws prohibited sexual orientation-based discrimination, the Supreme Court has never recognized gender and sexual minorities as a protected class. As discussed in Part II, Justice Kennedy's libertarian approach prevailed in *Romer*, *Lawrence*, and *Obergefell*. These cases form part of a broader trend in the Court toward "hybrid liberty/equality claims" that Kenji Yoshino helpfully dubbed "dignity claims."[516] By combining equal protection and due process in a single analysis, Kennedy and the

[511] *Id.* at 2321–22.
[512] *Id.* at 2322 (Sotomayor, J., dissenting).
[513] *See* Kenji Yoshino, *Rights of First Refusal*, 137 HARV. L. REV. 244, 245 (2023).
[514] *303 Creative*, 143 S Ct. at 2329–30 (Sotomayor, J., dissenting).
[515] *Id.* at 2322.
[516] Yoshino, *supra* note 183, at 749.

Court sidestepped the traditional tiers of scrutiny approach that had prevailed in previous eras with respect to race and sex-based discrimination. As a result, neither the LGBTQ+ community nor any subgroup therein (like same-sex married couples) has ever received comparable protection from the Court.

Returning to *303 Creative*, Justice Sotomayor is correct that gender and sexual minorities are a protected class both at the state-level in Colorado and under Title VII, thanks to *Bostock*. But in contrasting the *303 Creative* majority's approach toward anti-LGBTQ+ discrimination with the Court's jurisprudence on race and sex-based discrimination, Justice Sotomayor lets herself, other liberal justices, and Justice Kennedy off the hook. *303 Creative*, unfortunately, represents a continuation, rather than a departure, from the Court's jurisprudence both in privileging the First Amendment and in failing to recognize the LGBTQ+ community as a protected class at a *constitutional* level.

VI. Conclusion: *Institutional Self-Preservation v. Partisan Decision-Making*

In 2015, with the constitutional recognition of same-sex marriage, the culture wars on LGBTQ+ rights appeared to be nearing an end. The Supreme Court, through a series of cases including *Romer*, *Lawrence,* and *Windsor* had steadily expanded the ambit of LGBTQ+ rights and participated in the project of the global constitutionalism. While *Obergefell* signaled the end of the Court's engagement with foreign materials, national majorities supported the Supreme Court's ruling in that case, and it appeared that the LGBTQ+ community would continue to gain public acceptance and legal protection within the United States.

Now, a decade later, that optimism has evaporated, and the LGBTQ+ community is in a more precarious legal and social position than it was when *Obergefell* was decided.[517] As the country has become more sharply polarized, so too have Republican-led states passed reactionary laws that discriminate against sexual and gender minorities. Since 2020, at least ten states have banned gender-affirming healthcare for gender-diverse youth;[518] more than twenty states have limited transgender students from participating in sports in their chosen gender identity;[519] and a few states (notably Florida) have even prevented schools from discussing LGBTQ+ issues.[520]

[517] *See* Waldman, *supra* note 419, at 985–86.

[518] *See* Francesca Paris, *Bans on Transition Care for Young People Spread Across U.S.*, N.Y. Times (Apr. 17, 2023), https://www.nytimes.com/2023/04/15/upshot/bans-transgender-teenagers.html.

[519] *See Bans on Transgender Youth Participation in Sports*, Movement Advancement Project (MAP), https://www.lgbtmap.org/equality-maps/youth/sports_participation_bans (last visited June 14, 2024).

[520] *See* Dustin Jones & Jonathan Franklin, *Not Just Florida. More Than a Dozen States Propose So-Called "Don't Say Gay" Bills*, NPR (Apr. 10, 2022), https://www.npr.org/2022/04/10/1091543359/15-states-dont-say-gay-anti-transgender-bills.

The Supreme Court has, meanwhile, become more sharply partisan in its jurisprudence. The 6–3 conservative supermajority installed by President Trump has moved the law sharply to the right on a wide range of constitutional rights issues including abortion, the right to bear arms, school prayer, and affirmative action. But the Court has been more circumspect in the LGBTQ+ rights context. In *Dobbs*—arguably the most reactionary judgment issued by this Court—Justice Alito's majority opinion distinguished *Lawrence* and *Obergefell* from the abortion precedents and signaled that they would be safe.[521] While Justice Thomas wrote separately to argue that *Lawrence* and *Obergefell* (as well as several other "demonstrably erroneous" precedents) should be reconsidered, none of his colleagues joined his opinion.[522]

This appears to have been a strategic move by the other conservative justices. *Dobbs* represented the culmination of a decades-long conservative movement to overturn *Roe*. It was also the outcome of a successful Republican Party strategy to stack the federal judiciary—especially the Supreme Court—with bona fide conservative judges. In *Dobbs*, five conservative justices seemed willing to accept that rights to sexual privacy and same-sex marriage needed to remain in place to preserve some sociological legitimacy. This was a small price to pay, especially since they were only sustaining homonormative and culturally mainstream LGBTQ+ rights.

Thus, *Lawrence* and *Obergefell* were not in the judicial crosshairs. But the LGBTQ+ jurisprudence of the Second Roberts Court suggests that other strategic considerations are also at play. Recent decisions in this area—*Fulton, 303 CreativeLLC*, and *Bostock*—allowed the Court to push back against its critics and against the narrative that it is a partisan institution. *Fulton* and *303 Creative LLC* enabled the Court to show that it neither disdains precedent nor the struggles of minority groups. While these judgments are characteristic of the Court's penchant to treat the First Amendment as sacrosanct,[523] the opinions of conservative justices therein display at least rhetorical concern for the LGBTQ+ community. They also reach outcomes that broadly accord with precedent and, unlike the Court's jurisprudence in other areas, reflect mainstream public opinion. To wit, in 2022, President Biden signed into law the bipartisan Respect for Marriage Act.[524] It requires states to recognize same-sex and interracial marriages performed in other states, while also protecting religious liberty with respect to marriage.[525]

521 *Dobbs*, 142 S. Ct. at 2261.

522 *Id.* at 2301 (Thomas, J., concurring).

523 *See* Mary Anne Franks, The Cult of the Constitution 105–57 (2019) (explaining how First Amendment doctrine has evolved to privilege the interests of White men at the expense of women and minorities).

524 Respect for Marriage Act, Pub. L. 117–228, 136 Stat. 2305 (2022).

525 For more on the balance between LGBTQ+ rights and religious liberty in this law, see Douglas Laycock et al., *The Respect for Marriage Act: Living Together Despite Our Deepest Differences*, 2024 U. Ill. L. Rev. 511 (2024).

Bostock, meanwhile, had a different strategic value. Justice Gorsuch's majority opinion illustrated that a conservative court, using textualist methods, could expand statutory protection for traditionally marginalized sexual and gender diverse groups. This decision is a useful counterpoint to high-profile conservative judgments like *Dobbs* and *Students for Fair Admissions*, which have been criticized for their disregard, even contempt, of other historically disadvantaged communities.

Overall, recent LGBTQ+ cases highlight the self-preservationist tendencies of a Supreme Court that is often depicted as unmoored from institutional (or even legal) constraints. Unlike its predecessors, the Second Roberts Court is not interested in advancing liberal constitutionalism, much less engaging with a global community of courts. Moderate to progressive LGBTQ+ rights decisions help to preserve (whatever is left of) its reputation for impartiality and fidelity to precedent, and to reduce the likelihood of political reforms to the Court's institutional structure and operation.

4
LGBTQ+ Rights Amid Institutional Crises and Rising Ethnonationalism in India

I. Introduction

A. Background

We turn from the world's oldest democracy to its largest. Home to 1.4 billion people, India has twenty-two official languages and is the birthplace of four major religions: Buddhism, Hinduism, Jainism, and Sikhism. This pluralism, though, has not always been looked upon as an asset. When India gained independence in 1947—following 200 years of British colonial rule—there was widespread skepticism in the West that this sprawling subcontinent could be ruled as a single state, much less as a democracy.[1] Partition carved out modern-day Pakistan and Bangladesh from the new Indian republic. But there remained a sizeable Muslim minority population, a rigid caste system, and high levels of illiteracy and malnutrition that needed to be addressed. As Madhav Khosla has shown, the challenge for the framers of the Indian Constitution was thus unprecedented. They not only had to design context-specific democratic institutions but also had to mold a citizenry that was capable of exercising self-government.[2]

A Constituent Assembly (CA) was convened in 1947 to undertake this herculean task. It took almost three years to finally enact India's republican Constitution, which was adopted on January 26, 1950. The Constitution, which has endured to the present day, is incredibly detailed. Comprising almost 400 articles, 12 schedules, and 145,000 words, the Constitution reflects the CA's attention to the many challenges confronting India as well as the framers' desire to fundamentally transform the country and its citizens.

The CA understood that a strong central government was crucial to bring about the intended social and political transformation.[3] Thus, the Constitution

[1] Madhav Khosla, India's Founding Moment: The Constitution of a Most Surprising Democracy 4–9 (2020).

[2] *Id.* at 25–26.

[3] *Id.* at ch. 2; Granville Austin, The Indian Constitution: Cornerstone of a Nation 145–46 (2nd ed. 1999).

Courts and LGBTQ+ Rights in an Age of Judicial Retrenchment. Rehan Abeyratne, Oxford University Press.
 DOI: 10.1093/9780191995040.003.0004

established a parliamentary democracy in which a prime minister-led government, advised by a Council of Ministers (cabinet), exercises executive power.[4] But in a nod to the country's diversity and to constrain executive power, the Constitution created a bicameral parliament.[5] The government must maintain the support of a majority of members of the Lok Sabha (lower house) to remain in power. The Rajya Sabha (upper house) represents the federal states and was intended to serve as a check on the lower house.[6]

The Constitution departed from the British model of parliamentary sovereignty by creating a robust judiciary. At the judicial apex sits the Supreme Court of India (SCI).[7] The SCI and High Courts (together, the higher judiciary) are empowered to undertake strong-form judicial review and grant a range of constitutional remedies.[8] Part III of the Constitution sets forth fundamental rights, including the rights to life, liberty, and equality,[9] while Article 13 declares void any law that contravene fundamental rights.[10] Read together, these provisions permit the higher judiciary to strike down unconstitutional laws.

The Indian Constitution also provides the higher courts with extensive remedial authority. Articles 32 and 226 permit citizens to directly approach the SCI and High Courts, respectively, via "appropriate proceedings" to seek the enforcement of fundamental rights. These provisions empower the higher judiciary to grant various writs (including habeas corpus, mandamus, and quo warranto) to remedy rights violations.[11] Dr. B.R. Ambedkar, Chairman of the CA's Drafting Committee, believed Article 32 was the "most important" provision in the Constitution, referring to it as the document's "very soul."[12]

In addition to this original jurisdiction, SCI has appellate jurisdiction over cases in the High Courts.[13] It may also "grant special leave to appeal from any judgment, decree, determination, sentence or order in any cause or matter passed or made by

[4] India Const. art. 74(1). Executive power is formally wielded by the President of India but following the Forty-Second Amendment to the Constitution in 1977, the President must act on the advice of the Council of Ministers, headed by the Prime Minister.

[5] *Id.* arts. 79–81. The Chair of the CA's Drafting Committee, Dr. B.R. Ambedkar, made clear that India while India has a federal structure, states do not have the autonomy or powers of those in the United States. *See* The Framing of India's Constitution: Select Documents 421–45 (B. Shiva Rao ed., Vol. 4, 1967).

[6] For an overview and critique of the Indian Parliament, see M. Mohsin Alam Bhat, *The Parliament and State Legislatures of India*, *in* Routledge Handbook of Asian Parliaments 178 (Po Jen Yap & Rehan Abeyratne eds., 2023).

[7] India Const. art. 124.

[8] On the wide scope of judicial review powers, see Vikram Aditya Narayan & Jahnavi Sindhu, *A Historical Argument for Proportionality Under the Indian Constitution*, 2(1) Indian L. Rev. 51, 70–73 (2018).

[9] India Const. arts. 14, 19, 21.

[10] *Id.* art. 13.

[11] *Id.* art. 32.

[12] B. Shiva Rao, The Framing of India's Constitution: A Study 307 (Subhash C. Kashyap ed., 1968). *See also*, Austin, *supra* note 3, at chs. 3–4.

[13] India Const. arts. 132–34.

any court or tribunal in the territory of India."[14] Special Leave Petitions (SLPs), as we will discuss, have come to dominate the Court's docket at the expense of its writ jurisdiction.

Today, with broad jurisdiction, and its status as the apex court in the world's largest democracy, the SCI is often called "the most powerful court in the world" and a "people's court."[15] These monikers derived from the Court's populist turn in the 1980s,[16] particularly the advent of public interest litigation (PIL) and the recognition of a range of new constitutional rights.[17] All told, by the turn of the millennium, the SCI had become a major player in Indian politics and in the public consciousness. It had also become a more cosmopolitan court, not only relying on universal values and principles but also looking to international sources to guide its fundamental rights jurisprudence.[18]

B. Chapter Overview

This chapter explores the SCI's LGBTQ+ rights jurisprudence in the context of major institutional and political challenges facing the Court. Institutionally, the SCI has a chronically overloaded docket and has come under scrutiny for the unethical conduct of its justices and the misuse of the powers vested in the Chief Justice of India (CJI). Politically, the country has shifted from liberal democratic rule to more autocratic rule under Prime Minister Narendra Modi. Modi leads the Hindu nationalist Bharatiya Janata Party (BJP), which is hostile to liberal constitutionalism and has sought to centralize power in the executive. The SCI, with its broad public support and wide constitutional jurisdiction, might have served as a check on government power, but it has largely deferred to the executive on major constitutional issues.

The rights of gender and sexual minorities remained a site for progressive constitutional jurisprudence without much political blowback. But as Modi's grip on

[14] *Id.* art. 136.

[15] *See* Nick Robinson, *Structure Matters: The Impact of Court Structure on the Indian and U.S. Supreme Court*, 61 AM. J. COMP. L. 173, 176 (2013); APARNA CHANDRA ET AL., COURT ON TRIAL: A DATA DRIVEN ACCOUNT OF THE SUPREME COURT OF INDIA 1–3 (2023).

[16] For a critical account of this period, see ANUJ BHUWANIA, COURTING THE PEOPLE: PUBLIC INTEREST LITIGATION IN POST-EMERGENCY INDIA (2017).

[17] *See generally*, Rehan Abeyratne, *Socioeconomic Rights in the Indian Constitution: Toward a Broader Conception of Legitimacy*, 39 BROOK. J. INT'L L. 1 (2014).

[18] *See, e.g.*, Vishaka v. Rajasthan, (1997) 6 S.C.C. 241 (India) (drawing from the Convention on the Elimination of All Forms of Discrimination Against Women (CEDAW) to formulate national sexual harassment guidelines). The Indian Constitution, to be sure, had cosmopolitan elements from its inception, both in its commitment—set forth in the Preamble—to universal principles of justice, liberty, equality, and fraternity, and in that the constitutional text and jurisprudence have always "been situated at the major cross-currents of global constitutional law." *See* Sujit Choudhry et al., *Locating Indian Constitutionalism*, *in* OXFORD HANDBOOK OF THE INDIAN CONSTITUTION 1, 4–8 (Sujit Choudhry et al. eds., 2016).

power tightened, and the SCI's independence and integrity weakened, the Court has retrenched on LGBTQ+ rights too.

Part II engages with criticisms of the SCI's expanded jurisdiction, including those arising from the flood of SLPs in the Court's docket and the apparent judicial turn away from the poor and toward neoliberal or middle-class issues. Due to the large docket, the SCI sits in small benches (often consisting of two judges) to decide most cases. This arrangement has resulted in a haphazard and often contradictory jurisprudence, as different benches issue contrasting decisions on similar matters.

After laying out this institutional context, Part II turns to the early LGBTQ+ rights judicial decisions beginning with the Delhi High Court's landmark judgment in *Naz Foundation v. Gov't of NCT* (2009).[19] The High Court decriminalized same-sex intercourse by reading down Section 377 of the Indian Penal Code (IPC). A Victorian-era holdover from the colonial era, Section 377 criminalized "carnal intercourse against the order of nature." As the High Court explained, this provision had been used by law enforcement authorities to harass and victimize members of India's LGBTQ+ communities. The High Court's judgment drew on the testimony of various affected groups including those from rural areas and smaller cities. Moreover, it referred to foreign judgments not only from Western jurisdictions but from South Africa and Fiji as well. Its approach, therefore, was neither neoliberal nor elitist but grounded in the community and in careful comparative engagement.

Nonetheless, a two-judge bench of the SCI reversed the Delhi High Court, in a judgment that mischaracterized the lower court's decision as importing Western values into the Indian context and catering to the needs of a small urban elite. The SCI's judgment in this case—*Koushal v. Naz Foundation*(2013)—effectively recriminalized same-sex relations.[20] It invoked principles of the separation of powers and judicial restraint to rule that any changes to Section 377 would be left to Parliament. A few months later, a different two-judge SCI bench in *NALSA* (2014) adopted the Delhi High Court's approach.[21] While not directly commenting on the issues in *Koushal*, the *NALSA* bench implicitly repudiated that judgment by recognizing broad transgender rights and relying heavily on a range of foreign examples, including from Nepal and Pakistan, to reach its conclusions.

Part III discusses the shift in Indian constitutionalism under the Modi-led BJP government, focusing on his first term as Prime Minister (2014–19). Since 2014, the government has turned a primarily plural, secular, and democratic state into one that is more monolithic, Hindu, and autocratic. Under Modi, India's neoliberal economic trajectory has also been turbocharged, conferring soaring wealth on

[19] Naz Foundation v. Gov't of NCT, (2009) D.L.T. 277 (Delhi HC) (India).
[20] Koushal v. Naz Foundation, (2014) 1 S.C.C. 1 (India).
[21] NALSA v. Union of India, (2014) 5 S.C.C. 438 (India).

a privileged few and deepening socioeconomic inequality. Part IV further shows how the SCI retrenched in this period, declining to use its broad jurisdiction to stand against *prima facie* constitutional violations.

Part IV turns to LGBTQ+ rights during the early Modi years (2014–18). It examines how the SCI, led by CJI D.Y. Chandrachud, was able to maintain the progressive and cosmopolitan strands of its fundamental rights jurisprudence. The Court built on *NALSA* and the Delhi High Court's judgment in *Naz Foundation* to recognize a broad right to privacy in *Puttuswamy v. Union of India* (2017).[22] *Puttuswamy* paved the way for progressive judgments that, *inter alia*, decriminalized adultery[23] and allowed menstruating women to access a Hindu temple from which they had been banned.[24] Building on *Puttuswamy*, the SCI would finally overrule *Koushal* and decriminalize same-sex relations in *Navtej Johar v. Union of India* (2018).[25]

Part V explores LGBTQ+ rights in Modi's second term as Prime Minister (2019–23). Several institutional crises at the SCI that began in Modi's first term and worsened during the second term. These crises stemmed from abuses of power by successive CJIs and a lack of transparency in the assignment of benches and judicial appointments. The Modi government has exploited these crises to weaken the Court further and to advance its illiberal agenda with little judicial pushback. The SCI in recent years has largely deferred to the government or simply avoided ruling on major constitutional issues, particularly with respect to writ petitions that challenged core aspects of Modi's political agenda.

Part V then turns to examine the fate of LGBTQ+ rights in this new institutional environment with an emboldened and increasingly autocratic executive and a weakened SCI. It explains how the *NALSA* judgment was co-opted by the BJP government to enact legislation on transgender rights in 2019 that neither comported with the SCI's ruling nor recognized the plural needs of India's gender-diverse communities. A few years later, the government prevailed in *Supriyo @ Supriya Chakraborty v. Union of India* (2023).[26] The SCI unanimously ruled that same-sex marriage was not a fundamental right and, by a 3–2 majority, that the state was under no obligation to recognize civil unions. While the justices expressed concern for the challenges facing same-sex couples, the final judgment lacked bite. It did not issue any binding orders. Instead, the judgment simply noted that the government had announced its intent to form a committee to investigate these issues.

The chapter concludes in Part VI by reflecting on the trajectory of LGBTQ+ rights and how it informs our understanding of Indian constitutionalism.

[22] Puttuswamy v. Union of India, (2017) 10 S.C.C. 1 (India).
[23] Joseph Shine v. Union of India, (2018) S.C.C. 1676 (India).
[24] Indian Young Lawyers Association v. State of Kerala, (2019) 11 S.C.C. 1 (India) [hereinafter *Sabarimala*].
[25] Navtej Johar v. Union of India, 2018 I.N.S.C. 790 (India).
[26] Supriyo @ Supriya Chakraborty v. Union of India, 2023 I.N.S.C. 920 (India).

II. LGBTQ+ Rights in an Era of Transition (2001–14)

In December 2001, the Naz Foundation—a non-governmental organization (NGO) working to combat the HIV/AIDS epidemic in India—filed a writ petition before the Delhi High Court.[27] It alleged that Section 377 of the IPC violated the fundamental rights of sexual minorities, primarily "men who have sex with men" (MSM).[28] Section 377 was a Victorian-era prohibition on "carnal intercourse against the order of nature."[29] It had been used in postcolonial India primarily as a means to criminalize and harass MSMs, who were forced into the shadows to the detriment not only to their sense of dignity and self-worth but also to their health.[30] Taking advantage of the higher judiciary's relaxed standing rules, the Naz Foundation filed its petition in the public interest, arguing Section 377 substantially contributed to the burgeoning HIV/AIDS public health crisis in India.[31]

As this petition worked its way through the higher judiciary,[32] the SCI was contending with two developments that would reshape both how it operated and how it was perceived. Let us consider each in turn, before returning to the Naz Foundation petition and the LGBTQ+ rights judgments that ensued.

A. Neoliberalism and the Overflowing Docket

In 1991, P.V. Narasimha Rao became Prime Minister of India. He was a member of the once-dominant Indian National Congress (INC), which had shepherded India to independence and instituted socialist policies first under Nehru and more aggressively under Indira Gandhi. But Rao led India in a different direction. He launched the New Economic Policy, which aimed to deregulate India's economy, including the privatization of state-owned enterprises and liberalization of government licensing regimes.[33] In this new capitalist phase, India's middle class expanded, and social programs were redesigned in light of the market-based development policies of the Washington Consensus.

[27] Naz Foundation v. Gov't of NCT, *Civil Writ Petition Under Article 226 of the Constitution of India for the Issue of. a Writ/Order/Direction in the Nature of an Appropriate Writ/Order/Direction to the Respondents*, Writ Petition (Civil) No. 7455/2001 (Delhi HC).

[28] *Id.*; *Naz Foundation*, (2009) D.L.T. 277 at para. 6.

[29] Indian Penal Code 1860, § 377.

[30] *Naz Foundation*, (2009) D.L.T. 277 at para.7.

[31] *Id.* at para. 6.

[32] The petition was initially dismissed by the Delhi High Court for a lack of standing before the SCI sent it back to the High Court for reconsideration. *See* Robert Wintemute, *Lesbian, Gay, Bisexual and Transgender Human Rights in India: From Naz Foundation to Navtej Singh Johar and Beyond*, *in* Human Rights in India 152, 153 (Satvinder Juss ed., 2019).

[33] *See* Manoj Mate, *Globalization, Rights, and Judicial Review in the Supreme Court of India*, 25 Wash. Int'l L. J. 649 (2016).

Scholars have linked this economic turn toward neoliberalism to a similar turn in the PIL jurisdiction of the higher judiciary,[34] where justices became less concerned with the poor and disadvantaged segments in society, and more interested in enabling large-scale infrastructure works and boosting India's image as a new economic powerhouse. In one high-profile judgment, the SCI permitted the construction of the Narmada dam, even though it would displace 40 million people without a clear resettlement plan.[35] For the Court, this heavy price was worth the developmental benefits of a dam. It said: "It is a fact that people are displaced by projects from their ancestral homes. Displacement of these people would undoubtedly disconnect them from their past, culture, custom and traditions, but then it becomes necessary to harvest a river for [*sic*] larger good."[36] Similarly, as Anuj Bhuwania has shown, the Delhi High Court used PIL in the 2000s as a "slum demolition machine."[37] The High Court forcibly removed thousands from their homes by authorizing municipal authorities to demolish "unauthorized construction" and to "cleanup" the city's street vendors, beggars, and cycle-rickshaw drivers.[38] Bhuwania highlighted both the procedural unfairness of this process and its neglect of poor and marginalized communities. As he put it, "'[I]llegal' citizens were not even made party to the proceedings. All problems were blamed on the conspicuous urban poor, who were seen as obstructing the neat solutions proposed to make the city come up to scratch as a 'global city.'"[39]

Moving beyond these exemplar cases, other scholars have conducted large empirical studies to determine whether judges have become less receptive to cases filed by low income or marginalized groups. Varun Gauri examined the Supreme Court's docket from 1988–2007 to assess the extent to which the Court favored disadvantaged groups in PIL and fundamental rights litigation.[40] Gauri's data reveals that "advantaged" claimants were less likely than other claimants to prevail in fundamental rights cases until the late 1980s.[41] However, "advantaged" claimants were significantly more successful thereafter.[42] In the 1990s, 68 percent of such claimants prevailed in their cases compared to 47 percent of non-advantaged claimants; from 2000 to 2008, the ratio was 73 to 47 percent.[43]

[34] *See, e.g.*, Nick Robinson, *Expanding Judiciaries: India and the Rise of the Good Governance Court*, 8 Wash. U. Global Stud. L. Rev. 1 (2009); The Shifting Scales of Justice: The Supreme Court in Neo-liberal India (Mayur Suresh & Siddharth Narrain eds., 2014).

[35] Narmada Bachao Andolan v. Union of India, 2000 I.N.S.C. 518 (India).

[36] *Id.*

[37] Bhuwania, *supra* note 16, at ch. 3.

[38] *Id.* at 80–82, 99.

[39] *Id.* at 95.

[40] Varun Gauri, *Fundamental Rights and Public Interest Litigation in India: Overreaching or Underachieving?*, *in* The Shifting Scales of Justice, *supra* note 34, at 89.

[41] *Id.* at 98.

[42] *Id.*

[43] *Id.* at 98–99.

The findings, therefore, suggest a clear neoliberal turn in the 1990s toward favoring more powerful interests.

Shylashri Shankar conducted a similar study that focused on the rights to health and education in India.[44] Examining all the SCI and High Court cases from 1950 to 2006, she concluded, "The dominant pattern emerging from our models is a Supreme Court judge negotiated with the laws, political configurations, institutional, and societal concerns to construct judgments that were perceived as legitimate by these elements."[45] She also echoed Gauri in describing a shift in judicial attitudes over time. Specifically, she noted a "trend towards conservatism by the Supreme Court after 1993."[46]

A later study by Chandra, Hubbard, and Kalantry examined every SCI case published from 2010 to 2014 to determine the types of cases admitted to the Court.[47] The SCI's docket is divided into "admission" and "regular" matters.[48] The former refers primarily to SLPs and writ petitions.[49] A small number of these petitions along with appellate cases are scheduled for "regular" hearings.[50] The study found that the Court favors comparatively less powerful actors at the admissions stage in three distinct areas: individuals over the government in civil cases, defendants over the prosecution in criminal cases, and claimants in constitutional cases over non-constitutional claimants.[51] Crucially, the authors drew the opposite conclusion to previous studies with respect to win rates.[52] They noted that the SCI does not hear every case on the merits; rather, it selects a small subsection of the appellate cases it admits every year for a regular hearing.[53] Thus, lower win rates for less advantaged claimants (such as criminal defendants and those alleging constitutional violations) suggest preferential treatment for such claimants at the admissions stage. Put simply, the SCI admits relatively weaker cases for merits review in these categories because of its greater receptivity to those claimants, but many go on to lose on the merits. The authors concluded that the SCI remains a people's court, at least with respect to admissions.

The backdrop for this study, and for the book that Chandra, Hubbard, and Kalantry later coauthored,[54] is the rapidly expanding SCI docket. When the Court

[44] Shylashri Shankar, Scaling Justice: India's Supreme Court, Social Rights, and Civil Liberties 129 (2009).

[45] *Id.* at 166.

[46] *Id.* at 144.

[47] Aparna Chandra et al., *The Supreme Court of India: A People's Court?*, 1(2) Indian L. Rev. 146 (2017).

[48] *See* Tarunabh Khaitan, *The Indian Supreme Court's Identity Crisis: A Constitutional Court or Court of Appeals*, 4 Indian L. Rev. 1, 4 (2020).

[49] *Id.*

[50] *Id.*

[51] Chandra et al., *supra* note 47, at 147.

[52] *Id.*

[53] *Id.*

[54] *See* Chandra et al., *supra* note 15, at ch. 2.

opened in 1950, it admitted approximately 1,000 cases. By 1980, that figure had ballooned to more than 20,000. By the turn of the millennium, the Court admitted more than 30,000 cases with approximately 4,500 of those matters scheduled for hearings.[55] Since then, but for a brief dip during the COVID-19 pandemic, the SCI admitted at least 30,000 cases (often thousands more) per year.[56] In most years from 2000 to 2023, more than 5,000 cases were scheduled for hearing each year. Most of this expanded docket consists of discretionary SLPs against orders passed by lower courts.[57] SLPs constituted about 82 percent of the SCI's docket in 1993; by 2018, 99 percent of pending cases were SLPs.[58] As a result, the number of writ petitions—which permit constitutional rights claims to be filed directly before the SCI—declined, constituting only 2 percent of the Court's admissions docket in 2011.[59]

The SCI could impose some limits on its SLP jurisdiction but has thus far declined to do so. In a 2016 judgment, it held that "no effort should be made to restrict the powers of this Court under Article 136"—the provision pertaining to SLP jurisdiction.[60] As Rishad Chowdhury put it, the Court's overburdened docket is, therefore, "neither a historical inevitability nor primarily a resource-centric problem. It is . . . the product of choices on the part of the judges of the Supreme Court."[61]

These choices have had deleterious institutional consequences to which we will return in Part III. For now, let us focus on the doctrinal consequences. Parliament increased the number of justices on the SCI from twenty-six in 1986 to thirty-one in 2009 and thirty-four in 2019. To keep up with the ever-expanding docket, the SCI is divided into several "benches", which usually comprise two or three judges.[62] Cases that raise a "substantial question" of constitutional interpretation must be heard by a bench of at least five justices.[63] The SCI takes an average of four years—and often much longer—to dispose of regular matters.[64] Meanwhile, it disposes of 30–60 admission matters per day, most of which are decided within a few minutes.[65] The Court often disposes of these matters without reasons, leaving

[55] INDIAN JUDICIARY: ANNUAL REPORT 2022–23, VOLUME 1: SUPREME COURT 86–87 (2023) [hereinafter SUPREME COURT REPORT 2023].

[56] *Id.*

[57] *See* Nick Robinson, *A Quantitative Analysis of the Indian Supreme Court's Workload*, 10 J. EMPIRICAL LEGAL STUD. 570, 582 (2013); Khaitan, *supra* note 48, at 5 (noting that of the cases added to the docket in 2011, approximately 85 percent were SLPs, 2 percent were writs, and 3 percent were other appellate matters).

[58] CHANDRA ET AL., *supra* note 15, at 26–27.

[59] *Id.* at 27.

[60] *Id.*; Mathai @ Joby v. George, (2016) 7 S.C.C. 700 (India).

[61] Rishad Ahmed Chowdhury, *Missing the Wood for the Trees: The Unseen Crisis in the Supreme Court* 5 NUJS L. REV. 351, 353 (2012). *See also*, Robinson, *supra* note 57, at 582 (noting that the Supreme Court appears "quite willing to oblige" the expanded docket, which is growing at a faster rate than the High Court or lower court dockets).

[62] Robinson, *supra* note 15, at 184–85.

[63] India CONST. art. 145(3).

[64] Nick Robinson, *A Court Adrift*, FRONTLINE (May 3, 2013), http://www.frontline.in/cover-story/a-court-adrift/article4613892.ece.

[65] Khaitan, *supra* note 48, at 4.

litigants (and the public) in the dark as to why certain matters are admitted and others are not.[66]

In the SCI's defense, the sheer volume of cases and its multiple benches make it practically impossible for its justices to issue well-reasoned judgments in every case and to consistently abide by precedent.[67] A recent empirical study on the Supreme Court's use of precedent suggests that the justices deploy *stare decisis* in strategic fashion, choosing to eschew citations to precedent entirely in nearly half of their opinions and citing a few highly salient older cases in the remaining opinions.[68]

In sum, as Nick Robinson put it, the Court is "polyvocal"—it speaks in many different voices at once.[69] It is, therefore, difficult to characterize the institution along ideological lines.[70] Justices have varying preferences on which matters to admit or reject. They also have distinct approaches to legal interpretation.[71] The fate of litigants often turns on the bench to which their case is assigned, as some benches are likely to be more sympathetic to their claims than others. On constitutional matters, this leads to a schizophrenic jurisprudence where some SCI benches seek to move in a progressive and cosmopolitan direction, while others are conservative and inward looking. This is precisely what happened in the early LGBTQ+ rights cases.

B. Oscillating Between Judicial Poles

The Naz Foundation's writ petition on behalf of MSMs was finally scheduled for hearing at the Delhi High Court in 2008. By that time, a social movement had coalesced around advocacy to repeal Section 377 of the IPC. A coalition of twelve NGOs representing LGBTQ+ groups, children's rights, and women's rights called "Voices Against Section 377 IPC" submitted affidavits to the High Court documenting the effects of Section 377 on LGBTQ+ groups around the country, including incidents of police harassment, custodial torture, and sexual violence.[72]

The Delhi High Court, like the SCI, has a large caseload and does not sit *en banc*. This case was assigned to a two-judge bench comprising Chief Justice A.P. Shah and Justice S. Muralidhar. Shah would later become a vocal critic of the Supreme Court's lack of transparency and its silence in the face of Modi's constitutional

[66] *Id.*

[67] *See* Tarunabh Khaitan, Koushal v Naz*: Judges Vote to Recriminalise Homosexuality*, 78 MODERN L. REV. 672, 679 (2015) ("Given such volume, what is surprising is the respectable number of cases where judges do manage to give reasoned judgments").

[68] *See generally*, Andrew Green & Albert H. Yoon, *Triaging the Law: Developing the Common Law on the Supreme Court of India*, 14 J. EMPIRICAL LEGAL STUD. 683 (2017).

[69] Robinson, *supra* note 15, at 184.

[70] *Id.* at 185–86.

[71] *Id.* at 185.

[72] *See* Naz Foundation v. Government of NCT, *Voices Against 377 Intervention Petition on Section 377* (2006); *Naz Foundation*, (2009) D.L.T. 277 at paras. 19–22.

assault.[73] Muralidhar, in his previous career as an advocate, fought for justice on behalf of those displaced by the Narmada dam and for the victims of the Bhopal chemical disaster.[74] It was no surprise, then, that this bench issued a progressive judgment, but the jurisprudential moves therein took the law in boldly new directions that neither the High Court nor the SCI had previously recognized.

Section 377 prohibits "carnal intercourse against the order of nature," but its colonial drafters could not bring themselves to explain what this meant in practice.[75] Earlier judicial decisions had interpreted the provision to effectively bar sexual acts other than penile-vaginal sex and events leading up to it.[76] The Delhi High Court sharply broke from these precedents in *Naz Foundation*. It held that Section 377 was unconstitutional and read it down insofar as it criminalized private consensual acts by adults.[77] Specifically, the Court held that Section 377 ran afoul of Article 14 (right to equality), Article 15 (right to non-discrimination), and Article 21 (right to life and personal liberty).[78] Article 15 prohibits discrimination on various grounds including "sex." The petitioner argued that "sex" should be read expansively to cover sexual orientation-based discrimination. The purpose of Article 15, they argued, was to prevent differential treatment grounded in stereotypical or essentialized conceptions of sex.[79] Discrimination on the basis of sexual orientation too "is grounded in stereotypical judgments and generalization about the conduct of either sex" and thus should fall within the ambit of Article 15.[80]

The Delhi High Court accepted this argument and thus expanded Article 15 to cover discrimination on the basis of sexual orientation.[81] To reach that conclusion, the Court surveyed a range of international and comparative materials, including Comments of the Human Rights Committee as well as Canadian and

[73] Pradeep Thakur, *Entire Episode Was Shrouded in Secrecy: Justice AP Shah on Harassment Charges Against CJI*, Times of India (July 28, 2019), https://timesofindia.indiatimes.com/india/entire-episode-was-shrouded-in-secrecy-justice-ap-shah-on-harassment-charges-against-cji/articleshow/70423751.cms; Awstika Das, *Courts Remain Silent Spectators as Minorities Remain in Fear Amidst Rise of Illiberal, Communal Forces: Justice (Retired) AP Shah*, LiveLaw (Sept. 2, 2023), https://www.livelaw.in/top-stories/justice-ap-shah-courts-silent-spectators-communal-forces-236776.

[74] *SC Collegium Recommends Transfer of Justice Muralidhar from Delhi HC*, Wire (Feb. 19, 2020), https://thewire.in/law/supreme-court-collegium-justice-muralidhar.

[75] *See* Alok Gupta, *Section 377 and the Dignity of Indian Homosexuals*, 41 Econ. & Pol. Wkly. 4815, 4815–16 (Nov. 18, 2006).

[76] *See* Lohana Vasantlal Devchand v. State, (1968) 9 C.L.R. 1052 (Gujarat H.C.) (India); Childline India Foundation v. Allan John Waters, (2011) 2 S.C.C. (Cri.) 900 (India); Fazal Rab Choudhary v. State of Bihar (1982) 3 S.C.C. 9 (India). For a fuller discussion of the judicial history of Section 377, see Gautam Bhatia, The Transformative Constitution: A Radical Biography in Nine Acts (2019), at ch. 2.

[77] *Naz Foundation*, (2009) D.L.T. 277 at para. 132. By "reading down," I mean that the Court stopped short of invalidating the law altogether. Section 377 remained on the books—it just did not apply to consensual sexual activity conducted in private.

[78] *Id.* The petitioners also argued that Section 377 violated their right to freedoms of speech, assembly, association, and movement under Article 19(1) of the Constitution, but the Court found it unnecessary to rule on this issue. *See id.* at para. 126.

[79] *Id.* at para. 15.

[80] *Id.* at para. 99.

[81] *Id.* at para. 104.

South African jurisprudence. It also built upon the SCI's landmark 2007 judgment in *Anuj Garg v. Hotel Association of India*.[82] That case involved a constitutional challenge to a Punjab law that prohibited women from working in any premises in which alcohol or other intoxicating substance was sold. The government defended the law on the basis that it protected women. The SCI rejected this paternalistic rationale under Article 15, stating that "the rights of women as individuals rest beyond doubt at this stage."[83] The judgment emphasized the importance of women's autonomy and self-determination, including as to the sort of employment they wish to pursue.[84]

The High Court summarized the ruling in *Anuj Garg* before declaring:

> [*Anuj Garg*] held that Article 15's prohibition of sex discrimination implies the right to autonomy and self-determination, which places emphasis on individual choice. Therefore, a measure that disadvantages a vulnerable group . . . [based on] personal autonomy must be subject to *strict scrutiny*.[85]

Thus, the Delhi High Court held not only that sexual orientation was a prohibited ground under Article 15 but also that any law that differentiates on the basis of sexual orientation would be adjudicated under the searching "strict scrutiny" standard rather than the more deferential "reasonableness" standard.[86]

The High Court also expanded the scope of Article 21. Article 21's protection of the rights to life and personal dignity had been interpreted broadly by the SCI to encompass due process and a right to live with human dignity.[87] But the SCI had been less clear about whether this provision—or the Constitution generally—protected a right to privacy. Two judgments issued in the Court's early years by eight and six-judge benches, respectively, had declined to recognize a constitutional right to privacy.[88] Subsequent cases, decided by smaller benches, had mentioned a limited right to privacy in the context of personal communications and government surveillance[89] but had not established a right that would encompass sexual autonomy or identity.

[82] Anuj Garg v. Hotel Association of India, (2008) 3 S.C.C. 1 (India).

[83] *Id.* at para. 19.

[84] *Id.* at paras. 34–41. For an analysis of the broader effects of this judgment, see Shreya Atrey, *Feminist Constitutionalism: Mapping a Discourse in Contestation*, 20(2) INT'L J. CONST. L. 611, 629–31 (2022).

[85] *Naz Foundation*, (2009) D.L.T. 277 at para. 108 (emphasis added).

[86] *Id.* at para. 113.

[87] *See* Maneka Gandhi v. Union of India, (1978) 1 S.C.C. 248 (India); Francis Coralie Mullin v. Delhi, (1981) 1 S.C.C. 608 (India).

[88] *See* M.P. Sharma v. Satish Chandra, A.I.R. 1954 S.C. 380 (India); Kharak Singh v. State of U.P., A.I.R. 1963 S.C. 1295 (India).

[89] *See, e.g.*, Gobind v. State of Madhya Pradesh, (1975) 2 S.C.C. 148 (India); District Registrar & Collector v. Canara Bank, (2005) 1 S.C.C. 496 (India); State of Maharashtra v. Bharat Shanti Lal Shah, (2008) 13 S.C.C. 5 (India).

The Delhi High Court's judgment would broaden the right to privacy and place it squarely within Article 21. It cited a range of international and comparative materials to establish that privacy should fall under the right to life and personal liberty within the Indian Constitution.[90] In terms of foreign courts, the High Court relied primarily on the U.S. Supreme Court's judgment in *Lawrence v. Texas* (2003) and the South African Constitutional Court's ruling in *National Coalition for Gay and Lesbian Equality v. Minister of Justice* (1998). Both courts decriminalized same-sex intercourse, in part, on privacy grounds. *Lawrence* ruled that the Fourteenth Amendment's Due Process Clause required the government to respect the petitioners' private lives.[91] Justice Sachs' concurring judgment in *National Coalition*—which was cited at length in *Naz Foundation*—held that laws criminalizing same-sex relations in South Africa violated the right to privacy by touching upon a deep, invisible, and intimate side of these citizens' lives.[92] Stressing the importance of dignity and equality in the Constitutional Court's jurisprudence, Justice Sachs argued that differential group-based treatment resulted in disadvantage and scarred "the sense of dignity and self-worth" of LGBTQ+ individuals.[93]

The High Court cited European Court of Human Rights (ECtHR) judgments, including *Dudgeon v. United Kingdom* (1981) and *Norris v. Republic of Ireland* (1988) where the Court held that prohibitions on same-sex relations infringed upon the right to respect for private life enshrined in Article 8 of the European Convention on Human Rights.[94] It also referred to the U.N. Human Rights Committee's decision in *Toonen v. Australia* (1994), which held that Tasmania's anti-sodomy laws violated Article 17 of the International Covenant on Civil and Political Rights (ICCPR),[95] and the Yogyakarta Principles, which recognize that "all persons are entitled to . . . the right to privacy, regardless of sexual orientation or gender."[96]

To its credit, the High Court did not simply jump from the cosmopolitan *tour d'horizon* to declaring that a broad right to privacy should be adopted in the Indian context. It delved into academic research on the discriminatory impact of

[90] *See* Rehan Abeyratne & Nilesh Sinha, *Insular and Inconsistent: India's Naz Foundation Judgment in Comparative Perspective*, 39 Yale J. Int'l L. Online 74 (2014).

[91] *See* Lawrence v. Texas, 539 U.S. 558, 578–79 (2003).

[92] *Naz Foundation*, (2009) D.L.T. 277 at paras. 47, 81, 94.

[93] National Coalition for Gay and Lesbian Equality v. Minister of Justice, 1999 (1) S.A. 6 (C.C.) (S. Afr.) at para. 125.

[94] *Naz Foundation*, (2009) D.L.T. 277 at para. 53 (citing Dudgeon v. The United Kingdom, 45 Eur. Ct. H.R. (ser. A) (1981); Norris v. Republic of Ireland, 142 Eur. Ct. H.R. (ser. A) (1988)).

[95] *Id.* at para. 55 (citing Toonen v. Australia, No. 488/1992 CCPR/C/50/D/488/1992 (Mar. 31, 1994)). Article 17 provides, "No one shall be subjected to arbitrary or unlawful interference with his privacy."

[96] International Commission of Jurists, Yogyakarta Principles on the Application of Human Rights Law in Relation to Sexual Orientation and Gender Identity (2007) [hereinafter Yogyakarta Principles].

laws like Section 377 on LGBTQ+ communities and drew extensively from the evidence placed on the record. It explained how the affidavits and reports submitted by the "Voices Against Section 377 IPC" coalition "testify to a widespread use of Section 377 IPC to brutalise MSM and [*sic*] gay community."[97] The High Court went on to note how the "criminalisation of homosexuality condemns in perpetuity a sizeable section of society and forces them to live their lives in the shadow of harassment, exploitation, humiliation, cruel and degrading treatment."[98] Thus, the High Court concluded that Section 377 violates "the right to privacy and liberty embodied in Article 21" to the extent it applied to consensual sexual acts performed in private.[99]

Naz Foundation was met with acclaim from LGBTQ+ groups and from scholars, who praised its doctrinal innovations and its positive impact on sexual minorities in Delhi.[100] Neither the Delhi government nor the INC-led national government appealed the High Court's judgment.[101] But because of the procedural looseness of PIL, the Supreme Court allowed Suresh Kumar Koushal (an astrologer from Delhi with no connection to the case), along with an alliance of conservative religious groups, to lodge an appeal.

While the Naz Foundation and other petitioners had good fortune with the assignment of the Delhi High Court bench, they would not be so lucky at the SCI. The case was assigned to a two-judge bench, comprising the conservative Justices G.S. Singhvi and S.J. Mukhopadhaya. That this would be an unsympathetic bench was clear at the hearing stage. The transcript is peppered with inappropriate and homophobic comments, especially from Justice Mukhopadhaya. For instance, he asked whether "penetration by nose" or "if a mother breastfeeding a child" were covered by Section 377.[102] Justice Mukhopadhaya also repeatedly asked counsel if "an adult could seduce a person into becoming gay."[103] For context, he was concerned that the fundamental rights of those affected by Section 377 might "interfere with the fundamental rights of others."[104]

[97] *Naz Foundation*, (2009) D.L.T. 277 at para. 50.

[98] *Id.* at para. 52.

[99] *Id.*

[100] *See* Vikram Raghavan, *Navigating the Noteworthy and Nebulous in Naz Foundation*, 2(3) NUJS L. Rev. 397 (2009); Dipika Jain, Impact of the Naz Foundation Judgment on the Gay, Bisexual and Transgender People in Delhi: An Empirical Investigation (2012). For a critical account of the judgment, including its conflation of "homosexual" and "gay" communities with descriptive categories like "MSM," see Pawan Singh, *Complicating Privacy Further in the* Naz *Aftermath: Homonormativity and Queer Politics in India*, *in* Desire and Its Discontents: Queer Politics in Contemporary India 142 (Dipika Jain & Oishik Sircar eds., 2024).

[101] Indeed, at a later hearing before the Supreme Court, the Attorney General made clear that the government did not wish to defend the constitutionality of Section 377.

[102] *Koushal v. Naz Foundation—Record of Proceedings in the Supreme Court of India: 13 February–27 March, 2012*, https://www.globalhealthrights.org/wp-content/uploads/2013/12/Koushal-v.-Naz-Foundation-record-of-proceedings.pdf, at 73–74.

[103] *Id.* at 32.

[104] *Id.*

Thus, unsurprisingly, the SCI in *Koushal* (2013) rejected the Delhi High Court's legal conclusions as well as its cosmopolitan approach. The Court held that Section 377 did not discriminate against LGBTQ+ individuals or against any subclass thereof.[105] The Court portrayed Section 377 as a neutral law that specified "certain acts which if committed would constitute an offence" but did not discriminate against any particular group.[106] Thus, while it acknowledged that the police have misused Section 377, the Court held that the "mere fact" of such abuse did not affect the law's constitutionality.[107] It relied on principles of parliamentary sovereignty and the separation of powers to conclude that such misuse "might be a relevant factor for the Legislature to consider while judging the desirability of amending Section 377."[108]

Given the SCI's history of expansive fundamental rights jurisprudence, the turn to judicial restraint was disingenuous and not in-keeping with the Court's precedents. This is especially true here, as the Court's progressive PIL jurisprudence enabled an unrelated party like Koushal to file this appeal.

But the passage in *Koushal* that received the most attention (and criticism) related to the relative size and importance of India's LGBTQ+ communities. The Court wrote dismissively that the High Court had "overlooked that a miniscule fraction of the country's population" identify as LGBTQ+ and that fewer than "200 persons have been prosecuted" under Section 377 in its 150 years of operation.[109] Aside from the fact that the Constitution protects individual rights—and so the size of the affected group is legally irrelevant—this statement also fundamentally misapprehends how Section 377 operated in society. Its very existence pushed sexual minorities into the shadows for fear of harassment or violence from authorities. The Delhi High Court understood this dynamic, which underlay its conclusion that Section 377 violated the right to privacy.

After rejecting the High Court's conclusions with respect to Articles 14, 15, and 21, the SCI turned to its engagement with international and comparative materials. It said:

> In its anxiety to protect the so-called rights of LGBT persons . . . the High Court has extensively relied upon the judgments of other jurisdictions. Though these judgments shed considerable light on various aspects of this right and are informative in relation to the plight of sexual minorities, we feel that they cannot be applied blindfolded for deciding the constitutionality of the law enacted by the Indian legislature.[110]

105 *Koushal*, (2014) 1 S.C.C. 1 (India) at paras. 54–56.
106 *Id.* at para. 42.
107 *Id.* at para. 51.
108 *Id.*
109 *Id.* at para. 43.
110 *Id.* at para. 52.

This parochial approach to interpretation is again at odds with the SCI's precedents, including *Vishaka v. Rajasthan*,[111] and misconstrues the Delhi High Court's approach. The High Court did not apply foreign law "blindfolded"; rather, it engaged dialogically with comparative materials to help clarify the underlying values and assumptions in the Indian constitutional order.[112]

When the judgment was released in December 2013, *Koushal* was immediately criticized for its shoddy reasoning and regressive ruling.[113] But just four months later, in April 2014, a different two-judge bench of the SCI issued a progressive ruling on transgender rights in which it followed the Delhi High Court's approach in *Naz Foundation*.

That case, *NALSA*, was assigned to Justices K.S. Radhakrishnan and A.K. Sikri. As with the challenge to Section 377, the original petition in this case was filed by an NGO—NALSA—on behalf of the gender-diverse communities that it served.[114] Other petitions were filed by members of the Kinnar and Hijra communities—two other groups who had hitherto received scant recognition of their third-gender status and no legal protection against discrimination.[115] The petitioners sought declarations from the SCI that transgender persons could legally choose a gender different than the one assigned to them at birth as well as to identify as a third gender.[116]

Justice Radhakrishnan's principal opinion began with history of gender-diverse people in the Indian subcontinent, with a focus on the Hijra community.[117] He noted that they played an important role in precolonial India but were made outcasts under British rule by the Criminal Tribes Act, 1871, which labeled this community (and other gender non-confirming groups) as innately criminal.[118] Justice Radhakrishnan made clear that Section 377 of the IPC, by criminalizing acts "against the order of nature," had been used to harass and physically abuse transgender people.[119] However, since another bench had recently upheld Section

[111] *Vishaka*, (1997) 6 S.C.C. 24.

[112] *See* Sujit Choudhry, *How to Do Comparative Constitutional Law in India: Naz Foundation, Same-Sex Rights, and Dialogical Interpretation*, *in* COMPARATIVE CONSTITUTIONALISM IN SOUTH ASIA 45, 72–82 (Sunil Khilnani et al. eds., 2010).

[113] *See, e.g.*, Shreya Atrey, *Of Koushal v. Naz Foundation's Several Travesties: Discrimination and Democracy*, OXFORD HUM. RTS. HUB (Dec. 12, 2013), http://ohrh.law.ox.ac.uk/?p=3702; Gautam Bhatia, *The Unbearable Wrongness of Koushal v. Naz Foundation*, INDIAN CONST. LAW & PHIL. BLOG (Dec. 11, 2013), http://indconlawphil.wordpress.com/2013/12/11/the-unbearable-wrongness-of-koushal-vs-naz-foundation/.

[114] *NALSA*, (2014) 5 S.C.C. 438 at para. 3. For more on the many communities that the SCI fits under the "transgender" umbrella, see Dipika Jain, *Shifting Subjects of State Legibility: Gender Minorities and the Law in India*, 32 BERKELEY J. GENDER L. & JUST. 39 (2017).

[115] *NALSA*, (2014) 5 S.C.C. 438 at paras. 3–4.

[116] *Id.* at para. 2.

[117] *Id.* at paras. 12–16.

[118] *Id.* at para. 16.

[119] *Id.* at paras. 17–18.

377 in *Koushal*, Justice Radhakrishnan said that this bench would "express no opinion on it."[120]

While the *NALSA* bench did not formally question *Koushal*, its reasoning squarely contradicted that of the prior judgment.[121] *NALSA* held that transgender communities faced systemic discrimination that violated their Article 14 right to equality. Following the Delhi High Court in *Naz Foundation*, the SCI ruled that Article 15's prohibition on "sex"-based discrimination should be read to encompass discrimination on the basis of gender identity.[122] The SCI also extended its judgment in *Anuj Garg* to hold that "[s]elf-determination of gender is an integral part of personal autonomy and self-expression and falls within the realm of personal liberty guaranteed under Article 21."[123] Moreover, like the trailblazing *Naz Foundation* judgment, the SCI read Article 21 to encompass "one's right to privacy" in addition to dignity and autonomy.[124]

Justice Sikri in a separate opinion implicitly pushed back against the *Koushal* judgment's attempt to minimize the effects of Section 377. *Koushal* suggested that the Court need not rule for the petitioners, as LGBTQ+ groups constituted only a "miniscule fraction" of India's population.[125] Justice Sikri in *NALSA* responded as follows: "Rule of law demands protection of individual human rights . . . even though insignificant in numbers, [transgender persons] are still human beings and therefore they have every right to enjoy their human rights."[126]

With respect to comparative materials, the SCI in *NALSA* again rejected the approach adopted in *Koushal*. Both Justices Radhakrishnan and Sikri referred to international human rights instruments and the Yogyakarta Principles.[127] Radhakrishnan also referred to foreign case law from, *inter alia*, Australia, New Zealand, and the ECtHR, which recognized that gender is not immutable and permitted individuals to live in the gender of their choice.[128] He also referenced a "trend" in legislation across several countries that permits individuals who undergo partial or complete sexual reassignment surgery (SRS) to change their official gender markers.[129] Finally, as if to avoid charges of importing "Western" values

[120] *Id.* at para. 18.
[121] For more on the differences between *Koushal* and *NALSA*, see Arvind Narrain, *Vacillating between Empathy and Contempt: The Indian Judiciary and LGBT Rights*, *in* Envisioning Global LGBT Human Rights: (Neo)colonialism, Neoliberalism, Resistance and Hope 43, 59–61 (Nancy Nicol et al. eds., 2018).
[122] *NALSA*, (2014) 5 S.C.C. 438 at para. 69. The Court also held that transgender peoples' Article 16 right to equality of opportunity in public employment had been violated, but it combined its analysis thereof with the discussion of Article 15.
[123] *Id.*
[124] *Id.* at para. 67.
[125] *Koushal*, (2014) 1 S.C.C. 1 at para. 43.
[126] *NALSA*, (2014) 5 S.C.C. 438 at para. 123.
[127] *See, e.g.*, *id.* at paras. 21, 83 (citing Universal Declaration of Human Rights (1948) and Yogyakarta Principles, *supra* note 96).
[128] *Id.* at paras. 26–34.
[129] *Id.* at para. 35.

into Indian constitutional law,[130] Justice Radhakrishnan noted that the Supreme Courts of Nepal and Pakistan had recognized the fundamental rights of transgender people.[131]

The ruling in *NALSA* recognized a third gender for the purpose of safeguarding the rights of transgender communities, including hijras.[132] It declared that transgender persons have the right to choose their gender and directed the central and state governments to recognize a third gender.[133] It also issued a series of directions to these governments to improve socioeconomic conditions and legal protections for gender-diverse groups.[134] The Court noted that an Expert Committee had been established to study these issues and propose policy recommendations. It directed that those recommendations be implemented within six months of the judgment.[135]

We will return in Part V to the effects of this judgment and the legislation that was eventually adopted on transgender rights. For now, suffice it to say that the petitioners had mixed success in these early LGBTQ+ cases. The social movement that coalesced around Section 377 had its claims broadly recognized by the Delhi High Court in 2008, only to be reversed by a conservative SCI bench in 2013. Meanwhile, the gender-diverse groups that petitioned the SCI met with more success, prevailing in *NALSA* before a sympathetic bench.

More broadly, these cases demonstrate both the promise and potential for abuse of PIL. They show that the higher judiciary remained accessible to a range of petitioners, including historically marginalized groups with limited financial means or social capital. The *Naz Foundation* and *NALSA* judgments engaged deeply with the arguments and evidence presented by these groups. These judgments were sensitive to the historical and social context. They did not display the neoliberalism that has crept into other parts of the judicial docket, nor did they—pace *Koushal*—ring of elitism or a desire to transplant Western legal concepts in India.

But these cases also revealed a dark side of PIL. Its procedural laxity enabled Koushal and allied reactionary groups to appeal the *Naz Foundation* judgment to the Supreme Court, even though they had no role in the proceedings below. *Koushal* and *NALSA* also highlight the legal uncertainty that arises from the Court's heavy workload and fragmentation. With two SCI benches issuing diametrically

[130] *See Koushal*, (2014) 1 S.C.C. 1 at para. 52 (quoting with approval from Jagmohan Singh v. State of U.P. (1973) 1 S.C.C. 20 (India)), at para. 14 ("We have grave doubts about the expediency of transplanting Western experience in our country.").

[131] *NALSA*, (2014) 5 S.C.C. 438 at paras. 71–72 (citing Sunil Babu Pant v. Nepal Government, Writ Petition No. 917 of 2007 (2007) (Nepal); Dr. Mohammad Aslam Khaki v. Senior Superintendent of Police, Constitution Petition No. 43 of 2009 (2011) (Pak.)).

[132] *Id.* at para. 129(1).

[133] *Id.* at para. 129(2).

[134] *Id.* at para. 129(3)–129(9).

[135] *Id.* at para. 130.

opposed judgments, no one knew what the future would hold for LGBTQ+ rights or the answer to fundamental questions of constitutional law. Did Article 21 encompass a right to privacy? And was it appropriate to refer to foreign sources in adjudicating constitutional rights?

Amid this indeterminacy, the political ground shifted beneath the judiciary. The BJP, led by Narendra Modi, and its allies had won a landslide victory in the 2014 national elections. On May 26, 2014—one month after the *NALSA* judgment's release—Modi became Prime Minister of India. Under his autocratic leadership, the SCI's structural independence and decisional autonomy would come under enormous strain.

III. The Shift in Indian Constitutionalism under Modi (2014–19)

This Part examines how Indian constitutionalism was fundamentally transformed by the ascension of Narendra Modi to the office of Prime Minister in 2014. After describing the political, social, and economic effects of this new regime, I show how the SCI retrenched in its role as constitutional guardian on both structural and rights-based issues.

A. A New Political, Social, and Economic Order

Prior to 2014, aside from the Emergency (1975–77), parliamentary democracy had functioned relatively well in postcolonial India. The INC—the center-left party of Prime Ministers Jawaharlal Nehru and Indira Gandhi—dominated parliamentary elections until 1989. Thereafter, India entered a period of splintered political power characterized by fragile coalition governments and relatively weak prime ministers.[136] The 1990s also witnessed the emergence of Hindu nationalism as a serious political force. In December 1992, Hindu mobs demolished the Babri Masjid mosque in Ayodhya—which they claimed stood in the birthplace of the Hindu god Ram—setting off widespread communal violence.[137]

In the aftermath of Ayodhya, the BJP, the standard-bearer of Hindu nationalism, rose to become one of the two major national political parties (along with the INC) in the 1990s and 2000s. In this period, it led coalition governments twice: briefly (for less than two weeks) in 1996, and then from 1998 to 2004 under Prime Minister Atal Bihari Vajpayee.

[136] Milan Vaishnav & Jamie Hintson, The Dawn of India's Fourth Party System 4–5 (2019).

[137] Neelanjan Sircar, *Religion-as-Ethnicity and the Emerging Hindu Vote in India*, 10 Stud. Indian Pol. 79, 84–85 (2022); Brenda Cossman & Ratna Kapur, *Secularism's Last Sigh? The Hindu Right, the Courts, and India's Struggle for Democracy*, 38 Harv. Int'l L.J. 113, 117–19 (1997).

Following two consecutive terms of INC-led coalition governments, the BJP swept back into power in 2014. The BJP-led National Democratic Alliance won a landslide victory that year: the most dominant victory in thirty years and the first time since 1984 that a single party won a majority of seats in Parliament.[138] But it was not merely the scale of this electoral victory that marked 2014 as inaugurating a new era in Indian politics. The new Prime Minister, Narendra Modi, was fundamentally different than his predecessors.

Modi ran a personality-driven campaign leading up to the 2014 elections that was reminiscent of a presidential election rather than the party-based campaigns that had hitherto characterized parliamentary elections in India.[139] Slick holograms, foreign consultants, and extensive cross-country travel were the hallmarks of Modi's campaign. He and the BJP converted the campaign into an individual contest between Modi, who came from a non-elite, lower caste background, and the INC leader Rahul Gandhi, the privileged and high-caste scion of the Nehru–Gandhi dynasty.[140] This campaign proved so effective that it not only resulted in a dominant BJP victory but also relegated the INC to a mere 44 seats (out of 545), fewer than the requisite 55 seats needed to serve as the official opposition party.

Once in power, Modi systematically disempowered Parliament and other checks on his authority. His government defied convention and refused to appoint a leader of the opposition,[141] politicized the previously independent Election Commission,[142] and used executive ordinances to bypass Parliament in the lawmaking process.[143] As Tarun Khaitan has argued, these measures, taken collectively, constituted a systematic assault on democratic institutions in India that was unprecedented in the country's independent history.[144]

At a social level, Modi's victory in 2014 emboldened and gave political cover to the activities of the Sangh Parivar, a network of Hindu nationalist organizations led by the Rashtriya Swayamsevak Sangh (RSS).[145] Founded in 1925, the RSS is committed to the ideology of "Hindutva," which views India as a monocultural state built upon the values and traditions of ancient Hindu civilization.[146] The RSS

[138] VAISHNAV & HINTSON, *supra* note 136, at 8.

[139] The closest parallel was Prime Minister Indira Gandhi, who to a lesser degree, built a cult of personality, which she especially relied upon in the tarnished 1971 elections.

[140] CHRISTOPHE JAFFRELOT, MODI'S INDIA: HINDU NATIONALISM AND THE RISE OF ETHNIC DEMOCRACY 89–101 (Cynthia Schoch trans., 2021).

[141] Tarunabh Khaitan, *Killing a Constitution with a Thousand Cuts: Executive Aggrandizement and Party-State Fusion in India*, 14 L. & ETHICS HUM. RTS. 39, 64–65 (2020).

[142] JAFFRELOT, *supra* note 140, at 337–41.

[143] *See* Madhav S. Aney & Shubhankar Dam, *Decree Power in Parliamentary Systems: Theory and Evidence from India*, 84 J. POL. 1432, 1432–33 (2021).

[144] Khaitan, *supra* note 141, at 52–53.

[145] *See generally*, Pratap Bhanu Mehta, *Hindu Nationalism: From Ethnic Identity to Authoritarian Repression*, 10(1) STUD. INDIAN POL. 31 (2022).

[146] Hartosh Singh Bal, *The Broken Compact: Modi's India Replaces Constitutional Values with Those of the RSS*, CARAVAN (Oct. 20, 2023), https://caravanmagazine.in/politics/modi-india-constitutional-values-rss.

is intolerant of minority groups, especially those whose religious beliefs originated outside the Indian subcontinent. India's large Muslim minority is its bête noire. And like its main political branch—the BJP—the RSS has grown in strength and influence since the demolition of Babri Masjid in 1992.[147]

While the RSS has been influential at other times in postcolonial India—notably when one of its members assassinated Mahatma Gandhi in 1948 for being too conciliatory toward the Muslim community—it had never enjoyed national power. This changed in 2014. Modi had been an RSS member since the 1960s and worked for the organization for more than fifteen years before he was assigned to the BJP in 1987.[148] Unlike the previous BJP Prime Minister Vajpayee, who was a moderate within his party, Modi was best known for serving as Chief Minister of Gujarat during the 2002 pogroms that resulted in more than 1,000 Muslim deaths.[149]

After Modi became Prime Minister, the incidence of anti-Muslim violence rose alarmingly.[150] Much of this violence occurred in the northern state of Uttar Pradesh where mobs descended upon, and in many cases lynched, Muslim men for allegedly killing or mistreating cows.[151] This followed state-level legislation that shut down slaughterhouses, which were largely Muslim-owned, depriving a substantial subset of that community its livelihood. Several states also enacted "Love Jihad" laws prohibiting interfaith marriage.[152] Such laws have resulted in the arrest of several hundred Muslim men for allegedly seeking to convert Hindu women to Islam upon or after marrying them. These developments are representative of a virulent form of communalism that has emerged in the Modi era to weaken and marginalize the Muslim community.[153] RSS-fueled moral panics on sensitive issues such as cow slaughter and miscegenation are given the sanction of law, with law enforcement not only selectively targeting Muslims but also turning a blind eye toward Hindu vigilante violence.

At the economic level, the neoliberal reforms of the 1990s and 2000s have been turbocharged under the Modi government toward extreme consolidation and inequality. A handful of conglomerates, including the BJP-friendly Adani Group,

[147] *See* JAFFRELOT, *supra* note 140, at 11–22.

[148] *Id.* at 34–37.

[149] *Id.* at 39–44.

[150] *See* Ashutosh Varshney, *How India's Ruling Party Erodes Democracy*, 33(4) J. DEMOCRACY 104, 110–15 (2022).

[151] Sumit Ganguly, *Threats to Pluralism*, 30(1) J. DEMOCRACY 83, 87–88 (2019).

[152] Varshney, *supra* note 150, at 114; Hartosh Singh Bal, *Casting Them Out: Under Modi, Hindutva Provides Sanction for Crimes Against Humanity*, CARAVAN (Aug. 20, 2023), https://hindi.caravanmagazine.in/politics/under-modi-hindutva-provides-sanction-for-crimes-against-humanity (noting that eleven states had enacted "Love Jihad" laws by 2022).

[153] To be sure, communalism is neither entirely new nor anathema to Indian constitutionalism. Rather, the Indian Constitution contains key communal elements that have shaped the country's legal and political trajectory. *See generally*, MATHEW JOHN, INDIA'S COMMUNAL CONSTITUTION: LAW, RELIGION, AND THE MAKING OF A PEOPLE (2023).

have experienced immense growth, while most Indians suffer from wage stagnation, inflation, and economic uncertainty.[154] The World Inequality Lab found that "the rise of top-end inequality has been particularly pronounced in terms of wealth concentration" between 2014–15 and 2022–23.[155] The top 1 percent owned 40 percent of India's wealth in 2022–23, which makes India today more unequal than in the British colonial era and one of the most elite-dominated economies in the world.[156] As the number of billionaires in India tripled over the past decade, the median annual income is only around 1,200 U.S. dollars with 90 percent of the country making less than 3,900 dollars.[157]

In sum, India under Modi has become more autocratic in political decision-making, more communal in the construction of national identity, and more ruggedly capitalist in the economic sphere.

B. Caution in the SCI's Constitutional Jurisprudence

Amid these major societal changes, the SCI has adapted its approach to adjudicating constitutional matters since 2014. The Court has been cautious in its use of constitutional judicial review on matters relating to the Modi government's policies or its use of executive power. In some cases, the SCI admitted the relevant matter but deferred to the government in the ensuing judgment. On some of the most politically sensitive issues, the Court has avoided ruling altogether.

1. Money Bills and Ordinances

Consider, first, some prominent cases in which the SCI chose to weigh in. One case involved the constitutionality of the Modi's government use of money bills. Article 110 of the Indian Constitution enables the Speaker of the lower house to designate bills relating to financial matters as "money bills." Once certified as such by the Speaker, these bills can be passed solely with the support of a majority in the lower house—the upper house's approval is not required. The Modi government has used this mechanism to pass sweeping legislation outside the realm of ordinary financial matters.[158] The most glaring example is the Aadhaar Bill 2016, which implemented a nationwide biometric identification scheme. Certified by the

[154] Niharika Mandhana & Newley Purnell, *Modi's Vision for India Rests on Six Giant Companies*, Wall Street J. (June 21, 2023), https://www.wsj.com/articles/modi-india-economy-reliance-industries-adani-group-tata-d2c4f89e; Seema Chisti, *Survey Finds Deep Economic Discontent, Job Pessimism; 52% Say Modi's Policies Favor "Big Business,"* Wire (Feb. 15, 2024), https://thewire.in/economy/survey-finds-deep-economic-discontent-job-pessimism-52-say-modis-policies-favour-big-business.

[155] Nitin Kumar Bharti et al., *Income and Wealth Inequality in India 1922–2023: The Rise of the Billionaire Raj*, World Inequality Lab Working Paper No. 2024/09, at 1.

[156] *Id.* at 1–3.

[157] Alex Travelli, *5 Things to Know to Understand India's Economy Under Modi*, N.Y. Times (Apr. 1, 2024), https://www.nytimes.com/2024/04/01/business/india-economy-election-takeaways.html.

[158] *Id.*

Speaker as a money bill, it was signed into law with no involvement of the upper house. A five-judge bench of the Supreme Court upheld the constitutionality of the Aadhaar Act. The judgment focused on whether the act violated the constitutional right to privacy and other fundamental rights, effectively ignoring that its passage as a money bill was constitutionally suspect.[159] In dissent, Justice Chandrachud strongly opposed the judgment and made clear the constitutional stakes involved. He wrote:

> Superseding the authority of the Rajya Sabha is in conflict with the constitutional scheme and the legitimacy of democratic institutions. It constitutes a fraud on the Constitution. Passing of a Bill as a Money Bill, when it does not qualify for it, damages the delicate balance of bicameralism which is a part of the basic structure of the Constitution.[160]

The Modi government has since used this mechanism more frequently than any past government to pass legislation on controversial issues without any oversight from the upper house.[161]

Under Modi, the government also used the ordinance mechanism to bypass the upper house more regularly than its predecessors. Article 123(1) of the Indian Constitution provides that the President may enact ordinances "at any time, except when both Houses of Parliament are in session" and "circumstances exist which render it necessary for him to take immediate action." Interestingly, this is not an emergency provision—the President must simply be satisfied that enacting an ordinance is necessary.[162] Article 123(2) makes clear that ordinances "shall have the force and effect as an Act of Parliament," meaning that, in substance, they are no different from legislation. Moreover, the President is a ceremonial figure in India, who exercises power pursuant to the advice of the Prime Minister and Council of Ministers.[163] Thus, the Prime Minister effectively has the power to rule by decree.

In theory, the ordinance power is a limited one. Ordinances are supposed to be temporary and expire six weeks after Parliament reconvenes unless signed into law.[164] But prime ministers have circumvented this restriction by re-promulgating lapsed ordinances when Parliament adjourns.[165]

[159] Justice K.S. Puttuswamy v. Union of India (2019) 1 S.C.C. 1 (per Sikri, J.).

[160] *Id.* (per Chandrachud, J.) 762.

[161] Khaitan, *supra* note 141, at 66; Devyani Chhetri, *As Justice Chandrachud Calls Aadhaar Law "Unconstitutional", Government Increases Use of Controversial Short Cut*, Bloomberg Quint (Oct. 3, 2018), https://www.bloom bergquint.com/law-and-policy/as-justice-chandrachud-calls-aadhaar-law-unconstitutional-government-increases-use-of-controversial-short-cut.

[162] For a comprehensive account of the uses (and abuses) of ordinances in India prior to Modi, see Shubhankar Dam, Presidential Legislation in India (2014).

[163] India Const. art. 74(1) (as amended by the Forty-Second Amendment).

[164] Dam, *supra* note 162, at 4.

[165] Aney & Dam, *supra* note 143, at 1432–35.

The constitutionality of ordinances was challenged in *Krishna Kumar Singh v. State of Bihar* (2017).[166] The case, emerging out of a series of state-level ordinances in Bihar, concerned whether a lapsed ordinance continued to have legal effects. Justice Chandrachud's majority opinion for a seven-judge bench held that lapsed ordinances would ordinarily cease to have enduring legal effects. To rule otherwise, he said, would give ordinances a "degree of permanence . . . in derogation of parliamentary control and supremacy."[167] The Court reaffirmed the ruling in a precedent case that re-promulgation constituted a "fraud on the Constitution and a subversion of the democratic process."[168] The judgment further established some conditions for the executive to follow in promulgating ordinances.[169]

But the Court's bark was greater than its bite. The *Krishna Kumar Singh* judgment did not clarify whether the exceptions the Court had carved out in a prior case to permit the re-promulgation of ordinances remained good law. And while it ruled that lapsed ordinances ordinarily lack continuing legal effects, the Court provided that in cases of constitutional necessity or public interest, ordinances may confer legal rights and liabilities after ceasing legal operation. As Gaurav Mukherjee argued, the "lack of sharpness" of these tests "may lead to courts accepting a wide category of justifications from an executive government which is unwilling or unable to undo the effects of an ordinance."[170]

From 2014 to 2019, the Modi government issued fifty-five ordinances, the most of any government since the mid-1990s.[171] The government promulgated a further fourteen ordinances in 2020, many of which pertained to non-urgent matters such as Member of Parliament salaries, as well as controversial issues that should have been handled by Parliament, such as agricultural reform.[172] Along with the increased use of money bills, this is part of a coordinated effort to circumvent the upper house, evade accountability in Parliament, and weaken democratic institutions in India more broadly. Despite its rhetorical objections, the SCI has not put an end to these practices. It has also failed to take a stand against the Modi government's systematic institutional assault on parliamentary democracy in India.

2. Fundamental Rights

On fundamental rights, the SCI has been even more timid in the Modi era. The Court had long struggled with the "squeezing out" of its role as constitutional

166 Krishna Kumar Singh v. State of Bihar, (2017) 3 S.C.C. 1 (per Chandrachud, J.).
167 *Id.* at 77.
168 *Id.* at 84 (affirming the ruling in D.C. Wadhwa v. State of Bihar, A.I.R. 1987 S.C. 579 (India)).
169 *See* Gaurav Mukherjee, *The Supreme Court and Executive Law-Making: The Afterlife of Failed Ordinances in Krishna Kumar Singh II*, 1 Indian L.R. 312, 316–17 (2017).
170 *Id.* at 325.
171 Aney & Dam, *supra* note 143, at 1438.
172 Bhat, *supra* note 6.

guardian due to its overburdened docket and concurrent appellate role.[173] As discussed, Special Leave Petitions have come to dominate the SCI's docket at the expense of its fundamental rights jurisprudence. In 2016, only 4 percent of the SLP petitions admitted concerned constitutional matters. PIL, while still central in the public imagination of the Court, constitutes less than 1 percent of the docket and approximately 3 percent of the reported judgments.[174]

Moreover, the appearance of senior advocates, who wield great power and prestige in the Indian legal firmament, increases the likelihood that certain SLPs are admitted.[175] When a senior advocate appears on behalf of a petitioner, the SLP has a 60 percent chance of being admitted. In contrast, only 34 percent of SLPs are admitted when no senior advocate appears. As Khaitan has argued, this leaves "vulnerable appellants" at a disadvantage.[176]

With the SCI admitting as many as 70,000 cases per year during the Modi era,[177] these structural inequalities have only worsened. But there has also been a qualitative shift in the SCI's approach. The Court once deemed the world's most powerful now systematically avoids or delays ruling on major constitutional issues. Strategic avoidance, as Erin Delaney has argued, can be beneficial for a court's institutional legitimacy if it enables, *inter alia*, productive dialogue with the political branches.[178] She identified two factors that affect this dialogue: the timing of avoidance and the court's candor in acknowledging its choice.[179] For instance, avoidance may permit democratic processes to play out, leading to a political resolution to the issue raised in court. And judicial legitimacy would not suffer—and might even be boosted—if judges noted these considerations in dismissing or declining to admit the relevant case.

In the Indian context, however, both the suspect timing and lack of reasons for avoidance damage the SCI's institutional legitimacy. Over the past decade, the Court has evaded or delayed hearing constitutional challenges to suspect laws enacted by the Modi government.[180] The result is that those laws remain on the books, and the groups whose rights have been infringed are left without recourse.

[173] Khaitan, *supra* note 48, at 11.

[174] Chandra et al., *supra* note 15, at 27.

[175] *Id.* at ch. 3; Khaitan, *supra* note 48, at 18. *See also*, Marc Galanter & Nick Robinson, *India's Grand Advocates: A Legal Elite Flourishing in the Era of Globalization*, 20 Int'l J. Legal Profession 241 (2013) (analyzing the importance of a select few senior advocates, who play a central role in the functioning of the judicial system).

[176] Khaitan, *supra* note 48, at 28.

[177] Supreme Court Report 2023, *supra* note 55, at 87.

[178] Erin Delaney, *Analyzing Avoidance: Judicial Strategy in Comparative Perspective*, 66 Duke L.J. 1, 4 (2016).

[179] *Id.* at 5.

[180] It is worth noting that the High Courts have not been so evasive. They have stepped in to strike down unconstitutional laws and policies even in politically charged areas. *See* Alok Prasanna Kumar, *From CAA to NRC, India's High Courts Are Setting Higher Benchmarks than the Supreme Court*, Print (Mar. 17, 2020), https://theprint.in/opinion/from-caa-to-nrc-indias-high-courts-are-setting-higher-benchmarks-than-the-supreme-court/382138/.

As of early 2025, challenges to facially unconstitutional amendments to information laws,[181] to the Unlawful Activities (Prevention) Act, 1967,[182] and to sedition laws[183] remain pending before the SCI.

Moreover, the Court has not explained why it hears certain matters on a priority basis, while leaving others pending for several years.[184] Take, for instance, the Citizenship Amendment Act 2019 (CAA), a facially unconstitutional law that played to the communal politics of the BJP. This Act made religion, for the first time, an explicit criterion for obtaining Indian citizenship by prioritizing Hindus over Muslims and Christians. Nonetheless, the SCI declined to hear writ petitions challenging the constitutionality of the CAA.[185] At the same time, led by CJI Ranjan Gogoi, the SCI closely supervised and spurred on the National Register of Citizens (NRC) in the northeastern state of Assam to force its 33 million inhabitants to prove their Indian citizenship.[186] The Court moved the NRC process along at an expedited pace to strip 2 million (mostly Muslim) Assamese residents of their Indian citizenship and imprisoned thousands more in India's largest detention center for being "illegal migrants."[187]

The Court acted here, as Alok Prasanna Kumar put it, in a more "executive-minded" manner than the executive.[188] It issued regressive orders that disregarded the rights of the affected people, much in the vein of the "slum demolition machine" that Bhuwania described in the Delhi High Court.[189] And, as Gautam Bhatia has shown, many of the SCI's orders in the NRC case and during CJI Gogoi's tenure generally, were performed in secret under "sealed covers."[190] This allowed the SCI

[181] *What Is Wrong with You: SC Pulls Up Centre for Not Responding to Plea on RTI Act Over a Year*, Scroll (Feb. 22, 2021), https://scroll.in/latest/987648/what-is-wrong-with-you-sc-pulls-up-centre-for-not-responding-to-plea-on-rti-act-in-over-a-year.

[182] Foundation of Media Professionals v. Union of India, Writ Petition (Civil) No. 230/2022, Order Dated 26-9-2022 (India).

[183] S.G. Vombatkere v. Union of India, Writ Petition (Civil) No. 682/2021 (India).

[184] *See* Gautam Bhatia, Unsealed Covers: A Decade of the Constitution, the Courts and the State 402–41 (2023).

[185] Indian Union of Muslim League v. UOI, Writ Petition (Civil) No. 1470/2019 (India). For a record of the hearings, see Supreme Court of India https://main.sci.gov.in/case-status (last accessed on Mar. 19, 2024). *See also*, R. Balaji, *CAA Hearing in Supreme Court Put Off Again*, Telegraph (Dec. 7, 2022), https://www.telegraphindia.com/india/caa-hearing-in-supreme-court-put-off-again/cid/1902389.

[186] Sruthisagar Yamunan, *How the Supreme Court's Hardline Stance on Citizenship Deepened the Flaws in Assam's NRC*, Scroll (July 31, 2019), https://scroll.in/article/932176/how-the-supreme-court-s-hardline-stance-on-citizenship-deepened-the-flaws-in-assams-nrc; Anuj Bhuwania, *The Indian Supreme Court in the Modi Era*, IACL-AIDC Global Roundtable (Nov. 23, 2020), https://www.iacl-democracy-2020.org/blog/2016/3/23/blog-post-sample-9wntn-6ye75-hwawc-xx9lz-p6k2z-85m67-nkxzl-m76y3-gmmc6.

[187] *See* Assam Sanmilitia Mahasangha v. UOI, Writ Petition (Civil) No. 562/2012, Order Dated 17-12-2014 (India). *See also*, Shoaib Daniyal, *Supreme Court Has Taken Disturbingly Illegal Stance on Assam's Detention Centres*, Scroll (Apr. 26, 2019), *https://scroll.in/article/921353/the-daily-fix-supreme-court-has-taken-a-disturbingly-illiberal-stance-on-assams-detention-centres.*

[188] *See* Alok Prasanna Kumar, *"More Executive Minded than the Executive": The Supreme Court's Role in the Implementation of the NRC*, 31 NLSI Rev. 203 (2019).

[189] *Id.* at 205–08; Bhuwania, *supra* note 16, at ch. 3.

[190] Bhatia, *supra* note 184, at 406–08.

to shield both the government and itself from public scrutiny. Sealed covers prevent even the lawyers in certain cases from viewing relevant evidence and enable the Court to rule without providing reasons for its decisions. This practice, as Bhatia put it, is the "absolute antithesis of open justice."[191]

In other cases, the SCI has ruled against the government but subsequently failed to enforce its orders. For instance, the Court partially struck down legislation establishing "Aadhaar," holding that this biometric identification system infringed upon constitutional rights to privacy and citizenship.[192] The government simply ignored this ruling and enacted an ordinance amending the Aadhaar Act in contempt of the Supreme Court's judgment. Indeed, Aadhaar remains "mandated" along with multiple identity cards in contravention of fundamental rights, but the SCI has not stepped in to enforce its judgment.

Finally, due to a combination of its heavy workload and tendency to avoid conflict with the government, the SCI left suspect laws in place for years before ruling on their constitutionality. For instance, a writ petition concerning the validity of the electoral bond scheme was filed in 2018.[193] This opaque funding scheme permitted fully anonymous political donations,[194] which most benefited the BJP in elections.[195] The SCI finally issued a judgment in February 2024.[196] While the judgment held the scheme unconstitutional—and is a welcome departure from the Court's pattern of deference and avoidance[197]—its delay enabled the BJP to raise millions in election funds in the six years that the case was pending.[198]

Another writ petition challenged the constitutionality of executive orders issued in August 2019 that reduced Kashmir's autonomy under Article 370 of the Indian Constitution.[199] The Court finally issued a judgment in December 2023,

[191] *Id.* at 407.

[192] *Justice K.S. Puttuswamy*, (2019) 1 S.C.C. 1.

[193] Association for Democratic Reforms v. UOI, Writ Petition (Civil) No. 333/2015 (2018) (India); Pavan Kasturi, *How Long to Adjudicate?: Unpacking the Controversial Electoral Bonds Scheme*, BAR & BENCH (Apr. 16, 2023), https://www.barandbench.com/columns/how-long-to-adjudicate-unpacking-the-controversial-electoral-bonds-scheme.

[194] See Gautam Bhatia, *Here Is Why the Electoral Bond Scheme Must Go*, HINDU (March 26, 2021), https://www.thehindu.com/opinion/lead/here-is-why-the-electoral-bonds-scheme-must-go/article34163851.ece.

[195] See Poonam Agarwal et al., *Not 105, Only 19 Parties Got Electoral Bonds, BJP Pockets 67.8% in 3 Years*, QUINT (June 6, 2022), https://www.thequint.com/news/india/only-19-parties-received-money-from-electoral-bonds-bjp-got-68-investigation-bjp-reporters-collective-supreme-court-105-parties.

[196] Ass'n Democratic Reforms v. Union of India, 2024 I.N.S.C. 113 (India).

[197] Kieran Correia, *The Supreme Court's Electoral Bonds Judgment—I: Political Equality and Electoral Transparency*, CONST. L. & PHIL. (Feb. 23, 2024), https://indconlawphil.wordpress.com/2024/02/23/the-supreme-courts-electoral-bonds-judgment-i-political-equality-and-electoral-transparency/.

[198] *See* S. Ragotham, *The BJP's Near-Monopoly on Political Funding*, DECCAN HERALD (Oct. 9, 2022), https://www.deccanherald.com/specials/the-bjps-near-monopoly-on-political-funding-1151845.html.

[199] Dr. Shah Faesal v. Union of India, Writ Petition (Civil) No. 1099/2019 (2019); *Supreme Court Has Been Slow to Deal with Kashmir Petitions: United Nations High Commissioner for Human Rights*, LIVELAW (Oct. 29, 2019), https://www.livelaw.in/top-stories/supreme-court-has-been-slow-to-deal-with-kashmir-petitions-united-nations-high-commissioner-for-human-rights-149324. For a historical

upholding the government's constitutionally questionable route to enact this significant constitutional change.[200] Perhaps more troublingly, the SCI fell silent in response to writ petitions challenging the communications lockdown (including widespread internet outages) and the mass preventative detention regime imposed by the government after revoking Kashmir's special status.[201] This was a dark period for fundamental rights in India, as habeas corpus petitions—which had hitherto been heard on a priority basis—were left unaddressed. As Bhatia has argued, the SCI's silence in this context was reminiscent of the Emergency (1975–77), where the Court declined to grant habeas corpus petitions to Indira Gandhi's detained political opponents.[202]

Though the Court retrenched in its fundamental rights jurisdiction and permitted the Modi government to move India in an illiberal direction, the Court's sheer size—in terms of both its docket and the number of judges—made it difficult (at least initially) for the government to capture the institution. As Part IV explains, some justices were able to carve out space for a progressive constitutional jurisprudence in one area: the rights of gender and sexual minorities.

IV. Privacy and the Decriminalization of Same-Sex Relations

While India took a hard rightward turn politically under Modi, the politics and constitutional law around LGBTQ+ rights remained unsettled. As an initial matter, social attitudes became more liberal as India globalized and become more interconnected with the Western world. The World Values Survey reported that the share of Indian respondents who believed that "homosexuality is never justifiable" declined from 89 percent in 1990 (just prior to Prime Minister Rao's economic reforms) to 24 percent in 2014. Thus, the *Koushal* judgment, issued in December 2013, was out of line both jurisprudentially and with public opinion on the criminalization of homosexuality. The SCI in that

overview and analysis of the constitutional issues in Kashmir, see Sumit Ganguly, *Autocratization in Kashmir*, *in* Routledge Handbook of Autocratization in South Asia 49 (Sten Widmalm ed., 2021).

[200] In re: Article 370 of the Constitution, 2023 I.N.S.C. 1058 (India); Kieran Correia, *The Supreme Court's Article 370 Judgment—Unilateral Declarations and Self-concurrence as Constitutional Practice*, Const. L. & Phil. (Dec. 12, 2023), https://indconlawphil.wordpress.com/2023/12/12/guest-post-the-supreme-courts-article-370-judgment-unilateral-declarations-and-self-concurrence-as-constitutional-practice/.

[201] Bhatia, *supra* note 184, at 231–39.

[202] *Id.* at 236. The Court's silence has also enabled the Modi government to engage in mass eviction and land redistribution to encourage migration from other parts of India into Kashmir and to facilitate mass infrastructure projects that benefit regime-friendly industrial conglomerates. *See* Tariq Mir, *Kashmir: Crackdowns and Plunder*, N.Y. Rev. of Books (July 21, 2024), https://www.nybooks.com/online/2024/07/21/kashmir-crackdowns-and-plunder/.

case accused the Delhi High Court of importing foreign values to read down Section 377, when in fact Indian society had moved on from that regressive provision on its own.

Indeed, the public outcry that followed *Koushal*'s regressive ruling that recriminalized homosexuality,[203] even reached the highest levels of government.[204] Cabinet ministers in the INC-led national government promised to repeal Section 377 through legislative means.[205] Thereafter, when several parties, including the Naz Foundation, filed review petitions before the SCI seeking a rehearing on this issue, the government joined them. It filed a petition urging the Court to repeal Section 377. The Court rejected these petitions in January 2014,[206] but it was clear that it would at some point have to revisit this issue given the opposing judgments that separate benches had issued in *Koushal* and *NALSA*.

What is most noteworthy here is the continuity in the government's position. The Modi government—which came to power in mid-2014—similarly chose not to defend the constitutionality of Section 377 when the matter finally reached a constitutional bench of SCI in *Navtej Johar* (2018).

While we cannot know for certain what drove the Modi government's restraint on this issue, it appears that public opposition to Section 377 played a role. Senior BJP leader and Finance Minister Arun Jaitley said in 2015, "When you have millions of people involved in this (gay sex) you can't nudge them off," adding that he thought the SCI had taken a "conservative view" and that "I am for decriminalising gay sex."[207] A BJP spokesperson in 2015 similarly said, "We are for decriminalising homosexuality. That is the progressive way forward."[208] Even the RSS Joint General Secretary, Dattatreya Hosabale, adopted a strikingly liberal position, stating in 2016, "I don't think homosexuality should be considered a criminal offence as long as it does not affect the lives of others in society."[209] It is unlikely that such statements would have emerged if the ruling coalition believed that Section 377 commanded broad public support.

[203] *See, e.g.*, Danish Sheikh, *A Tale of Two Judgments: The Afterlives of a Defeat and a Victory for Queer Rights in India*, 8 LGBTQ+ POL'Y J. 57, 61 (2018) (noting that the "immediate public reaction" to *Koushal* was a series of mass protests across seventeen cities in India and twenty-two other cities around the world); COALITION FOR SEX WORKERS AND SEXUALITY MINORITY RIGHTS (CSMR), DIGNITY FIRST: ONE YEAR OF RESISTANCE TO RE-CRIMINALISATION OF LGBT LIVES (2014), http://feministlawarchives.pldindia.org/wp-content/uploads/Report-on-11Dec-Anniversary.pdf.

[204] Arvind Narrain & Arun Thiruvengadam, *Social Justice Lawyering and the Meaning of Indian Constitutionalism: A Case Study of the Alternative Law Forum*, 31 WIS. INT'L L. J. 525, 558 (2013).

[205] *Id.*

[206] Naz Foundation v. Koushal, Review Petition (Civil) No. 197 of 2014 (2014) (India).

[207] Ruhi Tewari, *Sometimes Homophobic, Sometimes Liberal: BJP'S Uneven Section 377 Journey*, PRINT (Sept. 6, 2018), https://theprint.in/india/governance/sometimes-homophobic-sometimes-liberal-bjps-uneven-section-377-journey/112767/.

[208] *Id.*

[209] *Id.*

A. The Constitutional Right to Privacy

After the SCI rejected the petitions for rehearing in *Koushal*, it took a circuitous route to eventually striking down Section 377. Recall that the Delhi High Court's *Naz Foundation* judgment declared an expansive right to privacy under the umbrella of the right to life and personal liberty in Article 21. In *NALSA*, the SCI made a similar interpretive move, reading privacy into Article 21 alongside dignity and autonomy. But *NALSA* was decided by a two-judge bench. The SCI in *M.P. Sharma v. Satish Chandra* and *Kharak Singh v. State of U.P.*—two prior judgments issued by larger benches—had declined to recognize this right.[210]

The SCI thus needed to clarify whether the right to privacy had constitutional status and, if so, how broadly it should be interpreted. The opportunity to do so arose in an unlikely way. In the litigation challenging the constitutionality of the Modi government's biometric identification scheme (Aadhaar), the Attorney General of India argued that the Constitution did not enshrine a fundamental right to privacy.[211] While the Court would eventually uphold the Aadhaar Act,[212] the question of whether privacy received constitutional protection was placed in a separate case before a nine-judge bench. Given that most SCI cases are decided by two-judge benches, and matters of "constitutional importance" require only a five-judge bench, the Court signaled that this was an issue of unusual significance and that its decision would carry tremendous precedential weight.[213]

The ensuing judgment in *Puttuswamy v. Union of India* (2017) unanimously held that the Constitution protects a fundamental right to privacy and interpreted the scope of the right generously.[214] Totaling more than 500 pages, and consisting of 6 separate opinions, this vast judgment makes several important rulings. First, it overruled *M.P. Sharma* and *Kharak Singh* to the extent that those judgments held that the Constitution does not protect a right to privacy.[215]

Second, and more importantly, the Court grounded the right to privacy across several of the enumerated fundamental rights in Part III of the Constitution. Justice Chelameswar, for instance, held that privacy was located in the right to freedom in Article 19 and the right to personal liberty in Article 21.[216] Justice Bobde also relied on those two rights in his opinion but went further to call privacy "an inarticulate major premise in Part III of the Constitution."[217] Justice Nariman, similarly,

[210] *See M.P. Sharma*, A.I.R. 1954 S.C. 380; *Kharak Singh*, A.I.R. 1963 S.C. 1295.

[211] Shreya Atrey & Gautam Bhatia, *New Beginnings: Indian Rights Jurisprudence After Puttuswamy*, 3(2) U. OXFORD HUM. RTS. HUB 1, 1 (2020).

[212] *Justice K.S. Puttuswamy*, (2019) 1 S.C.C. 1.

[213] Atrey & Bhatia, *supra* note 211, at 1 (noting that this was only the fifteenth time that the Court had ever assembled a nine-judge bench).

[214] *Puttuswamy*, (2017) 10 S.C.C. 1.

[215] *Id.* at paras. 27, 42 (per Nariman, J.); paras.7, 9 (per Chelameswar, J.).

[216] *Id.* at paras. 36–40 (per Chelameswar, J.).

[217] *Id.* at paras. 25, 30–31 (per Bobde, J.).

connected privacy to the overall structure of the Constitution; specifically, he linked it to the Constitution's Preamble, which seeks to secure "justice . . . liberty . . . equality . . . [and] fraternity" for all citizens.[218] The SCI thus framed the right to privacy in broad terms that could apply in numerous contexts.[219]

Third, on the right's broad application, Justice Chandrachud's plurality opinion included a long discussion on how privacy affects women and sexual minorities. Citing feminist scholarship, Chandrachud noted that "women have an inviolable interest in privacy" and that the right "must not be utilised as a cover to conceal and assert patriarchal mindsets."[220] He also took direct aim at *Koushal*, referring to the judgment as a "discordant note" in the SCI's constitutional jurisprudence.[221] He criticized the *Koushal* bench's reasoning, particularly its rejection of constitutional challenges to Section 377 on the grounds that LGBTQ+ people constitute "a miniscule fraction of the country's population."[222] As Justice Chandrachud put it:

> The purpose of elevating certain rights to the stature of guaranteed fundamental rights is to insulate their exercise from the distain of majorities . . . Discrete and insular minorities face grave dangers of discrimination for the simple reasons that their views, beliefs, or way of life does not accord with the "mainstream."[223]

Chandrachud went on to declare that sexual orientation is an "essential attribute" of the right to privacy, and that discrimination on the basis of sexual orientation is "deeply offensive to the dignity and self-worth of the individual."[224] He concluded that privacy and the protection of sexual orientation are guaranteed under Articles 14 (equality), 15 (non-discrimination), and 21 (life and personal liberty).[225]

Finally, the Court also implicitly rejected the *Koushal* bench's approach to foreign sources. Justice Chandrachud's opinion, for instance, included a section on India's commitments under international law, which, *inter alia*, cited the right to privacy under the ICCPR, as well as its commitments under the Convention on the Elimination of All Forms of Discrimination Against Women (CEDAW).[226] His opinion also engaged with privacy-related jurisprudence from the United Kingdom, United States, South Africa, and Canada.[227] Justice Nariman, meanwhile, surveyed the development of privacy in U.S. constitutional law to contrast

[218] *Id.* at para. 82 (per Nariman, J.).
[219] BHATIA, *supra* note 184, at 57.
[220] *Puttuswamy*, (2017) 10 S.C.C. 1 at para. 140 (per Chandrachud, J.).
[221] *Id.* at para. 124. The other "discordant note" mentioned was *A.D.M. Jabalpur v. Shiv Kant Shukla*—the notorious 1976 judgment in which the SCI refused to grant habeas corpus relief to Prime Minister Indira Gandhi's political opponents jailed during the Emergency.
[222] *Id.* at paras. 125–26.
[223] *Id.* at para. 126
[224] *Id.*
[225] *Id.*
[226] *Id.* at paras. 130–32 (citing *Vishaka*, (1997) 6 S.C.C. 241 and *NALSA*, (2014) 5 S.C.C. 438).
[227] *Id.* at para. 134.

the narrower American conception of the right with the expansive formulation that he and his colleagues adopted in *Puttuswamy*.[228]

In sum, *Puttuswamy* was a landmark judgment. It firmly entrenched a constitutional right to privacy and did so in broad doctrinal terms that spoke both to the values underlying the Constitution and to the minority and disadvantaged communities who may call upon its protection in tangible ways. As Bhatia put it, "all nine judges agreed that privacy was at the heart of individual self-determination, of dignity, autonomy, and liberty and *concretely* inseparable from the meaningful exercise of guaranteed freedoms."[229]

B. Reading Down Section 377

With its ringing endorsement of the right to privacy, and direct criticism of *Koushal*, *Puttuswamy* telegraphed the SCI's intent to decriminalize homosexuality. Since the Court had rejected petitions for rehearing in *Koushal*, it used its writ jurisdiction to hear a new set of petitions challenging the constitutionality of Section 377. The petitions in the new case, *Navtej Johar*, had a different tenor to the original petition filed by the Naz Foundation or the petitions filed on behalf of transgender communities in *NALSA*.[230] The five named petitioners in *Navtej Johar* were all prominent celebrities. For instance, Navtej Johar was a renowned Indian classical dancer; Ritu Dalmia was a celebrity chef; and Keshav Suri headed a luxury hotel chain and a prominent LGBTQ+ nightclub in Delhi.[231] While the petitions in *Koushal* and *NALSA* highlighted discriminatory and other illegal practices against LGBTQ+ groups from various social classes and parts of country, the *Navtej Johar* petition stressed the elite, transnational credentials of the named individuals and focused on the individual discrimination that each experienced.[232]

As discussed, the Modi government chose not to defend Section 377, much like the previous INC-led government in *Koushal*. And just as it did in *Koushal*, the Supreme Court in *Navtej Johar* permitted various conservative non-state actors, including the Trust God Ministries, to intervene in support of Section 377.[233] In its written submission, the government said that to the extent Section 377

[228] He also cited South African materials. *See id.* at paras. 54–60, 68–80 (per Nariman, J.).

[229] Bhatia, *supra* note 184, at 57 (emphasis in original).

[230] *See* Navtej Johar v. Union of India, *Petition Under Article 32 of the Constitution of India Seeking a Declaration That Section 377 of the Indian Penal Code 1860 Is Unconstitutional*, Writ Petition (Criminal) No. 76 of 2016.

[231] *Id.* at paras. 4–16.

[232] *Id.* at paras. 18–22. Other petitioners joined the litigation, but they too were mostly from urban and elite backgrounds, including a group of students, faculty, and alumni from the prestigious Indian Institutes of Technology (IITs). A notable exception is the Voices Against 377 coalition, which had also intervened in the *Naz Foundation* case. *See Navtej Johar*, 2018 I.N.S.C. 790 at paras. 49–51 (per Chandrachud, J.).

[233] *Navtej Johar*, 2018 I.N.S.C. 790 at paras. 39–65 (per Misra C.J.).

criminalizes consensual adult acts in private, it would leave the question of constitutionality "to the wisdom of the Court."[234] The government did, however, note that if the Court were to read down the provision to this extent, it may "wish to file [a] detailed affidavit in reply, for other issues and rights would have far reaching and wide ramifications."[235]

With this non-confrontational posture, the Modi government effectively invited the Court to read down Section 377. And that is precisely what transpired. The five-judge bench unanimously overruled *Koushal*.[236] It held that by criminalizing consensual sex acts conducted in private, Section 377 violated Articles 14, 15, 19, and 21 of the Constitution.[237] The judgment built on the broad doctrinal foundation laid in *Puttuswamy* to link the right to privacy of sexual minorities with their dignity and autonomy, all of which are located across enumerated rights to equality, non-discrimination, freedom (especially freedom of speech), and personal liberty. As in *Puttuswamy*, the *Navtej Johar* judgment is long and sprawling. It comprises four separate opinions.

The principal opinion was authored by CJI Misra on behalf of himself and Justice Khanwilkar. The Chief Justice grounded his opinion on a broad conception of democracy, describing the Constitution as "an organic charter of progressive rights."[238] He would go on to say that constitutional democracy should "transform the society progressively and inclusively" and that "discrimination of any kind strikes at the very core of any democratic society."[239] But amid this grand language of inclusion, the opinion adopts a classically liberal position on rights. For CJI Misra, the fundamental problem with Section 377 was that it limited individual capacity for self-determination and to live as one chooses.[240] As he put it:

> The eminence of identity which has been lucently stated in the *NALSA* case very aptly connects human rights and the constitutional guarantee of right to life and liberty with dignity. With the same spirit, we must recognize that the concept of identity which has a constitutional tenability cannot be pigeon-holed singularly to one's orientation as it may keep the individual choice at bay.[241]

Justice Nariman followed the CJI's approach in stressing that "the very purpose of . . . fundamental rights . . . is to withdraw the subject of liberty and dignity of the

[234] *Id.* at para. 36.
[235] *Id.* at para. 37.
[236] *Id.* at para. 253 (per Misra, C.J.); para. 96 (per Nariman, J.); para. 156 (per Chandrachud, J.); para. 21 (per Malhotra, J.).
[237] *Id.* at para. 253 (per Misra, C.J.); para. 95 (per Nariman, J.); paras. 30, 41, 78, 92 (per Chandrachud, J.); para. 21 (per Malhotra, J.).
[238] *Id.* at para. 82 (per Misra, C.J.).
[239] *Id.* at para. 253.
[240] Bhatia, *supra* note 184, at 63–64.
[241] *Navtej Johar*, 2018 I.N.S.C. 790 at para. 253 (per Misra, C.J.).

individual and place such subject beyond the reach of majoritarian governments."[242] He referred to Section 377 as "manifestly arbitrary . . . capricious and irrational" for criminalizing the consensual acts of "gay persons and transgenders" who we know, thanks to modern science and societal advancements, "are not persons suffering from mental disorder[s]."[243] Justice Nariman later criticized the *Koushal* judgment's declaration that LGBTQ+ groups constitute "only a miniscule fraction of the country's population" as "neither here nor there."[244] What is relevant, he concluded, is that "when privacy interests come in, and the state has no compelling reason to continue an existing law which penalizes same-sex couples who cause no harm to others," that law—Section 377—is unconstitutional.[245]

Justice Malhotra's opinion also highlighted the absence of a justification for Section 377. She used the SCI's traditional two-part test to determine the constitutionality of a differentiation under the right to equality in Article 14: namely (1) that there should be a reasonable classification based on intelligible differentia; and (2) the classification should have a rational nexus with the objective sought to be achieved.[246] She concluded that Section 377 failed on the first step:

> Section 377 creates an artificial dichotomy. The natural or innate sexual orientation of a person cannot be a ground for discrimination. Where a legislation discriminates on the basis of an intrinsic and core trait of an individual, it cannot form a reasonable classification based on an intelligible differentia.[247]

Thus, Justice Malhotra concluded that that Section 377 could not withstand constitutional scrutiny insofar as it criminalized "consensual sexual acts of adults . . . in private."[248]

As in *Puttuswamy*, Justice Chandrachud authored the most progressive and rhetorically powerful opinion. Two aspects of his opinion are especially noteworthy. First, Justice Chandrachud built on his *Puttuswamy* opinion, where he held that sexual orientation is protected within the right to privacy. He reiterated that point in *Navtej Johar*, declaring, "Sexual orientation is integral to the identity of the members of the LGBT communities. It is intrinsic to their dignity, inseparable from their autonomy and at the heart of their privacy."[249] But Chandrachud ventured further to explain how gender stereotypes lead to indirect discrimination. Canvassing

[242] *Id.* at para. 81 (per Nariman, J.).
[243] *Id.* at para. 82.
[244] *Id.* at para. 95.
[245] *Id.* at paras. 95–97.
[246] For a history and critical analysis of this doctrine, see Tarunabh Khaitan, *Equality: Legislative Review Under Article 14*, *in* OXFORD HANDBOOK OF THE INDIAN CONSTITUTION, *supra* note 18, at ch. 39.
[247] *Id.* at para. 14.3 (per Malhotra, J.).
[248] *Id.* at para. 21 (also noting that "Section 377 will continue to govern non-consensual sexual acts against adults, all acts of carnal intercourse against minors, and acts of bestiality").
[249] *Id.* at para. 148 (per Chandrachud, J.).

feminist and anti-discrimination scholarship,[250] Chandrachud built a sophisticated theory of intersectional discrimination grounded in the Article 15 prohibition on sex discrimination. Sex discrimination, he noted, often arises out of stereotypical notions of the roles men and women play in society. By criminalizing certain acts—like sodomy—Section 377 is similarly based on stereotypes of the kinds of sexual activity that are considered appropriate for men and women, respectively.

Hence, Justice Chandrachud concluded, Section 377 indirectly discriminates on the basis of sexual orientation, which in turn constitutes sex discrimination under Article 15.[251] He added that a formalistic account of Article 15 would miss these nuances and "fail to take into account the intersectional nature of sex discrimination."[252] Thus, sexual orientation "cannot be said to operate in isolation of other identities, especially from the socio-political and economic context."[253]

This leads to the second notable aspect of Justice Chandrachud's opinion—his careful attention to context. Much in the vein of the Delhi High Court's *Naz Foundation* judgment, he connected Section 377 to the long history of oppression and the lived realities of LGBTQ+ groups, including those from less affluent and socially connected parts of the country. For instance, Chandrachud noted how this law, by pushing sexual minorities into the shadows, prevented them from accessing medical services and maintaining their "sexual health."[254] Another section of the opinion was devoted to HIV/AIDS, where Chandrachud similarly linked Section 377 to the spread of the epidemic, particularly among MSMs and transgender groups.[255]

Justice Chandrachud's opinion finished with a rhetorical flourish that set out the transformative possibilities of this judgment and of constitutional law more broadly. He wrote:

> In recognising the rights of the LGBT community, the Constitution asserts itself as a text for governance which promotes true equality. It does so by questioning prevailing notions about the dominance of sexes and genders. In its transformational role, the Constitution directs our attention to resolving the polarities of sex and binarities of gender. In dealing with these issues we confront much that polarises our society. Our ability to survive as a free society will depend upon whether constitutional values can prevail over the impulses of the time.[256]

In sum, the *Navtej Johar* judgment categorically rejected not only the ruling in *Koushal* but also its constrained reading of constitutional rights and narrow

[250] *Id.* at paras. 44–47.
[251] *Id.* at para. 36.
[252] *Id.*
[253] *Id.*
[254] *Id.* at para. 72.
[255] *Id.* at para. 84.
[256] *Id.* at para. 153.

conception of the judicial role. *Navtej Johar* thus vindicated the bold doctrinal approach adopted by the Delhi High Court in *Naz Foundation*, with Justice Chandrachud especially echoing some of the more progressive themes in that judgment.

Navtej Johar also followed *Naz Foundation* (and *Puttuswamy*) in adopting a cosmopolitan approach.[257] Arguments raised by conservative intervenors grounded in tradition and the distinctiveness of Indian culture were consistently rejected by the justices. Each of them instead adopted a universal approach to rights, informed by international and comparative law. All four opinions, for instance, cited American and South African case law on LGBTQ+ rights, including *Lawrence v. Texas* (2003) and *National Coalition for Gay and Lesbian Equality v. Minister of Justice* (1998).[258] Several references were also made to the Yogyakarta Principles, the Universal Declaration of the Human Rights, the ICCPR, and the U.N. Human Rights Committee.[259] The justices also cited international scientific studies, including from the World Health Organization, to show how our understanding of the biology and psychological health of sexual minorities has evolved.[260]

Thus, *Navtej Johar* was a landmark judgment that finally decriminalized gay sex in India and vindicated the Delhi High Court's brave decision in *Naz Foundation* almost a decade earlier. But it was not the only progressive SCI judgment on gender and sexuality that followed from *Puttuswamy*. A few weeks later, on September 27, 2018, the same five-judge constitutional bench ruled in *Joseph Shine v. Union of India* that Section 497 of the IPC was unconstitutional.[261] This provision criminalized adultery and was understood exclusively in gendered terms, applying only in cases of marital infidelity committed by women. As in *Navtej Johar*, the Court ruled that the impugned provision was manifestly arbitrary in violation of Article 14 of the Constitution; that its gender stereotyping constituted sex discrimination under Article 15; and that its application only to women was demeaning and contrary to the right to dignity within Article 21.[262]

The following day, the same bench issued its judgment in *Indian Young Lawyers Association v. State of Kerala*, commonly referred to as the *Sabarimala* case. By a 4–1 margin, it ruled that the Sabarimala Temple in Kerala could not exclude women of menstruating age from its inner sanctum.[263] Because it involved religious affairs,

[257] For more on the cosmopolitan aspects of the judgment, see Sujit Choudhry, *Postcolonial Proportionality: Johar, Transformative Constitutionalism and Same-Sex Rights in India*, *in* The Global South and Comparative Constitutional Law (Philip Dann et al. eds., 2020).

[258] *See Navtej Johar*, 2018 I.N.S.C. 790 at paras. 159, 195 (per Misra, C.J.); paras. 36, 41 (per Nariman, J.); paras. 107, 112 (per Chandrachud, J.); paras. 13.1, 16.1 (per Malhotra, J.).

[259] *See, e.g., id.* at para. 141 (per Misra, C.J.); paras. 84–87 (per Nariman, J.); paras. 43, 99 (per Chandrachud, J.); paras. 15.1, 16.3 (per Malhotra, J.).

[260] *See, e.g., id.* at paras. 70, 73–74 (per Chandrachud, J.); paras. 13.4, 13.6 (per Malhotra, J.).

[261] *Joseph Shine*, (2018) S.C.C. 1676 at para. 56 (per Misra, C.J.).

[262] *Id.* at para. 86 (per Nariman, J.); para. 153 (per Chandrachud, J.); para. 171 (per Malhotra, J.).

[263] *Sabarimala*, (2019) 11 S.C.C. 1 at para. 144 (per Misra, C.J.).

the judgment took on a different tenor from *Navtej Johar* and *Joseph Shine*. CJI Misra, writing for himself and Justice Khanwilkar, held that the temple's constitutional right to manage its internal affairs under Article 26(b) of the Constitution was limited by a competing constitutional provision—Article 25(2)(b)—that permits state reforms toward opening "Hindu religious institutions of a public character to all classes and sections of Hindus."[264] Justice Nariman concurred in this ruling, and further held that the excluded women were denied their right to freely practice religion under Article 25(1).[265] Justice Chandrachud adopted a more creative approach. He held, *inter alia*, that by excluding women, the temple treated them as "untouchable" in violation of Article 17's prohibition on untouchability.[266] Justice Malhotra dissented, concluding that the temple's rights to manage its own affairs and to free religious practice prevailed over competing rights claims.[267]

Overall, these three judgments, following on the heels of *Puttuswamy*, significantly advanced the cause of gender and sexual orientation-based equality and helped the SCI maintain its reputation for independence and progressive decision-making during an otherwise turbulent period for the institution. As it turned out, however, September 2018 would be the high watermark for liberal constitutionalism at the Court and for LGBTQ+ rights.

V. An Institution in Crisis and a Shift on LGBTQ+ Rights (2019–23)

This Part examines the fate of LGBTQ+ rights as the Modi government entrenched its authority. It first explores the SCI's institutional crises, many of which were of its own making. It then discusses how the government has exerted undue influence on the Court since 2019. Against that backdrop, we turn to developments on transgender rights and same-sex marriage. While the *NALSA* judgment was cited with approval by *Puttuswamy* and *Navtej Johar*, government-sponsored legislation in 2019 that purported to entrench transgender rights did little to advance them in practice. In 2023, a widely anticipated SCI judgment on same-sex marriage ended in disappointment for the petitioners, as the Court deferred to the government on both the ruling and remedy. As we will see, these regressive developments resulted from the combination of an increasingly brazen and autocratic executive and a correspondingly timid and weakened apex court.

264 *Id.*
265 *Id.* at para. 177 (per Nariman, J.).
266 *Id.* at paras. 256–60 (per Chandrachud, J.).
267 *Id.* at para. 313 (per Malhotra, J.).

A. Institutional Strife at the SCI

As Indian democracy was in turmoil under Modi, the SCI experienced its own institutional crises. These crises were borne out of the enormous and unchecked power exercised by the CJI in two domains: bench assignments and judicial appointments.

1. Master of Roster

As discussed, the SCI's workload is divided across its thirty-four justices, who sit in separate benches. The benches are not populated at random. Rather, the CJI is the master of roster. He has the sole prerogative to determine bench composition and the cases each bench will hear. Given the polyvocal nature of the SCI, and the fact that cases often hinge on the bench assignment, the master of roster authority takes on greater importance. The CJI can—and does—affect case outcomes. He may, for instance, lock some justices out of deciding constitutional matters or give preference to justices that he favors.[268] As there are no legal rules or even guidelines on how to form judicial benches, the CJI is unfettered in the exercise of this authority.[269]

The CJI also has the listing power, which allows him to determine if and when a matter will be heard. He can override the automated queue of cases and may choose to speed up or delay hearings in particular cases. Some CJIs have prioritized matters for hearing, including on environmental, tax, and social justice issues by forming special benches outside the regular queue.[270] Meanwhile, some CJIs have declined to appoint constitutional benches during their tenure, with severe consequences for the enforcement of fundamental rights.[271] CJI Ramana (2021–22) constituted only one constitutional bench during his tenure while fifty-three constitutional cases were pending.[272] Similarly, during the tenure of CJI Bobde (2019–21), no constitutional matters were heard on the merits.[273]

[268] Robinson, *supra* note 15, at 187. I refer to the CJI as "he/him" as all CJIs to date have been men. On the absence of women in this post, see Dipika Jain, *Gendered Silences? The Lack of Women Chief Justices in India*, *in* JUDICIAL HEROINES? FEMALE CHIEF JUSTICES IN COMPARATIVE PERSPECTIVE (Erin Delaney & Rosalind Dixon eds., forthcoming).

[269] Shanti Bhushan v. Supreme Court of India (2018) 8 S.C.C. 396 (India); Asok Pande v. Supreme Court of India (2018) 5 S.C.C. 341 (India). Courts around the world have introduced randomized case assignments to avoid the potential conflicts of interest that the CJI's master of roster power invites. *See* DAVID KOSAŘ, THE PERILS OF JUDICIAL SELF-GOVERNMENT IN TRANSITIONAL SOCIETIES 55–56, 91–92 (2016).

[270] Robinson, *supra* note 15, at 191.

[271] Under Article 145(3) of the Constitution, only SCI benches comprising five or more judges can hear constitutional matters.

[272] Saurav Das, *Lots of Speeches, But No Action in Cases of National Importance: The Legacy of Chief Justice Ramana*, ARTICLE 14 (Aug. 24, 2022), https://article-14.com/post/lots-of-speeches-but-no-action-in-cases-of-national-importance-the-legacy-of-chief-justice-ramana-63058720be481.

[273] *See* BHATIA, *supra* note 184, at 417–29.

Over the past decade, the master of roster authority has been abused by several CJIs to such a degree that it calls the Court's independence and integrity into question. In 2019, an SCI staff member accused then-CJI Gogoi of sexual harassment and victimization. When her case appeared before the SCI, Gogoi did not recuse himself as master of roster. Even worse, he assigned the case to five-judge bench on which he sat and then proceeded to comment on the case.

Gogoi's predecessor, CJI Dipak Misra—the same CJI Misra who presided over the landmark *Puttuswamy* and *Navtej Johar* judgments—showed a similar contempt for judicial ethics and due process. Shortly after he assumed the position of CJI, a civil society group called the Campaign for Judicial Accountability and Reforms filed a complaint before the SCI alleging that Misra engaged in unethical conduct.[274] The case was referred to a five-judge bench given its constitutional import. The bench would have comprised Misra and the four most senior puisne justices. But Misra refused to recuse himself and, as master of roster, chose to transfer the case to a different bench seemingly out of concern that the original bench might rule against him. The new bench—which did not include the four senior puisne justices—dismissed the petition.

The four senior justices held a press conference in January 2018 to publicly criticize CJI Misra's use of the master of roster power. Justice Chelameswar, the most senior member of this group, called it "an extraordinary event in the history of this institution."[275] He went on to say, "[T]he administration of the Supreme Court is not in order and many things which are less than desirable" had taken place in recent months.[276] Chelameswar added that the four justices had voiced their concerns to CJI Misra in private and asked him to take "remedial measures," but they were unable to convince him and were thus "left no choice but to communicate it to the nation."[277]

These four justices also released a letter to the CJI, which specifically discussed his misuse of the master of roster power. The letter noted that the longstanding "privilege" given to the CJI to "form the roster and assign cases to different members/benches of the court is a convention designed for a disciplined and efficient transaction of business of the Court."[278] However, it went on to say that this does not confer "superior authority, legal or factual" on the CJI, who is "only the first among equals."[279] It further declared that "well-settled and time-honoured

[274] For background and details on the complaint and Misra's conduct, see Atul Dev, *The Darkest House: Dipak Misra's Shadow over the Supreme Court*, CARAVAN (July 1, 2018), https://caravanmagazine.in/law/dipak-misra-shadow-supreme-court.

[275] J. Venkatesan, *Top 4 SC Judges Revolt Against Chief Justice, Question Biased Decisions*, DECCAN CHRONICLE (Jan. 12, 2018), https://www.deccanchronicle.com/nation/current-affairs/120118/top-4-sc-judges-revolt-against-chief-justice-question-biased-decisions.html.

[276] *Id.*

[277] *Id.*

[278] *Full Text of the Letter Four Supreme Court Judges Wrote to India's Chief Justice*, QUARTZ (Jan. 12, 2018), https://qz.com/india/1178370/full-text-of-the-letter-four-supreme-court-judges-write-to-the-chief-justice-of-india.

[279] *Id.*

conventions guiding the Chief Justice" require him to assign cases to appropriate benches, both in terms of their composition and size.[280] But, the letter noted, CJI Misra failed to follow these conventions. It referred to instances where the CJI "selectively" assigned cases to benches "of their preference" without any rationale.[281] The four justices made clear, both in the letter and in their public statements, that they believed CJI Misra's conduct had damaged the SCI's independence and public image.[282]

2. Judicial Appointments

The CJI's other significant—and unaccountable—power pertains to judicial appointments. Article 124(2) of the Indian Constitution provides that the President of India appoints judges to the higher judiciary in "consultation" with the CJI.[283] Initially, this power was exercised in line with the plain text of the Constitution. Since the President is a largely ceremonial figure, the actual appointments power rested with the Prime Minister and cabinet.[284] The CJI was consulted on judicial appointments, but his advice was not binding.

In response to Prime Minister Indira Gandhi's attempts to capture and control the judiciary in the 1970s,[285] the SCI gradually wrested the appointments power away from the executive. In the *Second Judges' Case* (1994),[286] the Court ruled that "consultation" in Article 124 means a deliberative process between the executive and judicial branches,[287] taking "into account the views of all the consultees, giving the greatest weight to the opinion of the Chief Justice of India who . . . is best suited to know the worth of the appointee."[288] The Court held that if no consensus could be reached, the "final opinion" should be that of the CJI unless there were "very good reasons" to the contrary "known to the executive and disclosed to the Chief Justice of India."[289] This judgment established the "collegium"—a select group comprising the CJI and a few senior justices who would have the final word on judicial appointments. The *Third Judges' Case* (1999) entrenched the collegium system by confirming its structure and issuing guidelines

280 *Id.*

281 *Id.*

282 *Id.*; Venkatesan, *supra* note 275. For a fuller account of these events and the misuse of the master of roster power, see Rehan Abeyratne & Surbhi Karwa, *The Institutional Failings of India's Chief Justice in the Age of Modi*, INT'L J. CONST. L. (forthcoming).

283 INDIA CONST. arts. 124, 217.

284 *Id.* art. 74(1).

285 *See* T.R. Andhyarujina, *A Committed Judiciary: Indira Gandhi and Judicial Appointments, in* APPOINTMENT OF JUDGES TO THE SUPREME COURT OF INDIA: TRANSPARENCY, ACCOUNTABILITY AND INDEPENDENCE 18 (Arghya Sengupta & Ritwika Sharma eds., 2018).

286 Advocates-on-Record Ass'n v. Union of India, A.I.R. 1994 S.C. 268 (India).

287 *See id.* at paras. 40–41. Justice Verma found that "consultation" (rather than "concurrence") was adopted "merely to indicate that absolute discretion was not given to any one, not even to the Chief Justice of India as [sic] individual."

288 *Id.* at para. 41.

289 *Id.*

for the CJI in exercising his discretion in recommending judicial appointments and transfers.[290] This system, which continues today, requires the CJI to consult with the four most senior puisne justices of the Supreme Court in making judicial nominations. A majority of these justices may reject nominees put forward by the CJI.[291]

Since Modi and the BJP came to power in 2014, the judicial appointments power has again become a site of institutional confrontation between the executive and judiciary. One of the first major actions of the Modi government was to establish a National Judicial Appointments Commission (NJAC). It comprised six members: three Supreme Court justices (including the Chief Justice), the Union Minister of Law and Justice, and two "eminent persons" drawn from civil society.[292] However, before the Commission began its work, the SCI invalidated both the constitutional amendment and legislation that created it. The Court's principal holding in the *Fourth Judges' Case* (2016) was that by removing judicial primacy in the appointments process—only three out of the six members of the Commission were judges—the NJAC compromised the independence of the judiciary, which was part of the Constitution's basic structure.[293] This judgment is legally and logically problematic. It does not explain why the Constitution requires judges to have the final word on appointments. It also fails to address serious concerns with the collegium system including a lack of transparency in selection criteria and allegations of corruption in the nomination process.

In recent years, the lack of information that the collegium provides on judicial nominees has proved problematic. It has enabled the government to hide relevant—and potentially disqualifying—background information from the public on its preferred candidates. For instance, the collegium nominated Victoria Gowri to the Madras High Court in early 2023. Gowri had served for the ruling BJP-led government as standing counsel at the Madras High Court and as assistant solicitor general. She had made discriminatory remarks—possibly amounting to hate speech—about Christian and Muslim minorities, which were apparently unknown to the collegium when they recommended her appointment.[294] The record of these remarks was only revealed after her name was recommended. Writ petitions were filed challenging her appointment and CJI Chandrachud constituted a two-judge bench to hear the case. The ensuing judgment dismissed these petitions. It ruled

[290] In re: Appointment and Transfer of Judges, A.I.R. 1999 S.C. 1 (India).

[291] *Id.* at para. 41(3). For a detailed account of the SCI's takeover of the amendment power, see Rehan Abeyratne, *Upholding Judicial Supremacy: The NJAC Judgment in Comparative Perspective*, 49 Geo. Wash. Int'l L. Rev. 569 (2017).

[292] The Constitution (Ninety-Ninth Amendment) Act, 2014 (India), art. 3.

[293] Supreme Court Advocates-on-Record Association v. Union of India (2016) 4 S.C.C. 1 (India).

[294] Saurav Das, *'Problem of Christian, Love Jihad': A Future Judge's Bias Reveals Supreme Court Collegium's Enduring Opacity*, Article 14 (Jan. 30, 2023), https://article-14.com/post/-problem-of-christian-love-jihad-a-future-judge-s-bias-reveals-supreme-court-collegium-s-enduring-opacity-63d73360b1296.

that collegium recommendations are unreviewable and, more troublingly, that the SCI lacks authority to ask the collegium to reconsider recommendations, much less to issue writs (such as certiorari or mandamus) to quash them.[295] Thus, as with the master of roster authority, the SCI was unwilling to police itself with respect to the collegium, effectively shielding the latter from scrutiny.

Following the *Fourth Judges' Case* (2016), the SCI finally began a public consultation process to reform the collegium. In October 2017, the collegium, led by CJI Misra, decided that it would publish its resolutions on the appointment and transfer of judges.[296] The stated goal was to improve transparency in the process, by publicly disclosing the collegium's decisions and its reasons. An empirical study of these resolutions from 2017 to 2019 found that they were "mostly a formality" and "did not lead to an improved understanding of the collegium's functioning."[297] The reasons provided for the collegium's decisions were vague, consisting largely of "generic platitudes" rather than specific details. According to the study, the resolutions also appeared in some cases to have been written with an intent to obfuscate rather than reveal the reasons behind certain decisions.[298]

The study further noted that the practice of publishing collegium resolutions ended in October 2019.[299] Thereafter, the collegium only provided the list of nominated judges, with no information about the judges who were consulted, objections (if any) from the government, or reasons for its decisions.

In early 2023, under the helm of CJI Chandrachud, the collegium was finally subject to meaningful reforms. Detailed resolutions were published on the SCI website, which contained the collegium judges' deliberations and reasons.[300] This was part of a broader (and welcome) series of reforms undertaken in the SCI under Chandrachud's leadership.[301] They included digitizing cases and using artificial intelligence-based tools to help search through the Court's database, making it more accessible to the public.[302] Chandrachud's commitment to transparency would, however, place the SCI at odds with the government.

[295] Anna Mathews v. Supreme Court of India, Writ Petition (Civil) No. 148/2023 (2023) (India), paras. 10–11.

[296] Rangin Pallav Tripathy, *Supreme Court Collegium and Transparency: An Empirical Inquiry*, 56 Econ. & Pol. Wkly. 33, 33 (May 29, 2021).

[297] *Id.*

[298] *Id.*

[299] *Id.*

[300] *SC Takes Giant Leap Towards Reforms During First 100 Days of Justice Chandrachud's Tenure as CJI*, Econ. Times (Feb. 16, 2023), https://economictimes.indiatimes.com/news/india/sc-takes-giant-leap-towards-reforms-during-first-100-days-of-justice-chandrachuds-tenure-as-cji/articleshow/97988844.cms.

[301] *Id.*

[302] *Id.*; Shruti Kakkar, *My Work Will Speak: CJI Keeps His Word on Judicial Reforms*, New Indian Express, Apr. 10, 2023, https://www.newindianexpress.com/nation/2023/Apr/10/my-work-will-speak-cji-keeps-his-word-on-judicial-reforms-2564448.html.

B. Undue Influence on the SCI

Prime Minister Modi and the BJP won another landslide election in 2019, gaining an even larger majority in Parliament. It then turned Indian constitutionalism in a more autocratic direction, which is evident in its dealings with the SCI.

Consider, for instance, the operation of the collegium. As discussed, while this judicial body nominates judges, it is ultimately up to the President of India, on the advice of the Prime Minister, to formalize the appointments. Under Modi in recent years, several nominees were delayed without explanation.

In some cases, the reasons can be inferred from the nominees' background. Take, for instance, Justice Akil Kureshi, who had placed the Minister of Home Affairs Amit Shah in custody for an extrajudicial killing of which he was accused in Gujarat.[303] Kureshi was recommended for the post of Chief Justice of the Madhya Pradesh High Court in 2019, but the government returned the nomination. He was then transferred to the Tripura High Court, one of the smallest in the country. In 2021, Kureshi was the second most senior High Court judge and, by convention, should have been nominated for a seat on the SCI. However, the collegium recommended the appointment of several justices to the SCI that year and excluded Kureshi.[304] Here, the government appears to have pressured the collegium into passing over a nominee that it opposed.

Similarly, Justice S. Muralidhar—a progressive judge who was on the *Naz Foundation* bench—was transferred from the Delhi High Court to the less prestigious Punjab & Haryana High Court after he recommended police action against a sitting cabinet minister for alleged hate speech during communal riots in Delhi. Thereafter, the government selectively ignored Muralidhar as a candidate to serve on another High Court despite the collegium's recommendation. He was also not considered for elevation to the Supreme Court despite being one of the most senior judges on any High Court.[305]

Under CJI Chandrachud's leadership, the collegium finally issued resolutions in January 2023 that publicly disclosed the government's reasons for delaying the appointment of five nominees. The government opposed one nominee, *inter alia*, because it claimed his openly gay lifestyle would make him biased. The collegium, to its credit, rebutted this argument, noting that it would be "manifestly contrary to the principles laid down by the Supreme Court" to oppose a candidate for his sexual orientation or his advocacy for the rights of sexual minorities.[306] Two other

[303] Shoaib Daniyal, *"Why Have Collegium at All?": What Kureshi's Rejection Says About SC Independence in the Modi Era*, SCROLL.IN (Aug. 31, 2021), https://scroll.in/article/1004168/why-have-collegium-at-all-what-kureshis-rejection-says-about-sc-independence-in-the-modi-era.

[304] *Id.*

[305] Manu Sebastian, *"By Not Standing up For Justice Murlidhar, Supreme Court Collegium Fails Yet Another Independent Judge,"* LIVELAW (Aug. 8, 2023), https://www.livelaw.in/articles/justice-s-muralidhar-supreme-court-collegium-fails-yet-another-independent-judge-234634.

[306] Jannani M., *The Indian Supreme Court Collegium Picking Its Battle*, VERFASSUNGSBLOG (Jan. 27, 2023), https://verfassungsblog.de/the-indian-supreme-court-collegium-picking-its-battle/.

nominees were opposed due to their criticisms of the government. Again, the collegium noted that this was not a legitimate basis to stall nominations, as it infringed upon the nominees' constitutional right to freedom of speech under Article 19(1)(a) of the Constitution.[307]

The government responded forcefully to the collegium's disclosure of these deliberations. Law Minister Kiren Rijiju commented on the collegium in late 2022, referring to it as "alien" to the Constitution and criticizing the opacity of the process.[308] Following the SCI's publication of detailed resolutions in January 2023, Rijiju wrote a letter to CJI Chandrachud in which he proposed "the inclusion of a government nominee in the decision-making process for shortlisting of judges" and further noted the "need for representation on a search-cum-evaluation committee (SEC) for appointments of judges to the Supreme Court."[309]

What emerges from these incidents is the outline of a concerted government plan to unduly influence the SCI.[310] By declining to appoint qualified judges for social or political reasons, punitively transferring judges who rule against the government, and failing to disclose relevant information on its preferred nominees, the government exerts its authority over the appointments process.

Recent scholarly work has also shown that the Modi government has sought to influence sitting justices by luring them with retirement benefits.[311] It has offered some justices prestigious government posts upon their retirement. The incentive structure is clear: justices who rule in favor of the government are more likely to secure these plum positions.[312] SCI justices must retire at the age of sixty-five, which enables the government prepare these offers in advance. CJI Ranjan Gogoi, for example, was invited by the Modi government to join the Rajya Sabha (upper house of Parliament) when he retired from the bench in 2019. He accepted the post and has served in the Rajya Sabha since 2020.[313]

Gogoi's inappropriate handling of the sexual harassment case against him should have been led to his resignation from the bench and certainly should have militated against this legislative appointment. But he had clearly won favor with

[307] *Id.*

[308] Surendra Kumar Yadawa, *Understanding the Friction Between Executive and Judiciary and Why Collegium Needs More Transparency*, OUTLOOK (Mar. 12, 2023), https://www.outlookindia.com/national/understanding-the-friction-between-executive-and-judiciary-and-why-collegium-needs-more-transparency-news-269347.

[309] K. Chandru, *Ad-hocism in Appointing Judges of Higher Courts Must Stop*, FRONTLINE (Jan. 26, 2023), https://frontline.thehindu.com/the-nation/ad-hocism-in-appointing-judges-of-higher-courts-must-stop/article66407426.ece.

[310] For more on the government's maneuvers to influence the SCI, see Abeyratne & Karwa, *supra* note 282.

[311] *See* Madhav S. Aney et al., *Jobs for Justice(s): Institutional Corruption in the Supreme Court of India*, 64 J. L. & ECON. 479 (2021) .

[312] *Id.* at 508.

[313] Shubhankar Dam, *Active After Sunset: The Politics of Judicial Retirement in India*, 51 FED. L. REV. 31, 31–32 (2023).

the government through his judgments on matters of political importance. As discussed, the SCI under Gogoi's stewardship propelled the NRC process to deprive millions of (mostly Muslim) Assamese residents of their Indian citizenship. And just a week before his retirement, Gogoi led a five-judge bench that unanimously awarded the land in Ayodhya on which the Babri Masjid had stood to a government-created trust to build a Hindu temple.[314] Thus, he delivered the government its greatest symbolic victory.[315] The new temple consecrating the Hindu god Ram's birthplace was opened in January 2024. In his speech to inaugurate the temple, Prime Minister Modi expressed "gratitude to the judiciary of India for doing justice" and added that Lord Ram is the "spirit of the Indian Constitution."[316]

In other instances, justices have made untoward extrajudicial comments to signal their pro-government bona fides. The most notorious example is Justice Arun Mishra, who in giving a vote of thanks at a judicial conference, referred to Prime Minister Modi as an "internationally acclaimed visionary" and a "versatile genius, who thinks globally and acts locally."[317] Upon his retirement the following year, Mishra was appointed Chairperson of the National Human Rights Commission.[318]

Overall, the SCI's independence and reputation have come under severe strain in the past decade. The Court has remained silent on petitions alleging serious fundamental rights violations on behalf of marginalized or victimized groups, including detainees in Kashmir and Assam. When it has acted forcefully, it has often favored the government at the expense of minorities. The NRC case—where the SCI effectively took over the executive function and harshly enforced citizenship laws in Assam—is the most glaring example.

Internally, the CJI's master of roster power has been used to favor certain justices and punish others, as well as to form benches that appear to produce preordained outcomes. The SCI has declined to review or even issue guidelines to regulate this practice. Similarly, the collegium-led judicial appointments process has been

[314] M. Siddiq (D) Thr Lrs v. Mahant Suresh Das, Civil Appeal Nos. 10866–10867 of 2010 (2019) (India).

[315] The SCI did award the Uttar Pradesh Sunni Central Waqf Board a separate (and smaller) parcel of land to build a Mosque, but this was a dubious compromise as the Board had far more evidence—and better arguments—on the merits of the main property dispute. *See* Suhrith Parthasarathy & Gautam Bhatia, *Peace Bought by an Unequal Compromise*, Hindu (Nov. 15, 2019), https://www.thehindu.com/opinion/lead/peace-bought-by-an-unequal-compromise/article62106425.ece; John Sebastian & Faiza Rahman, *The Babri Masjid Judgment and the Sound of Silence*, Wire (Dec. 6. 2019), https://thewire.in/law/the-babri-masjid-judgment-and-the-sound-of-silence.

[316] Sharangee Dutta, *"Our Ram Lalla is Here": PM Says January 22 Marks New Era After Temple Opening*, India Today (Jan. 22, 2024), https://www.indiatoday.in/india/story/pm-modi-congratulates-nation-after-temple-ram-inauguration-ayodhya-our-ram-lalla-is-here-2492010-2024-01-22.

[317] *"Modi is a Versatile Genius Who Things Globally and Acts Locally": Supreme Court Judge Arun Mishra*, Scroll (Feb. 22, 2020), https://scroll.in/latest/953994/modi-is-a-versatile-genius-who-thinks-globally-and-acts-locally-supreme-court-judge-arun-mishra.

[318] *Nine Months After He Retired from SC, Justice Arun Mishra Is NHRC Chief*, Indian Express (June 3, 2021), https://indianexpress.com/article/india/justice-arun-mishra-nhrc-chairman-7340811/.

characterized (notwithstanding reforms by CJI Chandrachud) by a lack of transparency and fairness.[319]

The Modi government, for its part, has capitalized on the Court's internal crises. It has stalled disfavored judicial nominations and hidden potentially disqualifying background information on government-backed candidates. It has also lured sitting justices with postretirement benefits, which creates the impression—apparently borne out in some cases and extrajudicial comments—that some justices are too cozy with the government.[320]

These pieces combine to form a troubling picture of the SCI's inner workings, its decisional independence, and institutional autonomy.

C. Transgender Rights under Modi

1. Subverting the *NALSA* Judgment

Returning to LGBTQ+ rights, the Modi government adopted a different tack to subvert the SCI's landmark transgender rights judgment in *NALSA*. Two months after Modi became Prime Minister in May 2014, the government filed a petition before the SCI seeking a clarification of its judgment in *NALSA*.[321] The *NALSA* bench had, *inter alia*, ordered the central and state governments to treat transgender people as "socially and educationally backward classes of citizens," which would entitle them to "reservations" in university admissions and public sector jobs.[322] Reservations has long been a fraught political issue in India, with various lower caste groups seeking recognition as "backward classes", while more privileged groups have fought to limit (or even abolish) the practice.[323] The *NALSA* judgment's direction clearly struck a nerve with the government, as creating new reservations of this sort—and for groups as marginalized and unpopular as India's transgender communities—would be politically untenable.

The government's petition, however, did not seek to overturn this direction (or any others). Instead, it asked the Court to "properly define who transgender persons are" to ensure that relief is directed toward the appropriate communities.[324]

[319] *See* Abeyratne & Karwa, *supra* note 282.

[320] For more on CJI Gogoi and Justice Mishra's apparent complicity with the government, see Rana Ayyub, *The Destruction of India's Judicial Independence Is Almost Complete*, WASH. POST. (Mar. 24, 2020), https://www.washingtonpost.com/opinions/2020/03/24/destruction-indias-judicial-independence-is-almost-complete/.

[321] *Application for Clarification/Modification of Judgment and Order Dated 15.04.2014 Passed by This Hon'ble Court and to Pass Appropriate Directions on Behalf of Union of India*, I.A. No. __ of 2014 in Writ Petition (Civil) No. 400/2012 (2014) [hereinafter *Clarification Petition*].

[322] *NALSA*, (2014) 5 S.C.C. 438 at para. 129.

[323] *See* Vinay Sitapati, *Reservations*, *in* OXFORD HANDBOOK OF THE INDIAN CONSTITUTION, *supra* note 18, at ch. 40.

[324] *Clarification Petition*, *supra* note 321, at para. 4.

An Expert Committee, convened by the previous government, had labeled "all persons whose own sense of gender does not match with the gender assigned to them at birth" as "transgender."[325] The petition noted that this definition appeared to conflict with parts of the *NALSA* judgment, which created "an ambiguity between a transgender and lesbian, gay and bisexual persons."[326] The petition referred to paragraph 107 in Justice Sikri's opinion in which he said:

> The grammatical meaning of "transgender," therefore, is across or beyond gender. This has come to be known as umbrella term which includes Gay men, Lesbians, bisexuals, and cross dressers within its scope.[327]

Out of context, this statement appears to broaden the conception of "transgender" and may pose the implementational concerns that the government raised. But the very next sentence in Justice Sikri's opinion removed any doubt. He wrote, "However, while dealing with the present issue we are not concerned with this aforesaid wider meaning of the expression transgender."[328] Similarly, Justice Radhakrishnan's separate opinion made clear that sexual orientation and gender identity are "separate concepts."[329]

All of this suggests, as other commentators have noted, that the government did not file this petition in good faith.[330] Its aim was likely to delay the implementation of the directions in *NALSA*, rather than to gain a clearer understanding of what the SCI meant by "transgender."[331] If the government's aim were to delay, it succeeded. The SCI took two years to respond to the clarification petition. In 2016, the Court finally heard this matter and confirmed that transgender reservations would not apply to lesbian, gay, or bisexual individuals. It also expressed frustration with the government's tactics, stating, "We ask why we should not dismiss the petitions with costs . . . No clarification is required."[332]

When it was finally time to implement the *NALSA* directions, the Modi government drafted legislation that repurposed language in the judgment for its own political ends. *NALSA* was a landmark progressive judgment, but Justices

[325] *Id.* at para. 4.
[326] *Id.* at para. 6.
[327] *NALSA*, (2014) 5 S.C.C. 438 at para. 107 (per Sikri, J.).
[328] *Id.*
[329] *Id.* at para. 20 (per Radhakrishnan, J.).
[330] *See* Surabhi Shukla, *Why the Clarification Petition Filed by the Union of India in the Transgender Case Is Incorrect in Law and Bad Faith on the Question of Reservation*, 22 Wm. & Mary J. Women & L. 585 (2016).
[331] *See* Shreya Ila Anasuya, *Over Two years After Landmark Judgment, Transgender People Are Still Struggling*, Wire (May 15, 2016), https://thewire.in/gender/over-two-years-after-landmark-judgment-transgender-people-are-still-struggling.
[332] *SC Third-Gender Rap on Centre*, Telegraph (July 1, 2016), https://www.telegraphindia.com/india/sc-third-gender-rap-on-centre/cid/1516607.

Radhakrishnan and Sikri framed or articulated parts of their opinions in ways that could be misused.

First, Justice Radhakrishnan's opinion contains a section titled "Historical Background of Transgenders in India" in which he sought to demonstrate that various transgender communities have deep roots in the subcontinent. He referred, *inter alia*, to the role of the hijra community in the two major Hindu epics—the Ramayana and the Mahabharata—as well as in ancient Jain texts.[333] The primary purpose of this exercise appears to have been to show how transgender communities were subsequently mistreated by the British colonial government, whose Criminal Tribes Act 1871 deemed the hijra community "criminal" and "addicted to the systematic commission of non-bailable offences."[334] Such groups were subject to registration and surveillance, and they could be arrested without warrant. Justice Radhakrishnan may also have included this historical section to counter the *Koushal* judgment, which adopted a parochial view of Indian culture, and chastised the Delhi High Court for applying foreign precedents "blindfolded" to the Indian context.[335]

While Justice Radhakrishnan mentioned the prominent role hijras played "in the royal courts of the Islamic world" including during "Mughal rule in Medieval India,"[336] these passing references are dwarfed by his discussion of Vedic or Hindu culture. Thus, the opinion's use of history plays into the nationalist narrative of the RSS and BJP, which harks back to a Hindu golden age prior to Muslim or colonial rule.[337] It ignored, as Gee Imaan Semmalar put it, "the Muslim cultural context within which several hijra gharanas [households] have flourished beyond the restrictions of Hinduism, creating a syncretic culture that respects Islam within the transgender community."[338]

A second issue with the *NALSA* judgment is its inconsistent, at times even contradictory, use of the term "transgender."[339] Given the country's vast size and population, "transgender" refers to several distinct communities, each with separate religious, caste-based, and political histories.[340] This pluralism is not always recognized or fully accounted for in the two opinions. Justice Radhakrishnan

[333] *NALSA*, (2014) 5 S.C.C. 438 at paras. 12–15 (per Radhakrishnan, J.).

[334] *Id.* at para. 16; Criminal Tribes Act, 1871 (India).

[335] *Koushal*, (2014) 1 S.C.C. 1 at para. 52.

[336] *NALSA*, (2014) 5 S.C.C. 438 at para. 15 (per Radhakrishnan, J.).

[337] *See* Rahul Rao, Out of Time: The Queer Politics of Postcoloniality 186–87 (2020); Ila Nagar & Debanuj DasGupta, *Transgender Rights and Religiosities in India: NALSA Judgment and Beyond*, 29(3) GLQ: J. Lesbian & Gay Stud. 329, 332 (2023).

[338] Gee Imaan Semmalar, *Gender Outlawed: The Supreme Court Judgment on Third Gender and Its Implications*, Roundtable India (Apr. 19, 2014), https://www.roundtableindia.co.in/because-we-have-a-voice-too-the-supreme-court-judgment-on-third-gender-and-its-implications/.

[339] The government raised what appears to be a similar concern in its clarification petition. But it asked whether "transgender" applied covered gay men and lesbians, which, as discussed, did not need to be clarified.

[340] *See* Semmalar, *supra* note 338; Nagar & DasGupta, *supra* note 337, at 336–37.

initially noted that "transgender" in the Indian context refers to several communities, including "Hijras, eunuchs, Kothis, Aravanis, Jogappas, Shiv-Shakthis etc."[341] Later, though, he often equated "transgender" with "hijra," referring only to the latter group when it appears he meant the plurality of these communities.[342]

The declaration and directions at the end of the judgment also reflect this reductionist view of India's many gender-diverse communities. The two-judge bench declared that "Hijras, Eunuchs, apart from binary gender, be treated as 'third gender' for the purpose of safeguarding their rights."[343] This formulation *prima facie* denies the "third gender" option to India's many other gender-diverse groups.

Justice Sikri, meanwhile, essentialized trans identities in a different way. His opinion repeatedly stressed that transgender persons should be treated as a third gender "for the purposes of safeguarding and enforcing appropriately their rights guaranteed under the Constitution."[344] For some trans people and communities, this is a desired outcome. But others, including those who have chosen to live as either men or women, are excluded from much of Justice Sikri's analysis.[345]

This omission is, however, addressed at the end of the judgment, in which the two justices collectively declare: "Transgender persons' right to decide their self-identified gender is also upheld and the Centre and State Governments are directed to grant legal recognition of their gender identity such as male, female or as third gender."[346] While this statement provides broader relief than Justice Sikri's opinion would allow, "male" and "female" are terms that connote biological sex as opposed to socially constructed gender. Indeed, an overemphasis on biological sex (as opposed to gender as it operates in society) is a feature of both *NALSA* opinions,[347] and it has been criticized in the academic literature.[348] This aspect of *NALSA* not only undermined the judgment's progressive sweep but also opened the door to regressive legislative action.

2. The Transgender Rights Act 2019

After the *NALSA* judgment was released, a member of the Rajya Sabha, Tiruchi Siva, introduced the Rights of Transgender Persons Bill in Parliament.[349] The bill,

[341] *NALSA*, (2014) 5 S.C.C. 438 at paras. 12, 44 (per Radhakrishnan, J.).

[342] *See, e.g., id.* at para. 55 (stating that "Hijra/transgender persons . . . [face] extreme discrimination in all spheres of society").

[343] *Id.* at para. 129.

[344] *Id.* at para. 128 (per Sikri, J.).

[345] *See* Aniruddha Dutta, *Contradictory Tendencies: The Supreme Court's NALSA Judgment on Transgender Recognition and Rights*, 5 J. Indian L. & Soc. 225, 231 (2014).

[346] *Id.* at para. 129.

[347] *See, e.g., id.* at paras. 35–41 (per Radhakrishnan, J.) (conflating "transsexual" and "transgender" in a survey of foreign laws); paras. 103–05 (per Sikri, J.) (concluding that changes in gender identity are permissible after a "person has changed his/her sex" because of "advancement in medical science").

[348] *See* Dutta, *supra* note 345, at 229–31; Semmalar, *supra* note 338.

[349] Rights of Transgender Persons Bill, 2014 (as Introduced in the Rajya Sabha on 12 December 2014) (India), available at: http://164.100.47.4/BillsTexts/RSBillTexts/asintroduced/trangder-E.pdf.

drafted with the engagement of gender-diverse groups, sought to implement and build upon the progressive aspects of the SCI's judgment. Among other things, the bill recognized the right of transgender persons to self-identify in their chosen gender,[350] created new commissions and courts to investigate and adjudicate transgender issues,[351] and introduced reservations for transgender communities in public sector jobs and public universities.[352] It also defined "transgender" in plural and non-biological terms:

> [A] person, whose gender does not match with the gender assigned to that person at birth and includes trans-men and trans-women (whether or not they have undergone sex reassignment surgery or hormone therapy or laser therapy etc.), gender-queers and a number of socio-cultural identities such as—kinnars, hijras, aravanis, jogtas etc.[353]

The bill was unanimously passed by the Rajya Sabha in April 2015—the first private member's bill to be approved in the upper house in more than forty years.[354]

Meanwhile, the Modi government's Ministry of Social Justice and Empowerment drafted its own Transgender Persons (Protection of Rights) Bill 2016.[355] The bill was introduced in the Lok Sabha in August 2016 after the SCI issued its decision on the government's clarification petition. And the lower house's bill differed in significant respects from the Rajya Sabha's bill. Unlike the latter, the Lok Sabha bill failed to define terms such as "violence," "exploitation," "discrimination," and "abuse."[356] Thus, though one chapter of the latter bill prohibited discrimination against transgender persons,[357] it was framed broadly and would be difficult to enforce without key terms defined. Moreover, it introduced a burdensome and intrusive process to qualify as "transgender" to obtain various benefits. The Lok Sabha bill required gender-diverse people to obtain a Magistrate's certificate of transgender identity, which in turn required the approval of a District Screening Committee.[358] This committee would comprise government officials, medical staff, and a member of the relevant gender-diverse community.

350 *Id.* at cl. 3.
351 *Id.* at chs. VII–VIII.
352 *Id.* at cls. 21–22.
353 Id. at cl. 2(t).
354 Dipika Jain, *Law-Making By and For the People: A Case for Pre-Legislative Processes in India*, 20 Statute L. Rev. 1, 11 (2019).
355 Transgender Persons (Protection of Rights) Bill, 2016, Bill No. 210 of 2016 (as introduced in Lok Sabha, 1 August 2016) (India), available at: https://prsindia.org/files/bills_acts/bills_parliament/2016/Transgender_Persons_Bill,_2016_1.pdf.
356 *Id.* at ch. 1.
357 *Id.* at ch. 2.
358 *Id.* at ch. 3. For more on the differences between these bills, see Jennifer Ung Loh, *Transgender Identity, Sexual Versus Gender "Rights" and the Tools of the Indian State*, 119 Feminist Rev. 39, 47–49 (2018).

The final bill that was eventually adopted in December 2018, and enacted as the Transgender Persons (Protection of Rights) Act 2019, included both of these problematic elements.[359] It also introduced a biological component to determine transgender identity, requiring individuals to undergo sex-change surgery in order to officially change their gender.[360] Such individuals would then need to obtain a certificate from the Medical Superintendent or Chief Medical Officer of the institution where the surgery was performed and present that certificate to a Magistrate for approval.[361]

These onerous procedures not only raised serious dignitarian and privacy-related concerns but also contradicted the ruling in *NALSA*, which declared that individuals have the right to self-identify in their chosen gender regardless of whether they had undergone surgery.[362] As Dipika Jain has shown, concerns about these provisions were raised by gender-diverse communities and by members of Parliament, but they were largely rejected by the ruling party.[363]

The BJP-led government, then, was able to enact a law on transgender rights that purported to implement the *NALSA* ruling but in fact placed new obstacles in the path toward legal recognition and social acceptance for India's gender-diverse communities.[364] The government was assisted in this exercise by unfortunate choices of framing and language in *NALSA*, which essentialized trans identities and placed too much emphasis on biological sex.

At a political level, Justice Radhakrishnan's linking of gender diversity with a distinctly Hindu conception of Indian history played into the hands of the BJP and RSS.[365] In 2016, Prime Minister Modi asked Members of Parliament from his party to reach out to gender-diverse communities in their respective districts, setting them a target of meeting 500,000 people.[366] Calling the Lok Sabha bill a "great step for social reforms," he said to his party, "Humanity is not confined to male

[359] Transgender Persons (Protection of Rights) Act, 2019, (India) § § 2, 5. The District Screening Committee was removed from Section 5, but the Act still requires transgender individuals to apply for a certificate of identity from a District Magistrate.

[360] *Id.* at § 7.

[361] *Id.*

[362] *See NALSA*, (2014) 5 S.C.C. 438 at para. 129. This regressive move is also at odds with progressive developments on transgender rights in other South Asian countries, especially Nepal. *See* Holning Lau & Mara Malagodi, *Legal Gender Recognition in Comparative Context*, 45(2) U. PA. J. INT'L L. 269, 280–83 (2024); Dipika Jain & Debanuj DasGupta, *Law, Gender Identity, and the Uses of Human Rights: The Paradox of Recognition in South Asia*, 20(1) J. HUM. RTS. 110, 112–16 (2021).

[363] Jain, *supra* note 354, at 14–16.

[364] *See* Ajita Banerjie, *How the Transgender Bill Discriminates Against the Very People It Claims to Protect*, CARAVAN (Aug. 16, 2016), https://caravanmagazine.in/vantage/transgender-bill-discriminates-people-claims-protect.

[365] This political move is akin to Jasbir Puar's concept of homonationalism. *See* JASBIR K. PUAR, TERRORIST ASSEMBLAGES: HOMONATIONALISM IN QUEER TIMES (2007); Jasbir Puar, *Rethinking Homonationalism*, 45 INT'L J. MIDDLE EAST STUD. 336 (2013) (noting how the concept, initially developed in the U.S. context, has been deployed in academic and activist projects in India).

[366] Dhrubo Jyoti, *Progressive Modi? The PM Speaks on Transgenders, Dalits, and Kashmir*, HINDUSTAN TIMES (Aug. 18, 2016), https://www.hindustantimes.com/analysis/progressive-modi-the-pm-speaks-on-transgenders-dalits-and-kashmir/story-h4tjMaUjDglh8FSKcWfWtO.html.

or female. Go and meet them. Have meetings and rallies."[367] Modi thus realized the electoral advantage that he might gain from tapping into these marginalized communities and, in the end, his government saw that the Transgender Rights Act was passed.

A writ petition challenging the constitutionality of the Act was filed before the SCI in 2020 and remains pending as of early 2025.[368] Perhaps the SCI will eventually strike down portions of the Act and push the government to make the law more inclusive and less intrusive. But for now, the Modi government casts itself as the champion of transgender rights, with the Prime Minister, in February 2024, declaring in the Lok Sabha: "Those who are on the margins have been reassured that there is a government . . . We have given transgender persons an identity."[369]

D. The Elusive Promise of Same-Sex Marriage

We now turn to the highly politically charged issued of same-sex marriage. The SCI's unanimous decision in *Navtej Johar* (2018) that decriminalized gay sex seemed to presage a progressive judgment in favor of same-sex couples. If India were to follow the jurisprudential path of two of the world's most influential courts, this seemed the natural outcome. The South African Constitutional Court recognized a constitutional right to same-sex marriage in *Minister of Home Affairs v. Fourie* (2005),[370] six years after it decriminalized same-sex relations in *National Coalition for Gay and Lesbian Equality* (1999).[371] In the United States, it took much longer: the Supreme Court gave constitutional recognition to same-sex marriage in *Obergefell* (2015)[372] more than two decades after holding a sodomy ban unconstitutional in *Lawrence* (2003).[373]

The SCI considered the rights of same-sex couples in 2023, five years after its ruling in *Navtej Johar*. While India followed South Africa's timeline, the judgment in *Supriyo @ Supriya Chakraborty v. Union of India* would ultimately not produce a similar result.

1. The Politics of Same-Sex Marriage

Before we discuss the SCI's judgment in *Supriyo*, it is worth noting significant differences in the politics surrounding this case compared to *Navtej Johar*. In the

[367] *Id.*

[368] Swati Bidhan Baruah v. Union of India, Writ Petition (Civil) No. 51/2020 (India).

[369] *"We Worked for Transgender Community, Gave Them an Identity": PM Modi in Lok Sabha*, Times of India (Feb. 10, 2024), https://timesofindia.indiatimes.com/india/we-worked-for-transgender-community-gave-them-an-identity-pm-modi-in-lok-sabha/articleshow/107584910.cms.

[370] Minister of Home Affairs v. Fourie, 2006 (1) S.A. 524 (C.C.) (S. Afr.).

[371] National Coalition for Gay and Lesbian Equality, 1999 (1) S.A. 6 (C.C.).

[372] Obergefell v. Hodges, 135 S. Ct. 2584 (2015).

[373] Lawrence, 539 U.S. 558.

latter case, the Modi government did not seek to defend Section 377 and left its fate to the "wisdom of the Court."[374] This deferral permitted the SCI to maintain a strand of progressive jurisprudence and, hence, at least the appearance of judicial independence. It also enabled the government to distance itself from Section 377—an outdated colonial relic that lacked popular support.

In *Supriyo*, however, the government strongly opposed not only same-sex marriage but also any formal legal recognition of same-unions.[375] It played to the BJP's political base to accuse urban elites of trying to impose Western liberal values on an unwitting Indian society. And public opinion remained divided on same-sex marriage. For instance, a 2019 poll found that only 24 percent of respondents favored same-sex marriage, while 62 percent opposed it.[376] In 2021, India ranked 23rd out of 27 countries surveyed in terms of public support for same-sex marriage, with 44 percent of Indian respondents expressing support.[377] A June 2023 Pew survey found that a narrow majority (53 percent) of those surveyed supported same-sex marriage, while 47 percent opposed. This was a dramatic increase from Pew surveys in 2020 and 2014 in which only 37 percent and 15 percent of respondents, respectively, supported providing such legal recognition to same-sex couples.[378] It also appears that support for same-sex marriage and LGBTQ+ rights generally was not confined to the major metropoles. By 2023, smaller cities like Jodhpur and Palampur were holding pride events.[379]

Yet, these developments and the survey data do not indicate that same-sex marriage enjoyed sufficient public approval to cause the BJP to change its position on this issue. It was no surprise, then, that the government opposed same-sex marriage, nor that it mischaracterized the issue to suit its political ends. In response to the *Supriyo* petitioners seeking legal recognition of their unions, it declared:

[374] *Navtej Johar*, 2018 I.N.S.C. 790 at para. 36 (per Misra C.J.).

[375] *See* Geeta Pandey, *Same-Sex Marriage: India Awaits Historic Supreme Court Verdict*, BBC News (Oct. 16, 2023), https://www.bbc.com/news/world-asia-india-67026910.

[376] *Where Is the Love: 62 Per Cent Indians Say Same-Sex Marriages Not Accepted, Finds Mood of National Poll*, India Today (Feb. 4, 2019), https://www.indiatoday.in/web-exclusive/story/20190204-motn-same-sex-marriage-lgbt-rights-section-377-india-1439545-2019-01-25.

[377] *LGBT+ Pride 2021 Global Survey Points to a Generation Gap Around Gender Identity and Sexual Attraction*, Ipsos (June 9, 2021), https://www.ipsos.com/en/lgbt-pride-2021-global-survey-points-generation-gap-around-gender-identity-and-sexual-attraction. Another 14 percent of Indian respondents supported some kind of legal recognition for same-sex couples. The only countries with lower levels of public support for same-sex marriage than India were South Korea, Turkey, Russia, and Malaysia. Countries with greater levels of support included Mexico, China, and Brazil.

[378] Sneha Gubbala et al., *How People Around the World View Same-Sex Marriage*; Pew Research Center (Nov. 27, 2023), https://www.pewresearch.org/short-reads/2023/11/27/how-people-around-the-world-view-same-sex-marriage.

[379] *See* Rajesh Asnani, *Jaipur Diary: Jodhpur Hosts First LGBTQ Rally*, New Indian Express (June 25, 2023), https://www.newindianexpress.com/thesundaystandard/2023/Jun/25/jaipurdiaryjodhpur-hosts-first-lgbtq-rally-2588254.html; Dhrubo Jyoti, *Social Justice Matters: How a Pride Walk in Palampur Is Breaking Stereotypes*, Hindustan Times (Jan. 1, 2022), https://www.hindustantimes.com/opinion/social-justice-matters-how-a-pride-walk-in-palampur-is-breaking-stereotypes-101641038944972.html.

> The petitions, which *merely reflect urban elitist views*, cannot be compared with the appropriate legislature which reflects the views and voices of far wider spectrum and expands across the country.[380]

These petitioners unwittingly gave credence to the government's characterization of same-sex marriage. Most of them had elite educational backgrounds, maintained high-status (and high-paying) jobs, and were based in major cities. Take the lead petitioners, Supriya Chakraborty (Supriyo) and his partner Abhay Dang. Supriyo was a faculty member at the International Institute of Hotel Management in Hyderabad before starting his own event management company.[381] Abhay received an undergraduate degree from one of the prestigious IITs and, at the time of filing, was a Senior Software Development Manager.[382] After nine years together, they organized a 2-day commitment ceremony in their home city of Hyderabad with 100–150 guests that "fully lived up to the standards of a 'big fat Indian wedding.'"[383]

Many of the other petitioners were married overseas and sought to have those marriages recognized in India. For instance, a gay couple married in Washington D.C. sought to have their marriage recognized under the Foreign Marriage Act, 1969 (FMA).[384] They were denied at the Indian consulate in New York.[385] Another set of petitioners, again both Indian citizens, were legally married in New York but lived in India and sought legal recognition of their union.[386] A third set of petitioners were legally married in Australia in 2018. One of them had an Overseas Citizen of India (OCI) card that permits individuals of Indian origin to live, work, and own property in India. Spouses of OCIs are usually granted the same status. In this case, however, the spouse was denied an OCI card because same-sex marriages were not recognized under Indian law.[387]

Same-sex couples based in India also filed petitions to have their relationships recognized. As with the lead petition, these petitions were filed by couples based in major cities with elite educational and professional backgrounds. Consider, for

[380] Arpan Chaturvedi, *India Government Calls Same-Sex Marriage Appeals "Urban Elitist Views,"* REUTERS (Apr. 17, 2023), https://www.reuters.com/world/india/india-government-calls-same-sex-marriage-appeals-urban-elitist-views-2023-04-17/ (emphasis added).

[381] *See* Supriyo @ Supriya Chakraborty v. Union of India, Writ Petition (Civil) No. 1011/2022, *Petition of Supriyo Chakraborty & Abhay Dang* (filed Nov. 14, 2022) [hereinafter Petitioners' Brief] at para. 6.

[382] *Id.* at para. 9.

[383] *Id.* at para. 39.

[384] Foreign Marriage Act, 1979, § 4 (India) [hereinafter FMA].

[385] Vaibhav Jain v. Union of India, Transfer Petition (Civil) No. 14/ 2023 (originally filed in Delhi High Court, Oct. 2020), at para. 1. A similar petition was filed by two Indian citizens married in Denmark, who wished to have their marriage registered with a view, *inter alia*, to adopt a child in India. *See* Amburi Roy v. Union of India, Writ Petition (Civil) No. __ /2023 (filed Jan. 31, 2023), at paras. 1–13 [hereinafter Roy Petition].

[386] Nitin Karani v. Union of India, Writ Petition (Civil) No. __/2022 (filed Dec. 12, 2022), at paras. 10–20.

[387] Mellissa Ferrier v. Union of India, Transfer Petition (Civil) No. 3007/2022 (originally filed in Delhi High Court, Nov. 11, 2021), at para. 1.

instance, two petitions filed by Delhi-based couples that challenged the constitutionality of the Special Marriage Act, 1954 (SMA), which restricted marriage to heterosexual couples.[388] One half of the first couple was a lawyer and development economist, with two graduate degrees from Harvard.[389] He had experience at the bar, including appearances at the SCI, and consultancy positions with the Indian Ministry of Finance, the World Bank, and the Boston Consulting Group.[390] His partner was pursuing a Ph.D. at the London School of Economics, received an M.Phil. from Cambridge, and had held similarly high-profile consulting jobs.[391] The second petition was filed by two prominent mental health professionals. One was a clinical psychiatrist who founded Children First—one of India's leading child and adolescent health service providers.[392] Her partner earned a graduate degree in psychology before working at Children First as a psychologist and arts-based therapist.[393]

While each of these petitions alleged deeply felt and legally cognizable harms arising out of India's lack of recognition for same-sex couples, they all spoke to the experience of upper middle-class professionals. These petitions did not discuss societal discrimination along other major fault lines in Indian society such as caste, religion, or class. They failed to give voice to India's marginalized LGBTQ+ communities, who were also given short shrift in the government's tendentious framing of this issue as merely urban and elite.

A few petitions, however, countered this narrative. One petition detailed the experiences of a lesbian couple in which one partner, who was from the conservative Jat community in northern India, faced violence and death threats from her family due to her relationship.[394] Another petition, filed by Rituparna Borah, provided a range of testimony to counter the government's framing. A self-described "queer feminist activist" with fifteen years of advocacy experience at the time of filing, Borah hails from an indigenous community in Assam. She had also been part of the "Voices Against Section 377 IPC" coalition that had intervened in previous LGBTQ+ rights cases.[395] Borah and three other petitioners were part of the "National Network of Lesbian, Bisexual, and Intersex (LBI) Women and Trans persons" that had coordinated advocacy efforts on LGBTQ+ issues across India.[396] As they put it:

[388] Special Marriage Act, 1954, § 4 (India) [hereinafter SMA].

[389] Utkarsh Saxena v. Union of India, Writ Petition (Civil) No. __/2022 (filed Dec. 13, 2022), at paras. 3–4 [hereinafter Saxena Petition].

[390] *Id.* at para. 3.

[391] *Id.* at para. 4.

[392] Kavita Arora v. Union of India, Transfer Petition (Civil) No. 2842/2022 (originally filed in Delhi High Court, May 10, 2020), at paras. 15–17.

[393] *Id.* at paras. 20–21.

[394] Kajal v. Union of India, Writ Petition (Civil) No. __/2023 (filed Jan. 18, 2023), at paras. 6–17.

[395] Rituparna Borah v. Union of India, Writ Petition (Civil) No. __/2023, at paras. 1–5 [hereinafter Borah Petition].

[396] *Id.* at paras. 15–16.

> Petitioner Nos. 1–4 have assisted a significant number of . . . [LGBTQ+] couples hailing from all parts of the country, from the remotest of villages to the biggest of metropolis; from all religions, castes and also from adivasi communities. The common thread running through the lives of all LBT couples is the myriad forms of violence that they suffer from their natal families and local communities.[397]

The other six petitioners were couples that had reached out to Borah and other activists in the National Network.[398] Their submissions detailed not only discrimination but also violence they experienced at the hands of local communities and state authorities. These harms largely arose from the intersection of their gender and/or sexuality with socioeconomic status, caste, and other markers of identity.[399]

The Borah petition, then, provided a fuller picture of LGBTQ+ life in India and the range of harms that resulted from the state's failure to provide legal recognition to same-sex couples. But this petition could not counterbalance the sheer weight of the more elite petitioners, whose arguments all coalesced around cosmopolitan conceptions of dignity, free expression, and liberty. And as we shall see, the SCI in *Supriyo* largely framed the issues around these abstract concepts, rather than in the factual record provided by Borah and other petitioners.

2. The *Supriyo* Judgment

As we have seen, Justice Chandrachud championed LGBTQ+ rights in prior cases. He was part of the five-judge bench that unanimously ruled for the petitioners in *Puttuswamy* and *Navtej Johar*. Chandrachud's opinions ventured further than those of his colleagues to recognize harms inflicted on LGBTQ+ groups. For instance, his opinion in *Puttuswamy* raised issues that were not briefed or argued in that case.[400] Chandrachud took it upon himself to criticize the SCI's regressive ruling in *Koushal* and to detail how the absence of a constitutional right to privacy harmed gender and sexual minorities. In *Navtej Johar*, he surveyed a wide array of academic and foreign sources to recognize, *inter alia*, intersectional and indirect discrimination in violation of Article 15 of the Constitution. His *Navtej Johar* opinion also laid the groundwork for a progressive judgment on same-sex relationships. There, Justice Chandrachud held that the "choice of whom to partner" was "intrinsic to the constitutional protection of same-sex orientation."[401]

On November 9, 2022, Chandrachud became Chief Justice. In his first month as CJI, the Court released a "Sensitisation Module for the Judiciary on the

[397] *Id.* at para. 18.
[398] *Id.* at para. 17.
[399] *Id.* at paras. 22–44.
[400] The hearing in *Puttuswamy* was confined to the existence and scope of a constitutional right to privacy. LGBTQ+ issues did not arise. Moreover, a curative petition seeking to reverse *Koushal* was pending before the SCI at the time, so the matter was technically sub judice and should not have been the subject of discussion, much less extensive judicial writing in *Puttuswamy*.
[401] *Navtej Johar*, 2018 I.N.S.C. 790 at para. 156 (per Chandrachud, J.).

LGBTIQA+ Community."[402] The module provided definitions of key gender and sexual orientation-related terms, instructed judges on using appropriate terminology, and recommended protocols for dealing with LGBTQ+ participants in court. Chandrachud also instituted gender-neutral bathrooms at the SCI and made the Court's online portal gender neutral.[403]

These institutional reforms—while significant for the SCI and the judiciary—lacked broader legal significance. With the SCI in turmoil, and his retirement looming in 2024, Chandrachud appears to have been determined to use his powers as CJI to issue a landmark LGBTQ+ rights judgment. To that end, he bypassed ordinary procedures to ensure that the same-sex marriage case was heard and decided before he left the bench.

The writ petition in *Supriyo* was filed on November 14, 2022, and was admitted on November 25, 2022. Given the SCI's enormous workload, it would ordinarily have taken at least three or four years for the petition to be heard, and at least one year more for the judgment to be issued. CJI Chandrachud also took the unusual step of referring the case to a five-judge constitutional bench via an oral observation on January 6, 2023. Ordinarily, the Court issues a referral order explaining the "substantial question" of constitutional interpretation for which a five-judge bench is required.[404] Moreover, if similar matters are pending before the High Courts, the SCI usually waits for the lower courts to issue their rulings before proceeding. In this instance, both the Delhi and Kerala High Courts were in the midst of adjudicating same-sex marriage petitions.

CJI Chandrachud placed *Supriyo* before a constitutional bench without a referral order and without waiting for the lower court cases to conclude. The SCI transferred the pending High Court petitions to itself to create a consolidated same-sex marriage case.[405] The ten-day hearing began on April 18, 2023, and the judgment was issued six months later on October 17, 2023.[406]

[402] Supreme Court of India E-Committee, *Sensitisation Module for the Judiciary on LGBTIQA+ Community*, SUPREME COURT OF INDIA (Nov. 2022), https://cdnbbsr.s3waas.gov.in/s388ef51f0bf911e452e8dbb1d807a81ab/uploads/2023/05/2023050154.pdf.

[403] *See* Rewati Karan, *SC Walks the Talk on LGBTQIA+ Inclusivity, Sets up Gender-neutral Loos, Revamps Online Portal for Advocates*, PRINT (Apr. 13, 2023), https://theprint.in/judiciary/sc-walks-the-talk-on-lgbtqia-inclusivity-sets-up-gender-neutral-loos-revamps-online-portal-for-advocates/1515505/.

[404] INDIA CONST. art. 145(3) (requiring a minimum of five SCI justices to adjudicate "a substantial question" of constitutional interpretation). No referral order was issued in *Navtej Johar* either, though in that case the conflicting two-judge bench judgments in *Koushal* and *NALSA* provided a clear justification to convene a five-judge bench.

[405] Sarthak Gupta, *India Supreme Court Consolidates High Court Same-Sex Marriage Petitions*, JURIST NEWS (Jan. 6, 2023), https://www.jurist.org/news/2023/01/india-supreme-court-transfers-high-court-same-sex-marriage-petitions-to-itself/.

[406] For a detailed timeline and links to many of the petitions in this case, see *Plea for Marriage Equality*, SUPREME COURT OBSERVER, https://www.scobserver.in/cases/plea-for-marriage-equality (last visited May 28, 2024).

The CJI was responsible for this remarkably expedited schedule as well as the composition of the bench. As discussed, the CJI has the master of roster authority, which has been used in some instances to stack the bench in favor of a particular outcome. While it is not clear that CJI Chandrachud did so here, it is notable that he selected four justices from Delhi—India's sprawling capital city with a prominent LGBTQ+ population—to serve with him on the *Supriyo* bench.[407]

With the jurisprudential path paved by *Puttuswamy* and *Navtej Johar*, and the author of the most progressive opinions in those judgments presiding as CJI over a hand-selected bench, the SCI was set to deliver a landmark progressive judgment for same-sex couples.

But the Court did not reach the widely anticipated result.[408] The SCI unanimously held that marriage was not a fundamental right and that excluding same-sex couples from this institution did not violate Article 19(1)(a) (right to freedom of speech and expression) or Article 21 (right to life and personal liberty).[409] The other unanimous holding was that transgender persons have the right to marry opposite-sex spouses.

The justices disagreed on two major issues: (1) whether the state had a positive obligation to recognize same-sex civil unions, and (2) whether same-sex couples could adopt children.[410] On both issues, the Court ruled against same-sex couples. The principal majority opinion was authored by Justice Bhat, on behalf of himself and Justice Kohli. Justice Narasimha wrote separately but made clear that he was "in complete agreement" with Justice Bhat's reasoning and conclusions.[411] CJI Chandrachud, who arrived at the opposite (and more progressive) outcome on those issues, wrote the principal minority opinion. Justice Kaul broadly agreed with the CJI but also penned a short separate opinion.[412]

In ruling that marriage was not a fundamental right, the justices took different routes to the same destination. CJI Chandrachud (with Justice Kaul concurring) pointed out that the state created and regulated the "socio-legal institution of marriage."[413] The petitioners, he said, asked for the Court to recognize the benefits that flowed to married couples through the statutory and regulatory framework as a fundamental right. For CJI Chandrachud, this was not a sufficient basis on

[407] The justices were Ravindra Bhat, S.K. Kaul, Hima Kohli, and P.S. Narasimha. Bhat, Kaul, and Kohli received their law degrees in Delhi, practiced law at the Delhi Bar, and served as judges on the Delhi High Court. Narasimha practiced law at the SCI (located in Delhi) and served as Assistant Solicitor General of India from 2014 to 2018.

[408] *See* Hannah Ellis-Petersen, *Indian Government Labels Same-Sex Marriage Elitist as Supreme Court Hearing Begins*, GUARDIAN (Apr. 18, 2023) (reporting that lawyers and petitioners who brought the case were "optimistic").

[409] *Supriyo*, 2023 I.N.S.C. 920 at para. 340 (per Chandrachud, C.J.), para. 149 (per Bhat, J.).

[410] *Id.*

[411] *Id.* at para. 3 (per Narasimha, J.).

[412] *Id.* at para. 3 (per Kaul, J.).

[413] *Id.* at para. 182 (per Chandrachud, C.J.).

which to confer constitutional status on marriage. Other unenumerated rights that the SCI recognized in past cases like privacy or education were, respectively, necessary to effectuate other fundamental rights or central "to the values that the Constitution espouses."[414] Marriage, according to the CJI, fit into neither category. Thus, if marriage did not exist, the state would not be constitutionally obliged to create such an institution.[415]

Justice Bhat, writing for himself and Justice Kohli, focused instead on the pre-constitutional origins for marriage. As he put it, "[M]arriage existed and exists . . . as an institution prior to the state . . . This implies that state power to regulate marriage does not sit easy with the idea of marriage as a fundamental right."[416] He went on to note the difficulty in operationalizing a fundamental right to marriage, since it would have to apply horizontally to non-state actors (like religious bodies) that confer this status on couples.[417]

Justice Narasimha, for his part, viewed marriage through a pluralist lens. Because marriage was simultaneously regulated by "legislative interventions, customary practices, and religious beliefs," he concluded that it was too restricted to be a fundamental right.[418]

The Court also unanimously upheld the SMA and FMA. For context, the SMA was enacted to permit couples from different religions or castes to marry, while the FMA enabled Indian citizens married abroad to have their marriages recognized and registered under Indian law.[419] These laws coexist in a complex, pluralistic framework governing marriage in India alongside legislation aimed at specific religious groups such as the Hindu Marriage Act, 1955, and the Muslim Personal Law (Shariat Application) Act, 1937.[420]

The petitioners argued, *inter alia*, that the SMA and FMA violated Articles 14 and 15 of the Constitution by excluding same-sex couples from their ambit.[421] Section 4 of the SMA imposes several conditions on couples, including that the "male" must be at least 21 years old and the "female" at least 18 years old.[422] Section 4 of the FMA imposes the same age restrictions but refers instead to the "bridegroom" and the "bride."[423]

[414] *Id.* at para. 184.
[415] *Id.* at paras. 184–86.
[416] *Id.* at para. 45 (per Bhat, J.).
[417] *Id.* at paras. 45–46.
[418] *Id.* at para. 12 (per Narasimha, J.).
[419] *See* Akshat Agarwal, *Marriage Equality in India: Thinking Beyond Judicial Challenges to Secular Marriage Law*, 6(2) INDIAN L. REV. 170, 172–76 (2022).
[420] *See generally*, Flavia Agnes, *Personal Laws*, *in* OXFORD HANDBOOK OF THE INDIAN CONSTITUTION, *supra* note 18, at ch. 50; FARRAH AHMED, RELIGIOUS FREEDOM UNDER THE PERSONAL LAW SYSTEM (2016).
[421] Petitioners' Brief, *supra* note 381, at paras. II–XXX.
[422] SMA, *supra* note 388, at § 4.
[423] FMA, *supra* note 384, at § 4. In addition, §§ 13 and 18 of the FMA use the terms "husband" and "wife," as do several provisions of the SMA including §§ 2, 12, 15, 22, and 23.

The justices agreed that these statutes had discriminatory effects on same-sex couples but held that it was either unwise or beyond the Court's power to grant a remedy. CJI Chandrachud, for instance, said "this Court would be required to extensively read words into numerous provisions of the SMA" which it was "not equipped to undertake . . . because of its institutional limitations."[424] With respect to interpreting the FMA in a gender-neutral way, the CJI reached the same conclusion: "[S]uch an exercise would amount to judicial legislation."[425]

Justice Kaul declared that the Section 4 of the SMA violates the right to equality in Article 14 of the Constitution.[426] He then demurred, noting the "multifarious interpretive difficulties in reading down the SMA to include marriages between non-heterosexual relationships" and agreeing with the CJI that "due to limited institutional capacity, this Court does not possess an adequate form of remedy."[427]

Justice Bhat, meanwhile, applied the usual two-prong test to determine if the SMA's classification between same-sex and opposite-sex couples withstood Article 14 scrutiny.[428] He noted that "exclusion or under inclusion" were not discriminatory *per se*.[429] The SMA's exclusion of same-sex couples, he ruled, was not motivated by animus but by an intention to "enable marriage (as it was understood then, i.e., for heterosexual couples) for persons belonging to *different faiths*."[430] Justice Bhat further found that the gendered language in both Acts evinced a clear purpose: to solemnize marriages "between *a man and a woman*."[431] Thus, following CJI Chandrachud and Justice Kaul, he held that it was not permissible for the Court to rewrite the SMA and FMA by substituting gender neutral language for terms like "husband" and "wife."[432]

On the question of same-sex civil unions, CJI Chandrachud arrived at a more progressive conclusion. Here, he shed the cautious register of judicial restraint and returned to the soaring language that characterized his opinions in *Puttuswamy* and *Navtej Johar*. Building on those judgments, he ruled that same-sex unions were constitutionally protected through a combined reading of several constitutional rights. These include the right to non-discrimination (Article 15), freedom of speech and expression (Article 19(1)(a)), freedom to form associations (Article 19(1)(c)), and the right to life and personal liberty (Article 21).[433]

[424] *Supriyo*, 2023 I.N.S.C. 920 at para. 208 (per Chandrachud, C.J.).
[425] *Id.* at para. 210.
[426] *Id.* at para. 16 (per Kaul, J.).
[427] *Id.* at paras. 17–18.
[428] The two prongs are: (1) that there should be a reasonable classification based on intelligible differentia and (2) the classification should have a rational nexus with the objective sought to be achieved.
[429] *Supriyo*, 2023 I.N.S.C. 920 at paras. 79–82 (per Bhat, J.).
[430] *Id.* at para. 82 (emphasis in original).
[431] *Id.* at para. 99 (emphasis in original).
[432] *Id.* at paras. 99–100. Justice Narasimha agreed with Justice Bhat's reasoning. *See id.* at para. 4 (per Narasimha, J.).
[433] *Id.* at paras. 219, 223, 233, 252 (per Chandrachud, C.J.).

CJI Chandrachud also creatively interpreted two other rights—not invoked in past LGBTQ+ judgments—to confer protection on same-sex couples. First, he read Article 19(1)(e) of the Constitution, which grants citizens the right to "reside and settle" in any part of India, to include the right for LGBTQ+ persons to build a life "in a place of their choosing" and to "settle down . . . by entering into a lasting relationship" with whoever they choose.[434] Second, he invoked the "freedom of conscience," which is enshrined in Article 25—a provision aimed at protecting religious freedom. As Chandrachud explained, "All persons, including members of the queer community, have the right to judge the moral quality of their actions in their own lives, and . . . have the right to act on their judgment in a manner they see fit."[435]

Thus, CJI Chandrachud concluded that the right to form a union extends to all persons. The state's failure to recognize same-sex unions, and the benefits that flow therefrom, had a "disparate impact on queer couples."[436] He held that the state was obligated to provide recognition to same-sex unions and provide them with concomitant legal benefits.

Justice Kaul concurred on this issue. But his opinion focused on the societal benefits that would accrue from such recognition, including challenging "culturally ordained gender roles" and increasing "queer participation in public spaces" that in turn "will help facilitate an expansive social dialogue, cutting across communities and generations."[437]

Justice Bhat's opinion largely echoed Chandrachud's analysis on this issue, but he disagreed as to the remedy. Justice Bhat included a subsection titled "Discriminatory Impact on Queer Couples" where he found that the denial of marital benefits to same-sex couples had an "adverse discriminatory impact."[438] He also concluded that the "right to cohabit and live in a relationship in the privacy of one's home is fundamental, and enjoyed by all."[439]

Justice Bhat, however, would not require the state to recognize same-sex civil unions. He distinguished this case from other major fundamental rights judgments, including *Vishaka* and *NALSA*, where the SCI, respectively, issued guidelines toward a legal framework on sexual harassment and directed the state to protect transgender rights.[440] He said that those approaches would not work in *Supriyo* because the Court here "would have to fashion a parallel legal regime . . . [that] would cast responsibilities upon private citizens and not merely the state."[441] This legal regime would require "new umbrella legislation" as well as "amendments to

434 *Id.* at para. 226.
435 *Id.* at para. 239.
436 *Id.* at para. 340.
437 *Id.* at paras. 30–33 (per Kaul, J.).
438 *Id.* at para. 114 (per Bhat, J.).
439 *Id.* at para. 117.
440 *See Vishaka*, (1997) 6 S.C.C. at 251; *NALSA*, (2014) 5 S.C.C. 438 at para. 129.
441 *Supriyo*, 2023 I.N.S.C. 920 at para. 145 (per Bhat, J.).

existing statutes, rules, and regulations."[442] Such "policy decisions," he said, should be "left to the realm of the legislature and executive."[443]

A similar split emerged on adoption rights. Petitioners had challenged the constitutionality of the Juvenile Justice Act, 2015, which only permitted "couples" to adopt children,[444] as well as related regulations that required couples to be in a "stable marital relationship" for at least two years to be eligible.[445] All five justices agreed that these provisions indirectly discriminated against same-sex couples. But only CJI Chandrachud joined by Justice Kaul interpreted the term "couples" in the Act to include same-sex couples and would have struck down the corresponding regulations.[446] The other three justices, led by Justice Bhat, ruled that the Act applied only to married couples and upheld the regulations.[447]

For Justice Bhat, this issue, like same-sex civil unions, was best left to the political branches. He said that addressing the various concerns raised in this case "would require a comprehensive study . . . involving a multidisciplinary approach and polycentric resolution, for which the court is not an appropriate forum to provide suitable remedies."[448] Justice Bhat noted that the government had declared in the hearing that it would set up a "high-powered committee chaired by the Union Cabinet Secretary" to conduct this study.[449] He left it up to this committee to determine what relief, if any, to provide those affected by existing restrictions on marriage and adoption, as well as by the lack of legal recognition of same-sex unions.

Finally, on the issue of transgender marriage, the SCI confirmed that existing law recognized marriages involving transgender persons "in a heterosexual relationship."[450] CJI Chandrachud discussed the issue in depth, noting that the passage of the Transgender Rights Act 2019 sought to implement the *NALSA* judgment and combat discrimination against India's transgender communities.[451] He then provided a harmonious interpretation of this Act and the various laws governing marriage in India, including the SMA. The CJI noted that the terms "bride" and "bridegroom," "wife" and "husband," "male and female" differentiated on the basis of sex rather than gender.[452] Thus, he concluded that transgender persons in heterosexual relationships—such as between a cisgender man and transgender woman or between a transgender man and woman—were allowed to marry under any of India's marriage laws, including the personal laws.[453]

[442] *Id.* at para. 148.
[443] *Id.*
[444] Juvenile Justice Act, 2015, § 57 (India).
[445] Central Adoption Resource Agency (CARA) Adoption Regulations, § 5(3) (India).
[446] *Supriyo*, 2023 I.N.S.C. 920 at para. 340 (per Chandrachud, C.J.).
[447] *Id.* at para. 149 (per Bhat, J.).
[448] *Id.*
[449] *Id.*
[450] *Id.* at para. 277 (per Chandrachud, C.J.).
[451] *Id.* at paras. 265–74.
[452] *Id.* at paras. 275–77.
[453] *Id.* at para. 277. Justice Bhat concurred. *See id.* at para. 119 (per Bhat, J.). Justices Kaul and Narasimha did not discuss this issue.

3. Echoes of *Koushal*

All told, for a judgment that promised to follow the path laid by *Puttuswamy* and *Navtej Johar*, *Supriyo* ultimately resembled the much-maligned *Koushal* judgment. For a Court once dubbed the "most powerful in the world," it was striking to see all five justices here choosing to uphold the SMA and FMA after acknowledging that these statutes had discriminatory effects on same-sex couples. CJI Chandrachud noted the strangeness of this posture, including its inversion of the legal ruling and the remedy. He said:

> We are conscious that the court usually first determines if the law is unconstitutional and proceeds to decide on the relief. However, in this case, an exercise to determine whether the SMA is unconstitutional . . . would be futile because of the limitations of this Court's power to grant a remedy.[454]

The CJI went on to invoke the separation of powers and judicial restraint—the very principles underlying the *Koushal* judgment that he and his colleagues criticized in *Puttuswamy* and *Navtej Johar*. Echoing *Koushal*, Chandrachud concluded that it was left for "Parliament to determine" if the SMA should be changed and that the Court "must be careful not to tread into the legislative domain."[455]

Similarly, Justice Bhat's principal opinion only directed the government to create a "high-powered committee" that should take account "all relevant factors" and the views of "all stakeholders."[456]

This vague guidance did not require the government to implement any new legislation, nor did it provide any remedies for same-sex couples. Though the Court unanimously found that they were subject to discrimination, these couples will continue to experience both the dignitary and material harms resulting from the lack of legal recognition for their relationships.

By leaving this unconstitutional discrimination unaddressed, the *Supriyo* bench also contradicted its own precedents. It was disingenuous for the SCI to claim that it lacked the authority to impose an obligation on the government to recognize same-sex civil unions, when its precedents establish that (1) fundamental rights violations require a remedy; and (2) that the Court has broad remedial power, including—as we saw in *NALSA*—to issue binding directions for the state to enact appropriate legislation. The specific form of that legislation might have been left to the political branches, especially given the polycentric nature of the issue and the complex legal framework on marriage in India. Again, *NALSA* is instructive. The Transgender Rights Act 2019 departed substantially from the judgment because the SCI did not provide specific guidance. Considering how the Act turned out,

[454] *Id.* at para. 208 (per Chandrachud, C.J.).
[455] *Id.*
[456] *Id.* at para. 149 (per Bhat, J.).

perhaps the Court should have been more specific.[457] To be sure, that would have raised genuine separation of powers and institutional competence concerns. Such concerns did not arise in *Supriyo*, as the Court abdicated its responsibility to enforce fundamental rights.

Supriyo also resembled *Koushal* in its reluctance to draw on foreign legal sources. This is most apparent in Justice Bhat's principal opinion. As to whether marriage was a fundamental right, Justice Bhat reviewed the American case law on this question. He made the following observation:

> Many decisions by the US courts, have underlined the rationale for declaring the right to marry a fundamental right as being essential to the orderly pursuit of Happiness (as it appears in their Declaration of Independence) by free persons. This strand of reasoning is apparent from *Loving* to *Obergefell*.[458]

He said that this reasoning "is not sound" because the "importance of something to an individual does not *per se* justify considering it as a fundamental right."[459]

Justice Bhat mispresented the holding in *Obergefell*. As an initial matter, the Declaration of Independence played only a marginal role in the U.S. Supreme Court's marriage jurisprudence and did not even appear in Justice Kennedy's majority opinion in *Obergefell*. It only appeared in the dissenting opinions in that case.[460] More importantly, marriage's importance to individuals was not the sole basis on which American courts concluded that it was a fundamental right. Justice Kennedy in *Obergefell* derived four principles from the Supreme Court's precedents. One of them was "its importance to the committed individuals."[461] But the other three were no less important and could arguably inform the Indian context. They included: (1) that the choice of whom to marry is "inherent in the concept of individual autonomy," (2) that marriage "safeguards children and families," and (3) that "marriage is a keystone of our social order."[462]

Thus, while Justice Bhat ostensibly distinguished *Obergefell*, he did not actually engage with the majority opinion and, in fact, wrongly described its ruling. Later in his opinion, Justice Bhat summarily dismissed other foreign precedents, including the South African Constitutional Court's judgment in *Fourie*. He noted his agreement with "the reasoning given by . . . [the] Chief Justice that our courts should exercise caution when relying on the law in other jurisdictions. We should

[457] *See* Tarunabh Khaitan, *NALSA v Union of India: What Courts Say, What Courts Do*, UK Const. L. Ass'n (Apr. 24, 2014), https://ukconstitutionallaw.org/2014/04/24/tarunabh-khaitan-nalsa-v-union-of-india-what-courts-say-what-courts-do/.

[458] *Supriyo*, 2023 I.N.S.C. 920 at para. 48 (per Bhat, J.).

[459] *Id.* at para. 39.

[460] *Obergefell*, 135 S. Ct. at 2627 (Scalia, J., dissenting), 2639 (Thomas, J., dissenting).

[461] *Id.* at 2599.

[462] *Id.* at 2599–2601.

be mindful of distinct contextual framework within which those decisions have been given."[463]

Justice Bhat's language is reminiscent of *Koushal*, which had warned against applying foreign judgments to determine the constitutional of Indian law. But the most surprising aspect of Justice Bhat's discussion of this issue is that it paralleled what the Chief Justice wrote. In *Supriyo*, the CJI Chandrachud—who adopted the most cosmopolitan approach of any justice in *Puttuswamy* and *Navtej Johar*—suddenly changed course. He said, "[C]ourts in India must be circumspect in relying on the law in other jurisdictions, torn from the context in which those decisions have been crafted."[464] A generous reading of this about-face is that he is referring specifically to the use of foreign law in informing the constitutional recognition of marriage, which is a peculiarly context-specific and multifaceted institution. But CJI Chandrachud's analysis of foreign judgments, especially the South African Constitutional Court's decision in *Fourie*, do not support this reading. As he pointed out, the South African Marriage Act had a provision that referred to heterosexual relationships,[465] much like the SMA and FMA. It used terms like "husband," "wife," "bride," and "bridegroom."[466] So, on what basis did CJI Chandrachud distinguish *Fourie*? He identified two grounds, both of which were dubious.

First, he noted that "various provisions of the SMA (Sections 4, 27(1A), 31, 36, and 37) confine marriage to a union between heterosexual persons" as opposed to only one provision that did this in the South African statute.[467] This is a distinction without a difference. Both the Indian and South African legislation defined marriage in heterosexual terms. That the SMA did so repeatedly indicates only, if anything, that it is more constitutionally suspect than its South African counterpart.

Second, CJI Chandrachud pointed out that when the *Fourie* judgment was issued, South Africa already recognized same-sex civil unions. This does not bear on question of whether a statute that excludes same-sex couples from marriage should be upheld. Indeed, the CJI and his colleagues all recognized that, by confining marriage to opposite-sex couples, the SMA and FMA indirectly discriminated against same-sex couples. This is precisely what the South African Constitutional Court found in their context.[468] The difference was that the South African Court did not shirk the remedy. Justice Sachs' majority opinion held the relevant statute unconstitutional.[469] But, in light of polycentricity and separation of powers-based concerns, he suspended the declaration of invalidity for one year to enable the

[463] *Supriyo*, 2023 I.N.S.C. 920 at para. 106 (per Bhat, J.).
[464] *Id.* at para. 203 (per Chandrachud, C.J.).
[465] Marriage Act, No. 25 of 1961 § 30(1) (S. Afr.).
[466] SMA, *supra* note 388, at § 4; FMA, *supra* note 384, at § 4.
[467] *Supriyo*, 2023 I.N.S.C. 920 at para. 197 (per Chandrachud, C.J.).
[468] *Fourie*, 2006 (1) S.A. 524 (C.C.) at para. 114 (per Sachs, J.).
[469] *Id.* at para. 120.

South African Parliament to enact legislation that would recognize same-sex marriage.[470] Justice Sachs laid out in detail the various options available to Parliament, but made clear that if it failed to legislate within twelve months, gender-neutral language would be added to the existing Marriage Act to permit same-sex marriage.[471] As it turned out, Parliament complied. South Africa's Civil Union Act came into effect on November 30, 2006, precisely one year after *Fourie* was published on December 1, 2005.[472]

VI. Conclusion: Institutional and Reputational Self-Preservation

After *Navtej Johar* (2017), India seemed poised to follow South Africa in granting constitutional recognition to same-sex marriage only a handful of years later. The SCI's precedents pointed in a progressive direction. And the Court went out of its way to hear a case on same-sex marriage. CJI Chandrachud ensured that the matter would be heard on an expedited schedule, before a carefully selected five-judge bench. Despite all this, *Supriyo* failed to deliver on the promise of same-sex marriage. The judgment did not even recognize an alternate form of legal recognition for same-sex couples. The SCI directed the government only to form a "high-powered committee" and to consult the relevant stakeholders. There was no timeline prescribed, nor was the government required to enact legislation to remedy the discrimination against same-sex couples that the Court had unanimously recognized.

One might argue that the Court reached opposite outcomes in *Navtej Johar* and *Supriyo* because the latter involved more politically and legally complex issues. Section 377 was an unpopular provision—so unpopular that the Modi government did not defend its constitutionality. The SCI could also read down that law without worrying about the downstream legal effects. Decriminalizing sex between consenting adults did not raise a host of other concerns. By contrast, same-sex marriage remains a deeply divisive issue in Indian society. And marriage in India, unlike Section 377, touches upon multiple sources of law and legal frameworks. The institution is regulated by a patchwork of personal and civil laws, which made it difficult for the Court to issue a remedy without cascading (and possibly unintended) legal effects.

But this explanation is, at best, incomplete. The SCI could have ordered the government, after its "high-powered committee" considered the various issues in

[470] *Id.* at para. 161. Justice Sachs' opinion was joined by all the other justices on the bench, except Justice O'Regan, who agreed with his reasoning, but wanted a stronger remedy. She would have struck down the impugned provision of the Marriage Act with "immediate prospective effect." *Id.* at para. 173 (per O'Regan, J.).

[471] *Id.* at paras. 132–61 (per Sachs, J.).

[472] Civil Union Act, No. 17 of 2006 (S. Afr.) (permitting same-sex couples to marry or form civil unions).

detail, to enact legislation on same-sex civil unions. In addition (or alternatively), the SCI could have read down the gendered language in the SMA and FMA and struck down their onerous notice requirements, without touching upon personal laws or other issues within India's complex legal framework on marriage.[473] To mitigate separation of powers or backlash-related concerns, the Court could have suspended these orders for one or two years to give the government a chance to legislate, much like the South African Constitutional Court had done in *Fourie*. But the SCI chose none of these paths and declined to force government's hand. All of this suggests that a broader shift took place in Indian constitutional politics.

As discussed in Part V, the SCI has weathered a combination of internal crises and undue political influence over the past decade. By declining to stand up against the Modi government's blatant constitutional violations in other domains, and in failing to hold its own justices (including at least two CJIs) accountable for their misdeeds, the Court's reputation for impartiality and integrity was severely damaged. Meanwhile, the government had exerted influence over judicial appointments, by blocking well-qualified nominees that it opposed and pushing through problematic nominees that it supported. The government had also lured justices, including a former CJI, with political appointments upon their retirement from the bench.

Thus, by 2023—when *Supriyo* was decided—the SCI had little left of its institutional independence and its once-vaunted public reputation. It is no surprise that the Court adopted a self-preservationist approach. It deferred to the government in *Supriyo* as it had done on other high-stakes constitutional matters in this era. It was, after all, the Solicitor General who proposed that the government form a committee to consider same-sex unions. A majority of the Court was content to simply endorse this plan, rather than order the government to do more than it had offered.

Another indication of the Court's unwillingness in *Supriyo* to confront the government was its refusal to hear constitutional challenges to the notice and objections regime within the SMA. The SMA enables intercaste and interreligious marriage in India but requires couples to provide written notice in a "conspicuous" public place at least thirty days before they officially marry.[474] In that period, anyone can object to the marriage.[475] District marriage officers may prohibit marriages under the SMA if they uphold such objections.[476] This regime not only prevented many couples from entering unions of their choice but also led to harassment, intimidation, and violence against those seeking to enter marriages

[473] *See* Aishwarya Singh et al., *A Pathway for the Supreme Court in Ensuring Marriage Equality*, WIRE (Apr. 18, 2023), https://thewire.in/law/a-pathway-for-the-supreme-court-in-ensuring-marriage-equality.

[474] SMA, *supra* note 388, at §§ 5, 6.

[475] *Id.* at § 7.

[476] *Id.* at § 8.

that departed from patriarchal and casteist social norms.[477] The BJP government and its reactionary allies also used this notice provision to thwart Hindu-Muslim marriages, which they used to fan the "Love-Jihad" conspiracy theory of Muslim men seeking to marry unsuspecting Hindu women and convert them to Islam.[478]

For these reasons, at least three petitions in *Supriyo* challenged the SMA's notice and objections regime.[479] They argued, *inter alia*, that the regime violates the right to privacy of couples seeking to marry under the SMA and that it indirectly discriminates against gender and sexual minorities, whose relationships are frequently subject to opposition and violence.[480] Despite the evidence and *prima facie* constitutional violations presented to the SCI, the Court refused to hear arguments on this issue and did not address it in the *Supriyo* judgment.[481] The most plausible explanation for this judicial silence is that the Court did not wish to oppose the Modi government on this important plank of its social and religious agenda.

The *Supriyo* judgment thus resembles *Koushal* more than *Navtej Johar*, *Puttuswamy*, or *NALSA*. Like *Koushal*, the majority in *Supriyo* leant on the crutch of judicial restraint and overstated separation of powers concerns to leave *prima facie* discrimination unremedied. *Supriyo* also followed *Koushal* in its glib dismissal of foreign cases, especially *Fourie*, that might have led to a more progressive judgment that accorded with the SCI's precedents in this area.

But in one significant aspect, *Supriyo* diverges from *Koushal*. The latter infamously referred to India's LGBTQ+ groups as a "miniscule fraction" of the country's population and referred to their "so-called rights."[482] This contemptuous language implied that LGBTQ+ persons were not worthy of the SCI's attention. It also indicated that *Koushal* judgment—that upheld Section 377 despite all the evidence of its discriminatory effects—was driven, at least in part, by judicial animus.

While *Supriyo* similarly failed to remedy *prima facie* discrimination, it was not dismissive of the real challenges that same-sex couples, and LGBTQ+ persons generally, faced in Indian society. All the justices expressed empathy and concern for those affected by India's exclusionary marriage laws. This was not surprising with respect to CJI Chandrachud, whose past opinions had discussed the dignity

[477] *See* Rehan Mathur, *The Notice Regime Under the Special Marriage Act*, CONST. L. & PHIL. (May 17, 2023), https://indconlawphil.wordpress.com/2023/05/17/guest-post-the-notice-regime-under-the-special-marriage-act; Namita Bhandare & Surbhi Karwa, *How the Special Marriage Act Is Killing Love* (Oct. 19, 2020), ARTICLE 14, https://www.article-14.com/post/how-the-special-marriage-act-is-killing-love.

[478] *See, e.g.*, Hannah Ellis-Petersen & Ahmer Khan, *"They Cut Him into Pieces": India's "Love Jihad" Conspiracy Theory Turns Lethal*, GUARDIAN (Jan. 21, 2022), https://www.theguardian.com/world/2022/jan/21/they-cut-him-into-pieces-indias-love-jihad-conspiracy-theory-turns-lethal.

[479] *See* Saxena Petition, *supra* note 389; Borah Petition, *supra* note 395; Roy Petition, *supra* note 385.

[480] *See* Saxena Petition, *supra* note 389, at paras. 56–79.

[481] *Supriyo*, 2023 I.N.S.C. 920 at para. 40 (per Chandrachud, C.J.) ("[S]ome senior counsel and counsel sought to address this Court on the 'notice and objections regime' in the SMA . . . This Court has not heard arguments on this issue in the present proceedings").

[482] Koushal, (2014) 1 S.C.C. 1 at para. 43.

and moral worth of LGBTQ+ persons in depth. In *Supriyo*, his moral concern was most apparent in the discussion of same-sex civil unions. Citing Principle 24 of the Yogyakarta Principles on the right to found a family, he wrote:

> Depriving someone of the freedom to choose their life partner robs them of their autonomy, which in turn is an affront to their dignity. Preventing LGBTQ+ individuals from entering into unions also has the result of denying (in effect) the validity of their sexuality because their sexuality is the reason for such denial. This, too, would violate the right to autonomy which extends to choosing a gender identity and sexual orientation.[483]

CJI Chandrachud's opinion even included a section titled "Queerness is not urban or elite." Pushing back against the government's characterization of the issue, he referred to academic scholarship, newspaper reports, and evidence provided by petitioners to show LGBTQ+ persons in rural and poor communities, too, experienced stigma and material harms borne out of their gender identity or sexual orientation.[484] He concluded that while "queerness" might be more visible among urban and elite circles, "[t]his only means the marginalized are yet to be heard . . . Persons of any geographic location or background may be queer."[485]

Even the Justices in the majority, who ruled against civil unions and adoption rights for same-sex couples, had kind words for the affected communities. Justice Bhat, for instance, said, "[T]he Court is alive to the feelings of being left out, experienced by the queer community," and that "their desire, for social acceptability . . . we can certainly have deep empathy with."[486] Justice Narasimha, too, declared that he was "not oblivious to the concerns of the LGBTQ+ partners with respect to denial of certain benefits and privileges that are otherwise available only to married couples."[487]

In short, *Supriyo*'s language evokes *Navtej Johar* even though its substance is akin to *Koushal*. The SCI's turn to self-preservation, brought about by its weakened institutional position vis-à-vis the government, helps to explain the ruling in *Supriyo*. But what accounts for the yawning gap between that regressive outcome and the progressive rhetoric? Here, we should recall that judges write for multiple audiences.[488] The SCI's primary audience is the government. This was especially true by 2023, when Modi's autocratic rule left little room for judicial decisions that

483 *Supriyo*, 2023 I.N.S.C. 920 at para. 234 (per Chandrachud, C.J.).

484 *Id.* at paras. 85–94 (citing, *inter alia*, Maya Sharma, Loving Women: Being Lesbian in Unprivileged India (2006); Ruth Vanita, Love's Rite: Same-Sex Marriage in India and the West (2005)).

485 *Supriyo*, 2023 I.N.S.C. 920 at para. 94.

486 *Id.* at paras. 149, 168 (per Bhat, J.).

487 *Id.* at para. 19 (per Narasimha, J.).

488 *See* Lawrence Baum, Judges and Their Audiences: A Perspective on Judicial Behavior (2006); Nuno Garoupa & Tom Ginsburg, *Judicial Audiences and Reputation: Perspectives from Comparative Law*, 47 Colum. J. Transnational L. 452 (2009).

defied the government. *Supriyo* thus not only ruled against same-sex couples on the major issues of civil unions and adoption but also deferred to the government's proposal at the remedial stage.

But the government was not the only audience for whom the justices were writing. An important secondary audience was elites who comprised the justices' broader social and intellectual milieu. This includes the privileged, professional communities from which the lead petitions in *Navtej Johar* and *Supriyo* were drawn. An editorial published by one of the Navtej Johar petitioners, Ritu Dalmia, is revealing here. Dalmia, a celebrity chef "with seven restaurants," made clear that she was "a businesswoman, not an activist."[489] She then laid bare the core of her—and her fellow petitioners'—claims: "We are not asking to be treated as a minority; we're not asking for quotas and reservations; only dignity and privacy to be who we are."[490] Dalmia here sought to distance herself from the *NALSA* petitioners—who did, in fact, ask for reservations—as well as "the Dalits (former 'untouchables'), the Adivasis (indigenous people), the disabled, and so on—the ones that demand quotas and reservations."[491] As Saptarshi Mandal put it, by asking only for recognition, elites like Dalmia could be "victims" and "loftily abjure special treatment," which in turn "garnered massive support from the mainstream media and the intelligentsia" for LGBTQ+ rights.[492]

It is this (mostly) symbolic recognition that the *Supriyo* Court was able to provide to same-sex couples. All five justices recognized their travails and made clear that LGBTQ+ persons enjoyed the protection of the law and had the right to enter relationships, even if those relationships lacked the official sanction and benefits of marriage or civil unions.

Some justices also write for legal scholars and jurists engaged in the project of global constitutionalism. From the 1980s onwards, the SCI engaged in the global community of courts, and its judgments formed part of the comparative constitutional law canon. Many recent SCI justices were socialized into this world. The best example is CJI Chandrachud, who earned a doctorate in comparative constitutional law at Harvard Law School in the 1980s,[493] and whose father served as CJI too. It is clear in his LBGTQ+ jurisprudence especially that he writes, in part, for a global audience. His many references not only to human rights bodies and foreign judgments but also to feminist, queer theory, and other academic literature mark

[489] Ritu Dalmia, *Let's Talk About 377: Law Says I'm a Criminal, That's Unacceptable: Ritu Dalmia*, Hindustan Times (Feb. 5, 2018), https://www.hindustantimes.com/india-news/let-s-talk-about-377-the-law-says-i-m-a-criminal-and-that-s-unacceptable-ritu-dalmia/story-QvWPsqMpZqq7HCF3QcV4TJ.html.

[490] *Id.*

[491] Saptarshi Mandal, *The Fabulous and the Fascist*, Verfassungsblog (Apr. 15, 2024), https://verfassungsblog.de/the-fabulous-and-the-fascist.

[492] *Id.*

[493] *India Supreme Court Justice Offers Public Lecture on Global Social Justice*, U. Hawai'i News (May 31, 2018), https://www.hawaii.edu/news/2018/05/31/chandrachud-global-social-justice-lecture/.

CJI Chandrachud as a true cosmopolitan. He revealed this disposition most clearly in *Navtej Johar*, writing, "The Indian Constitution is based on an abiding faith in those constitutional values. In the march of civilizations across the spectrum of a compassionate global order, India cannot be left behind."[494]

The Court's elite audiences were paying careful attention to the judgment in *Supriyo*. While the outcome might have been disappointing, it could be attributed to the Court's precarious position in an increasingly illiberal and autocratic India. But through empathetic language, the justices were able to demonstrate their continued adherence to liberal constitutionalism both within India and abroad. This rhetoric also signaled that the justices hold progressive views that are consistent with their social milieu.

Maintaining a strain of liberal constitutionalism also enabled the Court to assuage its critics in these elite circles. Take CJI Dipak Misra, who had been accused of unethical conduct. As we saw in Part V, four senior justices took the unprecedented step of holding a joint press conference in January 2018 to criticize his use of the master of roster power. In September that year, the SCI issued some of its most progressive judgments on issues of gender and sexuality, including *Navtej Johar*. CJI Misra wrote powerful opinions for the majority in those cases, which helped boost his (and the Court's) public image in the face of multiple scandals.[495]

In sum, the path of LGBTQ+ rights provides key insights into the evolution of Indian constitutionalism in the twenty-two year period between the initial filing of the *Naz Foundation* petition (2001) and SCI's judgment in *Supriyo* (2023). Consider, first, what it reveals about the government's approach to the Court and to fundamental rights. When the BJP government initially assumed power, it undermined democratic checks on its authority but did not directly confront the Court. The SCI still had reserves of public support and had such a prominent role in Indian life that it was not an attractive political target. As we have seen, the government would go on to undermine the Court by capitalizing on the institution's internal crises and luring justices with retirement benefits. But, at least in the initial years, the government was content to allow the SCI to boost its reputation as a "people's court" on matters like Section 377 that were not central to the Hindu nationalist agenda. In later years, as Modi grew in strength and popular legitimacy and the SCI declined on both counts, the government would strongly oppose same-sex marriage and prevail in the *Supriyo* judgment (2023)which declined to recognize any form of same-sex unions.

Moreover, the BJP and its allies realized that some LGBTQ+ rights issues could be woven into the Hindutva narrative. To that end, it enacted the Transgender

[494] *Supriyo*, 2023 I.N.S.C. 920 at para. 127 (per Chandrachud, C.J.).

[495] *See* Nizam Pasha, *Section 377 Ruling May Be Landmark, But SC Is Yet to Pass the Real Test*, WIRE (Sept. 13, 2018), https://thewire.in/law/supreme-court-377-ruling (referring to *Navtej Johar* ruling as "low-hanging fruit waiting to be plucked by a court increasingly conscious of its public image and the media reportage of its proceedings").

Rights Act 2019, which enabled the Modi government to declare itself the champion of India's gender-diverse communities. The BJP, as discussed, reaped the political rewards of this move. In substance, however, the Act seized on some essentialist language in the *NALSA* judgment to protect only a limited subset of rights and provide narrower recognition of plural gender identities than the SCI—and many gender-diverse communities—had envisioned.

Turning to the SCI, it is difficult to make definitive statements about its institutional or jurisprudential trajectory given the large docket and variability in bench selection. Still, two broad conclusions emerge from the Court's LGBTQ+ rights cases. First, the space between the rhetoric and the impact of SCI's judgments in this area has widened. The Court continues to invoke the language of global constitutionalism even as it has retreated toward self-preservation in the Modi era. With transgender rights transfigured toward Hindu nationalist ends, and the promise of same-sex unions all but extinguished, the soaring rhetoric in *NALSA* and *Supriyo* rings hollow.

Second, while the pre-Modi LGBTQ+ rights jurisprudence was criticized unfairly as elitist and catering only to the large metropoles, the SCI judgments in *Navtej Johar* and *Supriyo* do not escape such critiques. As India has become more economically stratified and elite-dominated under Modi, LGBTQ+ rights petitions admitted by the Court have also come from increasingly elite circles. As opposed to the broad-based social movements from which the *Naz Foundation* and *NALSA* petitions emerged, *Navtej Johar* and *Supriyo* arose out of petitions filed by celebrities and white-collar professionals, respectively. This elitist turn reveals an apex court whose prime concern appears to be reputational. The SCI wants to be seen by privileged segments of Indian society and the international community as advancing liberal values even as much of its constitutional jurisprudence—including money bills, the NRC, Kashmir, and Aadhaar—threatens or subverts those values in practice.

5

LGBTQ+ Rights, Economic Freedom, and the Remaining Fragments of Liberal Constitutionalism in Hong Kong

I. Introduction

A. Background

Hong Kong is sui generis. A Special Administrative Region (SAR) of the People's Republic of China (PRC),[1] Hong Kong is more akin to an independent country than it is to Kansas, Kerala, or Guangdong. The Hong Kong SAR (or HKSAR) governs itself, with an (ostensibly) autonomous political system and an independent judiciary that are distinct from those of Mainland China.[2] It maintains a separate immigration system from the PRC in which it issues its own passports and confers permanent residence (which includes the rights to vote and own property) on citizens from countries around the world.[3] The HKSAR has its own currency, an independent tax system, and trade relationships with foreign governments.[4]

Hong Kong became an SAR of China on July 1, 1997, after 150 years of British colonial rule. Its "high degree of autonomy"[5] is enshrined the Basic Law—Hong Kong's main constitutional document, which incorporates aspects of both liberal and socialist constitutionalism.[6] This hybrid constitutional framework is overlaid upon a free market economy, giving the region a peculiar blend of authoritarian governance in some areas and fierce individualism in others. As one of the four "Asian Tigers" or "Little Dragons" that experienced rapid industrialization and

[1] Xianfa art. 31 (1982) (China) ("The state may establish special administrative regions when necessary").

[2] Basic Law of the Hong Kong Special Administrative Region of the People's Republic of China [hereinafter Basic Law], art. 2.

[3] *Id.* art. 154.

[4] *Id.* arts. 151, 153, 156.

[5] *Id.* art. 2.

[6] For an overview, see Albert Hung-yee Chen & Po Jen Yap, The Constitutional System of the HKSAR: A Contextual Analysis 34–64 (2023).

Courts and LGBTQ+ Rights in an Age of Judicial Retrenchment. Rehan Abeyratne, Oxford University Press.
 DOI: 10.1093/9780191995040.003.0005

high growth from the 1950s to 1990s,[7] Hong Kong's laissez-faire economic system was the jewel coveted by both British and PRC leaders. The British government and business elites wished to maintain their financial hub in East Asia, while the reform-minded Chinese Communist Party of the 1980s and 90s were keen to link their increasingly market-based economy with a global economic powerhouse.[8]

This period marked the triumph of neoliberalism, embodied in the deregulatory and market-friendly policies of the Reagan administration in the United States and the Thatcher government in the United Kingdom.[9] With its low taxes, lax capital controls, and ease of doing business, Hong Kong was admired not only by the economic elites that benefitted from this regime but also by neoliberalism's ideological champions. The prominent University of Chicago Professor Milton Friedman, for instance, visited Hong Kong many times and believed it to be a free market utopia.[10] Friedman even shot the opening scenes of his popular 1980 television show *Free to Choose* in Hong Kong's Victoria Harbour, saying, "[I]f you want to see how the free market really works, this is the place to come."[11]

What Friedman didn't say—but what British and Chinese elites understood—was that Hong Kong's extreme capitalism existed alongside (and depended on) undemocratic government.[12] Hong Kong has never been ruled by a popularly elected government.[13] It transitioned from a colonial government with a British Governor at the helm, to one dominated by local oligarchs and headed by a "Chief Executive."[14] Persistently high levels of income and wealth inequality, a lack of affordable housing, and the relatively meager provision of social services[15] remain unaddressed as the SAR government—like the colonial government before it—does not have to answer for its elite-driven policies at the polls. Meanwhile, civil liberties, including the rights to free expression, press, and assembly, were strictly limited in the colonial era[16] and remained in check ever since.[17]

While democracy was never realized in Hong Kong and even the limited political freedoms have been all but extinguished in recent years, economic liberty has

[7] *See generally*, EZRA F. VOGEL, THE FOUR LITTLE DRAGONS: THE SPREAD OF INDUSTRIALIZATION IN EAST ASIA (1993). The other three "Dragons" are Singapore, South Korea, and Taiwan.

[8] *See* Eric C. Ip, *The Constitution of Economic Liberty in Hong Kong*, 26 CONST. POL. ECON. 307, 313–17 (2015). *See also*, QUINN SLOBODIAN, CRACK-UP CAPITALISM: MARKET RADICALS AND THE DREAM OF A WORLD WITHOUT DEMOCRACY (2023), ch. 1.

[9] *See generally*, GARY GERSTLE, THE RISE AND FALL OF THE NEOLIBERAL ORDER (2022), chs. 4–5.

[10] Jamie Peck, *Milton Friedman's Favorite Economy: Hong Kong in the Neoliberal Imagination*, LPE PROJECT (Mar. 10, 2021), https://lpeproject.org/blog/hong-kong-as-neoliberal-devotional-object/.

[11] *Id. See also*, GONZALO VILLALTA PUIG & ERIC C. IP, THE FREEST MARKET IN THE WORLD: THE CONSTITUTIONAL LOGIC OF ECONOMIC LIBERTY IN CHINA'S HONG KONG 3–4 (2023).

[12] SLOBODIAN, *supra* note 8, at ch. 1; Ip, *supra* note 8, at 315.

[13] For an historical overview of governance in Hong Kong, see STEVE TSANG, A MODERN HISTORY OF HONG KONG 197–208, 228–44 (2015).

[14] Basic Law, art. 43; PUIG & IP, *supra* note 11, at 38; CHEN & YAP, *supra* note 6, at 6–14.

[15] PUIG & IP, *supra* note 11, at 150–66.

[16] *See generally*, MICHAEL NG, POLITICAL CENSORSHIP IN BRITISH HONG KONG: FREEDOM OF EXPRESSION AND THE LAW (1842–1997) (2022).

[17] *See* CHEN & YAP, *supra* note 6, ch. 6.

remained intact. Hong Kong was ranked the freest economy in the world for fifty-three years until falling to second place (behind Singapore) in 2023.[18] In this neoliberal sense, Hong Kong has long been—and continues to be—much freer than either the United States or India.

Courts in Hong Kong, however, operate in a more restricted political and institutional environment than in the other two case studies. Hong Kong maintains a common law legal system, distinct from the socialist civil law system on the Mainland, with its own judiciary.[19] While these courts operate independently for the most part, the National People's Congress Standing Committee (NPCSC)—a powerful, non-judicial body in Mainland China—has the ultimate power of interpretation over the Basic Law.[20] As a result, scholars often characterize constitutional rights adjudication in strategic terms: a balancing act between fundamental rights projection and the "political sensitivities of the central government in Beijing."[21]

Despite Beijing's looming presence, judicial review in Hong Kong operates in liberal constitutional terms. Fundamental rights are recognized and are justiciable under the Basic Law and the Bill of Rights Ordinance (BORO).[22] The latter was enacted in 1991 to make the International Covenant on Civil and Political Rights (ICCPR) domestically enforceable in Hong Kong.[23] BORO served to assure the Hong Kong people and, more importantly, British and other international business elites that Hong Kong would continue to abide by international human rights standards and protect private property following the handover of Hong Kong's sovereignty from Britain to China in 1997.[24]

Constitutional rights adjudication in Hong Kong has long been a cosmopolitan endeavor. Its judges look to foreign sources more than their counterparts in the United States or India, and frequently cite British, Canadian, and European authorities.[25] Moreover, Hong Kong (unlike the other case studies) has adopted structured proportionality analysis to adjudicate fundamental rights. Proportionality initially developed in Germany before migrating across the world

[18] Fraser Institute, Economic Freedom of the World: 2023 Annual Report (2023), https://www.fraserinstitute.org/studies/economic-freedom-of-the-world-21023-annual-report.

[19] Basic Law, arts. 8, 19.

[20] *Id.* art. 158.

[21] Po Jen Yap, Courts and Democracies in Asia 45 (2017). *See also*, Eric C. Ip, *The Democratic Foundations of Judicial Review Under Authoritarianism: Theory and Evidence from Hong Kong*, 12 Int'l J. Const. L. 330 (2014); Swati Jhaveri, *Reconstitutionalizing Politics in the Hong Kong Special Administrative Region of China*, 13 Asian J. Comp. L. 27 (2018); Julius Yam, *Judging Under Authoritarianism*, 87 Modern L. Rev. 894 (2023).

[22] Bill of Rights Ordinance, (1991) Cap. 383 (H.K.) [hereinafter BORO].

[23] For a detailed account of the origins and events leading to the passage of BORO, see The Hong Kong Bill of Rights: A Comparative Approach (Johannes Chan & Yash Ghai eds., 1993).

[24] Richard Swede, *One Territory–Three Systems? The Hong Kong Bill of Rights*, 44 Int'l Comp. L.Q. 358, 359–60 (1995).

[25] David S. Law, *Judicial Comparativism and Judicial Diplomacy*, 163 U. Penn. L. Rev. 927, 986–90 (2015).

to become the most widely used test to adjudicate rights claims.[26] Proportionality is an intrusive form of judicial review. In contrast to earlier, more deferential standards such as *Wednesbury* unreasonableness, it requires the government to provide evidence and reasons to justify restrictions on fundamental rights.[27]

B. Chapter Overview

This chapter examines how Hong Kong courts, wielding proportionality analysis in a constrained environment, have strategically advanced LGBTQ+ rights as the political and legal ground has shifted beneath them. Part II provides a brief overview of the constitutional framework that existed from the handover of sovereignty in 1997 until 2019. In this period, Hong Kong courts proceeded cautiously when operating in the shadow of the NPCSC and on politically sensitive matters such as the freedom of expression and assembly.[28] They also became increasingly deferential to the government in their application of proportionality analysis.[29]

Nonetheless, Hong Kong courts developed a reputation for independence and expanded the scope of several constitutional rights, including voting, travel, and social welfare rights. LGBTQ+ rights was a major site for progressive judicial decision-making. As Part III will show, courts from 1997 to 2019 were able to strike down colonial laws on sexual relations and incrementally expand the recognition and benefits of marriage without inviting censure from the HKSAR government or intervention by the NPCSC. They also relied heavily on foreign judgments from the United Kingdom, Canada, and the European Court of Human Rights (ECtHR), which helped to place Hong Kong squarely within the project of global constitutionalism.

Part IV outlines the major constitutional changes introduced by Beijing in 2020 and 2021, which brought the region more squarely under PRC control, and converted the constitutional system from hybrid to authoritarian. Progressive judicial decisions are now few and far between in Hong Kong. As Part V shows, LGBTQ+ rights appears to be the only remaining domain for courts to rule against the

[26] Vicki C. Jackson, *Constitutional Law in an Age of Proportionality*, 124 YALE L.J. 3094, 3096 (2015); Alec Stone Sweet & Jud Mathews, *Proportionality and Rights Projection in Asia: Hong Kong, Malaysia, South Korea, Taiwan—Whither Singapore?*, 29 SINGAPORE ACAD. L. J. 774, 775 (2017).

[27] *See* MOSHE COHEN-ELIYA & IDDO PORAT, PROPORTIONALITY AND CONSTITUTIONAL CULTURE 2 (2013) (noting two essential features of proportionality: "it is standard-based rather than categorical, and it is results-oriented rather than being a formal and conceptual doctrine").

[28] *See* Po Jen Yap, *10 Years of the Basic Law: The Rise, Retreat, and Resurgence of Judicial Power in Hong Kong*, 36 COMMON L. WORLD REV. 166, 167 (2007); Po Jen Yap, *Twenty Years of the Basic Law: Continuity and Changes in the Geoffrey Ma Court*, 49 HONG KONG L.J. 209, 210 (2019); Albert H.Y. Chen, *Constitutional Adjudication in Post-1997 Hong Kong*, 15 PAC. RIM L. & POL'Y J. 627, 629 (2006).

[29] *See generally*, Rehan Abeyratne, *More Structure, More Deference: Proportionality in Hong Kong*, *in* PROPORTIONALITY IN ASIA 25 (Po Jen Yap ed., 2020). *See also*, Alec Stone Sweet, *The Necessity of Balancing: Hong Kong's Flawed Approach to Proportionality, and Why It Matters*, 50 HONG KONG L.J. 541 (2020).

government in constitutional matters. Post–2020 rulings on transgender rights,[30] housing and estate benefits for same-sex couples,[31] and same-sex unions[32] bear out this trend. These judgments show how Hong Kong courts have built—in a common law, incremental fashion—on their progressive jurisprudence of earlier years. But the judgments are also more self-preservationist than their predecessors in two ways. First, they are strategically attuned to the new political reality. The same-sex union judgment, for instance, did not recognize a constitutional right to same-sex marriage. It held that the Hong Kong government was in violation of its obligation to fulfill the right to privacy of same-sex couples and suspended the declaration of invalidity for two years to enable the government to remedy the violation.[33] This non-confrontational approach is probably wise in the authoritarian context in which Hong Kong courts now operate.

Second, Hong Kong courts want to show that they are not merely rubber stamps. The Court of Final Appeal (CFA), in particular, has developed a strong reputation for independence and comparative engagement.[34] LGBTQ+ rights judgments allow the CFA (and the Hong Kong judiciary generally) to demonstrate independence and continued engagement in the transnational enterprise of global constitutionalism in at least one domain. These judgments also work to the benefit of Hong Kong's government, whose international reputation cratered following its crackdown on public protests in 2019,[35] the passage of a draconian National Security Law (NSL) in 2020,[36] and electoral changes in 2021 that eliminated political opposition.[37] It is helpful for an increasingly authoritarian government to show, especially to critics abroad, that it remains under some liberal constitutional constraints.[38] LGBTQ+ rights judgments are ideally suited to this task, as they garner widespread media attention—especially with respect to same-sex unions—while leaving the government unconstrained on national security and other politically sensitive matters.

The chapter concludes in Part VI by linking LGBTQ+ rights to economic freedom. I argue that an uneasy truce has emerged wherein both the courts and the

[30] Q v. Commissioner of Registration, [2023] H.K.C.F.A. 4.

[31] Infinger v. Hong Kong Housing Authority, [2023] H.K.C.A. 1178; Ng Hon Lam Edgar v. Secretary for Justice, [2023] H.K.C.A. 1224.

[32] Sham Tsz Kit v. Secretary for Justice, [2023] H.K.C.F.A. 28.

[33] *Id.* at para. 260.

[34] *See* Law, *supra* note 25, at 996–97.

[35] *See, e.g.*, Human Rights Watch, *Hong Kong: Crackdown amid COVID-19* (Apr. 20, 2020), https://www.hrw.org/news/2020/04/20/hong-kong-crackdown-amid-covid-19.

[36] Law of the People's Republic of China on Safeguarding National Security in the Hong Kong Special Administrative Region, GN (E) 72 of 2020 (H.K.) [hereinafter National Security Law or NSL]. *See also*, Surabhi Chopra & Eva Pils, *The Hong Kong National Security Law and the Struggle over Rule of Law and Democracy in Hong Kong*, 50(3) FED. L. REV. 292 (2022).

[37] *See* Simon N.M. Young, *Introductory Note to the Decision of the National People's Congress on Improving the Election System of the Hong Kong Special Administrative Region*, 60 INT'L L. MATERIALS 1 (2021).

[38] *See* Tamir Moustafa & Tom Ginsburg, *Introduction: The Functions of Courts in Authoritarian Politics*, *in* RULE BY LAW: THE POLITICS OF COURTS IN AUTHORITARIAN REGIMES 1, 5–7 (Tom Ginsburg & Tamir Moustafa eds., 2012).

political authorities tacitly understand that liberal rights recognition of a limited kind—such as requiring the government to provide a legal framework for same-sex unions—serves the common purpose of making Hong Kong a more attractive place to live and to do business. LGBTQ+ rights therefore help to legitimate not only the HKSAR's courts and authoritarian government but also its iniquitous economic system.

II. Constitutional Adjudication under "One Country, Two Systems" (1997–2019)

A. The Sino-British Joint Declaration and the Basic Law

Hong Kong's transfer from Britain to China in 1997 was managed under the terms of a 1984 treaty: the Sino-British Declaration.[39] Section 3 of the Declaration sets out the broad terms under which Hong Kong would be returned to the PRC. It comprises twelve subsections, most of which relate to the preservation of economic freedom, including that Hong Kong will "retain the status of a free port and a separate customs territory";[40] "retain the status of an international financial centre";[41] "will have independent finances";[42] and "may establish mutually beneficial economic relations with the United Kingdom and other countries."[43] Only one subsection protects "rights and freedoms, including those of the person, of speech, of the press, of assembly," among others.[44] And even that provision ends on a capitalist note, providing, "Private property, ownership of enterprises, legitimate right of inheritance and foreign investment will be protected by law."[45]

In terms of governance, the Declaration made clear that Hong Kong would be "directly under the authority of the Central People's Government."[46] While the region was vested with executive, legislative, and judicial power, it would not have control over foreign affairs or defense matters. This hybrid constitutional framework—colloquially known as "one country, two systems" (OCTS)—was codified in Hong Kong's Basic Law. The Sino-British Joint Declaration stipulated that the "basic policies" comprising OCTS "will remain unchanged for 50 years."[47]

[39] Joint Declaration of the Government of the United Kingdom of Great Britain and Northern Ireland and the Government of the People's Republic of China on the Question of Hong Kong, Dec. 19, 1984, 23391, 1399 U.N.T.S. 33 [hereinafter Sino-British Joint Declaration]. For a comprehensive account of the negotiations, legal effects, and continuing relevance of the Sino-British Joint Declaration, see C.L. Lim, Treaty for a Lost City (2022).

[40] Sino-British Joint Declaration, *supra* note 39, § 3(6).

[41] *Id.* § 3(7).

[42] *Id.* § 3(8).

[43] *Id.* § 3(9).

[44] *Id.* § 3(5).

[45] *Id.*

[46] *Id.* § 3(2).

[47] *Id.* § 3(12).

Not coincidentally, the Basic Law enshrines this sunset clause in primarily economic terms: "[T]he previous *capitalist* system and way of life shall remain unchanged for 50 years." Since the Basic Law came into effect on July 1, 1997, OCTS is supposed to remain in place at least until June 30, 2047.

The Basic Law and OCTS, in theory, require that the HKSAR exercises a 'high degree of autonomy' over its economic, political, and legal affairs.[48] In practice, however, Hong Kong's autonomy (outside the economic realm) has been deeply contested from the outset. Politically, Hong Kong formally divides powers between the executive, legislative, and judicial branches, but it is widely considered, in practice, to have an "executive-led" system.[49] The Chief Executive (CE) is not popularly elected; rather, she is selected by a corporatist, pro-establishment Election Committee, which (prior to 2021) consisted of 1,200 members.[50] The Legislative Council (LegCo) originally comprised sixty seats (increased to seventy in 2012), half of which were selected through similarly corporatist and establishment-leaning functional constituencies. The remaining LegCo members were popularly elected. Hong Kong, therefore, has never been a fully democratic policy. Prior to the illiberal turn in 2020–21, the HKSAR was described as a hybrid,[51] liberal authoritarian,[52] liberal non-democratic,[53] or semi-democratic jurisdiction.[54]

The Basic Law guarantees the independence of the judiciary and created the CFA to replace the Judicial Committee of the Privy Council as the SAR's court of final adjudication.[55] The colonial legal system (including the lower courts) and the laws previously in force in Hong Kong (including the common law) largely remain in place.[56] British rule lasted from the mid-nineteenth century until 1997. As a result, British precedents and principles form the basis upon which Hong Kong courts exercise review over legislation. Judges follow the principle of *stare decisis* in which precedents of the higher courts are binding not only on Hong Kong residents and the other branches of government but also on the courts themselves. Yet, despite this continuity and the fact that the CFA has last word on constitutional interpretation within Hong Kong, the NPCSC retains final interpretive authority over the Basic Law.[57]

[48] Basic Law, art. 2.

[49] *See* CHEN & YAP, *supra* note 6, at 91–93.

[50] ERIC C. IP, HYBRID CONSTITUTIONALISM: THE POLITICS OF CONSTITUTIONAL REVIEW IN THE CHINESE SPECIAL ADMINISTRATIVE REGIONS 15 (2019) ("Beijing can count on an overwhelming majority of Election Committee members . . . to ensure that only an acceptable candidate is chosen as Chief Executive").

[51] *Id.* at 3–10.

[52] Matthew Y.H. Wong, *Party Models in a Hybrid Regime: Hong Kong 2007–2012*, 15 CHINA REV. 67, 69 (2015).

[53] David S. Law, *Alternatives to Liberal Constitutional Democracy*, 77 MD. L. REV. 223, 237 (2017).

[54] *See* ELIZA W.Y. LEE ET AL., PUBLIC POLICYMAKING IN HONG KONG: CIVIC ENGAGEMENT AND STATE-SOCIETY RELATIONS IN A SEMI-DEMOCRACY 1 (2013).

[55] Basic Law, arts. 19, 82.

[56] *Id.* arts. 8, 81.

[57] *Id.* art. 158.

Though the Basic Law is widely regarded to be the "mini-constitution" of the HKSAR,[58] it did not replace BORO and the ICCPR to become the sole reference point in local fundamental rights jurisprudence.[59] The Basic Law is, therefore, distinct from the Bill of Rights in the U. S. Constitution and Part III (Fundamental Rights) of the Indian Constitution, which are the sole textual source of constitutional rights in their respective jurisdictions. Article 39 of the Basic Law provides:

> The provisions of the International Covenant on Civil and Political Rights . . . as applied to Hong Kong shall remain in force *and* shall be implemented through *the laws* of the Hong Kong Special Administrative Region.[60]

In addition to enforcing constitutional rights, Hong Kong courts are explicitly authorized to engage with foreign law.[61] Article 84 of the Basic Law permits courts to "refer to precedents of other common law jurisdictions." Moreover, the Basic Law permits the Chief Justice to invite judges from other common law jurisdictions to sit on the CFA as non-permanent judges.[62] To date, leading jurists from the United Kingdom, Australia, New Zealand, and Canada have served as "overseas non-permanent judges" on the CFA, including Lord Hoffman, Sir Anthony Mason, Lord Cooke, and Chief Justice Beverly McLachlin. Cases are heard by five-judge benches, comprising of the Chief Justice, three permanent (local) justices, and one non-permanent judge (often an overseas judge).[63]

The presence of overseas judges has been a mixed blessing. On one hand, the fact that eminent jurists agreed to serve on the CFA bolstered the Court's reputation as a respected and independent institution.[64] Moreover, foreign judges have on occasion cast the deciding vote on consequential progressive judgments, such as in the 3–2 split decision that required the Hong Kong government to recognize same-sex unions.[65] On the other hand, these judges tend to "parachute" in for a few months every year, treating the role as a cushy retirement sinecure or summer break from their full-time responsibilities on other courts.[66] There is also

[58] HKSAR v. Ma Wai Kwan, David, [1997] H.K.L.R.D. 761 (C.A.); Ng Ka Ling v. Director of Immigration, [1999] 2 H.K.C.F.A.R. 4.

[59] For a detailed analysis of the differences in the text and application of these sources of law, see Dinusha Panditaratne & Rehan Abeyratne, *Basic Law, Hong Kong Bill of Rights and the ICCPR*, *in* LAW OF THE HONG KONG CONSTITUTION (3rd ed., Johannes Chan & C.L. Lim eds., 2021).

[60] Basic Law, art. 39 (emphasis added).

[61] *See* Law, *supra* note 25, at 987.

[62] Basic Law, art. 82.

[63] *See* Simon N.M. Young & Antonio Da Roza, *The Judges*, *in* HONG KONG'S COURT OF FINAL APPEAL 259–61 (Simon N.M. Young & Yash Ghai eds., 2013).

[64] *Id.* at 257, 263–66; Rosalind Dixon & Vicki Jackson, *Hybrid Constitutional Courts: Foreign Judges on National Constitutional Courts*, 57 COLUM. J. TRANSNAT'L L. 283, 292 (2019) (noting that overseas judges on the CFA serve to "bolster its global reputation and independence").

[65] *Sham Tsz Kit*, [2023] H.K.C.F.A. at paras. 257–60.

[66] Jill Cottrell, *Fair Comment, Judges and Politics in Hong Kong*, 27 MELBOURNE U. L. REV. 33, 62 (2003).

something uncomfortably colonial about this arrangement, especially as the Chief Justice has never invited a judge from the Global South (or even a jurist of color) to serve on the CFA. This has made the Court more vulnerable to the criticism—often made in bad faith—that its progressive judgments import "Western" values that are alien to Hong Kong society.[67]

We return to these critiques at the end of this chapter. Let us now turn to the CFA's early constitutional jurisprudence to explore how it navigated the complex political landscape that characterized post-handover Hong Kong.

B. Judicial Deference to the NPCSC

The CFA forcefully asserted its jurisdiction over the Basic Law in its very first constitutional judgment: *Ng Ka Ling v. Director of Immigration* (1999) [*Ng Ka Ling No. 1*]. The Court in this case not only resolved the matter at hand but also opined on scope of its judicial review authority vis-à-vis the NPCSC. As an initial matter, the CFA declared that the Basic Law is a "living instrument intended to meet changing needs and circumstances."[68] Hong Kong courts should therefore adopt a "purposive" approach to Basic Law interpretation and a "generous" approach to fundamental rights and freedoms.[69] The CFA also asserted its authority to "examine whether legislation enacted by the legislature of the Region or acts of executive authorities of the Region are consistent with the Basic Law and, if found to be inconsistent, to hold them to be invalid."[70] This pronouncement of strong-form judicial review authority was uncontroversial given the constitutional status of the Basic Law and the preeminent role it conferred on the CFA.[71]

The Court went on to declare (in obiter) that it had the jurisdiction "and indeed the duty to declare invalidity if inconsistency is found" between "legislative acts of the National People's Congress or its Standing Committee" and the Basic Law.[72] In asserting this broad jurisdiction, the Court made clear that acts of the National People's Congress (NPC) are "acts of the sovereign" but noted that the Basic Law itself was enacted by the NPC pursuant to Article 31 of the PRC Constitution, which allows for the creation of SARs.[73] Having created the HKSAR and the Basic Law as the constitution for the region, the CFA noted that, as with any constitution, acts that are inconsistent with the Basic Law "are of no effect and are invalid."[74]

[67] Stuart Hargreaves, *Canaries or Colonials? The Reduced Prominence of "Overseas Judges" on Hong Kong's Court of Final Appeal*, 16 Asian J. Comp. L. 187, 209–11 (2021).
[68] *Ng Ka Ling No. 1*, (1999) 2 H.K.C.F.A.R. at 28.
[69] *Id.* at 28–29.
[70] *Id.* at 25.
[71] Basic Law, arts. 19(1), 80, 82.
[72] *Ng Ka Ling No. 1*, (1999) 2 H.K.C.F.A.R. at 26.
[73] *Id.*; Xianfa art. 31 (1982) (China).
[74] *Ng Ka Ling No. 1*, (1999) 2 H.K.C.F.A.R. at 26.

It falls upon the courts of the region, which are endowed with "independent judicial power" to adjudicate "questions of inconsistency and invalidity when they arise."[75] The CFA concluded, "It is therefore for the courts of the Region to determine whether an act of the National People's Congress or its Standing Committee is inconsistent with the Basic Law, subject of course to the provisions of the Basic Law itself."[76]

As it turned out, this *obiter dicta* would be the high watermark of the CFA's claim of jurisdiction over acts of the NPC and NPCSC in Hong Kong. The HKSAR government asked the CFA to clarify its judgment in *Ng Ka Ling No. 1*. The CFA responded with a terse second judgment [*Ng Ka Ling No. 2*] in which it conceded that the NPCSC had the authority to issue interpretations under Article 158 of the Basic Law that would bind the Hong Kong courts.[77] But it left open the possibility of holding such interpretations unconstitutional. It said:

> [T]he Court accepts that it cannot question, the authority of the National People's Congress or the Standing Committee to do any act which is in accordance with the provisions of the Basic Law and the procedure therein.[78]

This cleverly worded passage implies that if these institutions were to act contrary to the Basic Law, the Court could call those acts into question. However, the CFA never followed through on this implicit power.

Following *Ng Ka Ling No. 2*, the NPCSC issued an Interpretation of the relevant Basic Law provisions. This Interpretation effectively overruled the CFA's judgment in *Ng Ka Ling No. 1*,[79] and the CFA fell in line, declaring that the NPCSC's power to interpret the Basic Law "is in general and unqualified terms"[80] and that NPCSC Interpretations "can clarify and supplement laws."[81]

Hong Kong courts would show even broader deference to NPCSC Interpretations in later years. Consider, for instance, the legislative oath controversy in 2016. That year, Sixtus Leung and Yau Wai-Ching were elected to the LegCo.[82] Under Article 104 of the Basic Law and the Oaths and Declaration Ordinance, they were required to swear an oath of allegiance to the Basic Law and the HKSAR.[83] However, while taking the oath, Leung and Yau departed from the statutory

[75] *Id.*
[76] *Id.*
[77] Ng Ka Ling v. Director of Immigration (No. 2), [1999] 1 H.K.L.R.D. 577 (C.F.A.).
[78] *Id.* at 578.
[79] Interpretation by the Standing Committee of the National People's Congress Regarding Paragraph 4 in Article 22 and Category (3) of Paragraph 2 in Article 24 of the Basic Law of the Hong Kong Special Administrative Region of the People's Republic of China (June 26, 1999).
[80] Lau Kong Yung v. Director of Immigration, [1999] 3 H.K.L.R.D. 778, 798 (C.F.A.).
[81] Director of Immigration v. Chong Fong Yuen, [2001] 2 H.K.L.R.D. 533, 544 (C.F.A.).
[82] Chief Executive of the HKSAR v. President of the Legislative Council, [2017] 1 H.K.L.R.D. 460, 464 (C.A.).
[83] *Id.* at 464–65.

language by referring to a "Hong Kong nation" and using a derogatory term for China.[84] The oaths were, therefore, declared invalid. While the LegCo President was willing to allow them to retake their oaths, pro-establishment legislators staged a walkout to prevent that from happening. The CE and Secretary for Justice filed legal proceedings on the same day to have Leung and Yau disqualified. While the case was pending before the Court of First Instance (CFI), the NPCSC issued an Interpretation of Article 104.[85]

The Interpretation made clear that "anyone who fails to lawfully and validly take the oath" or "who declines to take the oath" may not assume public office.[86] It further stated that the oath was to be taken "sincerely and solemnly" and "accurately, completely, and solemnly read out."[87] If an oath was determined to be invalid, "no arrangement shall be made for retaking the oath."[88] The CFI subsequently ruled that Leung and Yau should be disqualified from LegCo office.[89]

On appeal, Leung and Yau raised several challenges. The most significant, for our purposes, were the claims they advanced on the scope and breadth of NPCSC jurisdiction. They argued that the NPCSC Interpretation should not be read to have retrospective effect and should therefore not affect this case.[90] They also contended that the Interpretation effectively amended the Basic Law, which would be unconstitutional since the NPCSC did not follow the formal amendment procedures set forth in Article 159 of the Basic Law.[91]

The Court of Appeal, led by Chief Judge Andrew Cheung, rejected these arguments. On the question of retrospective application, the Court said the Interpretation "sets out the true and proper meaning of art. 104 from day one. The question of whether it applies 'retrospectively' to any given set of facts whether pending before the court or not therefore cannot and does not arise."[92] This statement implies that NPCSC Interpretations can be applied to conduct that occurred prior to their publication, as was the case here with the lawmakers' improper oaths.

As to whether the Interpretation constituted a *de facto* amendment to the Basic Law, the Court stated, "this argument does not even get off the evidential ground

[84] Po Jen Yap & Eric Chan, *Legislative Oaths and Judicial Intervention in Hong Kong*, 47 Hong Kong L.J. 1, 3 (2017).

[85] The NPCSC issued this interpretation on its own accord, without a referral from the CFA or the HKSAR government. See Johannes M.M. Chan, *A Shrinking Space: A Dynamic Relationship Between the Judiciary in a Liberal Society of Hong Kong and a Socialist-Leninist Sovereign State*, 72 Current L. Problems 85, 107 (2019).

[86] Interpretation of Article 104 of the Basic Law of the Hong Kong Special Administrative Region of the People's Republic of China by the Standing Committee of the National People's Congress (November 7, 2016) s 2(1).

[87] *Id.* at s 2(2).

[88] *Id.* at s 2(4).

[89] Chief Executive of the Hong Kong Special Administrative Region v. President of the Legislative Council, [2016] 6 H.K.C. 417 (C.F.I.), para. 47.

[90] *Chief Executive of the HKSAR*, [2017] 1 H.K.L.R.D. at 469.

[91] *Id.*

[92] *Id.*

and must be rejected."[93] The Court noted that the NPCSC is governed by the civil law system of Mainland China. Given the differences between that system and the common law system of Hong Kong, the Court said it had no basis on which to judge the "proper scope of interpretation."[94]

At the end of his principal opinion, Chief Judge Cheung discussed in obiter whether the Hong Kong courts ever had the power to review the constitutionality of NPCSC interpretations.[95] He said that apart from references to the *Ng Ka Ling* cases on the right of abode, petitioners' counsel had "simply made no submission on this fundamental question of jurisdiction."[96] He concluded by stating plainly, "In my view, the Court has no jurisdiction to deal with the issue raised."[97]

The CFA declined to grant leave to hear this case, but it provided reasons for that determination. Significantly, it reaffirmed one of its past judgments that held, "The NPCSC's power to interpret the Basic Law is in general and unqualified terms."[98] Further, in dismissing the petitioners' retroactivity claim, it stated, "[The NPCSC] declares what the law is and has always been since the coming into effect of the Basic Law on 1 July 1997."[99] The implication is that the NPCSC's Interpretations are beyond the scope of judicial review in Hong Kong courts and, as the Court of Appeal judgment suggested, courts will not prevent their retrospective application. As Cora Chan put it, "The contrast with the bold position taken in 1999 [in *Ng Ka Ling No. 1*] . . . could not be starker."[100]

C. Judicial Deference to the HKSAR Government

In areas where the NPCSC has not intervened (or threatened to intervene), the Hong Kong judiciary developed a robust constitutional rights jurisprudence from 1997 to 2019. Courts in this era struck down restrictions on prisoner voting rights.[101] They also invalidated eligibility requirements for indigenous village elections[102] and for residents convicted of minor offences seeking to stand for election.[103]

[93] *Id.*

[94] *Id.* (adding that the perspective "of a common law lawyer, untrained in the civil law system . . . is, with respect, quite simply irrelevant").

[95] *Id.*

[96] *Id.* at 479–80.

[97] *Id.* at 480.

[98] Yau Wai Ching v. CE of the HKSAR, 20 H.K.C.F.A.R. 390, para. 35 (2017) (citing *Lau Kong Yung*, [1999] 3 H.K.L.R.D. at 798).

[99] *Id.*

[100] Cora Chan, *Thirty Years from Tiananmen: China, Hong Kong, and the Ongoing Experiment to Preserve Liberal Values in an Authoritarian State*, 17 Int'l J. Const. L. 439, 448 (2017).

[101] Chan Kin Sum v. Secretary for Justice, [2009] 2 H.K.L.R.D. 166 (C.F.I.).

[102] Secretary for Justice v. Chan Wah, [2000] 3 H.K.C.F.A.R. 459.

[103] Wong Hin Wai v. Secretary for Justice, [2012] 4 H.K.L.R.D. 70 (C.F.I.). *See also*, YAP, *supra* note 21, at 45 (noting a "distinct contradiction" in the judicial outcomes between these cases and those involving "major systemic electoral changes" or "high-stakes" elections, where the courts have sided

They gave substance to social welfare rights[104] and the right to travel.[105] In addition, they recognized that the right against cruel, inhuman, or degrading treatment or punishment is a non-derogable and absolute right from which the government's immigration policies are not exempted.[106]

In adjudicating fundamental rights claims under the Basic Law and BORO, Hong Kong courts, for the most part, rely on proportionality analysis.[107] Hong Kong initially adopted the three-prong variety of proportionality, which asked: (1) whether the government has legitimate aims for restricting fundamental rights; (2) whether the restrictions are rationally connected to those legitimate aims; and (3) whether the restrictions are proportionate (no more than necessary) to accomplish the legitimate aims.[108] Because BORO incorporates the ICCPR into Hong Kong law,[109] constitutional litigation on civil and political rights has often been framed in the Covenant's terms.

The application of the proportionality test has varied according to the political salience and sensitivities attached to particular rights. Cases involving the freedoms of expression and assembly, for instance, were handled with more deference to the government. Consider *HKSAR v. Ng Kung Siu* (1999).[110] The case concerned the freedom of expression in the context of flag desecration. During a public demonstration, two individuals defaced both the PRC national flag and the regional HKSAR flag. Both flags were cut or torn, and the Chinese character "shame" was written on them. These individuals (respondents) were convicted for violating two ordinances that criminalized flag desecration.[111]

The respondents argued that these criminal provisions violated their rights to freedom of speech and expression. Article 27 of the Basic Law provides, "Hong Kong residents shall have the freedom of speech, of the press, and of publication."[112] Article 16 of BORO (whose language mirrors Article 19 of the ICCPR) provides a more detailed—and limited—right to free expression. It provides, in relevant part, "Everyone shall have the right to freedom of expression," and that this

with the government); Simon N.M. Young, *Judicial Review of Elections in Hong Kong: Resolving a Contradiction*, *in* JUDICIAL REVIEW OF ELECTIONS IN ASIA 11 (Po Jen Yap ed., 2016) (noting a contradiction between "strong review of restrictions on voting and candidacy, but weak review of serious institutional inequalities").

[104] Kong Yunming v. Director of Social Welfare, [2013] 16 H.K.C.F.A.R. 950.
[105] Gurung Kesh Bahadur v. Director of Immigration, [2002] 5 H.K.C.F.A.R. 480.
[106] Ubamaka v. Secretary for Security, [2012] 15 H.K.C.F.A.R. 743.
[107] For a comprehensive account of proportionality in Hong Kong, see Abeyratne, *supra* note 29.
[108] *See* Leung Kwok Hung v. HKSAR, [2005] 3 H.K.L.R.D. 164 (C.F.A.).
[109] Basic Law, art. 39 ("The provisions of the International Covenant on Civil and Political Rights ... shall be implemented through the laws of the Hong Kong Special Administrative Region").
[110] HKSAR v. Ng Kung Siu, [1999] 3 H.K.L.R.D. 907 (C.F.A.).
[111] National Flag and National Emblem Ordinance, No. 116 of 1997, § 7 (H.K.); Regional Flag and Regional Emblem Ordinance, No. 117 of 1997, § 7 (H.K.).
[112] Basic Law, art. 27.

right may be subject to restrictions that are provided by law and are necessary for, among other things, "the protection of national security or of public order (ordre public)."[113]

As a preliminary matter, the CFA noted that the ICCPR had been incorporated into the Basic Law.[114] This meant that the permissible restrictions on the freedom of expression as expressly identified in the ICCPR and BORO would affect the Court's interpretation of Article 27 of the Basic Law. The Court then proceeded to examine whether the restriction was justified on the grounds of "public order (ordre public)"—a permissible limitation under the ICCPR and BORO on which the government relied.[115]

Applying the proportionality test, the Court had to determine whether the government's legitimate aim of protecting the flag was encompassed by "public order (ordre public)." The Court defined this term broadly, including within its scope "what is necessary for the protection of general welfare or for the collectivity as a whole."[116] Moreover, the Court noted, "what is necessary" is "a function of time, place and circumstances."[117] Thus, the Court held that flag protection promoted general welfare and the collective public interest because of their symbolic value in the context of the resumption of Chinese sovereignty over Hong Kong, and the "One Country, Two Systems" arrangement.[118]

The Court then considered the question of necessity: whether the restrictions imposed on free speech by these statutes were no more than necessary to achieve the legitimate aim. The Court found that the expressive activity (flag desecration) proscribed by the relevant ordinances was a "limited" restriction, banning only "one mode" of expression, and leaving untouched a "person's freedom to express the same message by other modes."[119] Thus, it held, "Having regard to what is only a limited restriction on the right to the freedom of expression, the test of necessity is satisfied. The limited restriction is proportionate to the aims sought to be achieved and does not go beyond what is proportionate."[120]

At several points, the Court stressed the importance of the national and regional flags as "unique symbol[s]" of national unity. This enabled a broad interpretation of "public order (ordre public)," which was very deferential to the government and the legitimacy of its stated aims. *Ng Kung Siu* also stressed that Hong Kong courts should consider political context when adjudicating fundamental rights claims. At

[113] BORO, arts. 16(2), 16(3); International Covenant on Civil and Political Rights arts. 19(2) & 19(3), Dec. 19, 1966, 999 U.N.T.S. 171 [hereinafter ICCPR].

[114] *Ng Kung Siu*, 3 H.K.L.R.D. at 920.

[115] *Id.* at 922.

[116] *Id.* at 924–25 (citing the Siracusa Principles on the Limitation and Derogation Provisions in the ICCPR, UN Doc E/CN.4/1984/4, Annex (1985)).

[117] *Id.* at 925.

[118] *Id.* (stating that the resumption of sovereignty fulfilled the "long-cherished common aspiration of the Chinese people").

[119] *Id.* at 921.

[120] *Id.* at 926.

the end of the judgment, the Court noted the novel circumstances in which it was operating and reiterated the significance of the handover of sovereignty. It said, "Hong Kong is at the early stage of the new order . . . 'one country, two systems' is a matter of fundamental importance, as is the reinforcement of national unity and territorial integrity."[121]

In subsequent freedom of expression cases, the HKSAR government successfully relied on the "public order (ordre public)" justification, particularly in defending laws that limited the right to stand for election and the right to free expression within the LegCo.[122]

A similar story unfolded on the freedom of assembly. In *Leung Kwok Hung v. HKSAR* (2005),[123] protestors who were convicted of organizing and assisting in an unlawful assembly challenged the constitutionality of the Public Order Ordinance (Cap. 245). They argued that it conferred excessive discretion on the Commissioner of Police to restrict the freedom of assembly, which is protected by Article 27 of the Basic Law and Article 17 of BORO. The ordinance permitted the Commissioner to restrict peaceful assemblies, *inter alia*, to uphold public order (ordre public).[124] The concept of public order (ordre public), as discussed, is found in the ICCPR and reproduced in BORO. Both texts require that restrictions on the freedom of assembly must be "in conformity with law" and necessary in a democratic society.[125]

The CFA noted that the phrasing "in conformity with law" is equivalent to "prescribed by law."[126] Any laws restricting the freedom of assembly, therefore, must be "adequately accessible" and "formulated with sufficient precision" for citizens to regulate their conduct.[127] Once a law clears this hurdle, it is then subjected to the proportionality test to determine if it is "necessary" in a democratic society.[128]

However, prior to applying proportionality, the CFA found that the scope of the Commissioner's discretion under the Public Order Ordinance was not sufficiently precise and, therefore, held that it failed to meet the "prescribed by law" requirement.[129] The Court then severed the term "public order," meaning "law and order" in the narrower sense, from its etymological cousin "public order (ordre public)," which, as discussed, has wider scope.[130] It held that the Commissioner's

[121] *Id.*

[122] *See* Chan Ho Tin v. Lo Ying Ki Alan, [2018] 2 H.K.L.R.D. 7 (C.F.I.); HKSAR v. Fong Kwok Shan Christine, (2017) 20 H.K.C.F.A.R. 425.

[123] Leung Kwok Hung v. HKSAR, [2005] 3 H.K.L.R.D. 164 (C.F.A.).

[124] *Id.* at para. 4; Public Order Ordinance, (1967) Cap. 245, § 14(1) (H.K.); BORO, art. 17 (listing public order (ordre public) as one of the permissible restrictions on right of peaceful assembly).

[125] ICCPR, art. 21; BORO, art. 17.

[126] *Leung Kwok Hung*, 3 H.K.L.R.D. at para. 18.

[127] *Id.* at para. 27.

[128] *Id.* at para. 36.

[129] *Id.* at para. 77.

[130] *Id.* at para. 82; Siracusa Principles, para. 22 (defining public order (ordre public) as the "sum of rules which ensure the functioning of society or the set of fundamental principles on which society is founded").

discretion to limit peaceful assemblies as part of their duty to uphold law and order was sufficiently precise and limited in scope to fulfill the "prescribed by law" requirement.[131] The CFA went on to hold that this more limited discretion was rationally connected to the legitimate aim of maintaining public order and was no more than necessary to achieve it.[132] Thus, after severance, the Commissioner's statutory discretion was upheld.[133]

In recent years, proportionality analysis has become more structured. In *Hysan Development Co Ltd v. Town Planning Board* (2016), the CFA followed Canadian and British jurisprudence to add a fourth step to the proportionality analysis.[134] The fourth step requires judges to engage in a broader balancing analysis, as it asks, "whether a fair balance has been struck between the general interest and the individual rights intruded on."[135] While this balancing requirement, in theory, should increase the scope of fundamental rights protection, it has proved inconsequential thus far.[136]

The more significant advent in *Hysan* was to formalize and expand a new standard of review. The CFA had previously held, in the context of socioeconomic rights, that government policies should be upheld unless they are "manifestly beyond the spectrum of reasonableness (or manifestly without reasonable foundation)."[137] *Hysan* followed those judgments in linking this deferential standard to the margin of appreciation doctrine cited in the ECtHR jurisprudence. The CFA in *Hysan* noted the difference in context between the Strasbourg Court and the CFA, as the former is a supranational court, and the margin afforded to member states is largely a function of this unique arrangement.[138] Thus, the concept as applied in Hong Kong is referred to as the "margin of discretion" to avoid confusion.[139]

As to whether the concept should apply in a domestic context, the Court noted that U.K. courts, too, following the ECtHR, had adopted the "manifest" standard of review in the socioeconomic policy realm, which provides a wide margin (or substantial deference) to the government.[140] The alternative standard is "reasonable necessity" in which courts ask whether a restriction is "no more than necessary" to advance the legitimate aim espoused by the government.[141] This was previously the default standard of review in proportionality analysis. However,

[131] *Leung Kwok Hung*, 3 H.K.L.R.D. at para. 83.
[132] *Id.* at paras. 90–93.
[133] *Id.* at para. 94.
[134] Hysan Development Co Ltd v. Town Planning Board, [2016] 19 H.K.C.F.A.R. 372.
[135] *Id.* at paras. 77–78.
[136] *See* Abeyratne, *supra* note 29, at 53–57. *See also*, Stone Sweet, *supra* note 29 (arguing that *Hysan* "fundamentally deformed" proportionality analysis by, among other things, "virtually never reaching [step] . . . 4 balancing").
[137] *See* Fok Chun Wa v. Hospital Authority, [2012] 15 H.K.C.F.A.R. 409, para. 76.
[138] *Hysan*, 19 H.K.C.F.A.R 372 at para. 89.
[139] *Id.* at para. 100.
[140] *Id.* at paras. 96, 98–99; R (Carson) v. Secretary of State for Work and Pensions, [2006] 1 AC 173.
[141] *Hysan*, 19 H.K.C.F.A.R 372 at para. 83.

Hysan extended the scope of the deferential "manifest" standard beyond the socioeconomic rights context by listing factors courts should consider in choosing whether this standard or "reasonable necessity" should apply in a particular case. The factors, drawn from ECtHR and British jurisprudence, are as follows:

> (i) [T]he significance of and degree of interference with the right in question; and (ii) the identity of the decision-maker as well as the nature and features of the encroaching measure relevant to setting the margin of discretion.[142]

Hong Kong courts have since applied the "manifest" standard to rule in favor of the government in cases, *inter alia*, involving sex discrimination in prisons and the right to stand for election to the LegCo.[143]

Overall, courts in Hong Kong were pragmatic in their fundamental rights jurisdiction from 1997 to 2019. They were cautious and deferential when NPCSC was involved and on politically sensitive matters such as the freedoms of expression and assembly. But courts in this period also ruled against the government and gave substance to several constitutional rights, including the rights to travel, vote/stand for election, and social welfare. As we will see in Part III, LGBTQ+ rights was also a major site for progressive rights jurisprudence. From 2006 to 2019, Hong Kong courts incrementally decriminalized same-sex relations and expanded the scope and benefits of marriage.

III. Developing a Progressive LGBTQ+ Rights Jurisprudence (2006–19)

Hong Kong courts were able to progressively expand the scope of LGBTQ+ rights, in part, because they were presented many opportunities to do so. Since the handover of sovereignty in 1997, the HKSAR government has resisted calls to introduce legislation banning discrimination on the basis of sexual orientation and gender identity.[144] The government has cited, among other things, a lack of "community support," "divergent views," and the potential for such legislation to create "arguments, divisions, and conflicts," to explain its reluctance on this matter.[145] To

[142] *Id.* at para. 107 (citing R (Lord Carlile of Berriew) v. Secretary of State for the Home Department, [2015] AC 945).

[143] *See* Leung Kwok Hung (Long Hair) v. Commissioner of Correctional Services, [2018] 2 H.K.L.R.D. 933 (C.A.) (overruled on statutory grounds in Leung Kwok Hung (Long Hair) v. Commissioner of Correctional Services, [2020] H.K.C.F.A. 37; Kwok Cheuk Kin v. Secretary for Constitutional and Mainland Affairs, [2017] H.K.C.F.A.R. 353).

[144] Amy Barrow, *Sexual Orientation, Gender Identity, and Equality in Hong Kong: Rights, Resistance, and Possibilities for Reform*, 15 Asian J. Comp. L. 126, 127–28 (2020).

[145] Marco Wan, *The Invention of Tradition; Same-Sex Marriage and Its Discontents in Hong Kong*, 18 Int'l J. Const. L. 539, 542 (2020) (noting that "the most persistent feature of the landscape of gay and

date, it has only adopted a voluntary Code of Practice against sexual orientation discrimination in the workplace, which only a few employers have adopted.[146]

Because of this legislative inertia, LGBTQ+ rights activists have turned to the judiciary for redress.[147] And through a series of judgments, courts have forced the government to modify several laws and policies that discriminated against LGBTQ+ persons. These cases fall into two broad categories: the first pertains to restrictions on same-sex conduct, while the second concerns status discrimination claims. In both categories, Hong Kong courts relied on universal values, often citing progressive foreign judgments, to broaden the scope of LGBTQ+ rights protection in incremental fashion.[148] By proceeding in small, cautious steps, the courts widened LGBTQ+ rights protection with little political fallout or resistance.

A. Same-Sex Conduct and "Intense" Scrutiny

Hong Kong courts used proportionality analysis to hold unconstitutional laws that discriminate against same-sex conduct. In 2006, the Court of Appeal in *(William Roy) Leung v. Secretary of Justice* had to determine whether a difference in the age of consent for homosexual and heterosexual sex under Section 118C of the Crimes Ordinance conflicted with the Basic Law and BORO.[149] The applicant challenged provisions in the Crimes Ordinance, which criminalized, among other things, "buggery" under the age of 21.[150] As a gay man, he claimed that the ordinance violated his right to equality, as the ordinance set a higher age limit for buggery (age 21) than heterosexual sex (age 16) and criminalized homosexual acts involving more than two people but not similar heterosexual acts.[151]

The Court, led by then-Chief Judge Geoffrey Ma, ruled in favor of the applicant, holding that the relevant provisions of the Crimes Ordinance constituted indirect discrimination based on sexual orientation, which violated the right to equality under Article 25 of the Basic Law and Article 22 of BORO.[152] The Court found that

lesbian rights in Hong Kong has been the government's staunch refusal to introduce a law proscribing sexual-orientation discrimination").

[146] Barrow, *supra* note 144, at 128; Constitutional and Mainland Affairs Bureau Hong Kong, Code of Practice Against Discrimination on the Ground of Sexual Orientation (2014), https://www.cmab.gov.hk/en/issues/full_code_of_practice.htm.

[147] Wan, *supra* note 145, at 543.

[148] *See* Martin Shapiro, *Stability and Change in Judicial Decision-Making: Incrementalism or Stare Decisis?*, 2 L. Transition Q. 134, 156–57 (1965) (noting that, at its core, incrementalism respects the status quo and moves forward only in "short, marginal steps carefully designed to allow for further modification in the light of further developments"). *Cf.* Jeff King, Judging Social Rights 293 (2012) (arguing that incrementalism is not necessarily a passive judicial strategy and should instead "be viewed as a *dynamic* and *searching* process that takes place in a controlled fashion").

[149] Leung v. Secretary for Justice, [2006] 4 H.K.L.R.D. 211, 217 (C.A.).

[150] Crimes Ordinance, (1972) Cap. 200, § 118C (H.K.).

[151] *Id.* §§ 118C, 118F (2) (a), 118H, 118J (2) (a).

[152] *Leung*, 4 H.K.L.R.D. at 231, 238–40.

the impugned age differential "significantly affects homosexual men in an adverse way compared with heterosexuals."[153] Though the prohibition on "buggery" under the age of 21 facially applied to all, in practice it worked special harm on gay men. The Court, therefore, concluded that it constituted "disguised discrimination" on the basis of sexual orientation, in violation of fundamental rights to equality and privacy.[154]

The government sought to justify the difference in age limit—16 for heterosexual sex, 21 for buggery—on the grounds of protecting "the young from sexual activities which are . . . for more mature persons."[155] It relied on the ECtHR precedent *Dudgeon v. United Kingdom*, which held that the criminalization of buggery in Northern Ireland was unconstitutional, but permitted countries to set age limits.[156] However, the Court of Appeal concluded that there was no evidence presented, including no medical reasons, as to why the age of consent should be lower for heterosexual sex.[157] Thus, the government failed to show a rational connection between its aims and the higher age restriction on buggery.

The Court also dismissed the government's contention, based again on the ECtHR jurisprudence, that the legislature was owed a margin of appreciation in this case. It said, "Where there is an apparent breach of rights based on race, sex or sexual orientation, the court will *scrutinise with intensity* the reasons said to constitute justification."[158]

This standard of "intense scrutiny" would apply in subsequent cases involving unconstitutional discrimination on the grounds of sex or sexual orientation. In *Secretary for Justice v. Yau Yuk Lung* (2006), the CFA applied intense scrutiny to hold unconstitutional a provision in the Crimes Ordinance (Cap. 200) that criminalized public homosexual intercourse between men (but did not criminalize any other public sexual acts).[159] In that case, Chief Justice Li authored a short opinion that was critical of the government's submissions. He said that the government did not address "the critical question . . . What must be established is a genuine need for differential treatment. That need cannot be established from the mere act of legislative enactment."[160] Thus, he held that the government failed to clear the first stage of the proportionality test: it did not identify legitimate aims.[161]

[153] *Id.* at 237.
[154] *Id.*
[155] *Id.*
[156] *Id.*; Dudgeon v. United Kingdom, 4 E.H.R.R. 149, Eur. Ct. H.R. (1981). *See also*, Barrow, *supra* note 144, at 127 (noting that British colonial government in Hong Kong took steps to decriminalize same-sex relations in 1991 after the *Dudgeon* judgment).
[157] *Leung*, 4 H.K.L.R.D. at 238–39.
[158] *Id.* at 239 (quoting Ghadian v. Godin-Mendoza, [2004] 2 AC 557 [19]) (internal quotation marks omitted) (emphasis added).
[159] Secretary of Justice v. Yau Yuk Lung, [2006] 4 H.K.L.R.D. 196, paras. 22, 30 (C.F.A.).
[160] *Id.* at para. 27.
[161] *Id.*

At the legislative level, the Crimes Ordinance was finally amended eight years after the *(William Roy) Leung* judgment to remove the age differential between consensual homosexual and heterosexual sex.[162] Such legislative developments follow the case law in proceeding incrementally. Rather than prohibit sexual orientation-based discrimination outright, the LegCo has intervened selectively and on narrow grounds. For instance, in 2009, same-sex couples were included in the domestic violence ordinance.[163] In 2015, new legislation recognized the right of cohabiting same-sex persons to make decisions on medical treatment of their partners, where the latter are unable to make decisions themselves.[164] But the LegCo has yet to enact legislation that gives full legal sanction to same-sex intimate conduct. As a result, cases along similar lines to *(William Roy) Leung* and *Yau Yuk Lung* re-emerge periodically.

In *HKSAR v. Yeung Ho Nam* (2019), the Court of Appeal once again dealt with the constitutionality of statutory age restrictions for homosexual and heterosexual conduct.[165] The applicant argued that Section 118C(a) of the Crimes Ordinance violated the right to equality under Article 25 of the Basic Law for imposing "a heavier sentence for the offence of homosexual buggery" than for "heterosexual buggery" under Section 124.[166] Relying on *(William Roy) Leung* and *Yau Yuk Lung*, he contended that the Court should scrutinize this differential treatment "with intensity."[167] The Court agreed that this was the appropriate standard of review. It then upheld the judgment below, which set forth a remedial interpretation of Section 118C (a) "making it in line with the sentence for unlawful sexual intercourse with a girl under section 124."[168] This interpretation, according to the Court, served to remedy the "obvious unequal treatment of homosexual males."[169] The Court added the following observations:

> There needs to be a proper and effective review of the laws and policies that discriminate against same-sex relationships, which should not be left for the courts to ultimately resolve through lengthy legal proceedings when there is no resistance to the challenge of the discriminatory nature of the law in question.[170]

Despite the Court's frustration with the political branches of the HKSAR, the Hong Kong judiciary from 2006 to 2019 effectively decriminalized same-sex conduct and ended some forms of discrimination against LGBTQ+ persons.

[162] Crimes Ordinance, (2014) Cap. 200, § 118C (H.K.). The delayed legislative amendment did not have much practical effect, as the CFA's judgment went into effect immediately.
[163] Domestic and Cohabitation Relationships Violence Ordinance, (2009) Cap. 189, § 2(1)(a) (H.K.).
[164] Electronic Health Record Sharing System Ordinance, (2015) Cap. 625, § 3(4)(f) (H.K.).
[165] HKSAR v. Yeung Ho Nam, [2019] H.K.C.A. 384.
[166] *Id.* at para. 24.
[167] *Id.* at paras. 24–26, 28.
[168] *Id.* at para. 46.
[169] *Id.* at para. 48.
[170] *Id.* at para. 49.

B. Status Discrimination Cases

Hong Kong courts in this period also adjudicated status discrimination claims against LGBTQ+ persons. These cases dealt with differential treatment in the marital rights and benefits of same-sex couples as well as gender-diverse persons. As with the cases on sexual conduct, the courts moved gradually toward greater rights protection. The rulings are mostly narrow, confined only to the specific circumstances at issue. In one instance where the CFA issued a far-reaching judgment, it delayed the declaration of invalidity to allow the government to modify the impugned laws, thereby pre-empting political blowback.

Let us begin with that judgment: *W v. Registrar of Marriages* (2013). The appellant was a postoperative transsexual woman who wished to marry her male partner.[171] She received a letter from the Hospital Authority following her medical procedures certifying that her "gender should now be changed to female."[172] She was then issued a new government identity card and passport that listed her sex as female.[173]

Nevertheless, the Registrar of Marriages ruled that she did not qualify as a "woman" under the Marriage Ordinance (Cap. 181) and the Matrimonial Causes Ordinance (Cap. 179).[174] The Marriage Ordinance, in relevant part, provides that every marriage shall be a "Christian marriage," which involves the "voluntary union for life of one man and one woman."[175] The Matrimonial Causes Ordinance further stipulates that marriages in which "the parties are not respectively male and female" are void.[176] Since same-sex marriage was prohibited, the appellant was not permitted to marry her partner following the registrar's ruling that she was not a "woman."[177]

The appellant's case rested principally on Article 37 of the Basic Law and Article 19(2) of BORO, which protect the freedom of marriage and recognize the right of men and women to marry, respectively.[178] The government's case relied on the British precedent *Corbett v. Corbett* (1970), which held that a postoperative female transsexual could not legally enter into a marriage in the United Kingdom.[179] *Corbett* further established that, in the context of marriage, only biological factors

[171] W v. Registrar of Marriages, [2013] 3 H.K.L.R.D. 90, 98 (C.F.A.).
[172] *Id.* at 104.
[173] *Id.*
[174] *Id.*
[175] Marriage Ordinance, (1876) Cap. 181, § 40 (H.K.).
[176] Matrimonial Causes Ordinance, (1967) Cap. 179, § 20(1)(d) (H.K.).
[177] *W*, 3 H.K.L.R.D. at 104.
[178] Basic Law, art. 37; BORO, art. 19(2). The appellant also invoked the right to privacy in Article 14 of BORO. While the right to equality was not formally raised (and hence this is not strictly a status discrimination case), the appellant's arguments and the CFA's reasoning sounded in the register of non-discrimination.
[179] Corbett v. Corbett, [1970] 2 ALL E.R. 33 (U.K.). The government argued that the ICCPR, upon which the Art. 19(2) of BORO is based, assumed a traditional view of marriage in line with *Corbett*.

were relevant in the consideration of the sex of an individual, and that these factors were fixed at birth.[180] The decision was cited with approval in a later case by the House of Lords. Lord Nicholls said that it represented "the present state of English Law regarding the sex of transsexual people."[181] Indeed, shortly after the *Corbett* judgment was issued, the British Parliament enacted the Nullity of Marriage Act 1971, which provided that future marriages in which "the parties are not respectively male and female" would be void.[182]

The CFA, per Chief Justice Ma and Justice Ribeiro, considered *Corbett* and related precedents at length but ultimately found them unpersuasive. The CFA considered the "evolution of the United Kingdom's position" on this issue in line with the jurisprudence of the ECtHR, which has binding effect on the United Kingdom since the passage of the Human Rights Act 1998.[183] The early ECtHR cases affirmed *Corbett* citing the "transitional stage" of the law in this area.[184] States were given "a wide margin of appreciation," and the ECtHR declined to adopt a new approach that moved away from biological criteria in determining sex for the purposes of marriage.[185] The ECtHR finally departed from these precedents in *Goodwin v. United Kingdom*.[186] *Goodwin*, like the cases before it, involved a post-operative female transsexual who was not permitted to marry her male partner. Due to advances in science and social convention, the ECtHR held that in the context of the right to marry under Article 12 of the European Convention of Human Rights (ECHR), biological factors could "no longer be decisive in denying legal recognition to the change of gender of a post-operative transsexual."[187] It went on to hold that the applicant in this case was denied "the very essence of her right to marry."[188]

Following a *tour d'horizon* of medical advancements and changes in societal norms, the CFA agreed with the *Goodwin* analysis. The Court also stressed the "long and painful ordeal" that transsexual people undergo to acquire a body that conforms to their "self-perception," and their "struggle for social recognition" of their new gender identity.[189] In light of this heavy burden, the Court concluded that for the law to exclude psychological factors in the determination of sex was "quite unjustifiable."[190] The CFA then followed the ECtHR in holding that the Registrar

[180] *Id.*; *W*, 3 H.K.L.R.D. at 108.
[181] *See* Bellinger v. Bellinger, [2003] 2 AC 467.
[182] Nullity of Marriage Act 1971 (U.K.) (quoted in *W*, 3 H.K.L.R.D. at 111).
[183] *W*, 3 H.K.L.R.D. at 118–24.
[184] *See, e.g.*, Rees v. United Kingdom, 9 E.H.R.R. 56, Eur. Ct. H.R. (1987).
[185] *See id.*; Cossey v. United Kingdom, 13 E.H.R.R. 622, Eur. Ct. H.R. (1991); Sheffield & Horsham v. United Kingdom, 27 E.H.R.R. 163, Eur. Ct. H.R. (1999).
[186] Goodwin v. United Kingdom, 35 E.H.R.R. 18, Eur. Ct. H.R. (2002).
[187] *Id.*; *W*, 3 H.K.L.R.D. at 121.
[188] *Goodwin*, 35 E.H.R.R. 18; *W*, 3 H.K.L.R.D. at 122.
[189] *W*, 3 H.K.L.R.D. at 125–31.
[190] *Id.* at 131.

of Marriages violated the "very essence of the right to marry guaranteed by art. 37 and art. 19(2)."[191] This was a brave pronouncement by the Court: it departed from cases on LGBTQ+ rights (and fundamental rights generally) by eschewing the proportionality test altogether.

Yet, in keeping with its incremental approach, the CFA adopted a creative remedy to soften the blow of this landmark judgment. The Court delayed the declaration of invalidity for one year. It acknowledged the "highly valuable and constructive role" the legislature may play in revising the law, highlighted several areas that would benefit from legislative input, and explained how legislative intervention would be preferable to any "line-drawing" by the judiciary.[192] However, if legislators failed to act within twelve months of the judgment to remedy the unconstitutional provisions, then the courts would step in and engage in the "highly undesirable" practice of devising "different tests for different purposes."[193] The government failed to act within twelve months, which led to the delayed declaration of invalidity coming into effect. *W* and persons similarly situated could therefore marry in Hong Kong. Still, as of early 2025 (more than a decade after the CFA's judgment in W), the HKSAR government and LegCo have still not revised the relevant law. This failure to act excluded other sexual minorities from the institution of marriage. For instance, as we will see in Part V, the government prevented individuals who had not undergone sexual reassignment surgery (SRS) from officially changing their gender. The CFA would be called upon again to determine the constitutionality of this restriction.

Meanwhile, public opinion on LGBTQ+ issues shifted significantly in the years following the *W* case. The Centre for Comparative and Public Law at the University of Hong Kong (HKU) published a report showing that support for same-sex rights generally increased dramatically from 2013 to 2017.[194] By 2017, more than 50 percent of Hong Kong residents supported same-sex marriage, compared to only 38 percent in 2013.[195] Moreover, 78 percent of respondents said that same-sex couples should have some or all the rights afforded to opposite-sex couples,[196] while 80 percent of respondents in a subsequent study had accepting views of transgender people.[197] Polls conducted in 2019 by The Chinese

[191] *Id.* at 133–34.
[192] *W*, 3 H.K.L.R.D. at 137–41.
[193] *Id.* at 140–44.
[194] Holning Lau et al., Support in Hong Kong For Same-Sex Couples' Rights Grew Over Four Years (2013–2017): Over Half of People in Hong Kong Now Support Same-Sex Marriage (2017).
[195] *Id.* at 1.
[196] *Id.* at 3.
[197] Kelley Loper et al., Public Attitudes Towards Transgender People and Antidiscrimination Legislation (2018). *See also*, Kelley Loper, *The Courts, Public Opinion and the Rights of Lesbian, Gay, Bisexual and Transgender Persons: A Hong Kong Study*, 20 Australian J. Asian L. 4(1) (2019) (analyzing the Hong Kong judiciary's use of societal consensus in LGBTQ+ rights cases).

University of Hong Kong revealed similar results, both with respect to same-sex marriage and equality for LGBTQ+ persons.[198] Compared to previous decades, where a majority of the Hong Kong public had negative views of LGBTQ+ people and were opposed to any legislation to protect their rights,[199] this was a dramatic shift.

In this context, Hong Kong courts issued a series of judgments on the recognition and treatment of same-sex married couples. In *QT v. Director of Immigration* (2018), a British national, whose spouse was employed in Hong Kong, was denied a dependent visa.[200] The couple entered into a valid same-sex civil partnership in England and met the relevant Immigration Department standards for a bona fide relationship that would ordinarily qualify QT for a dependent visa. QT challenged this decision on both administrative and constitutional law grounds. She argued that it was unreasonable in the *Wednesbury* sense and violated several of her constitutional rights, including the right to equality.[201]

Once again, the CFA departed from the standard proportionality test. Here, it combined administrative and constitutional law arguments into a single analysis. The Court noted that Article 154 of the Basic Law vests the Hong Kong government with immigration power over the HKSAR, which is exercised by the Director of Immigration. The Director enjoys wide discretion under the Immigration Ordinance to regulate entry and exit into Hong Kong for those without the right to abode.[202] He explained QT's visa denial as follows: the policy on admitting spouses as dependents "is based on . . . the concept of a married couple consisting of one male and one female."[203] Still, the Director conceded in this case that his discretion was constrained by the "principle of equality."[204] This placed the burden of justification on the government.[205] The Court would apply the proportionality test, which it held "was equally applicable" in adjudicating the impugned policy under *Wednesbury*.[206] It further held that Article 25 of the Basic Law and Article 22 of BORO, which protected the constitutional right to equality, were "indirectly relevant here."[207]

[198] *See CUHK Poll: 47% Supports Same Sex Marriage, More than Half Supports Adopting Children and Inheritances*, HK01, July 9, 2019; *CUHK Poll: 60% agree having laws to protect different sexual orientations, only 10% opposed*, HK01, Jan. 7, 2020.

[199] *See* Ying Tung Suen & Miu Yin Wong, *Male Homosexual in Hong Kong: A 20-Year Review of Public Attitudes Towards Homosexuality and Experiences of Discrimination Self-Reported by Gay Men*, *in* East Asian Men: Masculinity, Sexuality and Desire 69, 73–75 (Lin Xiaodong et al. eds., 2017).

[200] QT v. Director of Immigration, [2018] H.K.C.F.A. 28.

[201] *Id.* at para. 9; Associated Provincial Picture Houses Ltd. v. Wednesbury Corp. [1948] 1 KB 223, 229–30 (U.K.) (holding that laws or government policies would be struck down only if "so unreasonable that no reasonable authority could ever come to it").

[202] *QT*, [2018] H.K.C.F.A. 28 at para. 18.

[203] *Id.* at para. 8.

[204] *Id.* at para. 19.

[205] *Id.* at para. 83.

[206] *Id.* at para. 87.

[207] *Id.*

In applying the proportionality test, the CFA accepted at step one that the Director's two policy aims were legitimate: (1) to encourage talented individuals to join the HKSAR workforce, with their families; and (2) to maintain strict immigration controls. The government further stated—and QT did not contest—that it needed a bright-line rule to differentiate between those who did and did not qualify for dependent visas, as this would promote legal certainty and administrative convenience.[208]

At step two, the CFA held that the Director's exclusion of bona fide same-sex spouses was "counter-productive and plainly not rationally connected" to its aim of recruiting talent to Hong Kong.[209] As for strict immigration controls, the Court acknowledged the convenience of bright-line rules but pointed out that QT and her partner "are just as conveniently able to produce their civil partnership certificate. Excluding them on the basis of administrative convenience is irrational."[210] The Court, therefore, ruled in favor of QT.

Shortly before the CFA delivered its judgment in *QT*, the Court of Appeal below decided another case involving LGBTQ+ rights. *Leung Chun Kwong v. Secretary of Civil Service* (2018) involved challenges filed by a gay civil servant against two decisions—denying him civil service benefits and the ability to file joint taxes, respectively—that he claimed discriminated against him on the basis of sexual orientation.[211]

Justice Poon, who authored the main opinion, distinguished "core rights and obligations unique to marriage" for which differential treatment between married and unmarried persons (including same-sex couples) are self-evident and required no justification, from differential treatment falling outside this core that, unless justified, would constitute discrimination on the basis of sexual orientation.[212]

In this case, the Court of Appeal determined that the policies at issue were not unique to marriage and had to be justified through the proportionality test. Justice Poon considered the benefits and tax decisions together when applying the test. At step one, he rejected "allocation of limited public resources" and "administrative workability" as legitimate aims and relied instead on the aim of "protecting and not undermining the institution of marriage in the societal context of Hong Kong."[213] Justice Poon relied on "local . . . circumstances" and what he described as the "prevailing views of the community on marriage" at the second step, finding a rational connection between the differential treatment in spousal and tax benefits and the protection of marriage.[214] He said that because

208 *Id.* at para. 88.
209 *Id.* at para. 90.
210 *Id.* at paras. 95–97.
211 Leung Chun Kwong v. Secretary for Civil Service, [2018] H.K.C.A. 318, paras. 83–86; Basic Law, art. 25; BORO, art. 21.
212 *Leung Chun Kwong*, [2018] H.K.C.A. 318 at para. 83. The CFA's judgment in *QT* rejected this approach. See *QT*, [2018] H.K.C.F.A. at para. 66.
213 *Leung Chun Kwong*, [2018] H.K.C.A. 318 at paras. 124–25.
214 *Id.* at para. 126.

these benefits were closely associated with marriage, if they were extended to same-sex couples, "it would *per se* undermine, or be perceived by many to undermine, the status of marriage."[215]

On step three, Justice Poon adopted the less deferential "reasonable necessity" standard but again emphasized the local context to hold that the restriction on benefits was no more than necessary to protect marriage as an institution.[216] As to the fourth step, he noted the "perceived prejudice that the applicant may feel," yet concluded that such hardship is "reasonably balanced out by the immense public interests involved in protecting the status of marriage."[217]

Putting aside the conservative framing and outcome of this case which depart from precedents in this area,[218] it is worth noting that the Court of Appeal simply accepted the government's contention that a substantial majority of Hong Kong residents are opposed to same-sex marriage.[219] To the contrary, as the HKU Report shows, support for same-sex rights had increased substantially. When this judgment was issued, more than 50 percent of Hong Kong residents supported same-sex marriage.[220]

The CFA reversed the Court of Appeal's judgment. As an initial matter, it rejected Justice Poon's reliance on "prevailing views of the community on marriage."[221] The CFA held that such views were "simply not relevant to a consideration of the justification exercise."[222] When it applied the proportionality test, the first step was not at issue. All parties agreed that protecting the "traditional family as constituted by heterosexual marriage" was a legitimate aim.[223] However, the CFA did not find a rational connection between this aim and the denial of benefits to same-sex married couples. As the Court put it:

> [W]e cannot agree with the Court of Appeal's analysis. Restricting these financial benefits to opposite-sex married couples on the ground that heterosexual marriage is the only form of marriage recognised in Hong Kong law is circular and therefore proceeds on the fallacious basis rejected by the Court in *QT* . . . we are unable to accept the proposition that heterosexual marriage would be undermined by the extension of the employment and tax benefits to same-sex married couples.[224]

[215] *Id.*
[216] *Id.* at para. 128.
[217] *Id.* at para. 129.
[218] *See* Po Jen Yap, *Spouses Without Benefits: "Ring-Fencing" Marriage After W and QT Have Unbolted Its Gates*, 48 Hong Kong L.J. 365 (2018).
[219] *Leung Chun Kwong*, [2018] H.K.C.A. 318 at para. 126.
[220] Lau et al., *supra* note 194, at 1.
[221] Leung Chun Kwong v. Secretary for the Civil Service [2019] H.K.C.F.A. 19, para. 57.
[222] *Id.*
[223] *Id.* at para. 58.
[224] *Id.* at paras. 71–72.

Having decided that the government's case failed at step two, it was not necessary for the CFA to explain its reasoning at steps three and four of the proportionality test. The Court still noted in dicta that it would have applied the reasonable necessity test to adjudicate step three.[225] Thus, neither the Court of Appeal nor the CFA in *Leung Chun Kwong* mentioned, much less applied, "intense" scrutiny in the proportionality analysis, even though the case concerned discrimination on suspect grounds.

Still, by recognizing the immigration status and benefits of same-sex spouses married abroad, the *QT* and *Leung Chun Kwong* judgments appeared to pave the way for the judicial recognition of marriage equality within Hong Kong. More broadly, by advancing LGBTQ+ rights incrementally, and in citing foreign judgments to support their judgments, Hong Kong courts from 2006 to 2019 were able to pursue a progressive rights jurisprudence and demonstrate their fidelity to the project of global constitutionalism without inviting government censure or intervention from the NPCSC.

IV. From Hybrid to Authoritarian (2019–21)

If the legalization of same-sex unions appeared likely (if not inevitable) in early 2019, it seemed a remote possibility by the end of the year. Hong Kong experienced a major constitutional upheaval that summer. In June 2019, the Hong Kong government proposed a bill to amend the region's extradition policy.[226] If enacted, it would allow for criminal suspects in Hong Kong to be extradited to Mainland China.[227] Public opposition to the Extradition Bill was fierce. Mass protests erupted around the city, with the largest protest comprising approximately 2 million of Hong Kong's 7.5 million residents.[228]

While the proposed bill triggered these events, they also reflected longstanding public grievances on the lack of progress toward fully democratic elections and broader fears about the erosion of civil liberties.[229] The Basic Law provides that universal suffrage is the "ultimate aim" in both the CE and LegCo elections.[230] Though modest democratic reforms had been made since 1997, Hong Kong had not made significant strides in enabling the public to select its leaders.[231] Both the executive and legislative elections remained skewed in favor of corporate, pro-establishment

225 *Id.* at para. 79.

226 Anti-Extradition Law Amendment Bill (proposed to amend the Fugitive Offenders Ordinance), (2019) Cap. 503 (H.K.).

227 *See* Cora Chan, *Demise of "One Country Two Systems"? Reflections on the Hong Kong Rendition Saga*, 49 HONG KONG L. J. 447 (2019).

228 *See* Chopra & Pils, *supra* note 36, at 297.

229 *Id.* at 294–97.

230 Basic Law, arts. 45, 68.

231 For an overview and analysis of these reforms, see CHEN & YAP, *supra* note 6, at ch. 4.

interests in the form of the Election Committee that selected the CE and the functional constituencies that elected half the LegCo members. The "Occupy Central" or "Umbrella" movement in 2014 sought to bring about universal suffrage in the CE election through non-violent means.[232] The movement organized seventy-nine days of mass sit-ins on major public thoroughfares and other public spaces, before the government forcibly intervened.[233] The NPCSC responded by proposing a scheme in which the public would participate in selecting CE nominees but only among candidates preselected by Beijing. Unsurprisingly, the pan-democratic legislators—who backed the Occupy Movement and had long fought for universal suffrage—all voted against this proposal, leaving in place the existing, undemocratic selection process.[234]

Article 23 of the Basic Law requires the Hong Kong government to enact national security legislation. When the government attempted to do so in 2003, it was thwarted by mass protests.[235] But in 2019, the political environment had markedly changed. The Hong Kong public had grown wary of the PRC's encroachment on the region's autonomy, including on the individual freedoms enshrined in the Basic Law and BORO. The proposed extradition bill exacerbated these grievances and stoked public concerns that Hong Kong residents might be criminally prosecuted in the PRC. Moreover, the sheer scale of the 2019 protests, the international media coverage that ensued, and the violent confrontation between protestors and the Hong Kong police, made the Hong Kong government intransigent to public demands.[236] Unlike 2003, when the government backed down, or 2014 when election-related concessions were proposed, the local government and the PRC would respond only with force, first by backing the police to use increasingly severe means to suppress protests,[237] and then by enacting significant changes in Hong Kong's constitutional framework.

A. The National Security Law

Beijing took on a more interventionist role in Hong Kong affairs following the 2019 protests. Frustrated by the HKSAR government's inability to pass a national security law following months of civil unrest, Mainland authorities took it upon themselves to draft and enact such legislation. On May 22, 2020, the NPC—the legislature and highest lawmaking authority in the PRC—adopted a decision

[232] Chopra & Pils, *supra* note 36, at 297.
[233] *Id.*
[234] *Id.*
[235] *Id.* at 295.
[236] *See* CHEN & YAP, *supra* note 6, at 20–25.
[237] *See* JUN CHAN, ERIC YAN-HO LAI, & THOMAS E. KELLOGG, THE HONG KONG 2019 PROTEST MOVEMENT: A DATA ANALYSIS OF ARRESTS AND PROSECUTIONS (2023); Martin Purbrick, *A Report of the 2019 Hong Kong Protests*, 50(4) ASIAN AFF. 465 (2019).

authorizing the NPCSC to enact a national security law for Hong Kong.[238] The NPCSC drafted this law in secret. It was neither subjected to public consultation nor released in draft form prior to its promulgation.[239] The NSL was passed unanimously by the NPCSC and promulgated by Hong Kong's CE on the same day: June 30, 2020.[240]

Substantively, the NSL fundamentally altered Hong Kong's legal system and weakened judicial independence. It introduced four broad crimes: "secession," "subversion of state power," "terrorist activities," and "collusion with foreign governments" that are punishable with sentences up to life imprisonment.[241] These offences apply not just in the HKSAR but also extraterritorially including to non-residents with no connection to Hong Kong.[242] Under the NSL, juries may be replaced by three-judge panels.[243] Moreover, only judges preselected by the CE (in consultation with the Chief Justice) are permitted to adjudicate national security cases.[244] The NSL, in another unprecedented provision, also permits criminal cases originating in Hong Kong to be moved to Mainland China and, hence, prosecuted and tried by PRC authorities and courts, respectively.[245]

Though the NSL ushered in sweeping changes, its status vis-à-vis the Basic Law and BORO was not clear from its text. On the one hand, the NPCSC inserted a provision granting the NSL a quasi-constitutional status. Article 62 of the NSL provides, "This Law shall prevail where provisions of the local laws of the Hong Kong Special Administrative Region are inconsistent with this Law."[246] On the other hand, Articles 4 and 5 provide, "Human rights shall be respected and protected in safeguarding national security" and the "principle of the rule of law shall be adhered to," respectively.[247] As with NPCSC Interpretations and Decisions, then, Hong Kong courts would have to determine if the NSL was subject to judicial review and whether provisions therein could be held unconstitutional for inconsistency with the Basic Law or BORO.

[238] Decision of the National People's Congress on Establishing and Improving the Legal System and Enforcement Mechanisms for the Hong Kong Special Administrative Region to Safeguard National Security (Adopted at the Third Session of the Thirteenth National People's Congress on May 28, 2020), L.N. 135 of 2020.

[239] Kent Roach, *Echoes Enhanced to a Cacophony: Hong Kong's Security Law Compared to Illiberal Elements of the Security Laws of Liberal Democracies*, *in* THE NATIONAL SECURITY LAW OF HONG KONG: RESTORATION AND TRANSFORMATION 306 (Hualing Fu & Michael Hor eds., 2022).

[240] Decision of the Standing Committee of the National People's Congress on Adding a Law to the List of the National Laws in Annex III to the Basic Law of the Hong Kong Special Administrative Region of the People's Republic of China (Adopted at the Twentieth Session of the Standing Committee of the Thirteenth National People's Congress on June 30, 2020), Instrument A117; Promulgation of National Law 2020, Instrument A406.

[241] NSL, *supra* note 36, arts. 20–30.

[242] *Id.* at arts. 37–38.

[243] *Id.* at art. 46.

[244] *Id.* at art. 44.

[245] *Id.* at arts. 55–57.

[246] *Id.* at art. 62.

[247] *Id.* at arts. 4, 5.

The CFA addressed this issue in *HKSAR v. Lai Chee Ying* (2021). Jimmy Lai, the founder of the pro-democracy *Apple Daily* tabloid newspaper, was arrested in December 2020 on the charge of "collusion with a foreign country or with external elements to endanger national security" under Article 29(4) of the NSL.[248] He was initially denied bail by a magistrate based on NSL Article 42(2), which denies bail to defendants and criminal suspects "unless the judge has sufficient grounds for believing that [they] . . . will not continue to commit acts endangering national security."[249] The District Court subsequently granted Lai's bail application,[250] leading the prosecution to appeal the decision to the CFA, which granted leave to determine the "correct" interpretation of Article 42(2) of the NSL.[251]

The CFA rehearsed the events that led to the passage of the NSL, including the NPC Decision to authorize the NPCSC to formulate the law and the latter's listing of the NSL in Annex III of the Basic Law.[252] The CFA not only concluded that the NSL was passed in accordance with Article 18 of the Basic Law but also noted "that safeguarding national security is a matter outside the limits of the HKSAR's autonomy and within the purview of the Central Authorities, the [Central People's Government] . . . having an overarching responsibility for national security affairs relating to the HKSAR."[253]

It therefore follows, the Court held, that Hong Kong courts lack jurisdiction to review the constitutionality of the NSL.[254] It cited *Ng Ka Ling (No. 2)*, which had stated that the CFA could not question "the authority of the National People's Congress or the Standing Committee to do any act which is in accordance with the provisions of the Basic Law and the procedure therein."[255] This ambiguous formulation left open the possibility that the CFA could question NPC or NPCSC acts that do not accord with the Basic Law. Indeed, the defendant's counsel argued in *Lai Chee Ying* that the CFA should rely upon common law principles to conduct a weak form of review. Specifically, he asked the Court to invoke the principle of legality to "read down" Article 42(2) to the extent it infringed upon the presumption of innocence and the right to liberty.[256] The CFA, however, declined to do this. Instead, the Court asserted unambiguously that it has "no power to hold any provision of the NSL to be unconstitutional or invalid as incompatible with the Basic Law and Bill of Rights."[257]

248 HKSAR v. Lai Chee Ying, [2021] H.K.C.F.A. 3, at para. 2.
249 *Id.* at para. 3; NSL, *supra* note 36, at art. 42(2).
250 HKSAR v. Lai Chee Ying, [2020] H.K.C.F.I. 3161.
251 *Lai Chee Ying*, [2021] H.K.C.F.A. 3 at para. 7.
252 *Id.* at paras. 9–29. Article 18 of the Basic Law provides that PRC laws listed in Annex III may be applied in Hong Kong by way of local legislation or, as was the case here, through promulgation by the CE.
253 *Id.* at para. 32.
254 *Id.* at para. 37.
255 *Id.*; *Ng Ka Ling No. 2*, 1 H.K.L.R.D. at 578.
256 *Lai Chee Ying*, [2021] H.K.C.F.A. 3 at para. 33.
257 *Id.* at para. 42.

This higher level of deference is also evident in civil liberties judgments issued in 2020. The Court of Appeal, for instance, upheld restrictions on access to a public area outside the main government building complex, which had been fenced off following protests and subject to a stringent "Permission Scheme" for entry.[258] The CFA, meanwhile, reversed a lower court judgment that struck down regulations that banned face coverings (including masks) not just in "unlawful" or "unauthorized" assemblies but also in lawful public meetings and processions.[259] This ruling was remarkable for its timing, as it was issued during the COVID-19 pandemic when masks were legally mandated in public. When faced with the argument that the impugned regulations contradicted COVID-related mask mandates, and therefore were no longer justified under the proportionality test, the CFA simply dismissed these "supervening events" as "wholly irrelevant."[260] The constitutionality of the regulations banning face coverings, the Court said, had to be judged in the circumstances in October 2019 (prior to the pandemic) when they came into force even if "subsequent events have changed the legal context."[261] This extraordinary statement undermines the core of proportionality analysis, which is a fact-based, contextual inquiry that requires the government to justify the suitability and necessity of restrictions on fundamental rights.[262]

B. Electoral Changes

Alongside the NSL—which clamped down on public protests and restricted judicial power—the NPCSC overhauled the electoral system for both the CE and the LegCo to eliminate political opposition. It would also change the procedure for amending election-related rules. In 2004, the NPCSC issued an Interpretation of election-related provisions in the Basic Law, which guided subsequent reform exercises.[263] The process began with the CE issuing a report to the NPCSC as to whether changes were needed. The government would then conduct public consultations before proposing reforms to the NPCSC. If the NPCSC agreed that reforms were needed, the government would propose an amendment bill, which

[258] Cheung Tak Wing v. Director of Administration, [2020] H.K.C.A. 124.

[259] Kwok Wing Hang v. Chief Executive in Council, [2020] H.K.C.F.A. 22, paras. 6–18.

[260] *Id.* at paras. 142–43.

[261] *Id.* at para. 143.

[262] See Jamal Greene, *Foreword: Rights as Trumps*, 132 Harv. L. Rev. 30, 63 (2018) (noting that proportionality "does not require extensive analysis of constitutional text, history, or precedent. Rather, it requires reliable access to social facts."); Anne Peters, *A Plea for Proportionality: A Reply to Yun-chien Chang and Xin Dai*, 19(3) Int'l J. Const. L. 1135, 1140 (2021) (noting that steps 2 and 3 of the proportionality test require that "the restriction of the right must not be useless and it must be not more intense than needed in order to reach the public interest objective").

[263] Interpretation by the Standing Committee of the National People's Congress of Article 7 of Annex 1 and Article III of Annex 2 to the Basic Law of the Hong Kong Special Administrative Region of the Peoples' Republic of China, Instrument A107, 6 April 2004.

required the support of two-thirds of the LegCo, the consent of the CE, and, if the changes pertained to the CE election, the NPCSC's final approval to be enacted.[264] While the NPCSC played an important role, the public had a voice, and the Hong Kong government and LegCo led the process.

On May 11, 2021, the NPC authorized its Standing Committee to amend the electoral rules for selecting the CE. The NPCSC ignored its 2004 Interpretation for this round of reforms. It changed the electoral rules on its own, without consulting stakeholders within Hong Kong. As a result, both the public and the local government were cut out of the process. The NPCSC increased the size of the Election Committee that selects the CE from 1,200 to 1,500 members.[265] The new 300-member bloc consisted of Hong Kong deputies to the NPC, the Chinese People's Political Consultative Conference, as well as "representatives of Hong Kong members of relevant national organisations."[266] In other words, it transformed an already pro-establishment body into one that would make certain that only PRC-approved candidates would be eligible for the CE position. While the Election Committee previously included some members from the District Councils (popularly elected members of local governing boards), these members would now be eliminated from the Committee and replaced with government-appointed "representatives of members of areas committees."[267]

More significant changes were made to the LegCo elections. Prior to 2021, the LegCo consisted of seventy members, half of whom were popularly elected. Following the NPCSC's amendments in 2021, the LegCo was enlarged to ninety members, only twenty of whom would be popularly elected. Thirty seats are now filled by the functional constituencies. The remaining forty members are selected by the Election Committee, which had hitherto only played a role in CE elections.[268] The five functional constituency seats that consisted of District Council members were also eliminated.[269] If this were not enough, all potential candidates (for both the CE and LegCo) are screened by the National Security Unit of the Hong Kong police, and then reviewed by a National Security Committee (headed by the CE) as well as a vetting committee.[270] Thus, not only was the number of popularly elected seats reduced, but there was little to no possibility for genuine opposition candidates (such as the pan-democrats) to even contest those seats.

[264] *Id.*
[265] Basic Law, Annex I (as amended in 2021), § 2.
[266] *Id.*
[267] *Id.* at § 3.
[268] Basic Law, Annex II (as amended in 2021), § 1.
[269] *Id.* § 3.
[270] *Id.* § 5. For a detailed account of the changes to the LegCo, see Eric Chan, *The Legislative Council of Hong Kong*, *in* ROUTLEDGE HANDBOOK OF ASIAN PARLIAMENTS 158 (Po Jen Yap & Rehan Abeyratne eds., 2023).

All told, these electoral changes and the NSL altered the fundamental character of constitutionalism in Hong Kong.[271] While authoritarian elements always existed, and the corporatist, pro-establishment political bloc had consistently been in charge, they now operated without any democratic or political checks. Public protests and legislative opposition were no longer viable in the HKSAR.

V. LGBTQ+ Rights in Authoritarian Hong Kong

Progressive judicial advances on LGBTQ+ rights (or on any liberal constitutional rights) seemed unlikely in this new era. The NSL's vaguely defined crimes and suspension of common law legal protections chilled political organizing of all kinds. With hundreds of activists arrested,[272] more than fifty civil society groups disbanded,[273] and police permission required for any public gathering,[274] there was little scope to advocate for fundamental rights. Hong Kong's human rights lawyers also feared for safety and livelihood in the post–2020 environment, with many choosing to leave the city.[275] The most high-profile departure—and the most relevant for our purposes—was that of British solicitor Michael Vidler, who fled the city abruptly citing NSL-related concerns and harassment from PRC-based media outlets.[276] Vidler's firm had represented many LGBTQ+ rights claimants.[277]

Meanwhile, Chief Justice Geoffrey Ma stepped down in January 2021 and was replaced by the more conservative Andrew Cheung. Ma wrote the principal judgments in the *(William Roy) Leung* and *W* cases and presided over the CFA's judgment in *QT*. Cheung, meanwhile, sat on the Court of Appeal panel in *Leung Chun Kwong*, which denied tax and other benefits to same-sex couples—a decision overruled by the CFA.

These changes have led Hong Kong courts to significantly retrench in their constitutional rights jurisprudence, except on LGBTQ+ rights. If courts have become

[271] *See* Cora Chan, *From Legal Pluralism to Dual State: Evolution of the Relationship between the Chinese and Hong Kong Legal Orders*, 16(1) L. & Ethics Hum. Rts. 99 (2022).

[272] Thomas Kellogg & Charlotte Yeung, *Three Years In, Hong Kong's National Security Law Has Entrenched a New Status Quo*, China File (Sept. 6, 2023), https://www.chinafile.com/reporting-opinion/viewpoint/three-years-hong-kongs-national-security-law-has-entrenched-new-status.

[273] *Timeline: 58 Hong Kong Civil Society Groups Disband Following the Onset of the Security Law*, Hong Kong Free Press (June 30, 2022), https://hongkongfp.com/2022/06/30/explainer-over-50-groups-gone-in-11-months-how-hong-kongs-pro-democracy-forces-crumbled/.

[274] *Hong Kong: Stop Prosecuting Pro-Democracy Activists*, Hum. Rts. Watch (Sept. 25, 2020), https://www.hrw.org/news/2020/09/25/hong-kong-stop-prosecuting-pro-democracy-activists.

[275] James Pomfret et al., *Lawyers Exit Hong Kong as They Face Campaign of Intimidation*, Reuters (Dec. 29, 2022), https://www.reuters.com/investigates/special-report/china-lawyers-crackdown-exodus/.

[276] Almond Li, *Lawyer Michael Vidler Reflects on 19 Years of Equal Rights Advocacy in Hong Kong, and His Reasons for Leaving*, Hong Kong Free Press (June 2, 2022), https://hongkongfp.com/2022/06/02/lawyer-michael-vidler-reflects-on-19-years-of-equal-rights-advocacy-in-hong-kong-and-his-reasons-for-leaving/.

[277] *Id.*

more deferential to the government in other areas, what explains their continued commitment to LGBTQ+ rights?

We will explore this question by examining key judgments issued in 2023: on transgender rights, housing and estate benefits for same-sex couples, and same-sex unions, respectively. Each built incrementally on past CFA decisions, demonstrating that a progressive rights jurisprudence can be maintained in this domain if not in others. But these judgments—the same-sex union judgment, in particular—also show a heightened judicial awareness of the new political climate, where self-preservation appears to be the dominant strategic objective.

A. Changing Official Gender Markers

On February 6, 2023, the CFA ruled in favor of two transgender applicants, Henry Tse and Q, seeking to change the gender marker on their identification cards. The CFA held that the Hong Kong government's policy, which required applicants to undergo full SRS to change their gender markers, unconstitutionally infringed upon their right to privacy.

Recall that a decade earlier, the CFA held in *W* that laws preventing a post–SRS transgender person from marrying her opposite gender partner violated her constitutional right to marry. Eschewing the normal proportionality analysis, the CFA held that this restriction violated "the very essence of the right."[278] In other words, it was such an egregious rights violation that the government could not provide a justification.

The CFA in *W* delayed its declaration of invalidity by twelve months to give the government a chance to amend the relevant laws to comply with the ruling. When the government failed to do so by the one-year deadline, the applicant and those similarly situated were permitted to marry opposite-sex spouses.

Against this backdrop, the CFA issued its judgment in *Q v. Commissioner of Registration*. Henry Tse and Q (two female-to-male transgender persons) suffered from gender dysphoria for which they received physical and psychological medical treatment. Their medical treatment included, among other things, long-term hormone therapy and irreversible mastectomies. Neither was willing to undergo a complete SRS, which would have required more invasive surgery.[279] The Commissioner of Registration refused to permit them to change the gender markers on their Hong Kong Identity Cards (HKIDs).[280] Though both Tse and Q had obtained British passports with their new genders and chosen (male)

[278] *W*, 3 H.K.L.R.D. at 133–34.
[279] *Q*, [2023] H.K.C.F.A. 4 at paras. 4, 27, 33.
[280] *Id.* at para. 6.

forenames, the government's policy required a full SRS for these changes to be reflected on their identity cards.[281]

The applicants argued that this policy violated their right to privacy under Article 14 of BORO. Specifically, they claimed it was disproportionate for the government to require such invasive surgical procedures to change their gender markers.[282] The medical evidence presented to the Court showed that these procedures were not necessary for many gender-diverse persons (including the applicants), whose gender dysphoria had been effectively treated and who were already living in their chosen gender.[283] The CFA accepted the applicants' claim that the policy encroached upon their right to privacy.[284] But unlike the *W* judgment,[285] where it categorically ruled in favor of the applicant, the Court here followed its usual practice of undertaking proportionality analysis.

Tse and Q did not challenge the lower court's ruling that the government in this case had a legitimate aim ("to establish a fair, clear, certain, and objective administrative guideline") and that the policy was rationally connected thereto.[286] The judgment turned on the third step of the proportionality analysis: whether the restriction on applicants' right to privacy was "no more than necessary" to achieve the legitimate aim.[287] Here, the Commissioner of Registration advanced three justifications: first, a full SRS was the only workable, bright-line rule; second, administrative problems would arise due to the "incongruence between the external physical appearance" of the applicant and the gender marker if a different rule was adopted; and third, hormonal and psychiatric treatments were not "absolutely irreversible" such that if applicants were to stop the treatment, they might become pregnant and give birth.[288]

The CFA rejected all three justifications, relying heavily on comparative analysis. On the question of line-drawing, the Court cited the ECtHR judgment in *AP, Garçon & Nicot v. France* to conclude that medical treatment "should not be prescribed merely to promote administrative convenience or clarity."[289] Rather, it should only be administered in the best interests of the patient. The CFA noted that many transgender persons in Hong Kong felt pressured to undergo intensive surgery to have their gender officially changed on the HKID. Such pressure, said the Court, is "objectionable in principle" and the adoption of the Commissioner's bright-line rule therefore "weighs significantly against the Policy."[290]

281 *Id.* at paras. 23–34, 38–39.
282 *Id.* at para. 41.
283 *Id.* at paras. 8–20.
284 *Id.* at para. 46.
285 *See W*, 3 H.K.L.R.D. at 133–34.
286 Q, [2023] H.K.C.F.A. 4 at paras. 49–51.
287 *Id.* at paras. 52–62 (discussing why "reasonable necessity" was the appropriate margin of discretion in this case).
288 *Id.* at para. 63.
289 *Id.* at paras. 64–67 (citing AP, Garçon & Nicot v. France, App. No. 79885/12 (Apr. 6, 2017), Eur. Ct. H.R., https://hudoc.echr.coe.int/eng?i=001-172913).
290 Q, [2023] H.K.C.F.A. 4 at paras. 66–67.

The CFA proceeded to reject the Commissioner's argument that it would be unfeasible to adopt a different rule. The Court referred to the government's Interdepartmental Working Group on Gender Recognition consultation paper, which listed more than twenty jurisdictions around the world that permitted individuals to change the gender marker on identification documents upon the submission of medical evidence and documentation but did not require a complete SRS.[291] The Court highlighted the United Kingdom's Gender Recognition Act 2004 under which applicants must prove that they have gender dysphoria, lived with the acquired gender for at least two years, intend to continue living in the acquired gender until death, and met certain evidentiary requirements.[292] It further stressed that the applicants were not asking for a minimal regime of self-certification to change gender markers. Rather, their claim, with which the Court agreed, was that less intrusive lines could be drawn and administered effectively.[293]

On "external incongruence," the CFA determined that the government's policy exacerbated this problem.[294] As the Court noted, transgender persons regularly experience the "violation of their dignity and invasion of their privacy" when they are asked to produce identity cards on which the stated gender does not match their outward appearance.[295] Thus, the Commissioner's claim had it backwards: adopting a less stringent rule for changing gender markers would lessen, not worsen, the intrusion on the applicants' right to privacy.

Finally, as to the claim that the applicants had not irreversibly changed their gender, the CFA relied on medical experts to find that post-transition pregnancy is exceptionally rare. Hence, it would be "wholly disproportionate" to require the applicants to undergo a full SRS simply to avoid this contingency.[296]

For these reasons, the CFA ruled against the government on step three of the proportionality test.[297] It was, therefore, not necessary to rule on step four, which asks whether a fair balance has been struck between the policy's societal benefits and the intrusion on individual rights. Nonetheless, the Court noted in *obiter dicta* that it would have ruled for the applicants here. It said, "[T]he societal benefits of the Policy are . . . at best relatively slim," while imposing an "unacceptably harsh burden on the individuals concerned."[298]

The CFA, therefore, ruled in favor of the applicants, holding that the policy violated their right to privacy under Article 14 of the BORO. The Court added that

[291] *Id.* at para. 73 (citing Interdepartmental Working Group on Gender Recognition, *Consultation Paper 1: Gender Recognition*, June 2017, https://www.iwggr.gov.hk/eng/pdf/eSummary.pdf [hereinafter IWG Working Paper]).

[292] *Id.* at para. 74; Gender Recognition Act 2004 (United Kingdom), https://www.legislation.gov.uk/ukpga/2004/7/contents.

[293] *Q*, [2023] H.K.C.F.A. 4 at paras. 76–78.

[294] *Id.* at para. 87.

[295] *Id.* at paras. 87–90.

[296] *Id.* at paras. 97–102.

[297] *Id.* at paras. 103–04.

[298] *Id.* at paras. 105–07.

while it is "not for the Court to re-write the Commissioner's policy," there are "various models and approaches" that the government might consider in reformulating the policy to bring into compliance with Article 14.[299] However, given its failure to respond to similar prodding in the *W* judgment, the HKSAR government is unlikely to make any far-reaching changes to the existing framework on gender recognition. Indeed, the government delayed providing the lead petitioner in *Q*, Henry Tse, with a new identity card for more than a year. He finally received the card in April 2024 after challenging the delay in the High Court.[300]

B. Housing and Estate Benefits for Same-Sex Couples

The CFA's 2019 judgment in *Leung Chun Kwong*[301]—which held that same-sex spouses are entitled to government tax and medical benefits—led to more litigation seeking to extend benefits enjoyed by opposite-sex married couples to same-sex married couples. One case challenged the Hong Kong Housing Authority's (HA's) policy that excluded same-sex married couples from applying for Public Rental Housing (PRH).[302] The applicant, Nick Infinger, and his male partner (both Hong Kong permanent residents) were married in Canada. Infinger wrote to the HA requesting PRH accommodation for an "Ordinary Family."[303] Infringer listed his spouse as the only family member in the application and enclosed a copy of their marriage certificate. The HA responded that they were ineligible to apply as an "Ordinary Family."[304] The HA referred to its "Application Guide for Public Rental Housing," which specifies "that the relationship between the Infinger and family members must be either husband or wife, parent and child, grandparent and grandchild."[305] Infinger filed a judicial review, claiming that the policy violated his right to equality under Article 25 of the Basic Law and Article 22 of BORO.[306]

A second case challenged the constitutionality of a similar HA policy. Edgar Lam and his partner Li Yik Ho (Henry) were married in the United Kingdom. Lam lived in a PRH flat, which he sought to purchase as the couple's martial home under the HA Home Ownership Scheme (HOS) that offers subsidized housing to PRH tenants.[307] The HA did not recognize same-sex spouses under its "Family Member Policy" as authorized occupants or co-owners. Hence, though Li contributed

[299] *Id.* at paras. 108–10.

[300] Kelly Ho, *Hong Kong Trans Activist Gets New ID Card After "Incredibly Difficult" 7-Year Legal Battle*, Hong Kong Free Press (Apr. 29, 2024), https://hongkongfp.com/2024/04/29/hong-kong-trans-activist-gets-new-id-card-after-incredibly-difficult-7-year-legal-battle/.

[301] *Leung Chun Kwong*, [2019] H.K.C.F.A. 19 at paras. 71–72.

[302] *Infinger*, [2023] H.K.C.A. 1178 at para. 2.

[303] *Id.* at para. 28.

[304] *Id.* at para. 29.

[305] *Id.* at para. 13.

[306] *Id.* at para. 31.

[307] *Id.* at paras. 17, 33.

more than 90 percent of the financing, Lam was not allowed to include him on the HOS application.[308] Like Infinger, Lam filed a judicial review, claiming that this policy violated Articles 25 and 22 of the Basic Law and BORO, respectively.[309] Lam unfortunately passed away during the course of litigation, which led to Li being substituted as the main applicant.

The Court of First Instance heard these cases separately and ruled in favor of both Infinger and Lam.[310] The HA relied on what it called the "Family Aim" to defend its policies. The HA claimed that housing policies reflected this aim in three ways: (1) to support existing "traditional" families (meaning heterosexual married couples), (2) to support "traditional" families and their children, and (3) to support the institution of the "traditional family" by limiting the supply of PRH and HOS flats to opposite-sex married couples whose marriage plans or plans to have children might be influenced by the availability of affordable housing.[311]

The CFI accepted the "Family Aim" as a legitimate aim at the first step of the proportionality test in both cases. However, it held that the differential treatment accorded to Lam was not rationally connected to this aim. The Court found it "far-fetched" that opposite-sex couples would be discouraged from marriage or having children because a same-sex spouse was added to an HOS application.[312]

With respect to PRH (in Infinger's case), the Court held that the impugned policy preventing Infinger and his partner from renting a flat together was rationally connected to the Family Aim, since it made available more flats for opposite-sex couples.[313] But on step three, it held that the policy was not proportionate, as the HA failed to provide any evidence to show that this policy had a significant impact on the availability of housing for opposite-sex couples.[314] On step four, the Court in both cases, again citing a lack of evidence, concluded (in *obiter dicta*) that a fair balance had not been struck between the burden on the applicants' right to equality and the societal benefit achieved.[315]

The government appealed both decisions, which were consolidated before the Court of Appeal. Several questions were raised, including as to whether the lower court used the proper comparators, adopted the appropriate standard of review, and applied the proportionality analysis correctly.[316] The CFI had compared the applicants to similarly situated opposite-sex couples. The HA, however, stressed the "inherent procreative capacity" of opposite-sex couples as a ground to give

[308] *Id.* at paras. 33–36.
[309] *Id.* at para. 37.
[310] *See* Infinger v. Hong Kong Housing Authority, [2020] H.K.C.F.I. 329; Ng Hon Lam Edgar v. Secretary for Justice, [2020] H.K.C.F.I. 2412.
[311] *Infinger*, [2023] H.K.C.A. 1178 at para. 48.
[312] *Lam*, [2020] H.K.C.F.I. 2412 at paras. 54–60.
[313] *Infinger*, [2020] H.K.C.F.I. 329 at para. 51(2).
[314] *Id.* at para. 51(3).
[315] *Id.* at para. 51(4); *Lam*, [2020] H.K.C.F.I. 2412 at paras. 75–77.
[316] *Infinger*, [2023] H.K.C.A. 1178 at paras. 52–54.

them preferential treatment over same-sex couples in public housing.[317] The Court of Appeal rejected this argument, citing the House of Lords Judgment in *Ghadian v. Godin-Mendoza* at length, to support the propositions that (1) not all opposite-sex couples want to have or are capable of having children; (2) that same-sex couples might have children through in vitro fertilization or surrogates; and (3) that same-sex couples have similar emotional and financial needs that cohabitation helps to meet.[318]

Moreover, as the Court noted, the government had in a previous filing expressly stated that its housing policies were not aimed at reviving Hong Kong's flagging birth rate.[319] Infinger had relied on this assurance and had therefore not presented any evidence to rebut the connection between housing discrimination and Hong Kong's "population dynamics."[320] For these reasons, the Court of Appeal did not allow the government to raise this argument.

On the standard of review, the lower court had adopted a standard that fell "somewhere in between the middle and high end of the continuous spectrum of reasonableness."[321] The Court of Appeal upheld the use of this standard, noting that the CFA had "repeatedly emphasized that when core values relating to personal or human characteristics are involved, such as sexual orientation in the present case . . . the court's vigilant scrutiny by the more stringent standard of 'no more than necessary'" is appropriate.[322]

Finally, as to the application of the proportionality analysis, the Court of Appeal upheld the lower court's conclusion that there was no rational connection between the Family Aim and the HOS spousal policy. The Court agreed, in Lam's case, that it was "objectively far-fetched" to claim that adding a same-sex spouse to a flat already owned by his partner would materially affect the availability of such flats for opposite-sex couples.[323] The Court of Appeal further agreed with the lower court that, in Infinger's case, the HA had failed to provide evidence to show that its policy excluding same-sex couples from PRH was proportionate on step three.[324] It also held that the lower court fairly determined on step four that such housing policies placed "an unacceptably hard burden on same-sex couples married overseas."[325]

[317] *Id.* at para. 112.
[318] *Id.* at para 108 (citing Ghadian v. Godin-Mendoza, [2004] UKHL 30 (appeal taken from Eng.)).
[319] *Id.* at paras. 113–14.
[320] *Id.*
[321] *Id.* at para. 127.
[322] *Id.* at para. 130.
[323] *Id.* at para. 120(3).
[324] *Id.* at para. 161.
[325] *Id.* at para. 162. The government appealed these two CA decisions. In November 2024, the CFA unanimously dismissed the appeals, thereby ruling in favor of both Infinger and Lam. *See* Infinger v. Secretary of Justice [2024] H.K.C.F.A. 29; Ng Hon Lam Edgar v. Housing Authority, [2024] H.K.C.F.A. 29.

In a separate judgment (issued a few days later), the Court of Appeal again ruled in favor of Edgar Lam and his partner Henry Li. The case concerned whether the same HOS flat would devolve to Li upon Lam's death, as the Intestates' Estates Ordinance (Cap 73) and Inheritance (Provision for Family and Dependants) Ordinance (Cap 481) both defined marriage in heterosexual terms, explicitly referring to the "husband" and "wife."[326] Under the relevant HOS policy, therefore, Li would not be able to inherit the flat.

Li filed a judicial review and the CFI ruled in his favor.[327] It held that this exclusionary policy failed at step two of the proportionality analysis: it was not rationally connected to any of the aims advanced by the HA, including supporting the traditional institution of marriage, encouraging opposite-sex couples to get married, and maintaining a coherent legal framework in this domain.[328]

The government, on appeal, raised essentially the same arguments that it raised in the housing case, including that the comparators were inapposite; the lower court's heightened standard of review was not warranted; and that the proportionality analysis was not correctly applied.[329] The Court of Appeal dismissed all these arguments, holding that Li was entitled to inherit Lam's HOS flat, and that the inheritance provisions in these ordinances must be read to include the surviving spouse in a same-sex marriage.[330]

Overall, these were resounding wins for the applicants and for same-sex couples in Hong Kong. They extended the CFA's rulings in *QT* and *Leung Chun Kwong* to ensure that same-sex married couples are entitled to the housing and estate benefits of opposite-sex married couples. But these cases concerned the rights of same-sex couples that were legally married outside Hong Kong. The remedies sought, therefore, only benefitted those couples with the financial means and mobility to obtain such documentation abroad. Same-sex couples within Hong Kong continued to lack any legal recognition.

To be sure, the incremental approach to LGBTQ+ rights litigation had worked well for both the applicants and the courts in Hong Kong's shifting political environment. It had succeeded in its challenging outdated laws and discriminatory policies. And it laid the groundwork for litigation to move beyond piecemeal challenges to confront the big, underlying question: whether same-sex couples were entitled not just to the benefits of same-sex marriage but to the institution of marriage itself. We turn next to the landmark case that finally addressed this question.

326 *Lam*, [2023] H.K.C.A. 1224 at para. 1.
327 Ng Hon Lam Edgar v. Secretary for Justice, [2020] H.K.C.F.I. 2422 at para. 52.
328 *Id.* at paras. 42–45.
329 *Lam*, [2023] H.K.C.A. 1224 at para. 56.
330 *Id.* at paras. 103, 108–09. The CFA unanimously upheld this judgment in November 2024. *See* Ng Hon Lam Edgar v. Secretary for Justice, [2024] H.K.C.F.A. 30.

C. Same-Sex Unions

A few weeks before the Court of Appeal ruled in favor of Infinger and Lam, the CFA issued its long-awaited judgment on same-sex marriage in *Sham Tsz Kit v. Secretary for Justice* (2023). The applicant and his partner in this case were married in New York.[331] As a Hong Kong permanent resident, he sought legal recognition of that marriage in the HKSAR. To wit, he filed a judicial review, raising three claims: (1) that he had a constitutional right to same-sex marriage under the right to equality in Article 25 of the Basic Law and Article 22 of BORO; (2) that the absence of any alternative legal framework of same-sex partnerships violated, *inter alia*, his right to privacy under Article 14 of BORO; and (3) that the lack of recognition conferred on his New York marriage violated his constitutional right to equality.[332]

A few years earlier, the CFI heard a similar application for judicial review on this issue in *MK v. Government of the HKSAR* (2019).[333] The application was filed by a lesbian woman who claimed that the denial of her right to marry was unconstitutional as was the failure of the government to provide an alternative legal framework (such as civil unions) for same-sex couples.[334] Specifically, she claimed that the Marriage Ordinance and Matrimonial Causes Ordinance, which prohibited same-sex marriage, violated her rights to equality, freedom of conscience, and freedom of marriage.[335]

The CFI's judgment in that case focused on the right to marry in Article 37 of the Basic Law and Article 19 of BORO. It noted that when the Basic Law and BORO were adopted in the 1990s, no country recognized same-sex marriage.[336] Thus, "marriage" in these instruments was intended to apply only to heterosexual couples.[337] The Court further noted, citing *QT* and *Leung Chung Kwong*, that Hong Kong courts had consistently interpreted "marriage" as between a man and a woman.[338] Though the Court conceded that fundamental rights "ought to be interpreted generously," it concluded that the right to marry could not be read so broadly as to include same-sex couples.[339] With respect to the claim that the Hong Kong government should provide an alternative legal framework in lieu of same-sex marriage, the applicant relied on the ECtHR's judgment in *Oliari v. Italy*.[340] The European Court had held that the Italian government violated Article 8 of the

[331] *Sham Tsz Kit*, [2023] H.K.C.F.A. 28 at para. 2.
[332] *Id.* at para. 3.
[333] MK v. Government of the HKSAR, [2019] H.K.C.F.I. 2518.
[334] *Id.* at paras. 3–6.
[335] *Id.* at para. 6.
[336] *Id.* at para. 14.
[337] *Id.*
[338] *Id.* at para. 16.
[339] *Id.* at para. 20.
[340] Oliari v. Italy, 65 E.H.R.R. 26, Eur. Ct. H.R. (2017).

ECHR by failing to provide a legal framework to protect same-sex unions.[341] The Court in *MK* distinguished *Oliari* on the basis that "prevailing legal, social, and political circumstances" in Italy and surrounding regions were fundamentally different to those in Hong Kong.[342]

In *Sham Tsz Kit*, the CFI and Court of Appeal similarly ruled against the applicant.[343] When the case reached the Court of Final Appeal, the five-judge bench largely concurred with the lower courts. On Questions 1 and 3—as to whether the applicant's right to equality had been infringed—the CFA unanimously ruled in favor of the government. Justices Ribeiro and Fok in a joint opinion explained that the right to equality in this case had to be read in light of the right to marry in Article 37 of the Basic Law and Article 19 of BORO.[344] Adopting the reasoning in *MK*, Justice Ribeiro noted that the ICCPR (upon which BORO was based) expressly refers to "the right of men and women" to marry, and that neither the Basic Law nor BORO contemplated same-sex marriage.[345] Relying on the *lex specialis* principle, the Court held that marriage under these instruments could not be broadened to include same-sex couples.[346] The general right to equality, in other words, was trumped by the specific meaning of marriage within the Basic Law and BORO.

Chief Justice Andrew Cheung—who has a conservative track record on LGBTQ+ rights cases[347]—concurred with Justices Fok and Ribeiro on Questions 1 and 3 with respect to the right to equality.[348] He further rejected the applicant's argument on Question 2; namely, that the government's failure to provide an alternative legal framework for same-sex unions was inconsistent with the right to privacy in Article 14 of BORO.[349] Following the *MK* judgment, CJ Cheung distinguished *Oliari* and other European jurisprudence on the grounds of cultural and legal differences.[350] Aside from obvious statements to the effect that Hong Kong is not bound by the ECHR, CJ Cheung added that "very few of the developments described by the European court . . . apply in Hong Kong" and that no "clear general trend [toward the recognition of same-sex marriage] . . . can be seen in this part of the world."[351]

341 *Id.* at para. 186.
342 *MK*, [2019] H.K.C.F.I. 2518 at para. 51.
343 Sham Tsz Kit v. Secretary of Justice, [2020] 4 H.K.L.R.D. 930 (C.F.I.); Sham Tsz Kit v. Secretary of Justice, [2022] 4 H.K.L.R.D. 368 (C.A.). For critiques of the lower court judgments see Kelley Loper, *Equality, Dignity and Same-Sex Marriage: Reflections on Developments in Hong Kong*, 53 Hong Kong L.J. 38 (2023); Holning Lau & Xavier Dyer, *Comparative Law and Freedom to Marry in Hong Kong*, 53 Hong Kong L.J. 51 (2023).
344 *Sham Tsz Kit*, [2023] H.K.C.F.A. 28 at para. 95.
345 *Id.* at paras. 90–95, 107.
346 *Id.* at paras. 120–24.
347 *See, e.g., Leung Chun Kwong*, [2018] H.K.C.A. 318.
348 *Sham Tsz Kit*, [2023] H.K.C.F.A. 28 at paras. 4, 76.
349 *Id.* at para. 68.
350 *Id.* at paras. 54–59.
351 *Id.* at para. 58.

By contrast, Justices Ribeiro and Fok cited *Oliari* and other European precedents favorably in siding with the applicant on the need for a legal framework providing legal recognition to same-sex couples. Such recognition, they said, was "compellingly advocated" for two reasons.[352] First, it would help same-sex couples meet "basic social needs" that opposite-sex couples enjoy.[353] Second, the absence of legal recognition was "discriminatory and demeaning" to same-sex couples, leading to uncertainty in matters of property disposition, hospital visitation rights, and other areas where the law provides clear guidance to heterosexual married couples.[354] They then turned to whether this lack of recognition constituted a violation of the right to privacy under Article 14 of BORO. Here, the justices relied on ECtHR judgments that had interpreted "privacy" broadly to encompass the right to establish relationships and to have autonomy over one's private life.[355] They also relied on the CFA's judgment in *Q v. Commissioner of Registration*, which had held in the context of transgender rights that privacy is "inherently linked to a person's dignity."[356] They also characterized *QT* and *Leung Chun Kwong* cases as instances of "arbitrary interference in the private lives of members of same-sex unions as a result of the absence of basic legal recognition of their relationship."[357] Thus, these two justices held that the applicant and his partner were entitled to legal recognition "in an appropriate form of same-sex union."[358]

Justice Lam, in a separate opinion, expressed sympathy for the applicants' privacy-based claim. He said same-sex couples may have "legitimate objections to the repeated need or requirement to reveal private information . . . to substantiate their claim that they are in such relationship."[359] For Justice Lam, this sort of requirement would arbitrarily interfere in the private lives of same-sex couples—in violation of Article 14—and could be avoided if the government legally recognized their unions.[360] However, he sounded a similar cautionary note to the Chief Justice. He warned that the approach adopted by Justices Ribeiro and Fok too closely follows the ECtHR, whose jurisprudence "cannot be directly transplanted in Hong Kong."[361] In his view, this approach would not provide a sufficient

[352] *Id.* at para. 129.
[353] *Id.* at para. 130.
[354] *Id.* at para. 133.
[355] *Id.* at paras. 136–42 (citing, *inter alia*, Schalk & Kopf v. Austria, 53 E.H.R.R. 20, Eur. Ct. H.R. (2011); *Oliari*, 65 E.H.R.R. 26; Fedotova v. Russia, Application Nos. 40792/10, 30538/14 & 43439/14, Eur. Ct. H.R. (Jan. 17, 2023)).
[356] *Id.* at para. 143 (quoting Q, [2023] H.K.C.F.A. 4 at para. 46).
[357] *Id.* at para. 145.
[358] *Id.* at para. 146.
[359] *Id.* at para. 229.
[360] *Id.* Justice Lam recognized that the government had a duty under Article 14 of BORO to protect same-sex couples from interference in their private lives but did not join the Ribeiro/Fok judgment because he disagreed with their interpretation of rights. *Id.* at paras. 232–34.
[361] *Id.* at para. 234.

margin of discretion to the Hong Kong government in devising alternative legal arrangements for same-sex couples through a "political process."[362]

With the four permanent justices divided, the outcome of this case was determined by the overseas non-permanent judge on the panel: Patrick Keane, former Justice of the Australian High Court. In a short opinion, Justice Keane concurred with Justices Ribeiro and Fok. He held that Article 14 of BORO imposed positive obligations on the government to remedy the "state of affairs" that same-sex couples in Hong Kong experienced, in which their "privacy and dignity . . . are subject to arbitrary or unlawful interference."[363]

In sum, while all five justices declined to recognize same-sex marriage, the CFA by a 3–2 margin ruled that the government was "in violation of its positive obligation under Article 14 . . . to establish an alternative framework for legal recognition of same-sex partnerships (such as registered civil partnerships or civil unions)."[364] It further directed that this declaration be suspended for two years to "afford the Government time to comply with its aforesaid obligation."[365] In a separate "Judgement on Relief," the CFA made clear that both parties may file further applications with respect to the suspension order. The applicant may approach the Court for relief if the government fails to comply with the order, while the government may file for an extension beyond the two-year timeframe if necessary.[366] We do not know, as of early 2025, whether and in what form same-sex couples will have their partnerships recognized in Hong Kong.

D. Moving Toward Judicial Self-Preservation

How do we account for the post–2020 judicial developments on LGBTQ+ rights? From a doctrinal perspective, Hong Kong is a common law jurisdiction, and its courts have generally abided by precedent while incrementally advancing LGBTQ+ rights. Indeed, many of the recent judgments follow logically from prior cases. The CFA laid the foundation in earlier judgments recognizing fundamental transgender and same-sex partnership rights. *Q v. Commissioner of Registration* extended Court's landmark ruling in *W* to gender-diverse persons who had not undergone the full SRS procedure. Similarly, the housing and estate benefits conferred to Infinger and Lam, respectively, built upon the spousal visa provided to the applicant in *QT* and the tax and medical benefits extended to a civil servant and his spouse in *Leung Chun Kwong*.

[362] *Id.* at paras. 244–52.
[363] *Id.* at paras. 258–59.
[364] *Id.* at para. 260(b).
[365] *Id.*
[366] *Sham Tsz Kit*, [2023] H.K.C.F.A. 31 at paras. 6–10.

But doctrine alone cannot explain why the CFA ruled as it did in *Sham Tsz Kit*. If anything, it points to a different outcome. The relevant precedents—like *Leung Chun Kwong* and *QT*—appeared to be stops along the road to the judicial recognition of same-sex marriage. Moreover, public sentiment had turned decisively in favor of same-sex marriage. The Centre for Comparative and Public Law published an updated study in 2023 showing that 60 percent of respondents approved of same-sex marriage, while 17 percent were opposed to it (23 percent were neutral).[367] A decade earlier, only 38 percent of those surveyed expressed support for same-sex marriage, while in 2017, the respondents were equally divided with 50 percent in favor.[368]

With its precedents and public opinion pointing toward a landmark progressive ruling, the CFA nonetheless declined to recognize same-sex marriage in *Sham Tsz Kit*. All five justices rejected the applicant's arguments that the failure to recognize same-sex marriage violated his right to equality under both the Basic Law and BORO. The Court relied on uncharacteristically formalist reasoning to reach this conclusion. Justices Ribeiro and Fok (who authored the principal opinion) stressed that marriage was limited to unions between men and women at the time the Basic Law and the ICCPR were adopted.[369] This is at odds with the CFA's precedents on LGBTQ+ rights, which dismissed arguments from tradition in the context of same-sex marriage benefits and struck down laws based on outdated views on gender and sexuality.[370] Moreover, the CFA has consistently maintained that it adopts a "purposive" and "generous" approach to constitutional interpretation, not one based on textualism or original meaning.[371]

Of course, the Court did partially rule in the applicant's favor, holding by a 3–2 margin that the denial of any legal recognition to same-sex couples violated their right to privacy. The reasoning to reach this conclusion, however, was strained. Justices Ribeiro and Fok, and separately Justice Keane, stressed that same-sex couples had to repeatedly bear the costs and publicity of litigation, which required them to reveal intimate details of their personal lives. While these points are valid, they demonstrate how privacy is an awkward legal vessel through which to recognize same-sex unions. The applicant was not asking to be left alone, as he might have if challenging a criminal prohibition on same-sex conduct. Rather, he was seeking to have his partnership officially and publicly recognized. His primary argument was that he and his partner were treated differently than opposite-sex couples and that their exclusion from the institution of marriage was discriminatory. Equality is at the crux of their argument, as it was for the petitioners in the

[367] Holning Lau et al., Support in Hong Kong For Same-Sex Couples' Rights Grew Over Ten Years (2013–2023): 60 Percent Now Support Same-Sex Marriage (2023).

[368] *Id.*

[369] *See Sham Tsz Kit*, [2023] H.K.C.F.A. 28 at paras. 88–95.

[370] *See, e.g.*, *Leung Chun Kwong*, [2019] H.K.C.F.A. 19; *W*, 3 H.K.L.R.D. 90.

[371] *See, e.g.*, *Ng Ka Ling No. 1*, (1999) 2 H.K.C.F.A.R. at 28–29.

United States and India who demanded access to the institution and protections of marriage.[372]

So why did the CFA rule for the applicant in *Sham Tsz Kit* solely on privacy grounds? It appears that the Court strategically limited the scope of its judgment in two ways. One, as discussed, is remedial. By providing the government two years to devise its own solution, the Court sought to preempt, or at least diffuse, political backlash. The other, more subtle strategic move was to decide the case only on right to privacy grounds under BORO. This enabled the Court to rule partially for the applicant and to signal its continued adherence to global constitutionalism. It was able to cite *Oliari* and European precedents to conclude that the Hong Kong government was in violation of its obligations under BORO and, in turn, its international human rights obligations under the ICCPR.

At the same time, the CFA avoided direct confrontations with the Hong Kong government and the PRC. The government would have probably lashed out if the Court ruled that the traditional institution of marriage be extended to same-sex couples. Then there was the threat of NPCSC intervention. Had the Court ruled on right to equality grounds or expanded the definition of "marriage" under the Basic Law, the NPCSC might have issued an Interpretation. It is, after all, the ultimate interpreter of the Basic Law.[373] But the NPCSC has no jurisdiction over BORO. By ruling for the applicant only on the right to privacy—which is enshrined in BORO, with no analog in the Basic Law—the CFA ensured that the NPCSC could not override its judgment. This implication was not lost on the political leadership. Pro-establishment legislator and Convenor of the Executive Council, Regina Ip, put it plainly: "I think the CFA made a very clever judgment" by "wisely avoiding" the possibility of NPCSC involvement.[374]

One might wonder why the CFA jumped through these hoops to rule for the applicant on privacy grounds: Why not just hold in favor of the government on all counts? As an initial matter, it is worth noting that the two most recent permanent justices elevated to the bench, Chief Justice Cheung (appointed to the Court in 2018; made Chief Justice in 2021) and Justice Lam (appointed in 2021) ruled for the government on all three questions raised. The justices who were appointed in less authoritarian and politically fraught times—Justice Ribeiro (appointed in 2000) and Justice Fok (appointed in 2013)—ruled in favor of the applicant on the right to privacy, alongside Non-Permanent Judge Patrick Keane who joined the CFA in 2023 from the High Court of Australia. Once Justices Ribeiro and Lam retire, their replacements will almost certainly be more conservative in their

[372] *See* Obergefell v. Hodges, 135 S. Ct. 2584 (2015); Supriyo @ Supriya Chakraborty v. Union of India, Writ Petition (Civil) No. 1011 of 2022 (2023) (India).

[373] Basic Law, art. 158.

[374] Bruce Einhorn & Kari Lindberg, *HK LGBTQ Ruling "Wisely" Avoids China Rewrite, Adviser Says*, Bloomberg (Sept. 6, 2023), https://www.bloomberg.com/news/articles/2023-09-06/hong-kong-lgbtq-ruling-avoids-beijing-rewrite-top-adviser-says.

interpretive approach and less inclined to stick their necks out for minority groups. The CFA will probably shift decisively against liberal constitutionalism, even of the limited, strategic sort that narrowly prevailed in *Sham Tsz Kit*.

Moving beyond specific personnel, there was a broader self-preservationist interest served by ruling for the applicants. The CFA has been subject to criticism and reputational damage along several fronts. First, it has been set back by the high-profile departures of overseas non-permanent judges. Judge James Spigelman from Australia left the Court in September 2022 (prior to the end of his appointed term) due to concerns about the NSL.[375] In June 2021, Baroness Hale, former President of the U.K. Supreme Court, announced that she would not seek reappointment at the end of her term that year. She said to the *Times* of London: "The jury is out on how they will be able to operate the new national security law. There are all sorts of question marks up in the air."[376] Finally, in March 2022, two more British judges—Lord Reed and Lord Hodge—both ended their tenures on the CFA in the middle of their terms.[377] Lord Reed made the most pointed remarks to date on this issue, stating:

> The judges of the Supreme Court cannot continue to sit in Hong Kong without appearing to endorse an administration which has departed from values of political freedom, and freedom of expression, to which the Justices of the Supreme Court are deeply committed.[378]

In a second and related development, foreign governments have questioned whether the CFA remains an independent court in authoritarian Hong Kong. Just prior to the Baroness Hale's resignation, the U.K. Foreign Secretary announced that the British government would review its practice of allowing its judges to serve on the CFA.[379] No further action was taken. But it appears that Baroness Hale's departure, followed by Lords Reed and Hodge, were influenced by the British government's uneasiness with their presence on the CFA and its vocal opposition to Hong Kong's constitutional shakeup.[380]

[375] Gary Cheung et al., *Veteran Australian Judge James Spigelman Resigns from Hong Kong's Top Court, Citing National Security Law*, South China Morning Post (Sept. 18, 2020), https://www.scmp.com/news/hong-kong/law-and-crime/article/3102051/veteran-australian-judge-james-spigelman-resigns-hong.

[376] *Senior British Judges to Quit Top Hong Kong Court: Media*, RFI (June 4, 2021), https://www.rfi.fr/en/senior-british-judge-to-quit-top-hong-kong-court-media.

[377] Lee Yuk Yue & Lu Xi, *Top British Judges Quit Hong Kong Final Appeal Court, Citing National Security Law*, Radio Free Asia (Mar. 30, 2022), https://www.rfa.org/english/news/china/judges-03302022121200.html.

[378] *Id.*

[379] *Foreign Secretary Supports the Withdrawal of Serving UK Judges from the Hong Kong Court of Final Appeal*, U.K. Gov't (Mar. 30, 2022), https://www.gov.uk/government/news/foreign-secretary-supports-the-withdrawal-of-serving-uk-judges-from-the-hong-kong-court-of-final-appeal.

[380] *See, e.g., Britain Says China Has "Broken Its Promises" on Hong Kong*, DW (Dec. 11, 2020), https://www.dw.com/en/uk-says-china-has-broken-its-promises-on-hong-kong/a-55575800 (alleging that China violated the terms of the Sino-British Joint Declaration (1984)).

In May 2023, the American Congressional-Executive Commission on China published a report analyzing the role of judges under the NSL.[381] The report listed all the judges who were known to have been selected to adjudicate national cases.[382] It then showed how these judges "have affirmed and extended NSL provisions in ways that undermine procedural rights," including denying bail and jury trials, permitting broad police searches and seizures (including of journalistic materials), and infringing upon fundamental rights to speech, press, and association.[383] In November 2023, a bipartisan group in the U.S. House of Representatives introduced a bill that would impose sanctions on various Hong Kong officials it deemed responsible for implementing the NSL, including several judges who had ruled in national security cases.[384]

Within this environment, Hong Kong courts can bolster their international reputation by ruling against the government, especially on a high-profile issue like same-sex unions that would receive positive coverage from Western media outlets.[385] While the *Sham Tsz Kit* judgment did not assuage foreign governments, it usefully demonstrated that Hong Kong's judiciary retains some independence, at least outside the national security context.[386]

Hong Kong's legal firmament is keenly aware of the need to maintain appearances. Outside the courtroom, judges and the legal profession have pushed back against the perception that the judiciary is no longer independent. Chief Justice Cheung, in his January 2023 speech opening the new legal year, said, "Whether as designated judges under the Hong Kong National Security Law or not, [judges] . . . have all applied the law to the best of their ability, in accordance with the evidence presented before them."[387] He added in the proceeding press

[381] *See* Congressional-Executive Commission on China, One City, Two Legal Systems: Hong Kong Judges' Role in Rights Violations under the National Security Law (May 2023) [hereinafter CECC Report].

[382] *Id.* at 4–5.

[383] *Id.* at 5–11.

[384] James Lee, *US Lawmakers Introduce Bill to Sanction Hong Kong Judges and Prosecutors; Gov't Slams 'Despicable' Intimidation*, Hong Kong Free Press (Nov. 3, 2023), https://hongkongfp.com/2023/11/03/us-lawmakers-introduce-bill-to-sanction-hong-kong-judges-and-prosecutors-govt-slams-despicable-intimidation/.

[385] *See, e.g.*, Helen Davidson, *Hong Kong's Top Court Rules in Favor of Legal Recognition for Same-Sex Couples*, Guardian (Sept. 5, 2023), https://www.theguardian.com/world/2023/sep/05/hong-kong-top-court-legal-recognition-same-sex-couples; Derrick Bryson Taylor, *Hong Kong Must Have Framework to Recognize Same-Sex Unions, Court Rules*, N.Y. Times (Sept. 5, 2023), https://www.nytimes.com/2023/09/05/world/asia/hong-kong-same-sex-partnership-court-ruling.html.

[386] *See* Julius Yam, *Approaching the Legitimacy Paradox in Hong Kong: Lessons for Hybrid Regime Courts*, 46 L. & Soc. Inquiry 153, 167–68 (2021) (contrasting "medium-stakes cases" such as those on LGBTQ+ rights—where courts promote liberal values with a "minimal risk of sanctions"—with "high-stakes cases" on issues that touch upon Chinese sovereign interests in which they are more deferential).

[387] *CJ's speech at Ceremonial Opening of Legal Year 2023*, HKSAR Gov't, https://www.info.gov.hk/gia/general/202301/16/P2023011600599.htm.

conference, "Our court is very independent in terms of exercising our judicial rights, we handle it very solemnly."[388]

Meanwhile, both the Hong Kong Bar Association and Law Society strongly condemned the introduction of the 2023 U.S. sanctions bill that targeted judges, stressing that its passage would undermine judicial independence.[389] The Bar Association, which has historically been more independent and outspoken than the Law Society, added that it was "justifiably confident that Hong Kong judges have always and will continue to operate independently and apolitically."[390]

A third, and primarily domestic, criticism levelled at the CFA concerns the continuing presence of overseas non-permanent judges on the bench. As discussed, the Chief Justice may invite prominent jurists from abroad to serve on the CFA. This practice was initiated by the inaugural Chief Justice Andrew Li and continues to the present day.[391] The eminent jurists who have served in this capacity have thus far all hailed from the United Kingdom, Canada, Australia, and New Zealand. Some are appointed after retirement, while others serve on the CFA concurrently as they continue to sit on the apex courts in their home jurisdictions.[392] These judges, who are appointed for (renewable) three-year periods, bring prestige and experience from other jurisdictions to the CFA. They also helped in the early years of the HKSAR to establish the CFA's international reputation for independence and to build networks with courts in the Global North.[393] But, as Simon Young has shown, the presence of these judges has consistently been criticized within Hong Kong. Three main concerns emerge: namely, "ignorance of local law and circumstances, divided patriotic ties, and the sense they are no longer needed."[394]

The latter two concerns have become stronger in recent years. Consider, first, the notion that these judges are no longer necessary. In short, critics argue that the CFA has now been around for a quarter century, and it no longer requires the assistance of prominent foreign jurists (if it ever did) to develop its jurisprudence. And though there is a chronic shortage of judges at the lower levels of the judiciary, this does not extend to the CFA. A highly developed region like Hong Kong, with a population of 7.5 million, is not short of lawyers with elite qualifications and experience.[395] There is also

[388] Jessie Pang & Greg Torode, *Hong Kong Judge Defends Judiciary amid Fears of Ebbing Independence*, REUTERS (Jan. 17, 2023), https://www.reuters.com/world/asia-pacific/hong-kong-judge-defends-judiciary-amid-fears-ebbing-independence-2023-01-16/.

[389] Lee, *supra* note 384.

[390] *Id.*

[391] Basic Law, art. 82; Hargreaves, *supra* note 67, at 192–95.

[392] *Overseas Non-Permanent Judges*, HONG KONG COURT OF FINAL APPEAL, https://www.hkcfa.hk/en/about/who/judges/npjs/index.html.

[393] Young & Da Roza, *supra* note 63, at 263–65; Law, *supra* note 25, at 996–97.

[394] Simon N.M. Young, *Domestic Criticisms of Foreign Judges: The Case of Hong Kong*, *in* CAMBRIDGE HANDBOOK OF FOREIGN JUDGES ON DOMESTIC COURTS 284, 285 (Anna Dziedzic & Simon N.M. Young eds., 2023).

[395] Hargreaves, *supra* note 67, at 198–200.

the uncomfortably colonial character of the overseas judges, all of whom have been white and have come from either the United Kingdom or its "White Dominions."[396] This, combined with the fact that all but two of these judges have been male, and often fly in for a brief periods,[397] creates a (fair) perception that they do not represent the local community or its interests.

Though the Chief Justice could invite more female overseas non-permanent judges, or judges from India, Malaysia, Kenya, or Jamaica (among many other common law jurisdictions) to serve on the CFA, there appears to be no change forthcoming. To the contrary, current and former local judges on the Court have publicly expressed their admiration and support for the overseas non-permanent judges. Justice Kemal Bokhary, who served as a permanent judge from 1997 to 2012 and continues to serve as a non-permanent judge, said in a 2019 speech, "Sir Anthony Mason and Lords Cooke, Nicholls and Hoffmann are among the first overseas judges appointed to the Court of Final Appeal . . . I sat at their feet to learn of their wisdom."[398] Justice Fok—who is currently a permanent judge on the CFA—authored a chapter on the role and impact of overseas non-permanent judges on the CFA. Calling the contribution of these judges to Hong Kong's legal development "immense," and noting that the Court's standing has been "raised by their participation,"[399] Fok concluded on a personal and cautionary note. He wrote, "[I]t is a privilege and a pleasure to sit with them and they have our full respect, admiration and gratitude. It would be a loss . . . if they were no longer able to participate."[400]

The other concern that has gained prominence in recent years is that overseas judges have divided loyalties. For the last decade, and especially in the post–2020 authoritarian era, the PRC and the Hong Kong government have sought to rein in the judiciary on patriotism-related grounds. In 2014, in response to "Occupy Central," the State Council (China's highest administrative organ) issued a White Paper on the Practice of One Country, Two Systems in the HKSAR. The paper aimed to comprehensively set out how Hong Kong should be governed.[401] One subsection, titled "The Hong Kong People Who Govern Hong Kong Should Above All Be Patriotic," specified that "all those who administrate Hong Kong" including

[396] *Id.* at 216–17.

[397] Young & Da Roza, *supra* note 63, at 263 (noting that overseas non-permanent judges usually fly to Hong Kong to hear cases in "one-month stints").

[398] Kemal Bokhary, *Keynote Address at the Towering Judges Conference Held at The Chinese University of Hong Kong* (Jan. 25, 2019) at para. 17.

[399] Joseph Fok, *Judges from Other Common Law Jurisdictions on the Hong Kong Court of Final Appeal*, *in* CAMBRIDGE HANDBOOK OF FOREIGN JUDGES ON DOMESTIC COURTS 41, 55 (Anna Dziedzic & Simon N.M. Young eds., 2023).

[400] *Id.*

[401] *The Practice of the "One Country, Two Systems" Policy in the Hong Kong Special Administrative Region*, STATE COUNCIL OF THE PEOPLE'S REPUBLIC OF CHINA, https://english.www.gov.cn/archive/white_paper/2014/08/23/content_281474982986578.htm.

"judges of the courts at different levels" have the responsibility of "correctly understanding and implementing the Basic Law."[402] The subtext: judges must be aligned with other authorities (like executive and legislative officials) in ensuring that the one, "correct" interpretation of the Basic Law is upheld. This autocratic understanding of judging and legal interpretation is at odds with the liberal, common law approach adopted by Hong Kong courts. The State Council, of course, knew this. By including judges in this guidance, it sent a clear signal that the CFA, including the overseas non-permanent judges, must toe the line, especially when it comes to politically sensitive matters.

The CFA got the message. As Stuart Hargreaves has shown, the percentage of opinions authored by overseas judges declined from roughly 25 percent from 1997–2010 to 19 percent from 2014–19.[403] And overseas judges no longer write opinions on matters relating to Hong Kong-China relations or fundamental rights.[404] The general practice of one overseas judge sitting in almost every substantive case, however, remains unchanged. Thus, the CFA appears to have strategically reduced the prominence of overseas judges in a nod to the White Paper (and the domestic criticisms generally), while keeping these judges on the bench to preserve international confidence.[405]

The NSL brought the issue of judicial patriotism into sharp relief. Though the government has not adopted an official policy that prevents overseas judges from serving on NSL-related cases, it seems that they are excluded as a practical matter. To date, none of the overseas judges on the CFA have been designated as national security judges by the CE.[406] Moreover, no overseas judge was assigned to the *Lai Chee Ying* case. The bench instead included two local non-permanent judges (Patrick Chan and Frank Stock), who had been designated as national security judges, and who unsurprisingly joined the full Court's opinion holding that the NSL could not be subject to judicial review.[407]

All told, it appears that some overseas non-permanent judges will remain on the CFA, though their role is diminished. It is crucial for the Court's image to continue attracting eminent jurists from abroad. Its judicial output must, therefore, reflect both independence and continued engagement with foreign law, especially that of Western liberal democracies. The LGBTQ+ rights judgments are helpful on both fronts. They enable the Court to show that it can still rule (at least partially) against

[402] *Id.* at § V(3).
[403] Hargreaves, *supra* note 67, at 206–09.
[404] *Id.* at 217. Justice Keane's short concurring opinion in *Sham Tsz Kit* is a notable exception.
[405] *Id.*
[406] *See* Stuart Hargreaves, *Hong Kong's Overseas Judges Under the National Security Law*, *in* ROUTLEDGE HANDBOOK OF CONSTITUTIONAL LAW IN GREATER CHINA 356 (Ngoc Son Bui et al. eds., 2023); CECC Report, *supra* note 381, at 4–5.
[407] *See Lai Chee Ying*, [2021] H.K.C.F.A. 3.

the government and that it continues to cite and adopt jurisprudence from, *inter alia*, the ECtHR.[408]

E. The Government's Fine Line on Judicial Independence

In *Sham Tsz Kit*, an Australian non-permanent judge cast the deciding vote for the applicants in *Sham Tsz Kit*. While this might have fueled anti-Western rhetoric and led to a rehearsal of all the domestic criticisms of overseas judges, the Hong Kong government was reserved in its reaction to the judgment. When asked for comment, a government spokesperson said, "Since the parties may lodge written submissions on relief as directed by the court, the case has not completely concluded and it is inappropriate to give any comment at this juncture."[409] Regina Ip, Convenor of the Executive Council was similarly reserved. She acknowledged that "the government will need to put a bill to the Legislative Council" but stressed that it "has wide discretion on timing."[410]

What should we make of the government's muted response? On one hand, it signals continuity in the official position on same-sex marriage and on LGBTQ+ rights overall. While the public has warmed to same-sex unions—and to the recognition of LGBTQ+ rights generally—the Hong Kong government has not budged. Chief Executive Carrie Lam, for instance, referred to same-sex marriage as a "very controversial issue" and said that, despite the CFA's recognition of same-sex marriage benefits, Hong Kong was unlikely to legislate on marriage equality.[411] In 2019, the Court of First Instance remarked that the government should "undertake a comprehensive review" of the legal framework on same-sex couples.[412] The Court warned that in the absence of such a review, "specific legislations, or policies or decisions of the Government" would be challenged in court on "an *ad-hoc* basis, resulting in an incoherent state of the law at different times."[413] This is precisely what came to pass. The government has not only failed to legislate on this issue but continues to appeal adverse judgments, including the Court of Appeal rulings in favor of Infinger and Lam that simply applied prior CFA precedents to cover more same-sex couple benefits.

[408] *See, e.g.*, *Q*, [2023] H.K.C.F.A. 4 at para.66 (citing *AP, Garçon & Nicot*, App. No. 79885/12, Eur. Ct. H.R.); *Sham Tsz Kit*, [2023] H.K.C.F.A. 28 at paras. 136–41 (relying on the "Strasbourg Court's jurisprudence" to establish what the right to privacy in Article 14 of BORO requires).

[409] Einhorn & Lindberg, *supra* note 374.

[410] *Id.*

[411] *Carrie Lam Says Gay Marriage Remains Controversial*, STANDARD (Mar. 21, 2019), https://www.thestandard.com.hk/breaking-news/section/3/124527/Carrie-Lam-says-gay-marriage-remains-controversial.

[412] *MK*, [2019] H.K.C.F.I. 2518 at para. 57.

[413] *Id.*

The government has also ignored similar prodding from the CFA on transgender rights. Following the *W* judgment in 2013, the government failed to act within the specified timeframe to amend the impugned marriage ordinances that prevented a postoperative transgender person from marrying her opposite-sex spouse. The CFA in *W* further recommended a review of the existing legal framework on gender recognition. The government in response created the Interdepartmental Working Group (IWG) on Gender Recognition "to consider legislation and incidental administrative measures that may be required to protect the rights of transsexual persons in Hong Kong in all legal contexts and to make such recommendations for reform as may be appropriate."[414] Despite setting out a consultation paper in 2017,[415] the IWG has still not (as of early 2025) published a final report and the government has not legislated to protect the rights of gender-diverse persons.

With this track record, the muted response to *Sham Tsz Kit* is troubling. It may signal that the government plans to ignore the CFA's order and leave same-sex couples in the lurch. Unlike in *W*, where the applicant was able to marry once the suspension order expired, it is not clear what relief same-sex couples would receive if the government fails to act.

On the other hand, in Hong Kong's present political climate, one might ask why the government did not seek to delegitimize the CFA following this judgment. This would have been an opportunity to rail against the incursions of "foreign forces" and imported "Western" values,[416] especially since the decisive opinion was issued by an Australian judge.

To resolve this puzzle, we need to look more broadly at the government's rhetoric on judicial independence. Over the past few years, there appears to be a coordinated effort by the government and PRC authorities to keep (at least the appearance of) judicial independence intact. The constitutional overhaul in 2020–21, for instance, did not directly affect the CFA. The NSL (2020) enabled the CE to choose which of its justices would adjudicate national security cases, and the Court in *Lai Chee Ying* declined to exercise judicial review over the NSL. But the CFA remained structurally intact. Its composition, appointments process, and jurisdiction remain formally unchanged. This stands in stark contrast to the LegCo, which was transformed from partially democratic institution with a lively opposition to an autocratic one with opposing voices eliminated.

[414] *Public Consultation on Gender Recognition Launched Today*, HKSAR Gov'T (June 23, 2017), https://www.info.gov.hk/gia/general/201706/23/P2017062300575.htm.

[415] *See* IWG Working Paper, *supra* note 291.

[416] *See, e.g.*, Gigi Lee et al., *Hong Kong Introduces Security Law Targeting "Foreign Forces" in City*, RADIO FREE ASIA (Jan. 30, 2024), https://www.rfa.org/english/news/china/hongkong-article23-013 02024194009.html; Keith B. Richburg, *Beijing's Cancel Culture Is Crushing Hong Kong*, ASPI (Apr. 8, 2021), https://www.aspistrategist.org.au/beijings-cancel-culture-is-crushing-hong-kong/.

Similarly, at an ideological level, the Hong Kong government has veered toward Beijing's view of contested concepts like separation of powers but has remained consistent in its rhetoric on judicial independence. The Basic Law, like most modern constitutions, divides power between the executive, legislative, and judicial branches of government, dedicating a separate section to the powers and responsibilities of each.[417] In a statement to the Basic Law Drafting Committee in 1987, then-Chinese leader Deng Xiaoping expressed the PRC's view that "For a century and a half Hong Kong has been operating under a system different from those of Great Britain and the United States. I am afraid it would not be appropriate for its system to be a total copy of theirs with, for example, the separation of the three powers."[418] Ever since, the PRC has maintained that the separation of powers does not apply in Hong Kong.[419]

Yet, Hong Kong courts have consistently reiterated that the separation of powers—in the liberal sense of guarding against autocratic government—is "woven into the fabric of the Basic Law."[420] Public statements from Hong Kong's two former Chief Justices confirm this understanding. In 2014, Chief Justice Geoffrey Ma said, "The Basic Law sets out clearly the principle of the separation of powers."[421] His predecessor, Chief Justice Andrew Li, referred to judicial independence in 2001 as a principle that "lies at the heart of the separation of powers among the executive, the legislative and the judicial branches, providing checks and balances against one another."[422]

The Hong Kong government refrained from taking a position on this issue until the region's authoritarian turn in 2020. To demonstrate the government's alignment with Beijing, CE Carrie Lam explicitly adopted the PRC position and declared that "many people misunderstand" how HKSAR is governed.[423] She said Hong Kong has an "executive-led system" with a "division of labour" between the three branches.[424] Secretary of Justice Teresa Chang elaborated further that such a

[417] Basic Law, ch. IV.

[418] Deng Xiaoping, *Speech at a Meeting with the Members of the Committee for Drafting the Basic Law of the Hong Kong Special Administrative Region* (Apr. 16, 1987).

[419] *HK has never adopted Western "separation of powers" concept: State Council*, GLOBAL TIMES (Sept. 7, 2020), https://www.globaltimes.cn/content/1200196.shtml.

[420] *Lau Kwok Fai v. Secretary for Justice* [2003] HKEC 711 (C.F.I.) at para. 19. *See also*, P.Y. Lo & Albert H.Y. Chen, *The Judicial Perspective of "Separation of Powers" in the Hong Kong Special Administrative Region of China*, 5(2) J. INT'L COMP. L. 337 (2018).

[421] *CJ's speech at Ceremonial Opening of the Legal Year 2014*, HKSAR GOV'T, https://www.info.gov.hk/gia/general/201401/13/P201401130352.htm.

[422] Rhoda Kwan, *Explainer: Understanding Hong Kong's Debate Around the Separation of Powers and an Executive-Led System*, HONG KONG FREE PRESS (Sept. 26, 2020), https://hongkongfp.com/2020/09/26/explainer-understanding-hong-kongs-debate-around-the-separation-of-powers-and-an-executive-led-system/.

[423] Jennifer Creery, *No Separation of Powers in Hong Kong says Chief Exec. Carrie Lam, Despite Previous Comments from Top Judges*, HONG KONG FREE PRESS (Sept. 1, 2020), https://hongkongfp.com/2020/09/01/no-separation-of-powers-in-hong-kong-says-chief-exec-carrie-lam-despite-previous-comments-from-top-judges.

[424] *Id.*

division of labor enables the three branches to "complement each other with a view to upholding national unity and territorial integrity, maintaining the prosperity and stability of Hong Kong."[425]

PRC and Hong Kong authorities, however, have not pursued a similar ideological offensive with respect to judicial independence. To the contrary, they defend it vigorously when provoked. The China Liaison Office in 2020, for instance, described Hong Kong's constitutional framework as comprising "the division of the three powers, executive-led, judicial independence, the executive reports to the central government on behalf of the HKSAR."[426] In a 2021 press conference, CE Carrie Lam declared that she, as Chief Executive, had a duty to uphold judicial independence.[427] A few years later, when Lords Reed and Hodge abruptly left the CFA, Lam expressed regret at their decision. She declared that Hong Kong's "continued success . . . [was] underpinned by an independent judiciary which exercises judicial powers, including that of final adjudication, free from any interference."[428] Lam went on to say, "We appreciate fully the valuable contribution of judges from other common law jurisdictions sitting on the CFA for the past 25 years."[429] Lam also "vehemently refute[d]" any suggestion that these judges left as a result of the NSL.[430] In 2023, Lam's successor, CE John Lee strongly condemned the proposed U.S. sanctions against judges designated to sit on national security cases. Lee said, "Their obstruction of justice not only violates the rule of law, but also violates judicial independence that the US claims is guaranteed in their own constitution."[431] In a televised address a few months earlier, Lee made a sarcastic and telling remark: "We just had a case in which the government was sued and lost. Hong Kong has no human rights? That's impossible!"[432] The implication is that judicial independence must be intact since the government does not always prevail in court.

Taken together, these statements show that the government treats judicial independence as a principle that is worth defending at least rhetorically, if not

[425] Jennifer Creery, *Justice Sec. Says Hong Kong has an "Executive-Led" Political System in Row over Separation of Powers*, Hong Kong Free Press (Sept. 7, 2020), https://hongkongfp.com/2020/09/07/justice-sec-says-hong-kong-has-an-executive-led-political-system-in-row-over-separation-of-powers/.

[426] *Liaison Office of Central Gov't in HKSAR Clarifies Hong Kong's Political system as "Executive-Led"*, (Sept. 7, 2020), http://www.xinhuanet.com/english/2020–09/07/c_139349904.htm.

[427] *Judicial Independence Upheld*, News.Gov.HK (Feb. 2, 2021), https://www.news.gov.hk/eng/2021/02/20210202/20210202_101728_595.html.

[428] *Chief Executive Regrets Resignation of Two UK Non-Permanent Judges of Court of Final Appeal*, HKSAR Gov't, https://www.info.gov.hk/gia/general/202203/30/P2022033000658.htm.

[429] *Id.*

[430] *Id.*

[431] Kahon Chan, *Hong Kong's John Lee "Strongly" Condemns US Bill to Sanction 49 City Officials, Says Bid to Intimidate Judges Contradicts American Constitution*, South China Morning Post (Nov. 4, 2023), https://www.scmp.com/news/hong-kong/politics/article/3240334/hong-kong-leader-john-lee-strongly-condemns-us-bill-seeking-sanction-49-local-officials-says-attempt.

[432] Candace Chau, *Hong Kong Falls from Top 20 in Global Rule of Law Index*, Hong Kong Free Press (Oct. 26, 2022), https://hongkongfp.com/2022/10/26/hong-kong-falls-from-top-20-in-global-rule-of-law-index/.

substantively. The question that remains is *why* they chose to defend this liberal constitutional principle and not, say, democracy or the separation of powers, which were cast aside in the post–2020 constitutional overhaul. We turn to that question next.

VI. Conclusion—An Uneasy Truce

When Hong Kong was transferred from British to Chinese sovereignty in 1997, the priority for both countries was to maintain the region's status as a global hub for international finance and trade. Economic freedom remains the lodestar of the HKSAR's constitutional order.[433] And Hong Kong remains a major international financial center. It is the primary entry point for international businesses to access Chinese markets and for Chinese businesses to access foreign capital.[434] Thus, following all the negative press coverage it received since 2019, the Hong Kong government has been keen to spread the word that the city is economically prosperous again, especially for major transnational corporations and the ultrawealthy.[435]

It is no surprise, then, that the government reacts with pantomime outrage when Hong Kong receives bad press in areas that may sway economic elites from doing business or investing in the region. In 2023, the Fraser Institute—a Canadian think tank—published its annual *Economic Freedom in the World* report. And for the first time in more than fifty years, Hong Kong was not ranked as the world's freest economy.[436] The report cited the crackdown on civil rights and political dissent to explain Hong Kong's demotion to second place (behind Singapore).[437] The government issued a press release immediately thereafter, referring to claims of suppression as "factually wrong and totally groundless," and adding that "Hong Kong has entered a new stage of advancing from stability to prosperity."[438]

[433] *See* Basic Law, ch. V; Puig & Ip, *supra* note 11, at ch. 7.

[434] Basic Law, art. 112 ("No foreign exchange control policies shall be applied in the Hong Kong Special Administrative Region. The Hong Kong dollar shall be freely convertible. The Government . . . shall safeguard the free flow of capital within, into and out of the Region"); Kiuyan Wan et al., *Chinese Firms Are Dominating Key Parts of Hong Kong's Economy*, Bloomberg (June 27, 2022), https://www.bloomberg.com/news/articles/2022-06-26/chinese-firms-are-dominating-key-parts-of-hong-kong-s-economy. *See also*, Chen & Yap, *supra* note 6, at 213 ("Hong Kong's future depends on the mainland's perception of the former's utility to China's overall economic development").

[435] *See, e.g.*, Jessie Yeung & Kristie Lu Stout, *Hong Kong says it's back open for business. Will the world buy it?*, CNN (Nov. 5, 2022), https://edition.cnn.com/2022/11/05/asia/hong-kong-reopen-finance-summit-rugby-sevens-intl-hnk/index.html; Altrata, World Ultra Wealth Report 2023 (September 2023), https://info.altrata.com/world-ultra-wealth-report-2023-pdf (showing that more ultra-high net worth individuals [worth at least 30 million U.S. dollars] lived in Hong Kong than any other city in 2023 even as its overall population had shrunk more than 20 percent since 2022).

[436] Fraser Institute, Economic Freedom of the World: 2023 Annual Report vii (2023), https://www.fraserinstitute.org/sites/default/files/economic-freedom-of-the-world-2023.pdf.

[437] *Id.*

[438] Hans Tse, *Hong Kong Loses Edge to Singapore as World's Freest Economy, as Think Tank Cites Interference and Waning Rule of Law*, Hong Kong Free Press (Sept. 20, 2023), https://hongkongfp.

The government had a similar rhetorical response to Hong Kong's decline in the World Justice Project Rule of Law Index. Hong Kong fell from sixteenth position in 2020 to twenty-third in 2023 due to the authoritarian legal changes—including the passage of the NSL—that had occurred in that period.[439] The government deflected criticism and noted that the region had a higher score in the subcategory of "Order and Security" in 2023. A government spokesperson said, "The NSL has provided the necessary conditions for ensuring the long-term prosperity and stability of Hong Kong."[440]

This theme of prosperity and stability was central to President Xi Jinping's 2022 speech that commemorated twenty-five years of the handover of sovereignty. Referring to "one country, two systems" as an "unprecedented innovation," Xi declared that its "fundamental purpose is to safeguard China's sovereignty, security, and development interests and to maintain long-term prosperity and stability in Hong Kong."[441] After emphasizing that Chinese sovereign interests must be upheld, and that "patriots" must continue to administer the region, Xi said that Hong Kong's "distinctive status and advantages" should be maintained.[442] Of course, there was no mention of political freedoms or liberalism. Hong Kong's distinctiveness was framed in purely economic terms. As Xi put it:

> The central government fully supports Hong Kong in its effort to . . . improve its presence as an international financial, shipping, and trading center, to keep its business environment free, open, and regulated, and to maintain the common law, so as to expand and facilitate its exchanges with the world.[443]

If stability followed by economic prosperity is the official story of post–2020 Hong Kong, it becomes clear why the government is sensitive to criticism on judicial independence. Hong Kong requires an at least minimally independent judiciary to maintain its status as a major financial and trade hub. Like the rule of law and economic freedom, judicial independence—at least in commercial affairs—matters to investors and companies doing business in the region. As Rosalind Dixon and Vicki Jackson have pointed out, the appointment of overseas judges to the CFA

com/2023/09/20/hong-kong-loses-edge-as-worlds-freest-economy-as-think-tank-cites-beijing-interference-and-waning-rule-of-law/.

[439] Chau, *supra* note 432; World Justice Project Rule of Law Index (2023), https://worldjusticeproject.org/rule-of-law-index/.

[440] *HKSAR Government's Response to 2023 World Justice Project Rule of Law Index*, Gov't of the HKSAR (Oct. 25, 2023), https://www.info.gov.hk/gia/general/202310/25/P2023102500827.htm.

[441] *Full Text of Xi Jinping's Address at the Meeting Celebrating the 25th Anniversary of Hong Kong's Return to the Motherland and the Inaugural Ceremony of the Sixth-Term government of the Hong Kong Special Administrative Region*, Xinhua (July 2, 2022), https://english.news.cn/20220702/84161c1f78fc4cd3ad239d059e1b400f/c.html.

[442] *Id.*

[443] *Id.*

served, *inter alia*, to reassure the business community that "there would be continuity in the general legal-commercial regime following the handover of sovereignty" from Britain to China.[444]

More broadly, as Tamir Moustafa and Tom Ginsburg argue, courts can play a legitimating role for authoritarian regimes. Regimes with "questionable legitimacy" may strategically preserve judicial institutions "that give the image, if not the full effect, of constraints on arbitrary rule."[445] In some cases, the targets of legitimation are external.[446] Take Singapore, for example. Over past few decades, the authoritarian city-state has built a highly professional and efficient judicial system, which, in turn, helped to attract foreign investment and led many multinational companies to set up regional headquarters there.[447] Hong Kong's leaders have apparently taken note.

Let us now return to *Sham Tsz Kit* and the question of why the government did not criticize the CFA following its judgment requiring the legal recognition of same-sex unions. From the perspective of legitimation, especially to an external audience, the judgment benefits the government: a high-profile loss at the CFA on an issue that resonates internationally. The government can point to this judgment to show that it must still abide by (some) liberal constitutional rights, while it remains unchecked on national security and faces no political opposition. Indeed, *Sham Tsz Kit* received positive coverage from liberal media outlets like the *New York Times* and the *Guardian*, though each noted that this was not a complete victory for same-sex couples.[448]

The judicial recognition of same-sex partnerships also fits within the official narrative of economic freedom and prosperity. In *Sham Tsz Kit*, the decisive opinion of Non-Permanent Judge Patrick Keane relied almost exclusively on the CFA's 2018 judgment in *QT* to buttress its analysis and conclusion.[449] This initially appears to be a curious choice, as Justice Keane's opinion rested on the right to privacy enshrined in Article 14 of BORO, which was not discussed at all in *QT*. But as he explains, the immigration policy at issue in that case was *Wednesbury* unreasonable, meaning that it arbitrarily interfered in the applicant's private life.[450] Thus, Justice Keane went on to say, "[I]t can be seen that the absence of legal recognition of same-sex relationships is an occasion of arbitrary interference with the right to privacy . . . [and] is contrary to [Article 14 of BORO]."[451]

[444] Dixon & Jackson, *supra* note 64, at 328; YASH GHAI, HONG KONG'S NEW CONSTITUTIONAL ORDER: THE RESUMPTION OF CHINESE SOVEREIGNTY AND THE BASIC LAW 332–33 (1997).

[445] Moustafa & Ginsburg, *supra* note 38, at 5.

[446] *Id.* at 6–7.

[447] *See* Gordon Silverstein, *Singapore: The Exception That Proves Rules Matter, in* RULE BY LAW: THE POLITICS OF COURTS IN AUTHORITARIAN REGIMES 73, 78–83 (Tom Ginsburg & Tamir Moustafa eds., 2012).

[448] Davidson, *supra* note 385; Taylor, *supra* note 385.

[449] *Sham Tsz Kit*, [2023] H.K.C.F.A. 28 at paras. 258–59 (citing *QT*, [2018] H.K.C.F.A. 28).

[450] *Id.* at para. 259 (referring to *Associated Provincial Picture Houses* Ltd. v. Wednesbury Corp. [1948] 1 KB 223 (U.K.)).

[451] *Id.*

A closer look at *QT* reveals the economic stakes underlying the CFA's ruling. *QT* was the first in this line of precedent recognizing the legal status and benefits of same-sex couples. The applicant—a British woman—was denied a dependent visa to join her partner, who had been employed in Hong Kong. The denial was based on an Immigration Department policy that sought to balance two objectives: (1) encouraging "people with the right talent and skills to come to Hong Kong by giving them the choice of bringing in their dependants" and (2) maintaining strict controls given the region's small size and population density.[452] Same-sex spouses were excluded on the grounds of needing to maintain strict controls. The CFA ruled that there was no rational connection between the visa rejection and the government's policy aims.[453] The Court laid out this incongruity in plain terms: if the goal was to recruit the best workers to live and work in Hong Kong, it was "counter-productive" to flatly ban same-sex spouses from obtaining dependent visas.[454]

The economic subtext of this conclusion, on which the landmark same-sex union judgment (*Sham Tsz Kit*) would later hinge, was evident. Indeed, a group of twelve multinational banks and law firms sought to intervene in *QT*. They did so, as Morgan Stanley's regional Head of Diversity and Inclusion put it, because "It is critically important that we have policies and benefits in place that allow us to attract and retain the best talent."[455] While the CFA rejected the application to intervene, its justices were aware of the broader economic ramifications of their judgment.[456] If the existing immigration policy were to stand, Hong Kong would have been at a disadvantage in the global marketplace for elite talent by discriminating against—and thereby discouraging employment visa applications from—those in committed same-sex partnerships. After the *QT* judgment came down, law firms like Herbert Smith Freehills and Deacons issued statements declaring how they were "proud to have . . . lent support to QT's case,"[457] and that "[E]mployers could look forward to witnessing more talents enter Hong Kong's workforce as a result of the decision."[458]

[452] *QT*, [2018] H.K.C.F.A. 28 at para. 6.

[453] *Id.* at para. 99

[454] *Id.* at para. 90.

[455] *Hong Kong Case Could Lead to Visas for Same Sex Partners*, CIPD (Feb. 12, 2018), https://www.cipd.org/en/about/news-archive/hong-kong-visas-same-sex-partners/.

[456] *See* Karen Cheung, *Hong Kong's Top Court Rejects Bid by Banks and Law Firms to Intervene in LGBT Appeal*, Hong Kong Free Press (May 2, 2018), https://hongkongfp.com/2018/05/02/hong-kongs-top-court-rejects-bid-banks-law-firms-intervene-lgbt-appeal/; *QT*, [2018] H.K.C.F.A. 28 at para. 90 ("As is evident from the attempted intervention of the Banks and Law Firms, the ability to bring in dependants is an important issue for persons deciding whether to move to Hong Kong").

[457] *Hong Kong: Court of Final Appeal Rejects Policy on Dependant Spousal Visas for Same-Sex Couples*, Herbert Smith Freehills (Aug. 16, 2018), https://www.herbertsmithfreehills.com/notes/asiadisputes/2018-08/hong-kong-court-of-final-appeal-rejects-policy-on-dependant-spousal-visas-for-same-sex-couples/.

[458] *Victory for Same-Sex Civil Partners in Dependant Visa Case*, Deacons (July 26, 2018), https://www.deacons.com/2018/07/26/victory-for-same-sex-civil-partners-in-dependant-visa-case/.

The CFA thus advanced both LGBTQ+ rights and the HKSAR's elite-driven economic agenda through *QT* and *Sham Tsz Kit*. In doing so, it channeled what Lisa Duggan has dubbed "homonormativity."[459] These judgments do not contest either the dominant neoliberal or heterosexual paradigms.[460] Rather, they recognize LGBTQ+ rights in a manner that sustains neoliberalism and sanitizes sexual minorities by granting them access to the heterosexual institution of marriage and the spousal benefits thereof.

In sum, an uneasy truce has emerged on the progressive judicial recognition of LGBTQ+ rights. The CFA and the lower courts, chastened by the NSL and the authoritarian turn in Hong Kong, now must tread more carefully than ever to ensure their self-preservation. Indeed, in March 2024, Hong Kong passed its own legislation on national security in 2024 that builds upon the NSL. It criminalizes vague offences including "external interference" and "incitement to disaffection" and imposes a presumption of hearing bail applications in closed court.[461] Shortly after its passage, three more overseas judges left the CFA. One cited the "political situation" for their departure,[462] while another bluntly declared that judges in Hong Kong now "operate in an impossible political environment" where "the rule of law is profoundly compromised in any area about which the government feels strongly."[463]

As we saw in Part II, courts in Hong Kong have always been cautious when approaching constitutional cases on politically sensitive issues and have provided the government a wide margin of discretion. But on lower stakes issues, they have applied the proportionality test to progressive ends in some cases involving, *inter alia*, the rights to travel, vote/stand for election, and social welfare.

Since 2020, the CFA has not issued progressive judgments in any of those areas, nor on any novel rights claims. In *Lai Chee Ying*, the Court held for the first time that a Hong Kong law—the NSL—lay beyond its judicial review authority.[464] LGBTQ+ rights is the one area in which the CFA and other courts in Hong Kong have maintained a progressive constitutional jurisprudence in the post–2020 authoritarian period. By affirming housing and estate benefits for same-sex couples,[465]

[459] Lisa Duggan, *The New Homonormativity: The Sexual Politics of Neoliberalism*, *in* Materializing Democracy: Toward a Revitalized Cultural Politics 175 (Russ Castronovo & Dana D. Nelson eds., 2002).

[460] *Id.* at 179.

[461] *See* Safeguarding National Security Ordinance, No. 6 of 2024 (H.K.), §§ 19, 52–54, 87.

[462] Tom Grundy, *Canadian Judge Beverley McLachlin to Step Down from Top Court in July—Announced Days After 2 UK Judges Quit*, Hong Kong Free Press (June 11, 2024), https://hongkongfp.com/2024/06/11/canadian-judge-beverley-mclachlin-to-step-down-from-top-court-in-july-announced-days-after-2-uk-judges-quit/.

[463] Jonathan Sumption, *The Rule of Law in Hong Kong Is in Grave Danger*, Financial Times (June 10, 2024), https://www.ft.com/content/60c825be-b70a-4152-895f-f6127974570a (citing the High Court's May 30, 2024, conviction of fourteen pro-democracy politicians under the NSL as exemplifying these concerns).

[464] *Lai Chee Ying*, [2021] H.K.C.F.A. 3 at para. 42.

[465] *Infinger*, [2023] H.K.C.A. 1178; *Lam*, [2023] H.K.C.A. 1224.

permitting individuals who have not undergone a full-SRS to change their gender markers,[466] and requiring the government to recognize same-sex unions,[467] Hong Kong courts have been able to secure a space for progressive, liberal constitutional rights jurisprudence. Within the LGBTQ+ rights domain, they can demonstrate their (partial) independence and sustained judicial commitment to global constitutionalism in an increasingly hostile environment.

Meanwhile, LGBTQ+ rights judgments play a legitimating role for a government that is keen to downplay the degree to which Hong Kong's constitutional order has moved toward authoritarianism. The Hong Kong government and PRC authorities, as discussed, wish to preserve the appearance of judicial independence. They therefore defend the principle as an integral part of the region's constitutional framework. In keeping with that rhetorical commitment, they have refrained from publicly criticizing the courts in the realm of LGBTQ+ rights, even when high-profile judgments like *Sham Tsz Kit* do not reach their preferred conclusions. Such incremental advances are acceptable to the authorities because they do not threaten or destabilize extant power structures. Judicial decisions that permit changes to official gender markers, expand benefits or same-sex couples, and provide legal recognition to same-sex unions leave government authority untouched on political matters and with respect to law and order.

The expanding sphere of LGBTQ+ rights also serves a useful economic purpose. The official story of Hong Kong post-2020 is one of renewed stability and continued prosperity. *QT* and *Sham Tsz Kit* legitimate that narrative by encouraging LGBTQ+ professionals from around the world to join Hong Kong's workforce. Looking ahead, and beyond legitimation, it is in the government's economic interest to abide by the *Sham Tsz Kit* ruling and recognize same-sex unions. Such recognition would put Hong Kong ahead of regional rivals like Singapore, who have been less accommodating of gender and sexual minorities.[468] This, in turn, would enable Hong Kong to outcompete Singapore in recruiting high-skilled LGBTQ+ workers and perhaps even to reclaim the coveted title of world's freest economy.

[466] *Q*, [2023] H.K.C.F.A. 4.

[467] *Sham Tsz Kit*, [2023] H.K.C.F.A. 28.

[468] Singapore's Parliament decriminalized sex between men in 2022. However, it also amended the country's constitution to ensure that only the legislature (and not the courts) may regulate and define the institution of marriage. Singapore also maintains strictly binary definitions of gender, requiring individuals to undergo full SRS to change their official gender markers. *See* SINGAPORE CONST., art. 156 (as amended by Act 40 of 2022, w.e.f. Jan. 3, 2023); *Singapore Lifts Gay Sex Ban But Blocks Path Towards Marriage Equality*, GUARDIAN (Nov. 30, 2022), https://www.theguardian.com/world/2022/nov/30/singapore-lifts-gay-sex-ban-but-blocks-path-toward-marriage-equality; Kristen Gelineau, *Dubbed Torture, ID Policies Leave Transgender People Sterile*, AP NEWS (Nov. 11, 2022), https://apnews.com/article/transgender-sterilization-e2cd525389eb17bf5201fa0fcbabdbf3.

6

Conclusion

I. The Exceptionalism of LGBTQ+ Rights

The decline of liberal constitutionalism since 2005 has been accompanied by a judicial retrenchment in constitutional rights adjudication. Courts were once institutional leaders in entrenching rights at home and in diffusing rights around the world. These days they are often cast in defensive roles—to stem the tide of rising authoritarianism and to shield rights that were previously recognized.

Within this broader story of liberal and judicial decline, LGBTQ+ rights appear, at least in some jurisdictions, to be a bright spot. This book has explored the judicial adjudication of LGBTQ+ rights in the United States, India, and Hong Kong, as each society encountered serious challenges to their respective liberal constitutional orders. Chapters 3, 4, and 5 showed how LGBTQ+ rights have been exceptional: a site of progressive (or at least, less regressive) rights jurisprudence as the U.S. Supreme Court, the Supreme Court of India (SCI), and the Hong Kong Court of Final Appeal (CFA), respectively, retreated on or overturned other liberal rights.

I argued that all three courts treated LGBTQ+ rights differently than other rights for two strategic reasons: (1) to maintain a progressive rights jurisprudence with minimal political backlash and (2) to salvage whatever remains of their reputation for impartiality and independence in highly politicized and contentious environments. I further argued that, in each society, we have seen a shift toward the second objective over time. That is, courts (and judges therein) have become increasingly concerned about self-preservation as their sociological legitimacy declines and their institutional power is threatened.

While the case studies alone yield useful insights, it is also generative to compare them along several dimensions, including the degree to which courts shifted between strategic objectives, the audiences for whom judges write, and the normative implications of this judicial practice. I conclude with some observations and tentative conclusions about the future of LGBTQ+ rights and liberal constitutionalism in the three societies.

II. From Progressive to Self-Preserving

Consider, first, how each court has shifted toward institutional self-preservation in recent years. In the United States, the shift was more pronounced and more

Courts and LGBTQ+ Rights in an Age of Judicial Retrenchment. Rehan Abeyratne, Oxford University Press.
 DOI: 10.1093/9780191995040.003.0006

categorical than in India or Hong Kong. This is, in part, because of the "attitudinal" nature of the U.S. Supreme Court, where the justices' individual ideologies influence the case law to a significant degree.[1] When the Court was ideologically balanced, with Anthony Kennedy as the swing justice, LGBTQ+ rights was one of the few areas in which he voted consistently with the liberal justices and sought to engage with the project of global constitutionalism. Many of his colleagues in the 1990s and 2000s shared an interest in the latter, including Justices Breyer, O'Connor, and Ginsburg.

Today, the Supreme Court not only lacks ideological balance with its 6–3 conservative supermajority but also lacks a single justice that shows interest in global constitutionalism. The inauguration of what I call the Second Roberts Court in 2018 (when Kennedy was replaced by Brett Kavanaugh) shifted constitutional law sharply to the political right. This Court has little interest in advancing, much less preserving, liberal constitutionalism, but it does have an interest in maintaining some sociological legitimacy and in preempting reforms to its structure or operations. Recent LGBTQ+ rights decisions thus appear to serve a legitimating purpose. *Bostock* usefully demonstrated that the Court's conservative justices, employing textualism, can still reach a progressive result.[2] *Fulton* and *303 Creative* show that the Court is cognizant of the challenges facing the LGBTQ+ community and is respectful of precedent, even as these decisions ruled in favor of religious exemptions to anti-discrimination laws.[3]

Similarly, in India, the SCI has shifted toward self-preservation, if not as markedly as in the United States. Because of its large size and polyvocality, it is harder to discern institutional patterns in the SCI. The early LGBTQ+ cases illustrated this unpredictability. While one SCI bench reversed a progressive Delhi High Court judgment that decriminalized gay sex,[4] another bench recognized the rights of India's gender-diverse communities a few months later.[5] As discussed in Chapter 4, these cases reflected the randomness of bench allocation and that certain justices were far more progressive than others.

Yet, as we saw, the SCI has been strongly affected by the ascent of Narendra Modi and the BJP to national political power in 2014. The LGBTQ+ cases in the Modi era illustrate how the SCI justices maintained a rhetorical commitment to gender and sexually diverse communities even as their judgments were carefully calibrated to avoid political conflict. The Court's decision in *Navtej Johar* (2018), for instance, finally read down Section 377 of the Indian Penal Code, nearly a decade after the Delhi High Court had done so in *Naz Foundation*.[6] By this time, Section 377 had

[1] *See* Jeffrey A. Segal & Harold J. Spaeth, The Supreme Court and the Attitudinal Model Revisited (2002).

[2] *See* Bostock v. Clayton County, 140 S. Ct. 1731 (2020).

[3] *See* Fulton v. City of Philadelphia, 141 S. Ct. 1868 (2021); 303 Creative LLC v. Elenis, 143 S. Ct. 2298 (2023).

[4] *See* Naz Foundation v. Gov't of NCT, (2009) D.L.T. 277 (Delhi HC) (India).

[5] *See* NALSA v. Union of India, (2014) 5 S.C.C. 438 (India).

[6] *See* Navtej Johar v. Union of India, 2018 I.N.S.C. 790 (India).

little public support, and the Modi government did not even defend its constitutionality. In 2023, Chief Justice Chandrachud expedited proceedings on same-sex marriage in an apparent attempt to secure a landmark progressive judgment before his tenure as CJI ended. Yet, though Chandrachud selected the five-judge bench in *Supriyo* and came out in favor of same-sex unions, he found himself in the minority. Three of his five colleagues on the *Supriyo* bench ruled that the central government had only to form a "high-powered committee" to consider what might be done with respect to same-sex couples.[7] The government was not required to produce any new legislation or to amend constitutionally suspect laws such as the Special Marriage Act.

In Hong Kong, there was an even less discernable shift between the progressive and self-preserving objectives. Ever since its inception in 1997, the CFA has had to tread carefully between the liberal and authoritarian elements of the "one country, two systems" model. Thus, self-preservation in the literal sense of surviving as a liberal constitutional court in Greater China has always been an important objective for the CFA. As we saw in Chapter 5, the CFA had more leeway in its first two decades of operation but only in areas that did not raise Beijing's hackles. Hong Kong maintained a semi-democratic political system in those years and the CFA could incrementally advance LGBTQ+ rights without fear of reprisal.

But the mass protests in 2019, the ensuing political crackdown in 2020, and constitutional overhaul by 2021 diminished the prospects for progressive judicial decision-making. Hong Kong is no longer even partially democratic, and there is little political forbearance (either within the SAR or from the PRC) for judgments that deviate from the official political line. It is no surprise, then, that the CFA was closely divided and exceptionally cautious in *Sham Tsz Kit*.[8] While the Court held that the government violated its obligations to same-sex couples, it circumscribed the ruling to avoid NPCSC intervention and to provide the government two years to craft its own legislative solution.

III. The Changing Audiences for LGBTQ+ Rights Judgments

The strategic value of LGBTQ+ rights is thrown into sharper relief when we examine the judicial audiences in the United States, India, and Hong Kong, respectively.[9] The U.S. Supreme Court, as we saw in Chapter 3, was once heavily invested in the project of global constitutionalism. Justice Kennedy especially cared about the international (specifically, European) reception to his jurisprudence. This is

[7] Supriyo @ Supriya Chakraborty v. Union of India, 2023 I.N.S.C. 920 (India), para 149 (per Bhat, J.).

[8] *See* Sham Tsz Kit v. Secretary for Justice, [2023] H.K.C.F.A. 28.

[9] *See* Nuno Garoupa & Tom Ginsburg, *Judicial Audiences and Reputation: Perspectives from Comparative Law*, 47 COLUM. J. TRANSNAT'L L. 452 (2009).

evident in his *Lawrence* (2003) majority opinion. Kennedy cited the Wolfenden Report (1957) and the European Court of Human Rights (ECtHR) decision in *Dudgeon v. United Kingdom* to show that the right to engage in same-sex relations was "accepted as an integral part of human freedom in many other countries."[10] The backlash that followed *Lawrence* and other cosmopolitan Supreme Court decisions of the early 2000s would lead Kennedy and his colleagues to step back from explicitly engaging with foreign materials. *Obergefell* was decided after many other countries (including Canada, the United Kingdom, and much of Western Europe) had legalized same-sex marriage, but Kennedy refrained from citing any of this in his majority opinion.[11]

Kennedy's retirement in 2018, followed by Justice Ginsburg's death in 2020, fundamentally reshaped the Supreme Court into a partisan and far more radical institution. This new Court—the Second Roberts Court—appears to write for an exclusively domestic audience. In part, this is due to a cultural shift in constitutional interpretation. With even some Democratic-appointed justices identifying as originalists since 2010, there is little scope to rely on evolving standards or an emerging consensus at home, much less abroad, in adjudicating constitutional rights.

But the turn to domestic audiences also results from the Republican strategy, led by the Federalist Society, to appoint justices who were carefully vetted to hold strong conservative values and would be unlikely to fall prey to the Greenhouse Effect.[12] Republican-appointees to the Supreme Court from 2005 onwards have shown less interest than their predecessors in writing for mainstream news sources or producing judgments that align with public opinion.

The absence of term limits combined with the practice of justices signing opinions, including a high number of concurring and dissenting opinions, enable each Supreme Court justice to develop their jurisprudence over a long period and to target specific groups. As Lawrence Baum has explained, each justice therefore has a "personal audience."[13] In the First Roberts Court (2005–17), as political and judicial polarization increased, conservative justices like Scalia, Thomas, and Alito appeared to be writing exclusively for conservative audiences such as the Federalist Society and like-minded law professors.

Following the bitter nomination battles from 2016 to 2020, and the mounting political calls to rein in what had clearly become a partisan and corrupt Court, the conservative justices needed legitimation among the broader public. And, as Chapter 3 explained, LGBTQ+ rights played a useful role in that endeavor. Decisions like *Fulton* and *303 Creative* demonstrated that the Court respects

[10] Lawrence v. Texas, 539 U.S. 558, 577 (2003).

[11] *See* Obergefell v. Hodges, 135 S. Ct. 2584 (2015).

[12] *See* Amanda Hollis-Brusky, Ideas with Consequences: The Federalist Society and the Conservative Counterrevolution (2014), at ch. 1.

[13] Lawrence Baum, Judges and Their Audiences: A Perspective on Judicial Behavior 125 (2006).

precedent and can show rhetorical concern for both LGBTQ+ rights and religious liberty, much as the bipartisan Respect for Marriage Act (2022) sought to achieve.[14] *Bostock*, meanwhile, allowed the Court's conservative supermajority to demonstrate to a mainstream domestic audience that it does not invariably rule along partisan lines and that the justices are not simply Republican politicians in robes.[15]

In India, the primary judicial audience for LGBTQ+ rights has changed in a similarly revealing way. Chapter 4 showed how earlier progressive judgments in *Naz Foundation* and *NALSA* not only engaged with international sources but also considered the challenges faced by several LGBTQ+ communities within India. Both cases emerged from petitions filed by NGOs on behalf of some of the most marginalized of those groups. Later cases like *Navtej Johar* and *Supriyo* were elite-driven, emerging from petitions filed by five celebrities and high-skilled professionals (including those based in North America and Europe), respectively. These petitions illuminated the challenges facing a tiny high-status, transnational subset of the millions of LGBTQ+ people in India. Yet, among the many petitions filed before the SCI, these were the only ones to make it through the admissions process and to be placed before widely publicized hearings.

Facing undue influence from the Modi government and several internal crises, the SCI benefitted from the positive attention drawn by these cases and their high-status petitioners. At a rhetorical level, the *Navtej Johar* and *Supriyo* judgments seemed targeted at a similar, elite demographic to their respective petitioners. This includes media outlets, both at home and abroad, who had been paying close attention to these cases. But the main audience for *Supriyo* was not cosmopolitan elites, much less the broader Indian public. By 2023, when this judgment was released, the Court was writing primarily for the Modi regime, making clear that, despite all the lofty rhetoric, it would not force the government's hand on same-sex marriage. The Court's audience has thus not only changed but shrunk. While the SCI once wrote for a multitude of LGBTQ+ communities and the broader Indian public, it appeared in *Supriyo* to target only two small audiences: the government and a privileged segment of both local and global civil society.

Courts in Hong Kong, too, increasingly write for a governmental audience. Unlike the United States or India, however, they must be mindful of both the HKSAR and PRC governments. While the two have largely converged in their objectives, the LGBTQ+ judgments of recent years suggest that the local government maintains some distinct interests. The convergence between governments has been clear since the adoption of the National Security Law in 2020, which curbed judicial independence and made clear—as if further confirmation was needed—that courts should steer clear of enforcing politically sensitive rights like

[14] *See Fulton*, 141 S. Ct. 1868; *303 Creative LLC*, 143 S. Ct. 2298; Respect for Marriage Act, Pub. L. 117-228, 136 Stat. 2305 (2022).

[15] *See Bostock*, 140 S. Ct. 1731.

the freedoms of speech and assembly.[16] Changes to the Legislative Council in 2021 further cemented a monolithic, pro-Beijing government in Hong Kong.[17] While there was once a lively opposition in the LegCo, including a coalition of Pan-Democrats, it is now practically impossible for such candidates to even contest, much less occupy, legislative seats.

LGBTQ+ rights judgments play a legitimating role for the judiciary and for the HKSAR generally among external audiences.[18] Recall that the HKSAR and the CFA were only established in 1997. As a new apex court operating in a unique jurisdiction, the CFA quickly developed a reputation for producing high-quality, common law judgments, while also engaging extensively with foreign materials. At a doctrinal level, the CFA's adoption and continued use of the proportionality test in constitutional rights adjudication have enabled it to engage with case law from around the world, especially from the United Kingdom, Canada, and the ECtHR. Moreover, as discussed in Chapter 5, the presence of overseas non-permanent judges has aided the Court's international reputation, even if it caused some consternation among the Hong Kong and PRC political leadership. These judges, and the Court's comparative engagement, placed the CFA squarely within the global community of courts and assured international investors that Hong Kong remained open for business despite the handover of sovereignty from Britain to China.

After the constitutional overhaul in 2020–21, the few remaining overseas judges and the Court's continued comparative engagement continue to serve an external legitimating role. But the external audience has changed in two ways. First, though the PRC has brought the HKSAR more squarely under its control, Hong Kong still maintains formal autonomy from the Mainland. The PRC leadership has thus become a more important external audience for Hong Kong's courts, as the latter are now more closely scrutinized by Beijing, with the looming threat of further limits on judicial power if they overstep the new red lines.

Second, because of the damage to Hong Kong's reputation in recent years, the local government has tried to rebrand the city and encourage international business elites to return. Though it formally opposes the progressive LGBTQ+ jurisprudence that Hong Kong courts have produced in recent years, these decisions serve a useful role for the government. Judicial rulings on transgender rights,[19] housing and estate benefits for same-sex couples,[20] and same-sex unions[21] helped

[16] Law of the People's Republic of China on Safeguarding National Security in the Hong Kong Special Administrative Region, GN (E) 72 of 2020 (H.K.).

[17] Basic Law, Annex II (as amended in 2021), § 1.

[18] *See* Tamir Moustafa & Tom Ginsburg, *Introduction: The Functions of Courts in Authoritarian Politics*, *in* Rule by Law: The Politics of Courts in Authoritarian Regimes 1 (Tom Ginsburg & Tamir Moustafa eds., 2012).

[19] Q v. Commissioner of Registration, [2023] H.K.C.F.A. 4.

[20] Infinger v. Hong Kong Housing Authority, [2024] H.K.C.F.A. 29; Ng Hon Lam Edgar v. Secretary for Justice, [2024] H.K.C.F.A. 30.

[21] *Sham Tsz Kit*, [2023] H.K.C.F.A. 28.

to differentiate Hong Kong from its economic competitors. Most other major Asian business centers, including Singapore, are less accommodating of LGBTQ+ residents. Among other things, they do not recognize same-sex marriage or the benefits that flow from it. Thus, LGBTQ+ professionals (and their spouses) in the global workforce have become an important audience for the CFA and, in turn, for Hong Kong's government.

IV. Pinkwashing or Necessary Adaptation?

The book has laid out how courts in the United States, India, and Hong Kong have used LGBTQ+ rights to advance strategic objectives. In each case study, I showed how the move toward self-preservation has often been accompanied by legal outcomes that fall short of judicial rhetoric. This phenomenon raises normative questions about the interests served by the strategic judicial approach and its desirability going forward.

Critical international legal scholars have developed the useful concept of "pinkwashing."[22] The term describes a government strategy to divert attention away from severe human rights abuses by highlighting advances on LGBTQ+ issues.[23] Scholars have similarly shown how autocrats and other bad faith political actors have purported to advance gender equality when, in fact, they undermine the rights or status of women in society.[24] Charges of pinkwashing carry more weight when ascribed to those who intentionally or knowingly promote LGBTQ+ rights to maintain a veneer of legitimacy and obscure other problematic practices. A weaker form of pinkwashing arises when institutions or their members unduly benefit from positive LGBTQ+ developments, even if they acted without the specific knowledge or intention of such gains.[25]

Have the U.S. Supreme Court, SCI, and CFA engaged in this practice? In other words, is it fair to characterize their LGBTQ+ decisions as judicial pinkwashing? My view is that at least some of each court's LGBTQ+ jurisprudence—including the more self-preservative judgments of recent years—falls somewhere on the spectrum between the stronger and weaker forms of pinkwashing. I have shown

[22] *See* Jasbir Puar, *Rethinking Homonationalism*, 45 INT'L J. MIDDLE EAST STUD. 336, 337–38 (2013); Aeyal Gross, *The Politics of LGBT Rights in Israel and Beyond: Nationality, Normativity, and Queer Politics*, 46 COLUM. HUM. RTS. L. REV. 81, 88 (2015).

[23] *See* Aeyal Gross, *Post/Colonial Queer Globalisation and International Human Rights: Images of LGBT Rights*, 4 JINDAL GLOBAL L. REV. 99, 109 (2013); Diane Otto, *Gender and Sexual Diversity: A Question of Humanity?*, 17 MELBOURNE J. INT'L L. 1, 10–11 (2016).

[24] *See, e.g.*, Elin Bjarnegård & Daniela Donno, *Window-Dressing or Window of Opportunity? Assessing the Advancement of Gender Equality in Autocracies*, 20(1) POL. & GENDER 1 (2023); Agnieszka Graff et al., *Introduction: Gender and the Rise of the Global Right*, 44 SIGNS: J. WOMEN IN CULTURE & SOC. 541 (2019).

[25] *See* Rosalind Dixon, Abusive Feminism (draft on file with author) (describing a similar distinction between stronger and weaker forms of abusive feminism).

that these decisions had pinkwashing effects and pointed to evidence that judges, to varying degrees, seemed aware and perhaps even intended for such effects to come about.

A more interesting question is whether such pinkwashing may be defensible, nonetheless. The answer depends on the degree to which judicial independence, in terms of both decisional and institutional autonomy, is threatened and how courts have used LGBTQ+ rights in response to those threats. Where liberal constitutionalism is likely to be extinguished soon, or at least reduced to a bare, skeletal form, incremental advances on LGBTQ+ rights to avoid political retaliation or power-stripping might be the best a court can do. The CFA arguably finds itself in this predicament today, with both the local government and PRC probing its every move. The recent LGBTQ+ jurisprudence in Hong Kong has clear pinkwashing effects for both the judiciary and the SAR government, but at least with respect to courts, that may not be such a bad thing. After all, no other public institutions even make liberal constitutional noises in Hong Kong today.

Where there is a dominant, illiberal government that could be defeated at the ballot box, courts, like the SCI, may resort to pinkwashing in the short to medium term with a view to potentially recovering a broader progressive agenda in the future. A generous view would be that SCI justices, through their LGBTQ+ jurisprudence, adapted the project of liberal constitutionalism to survive the current political moment and to ensure that the court (and some degree of judicial independence) remains intact. A more cynical view is that at least some justices are using the language of LGBTQ+ rights to keep up appearances with an elite audience while toeing the Modi government line in substance. This may serve to keep them in good standing for postretirement posts, among other benefits. The latter scenario is worrying, especially if it turns out that Modi and his allies remain in power for many more years and co-opt the SCI in toto.

Finally, if a court does not face serious threats from illiberal political forces and its position on LGBTQ+ rights serves to mask a regressive judicial agenda, that would raise serious normative concerns. This is arguably what conservative justices on the U.S. Supreme Court did with *Bostock* and in their repeated assertions in *Dobbs* that LGBTQ+ precedents like *Lawrence* and *Obergefell* were safe.[26] We do not know precisely how much each member of the present conservative supermajority on the Court intended to pinkwash or knew that reputational gains would follow from their relative moderation on LGBTQ+ rights vis-à-vis other minority rights. But, as we saw in Chapter 3, many of these justices care about their reputation and that of the Court. And we know it would serve the Supreme Court well to align with public opinion on a matter like same-sex marriage, which not only

[26] *Bostock*, 140 S. Ct. at 1754; *Dobbs v. Jackson Women's Health Organization*, 142 S. Ct. 2228, 2277–80 (2022).

enjoys broad public support but is also not central to the Republican Party's political agenda.

Reasonable minds may differ as to where Supreme Court's LGBTQ+ jurisprudence falls on the spectrum of pinkwashing. What is clear is that this Court, comparatively, has the weakest normative case for a reputational lift. Pinkwashing may enable the CFA (and possibly the SCI) to "live to fight another day."[27] In the American context, however, it merely distracts attention from the Supreme Court's partisan (and often illiberal) agenda.

V. The Future of LGBTQ+ Rights and Liberal Constitutionalism

What does the foregoing analysis tell us about LGBTQ+ rights and liberal constitutionalism going forward? The court-led, progressive advances on LGBTQ+ rights covered in this book are, of course, worthy of celebration. But they entail several costs. Judicially created rights protections are usually easier to reverse than those entrenched by legislation. If a bare majority of an apex court recognizes same-sex marriage, a small shift in bench composition or in the judges' strategic calculus can lead to judgments that cut back on or even overrule progressive precedents. The U.S. Supreme Court in *Obergefell* recognized same-sex marriage by a 5–4 majority. Today, with a 6–3 conservative supermajority, the Court has carved out various exceptions to anti-discrimination laws that were intended to protect LGBTQ+ persons. Moreover, it has reversed important gender-related precedents like *Roe v. Wade* that protected women's access to abortion.[28] In *Dobbs*, which overturned *Roe*, Justice Clarence Thomas' concurring opinion listed *Lawrence* and *Obergefell* among several other "demonstrably erroneous" precedents that the Court should overturn.[29] While Thomas' position did not receive the support of his fellow justices in *Dobbs*, it should not be dismissed as purely speculative either.

More broadly, there is a tendency to conceive of major court victories as points along a spectrum toward a definite endpoint. But litigation on these matters is messy and leads to results that are neither linear nor teleological. Many commentators, for instance, expected the SCI after its judgments in *Puttuswamy* and *Navtej Johar* to recognize same-sex marriage in *Supriyo* or at least to grant same-sex couples some form of legal recognition. That did not transpire.

Same-sex marriage, in any event, does not mark the endpoint of advocacy or litigation. In the United States, same-sex couples continue to face discrimination post-*Obergefell*, as do the transgender community and unmarried LGBTQ+

[27] Rosalind Dixon & Samuel Issacharoff, *Living to Fight Another Day: Judicial Deferral in Defense of Democracy*, 2016 Wis. L. Rev. 683 (2016).

[28] Roe v. Wade, 410 U.S. 113 (1973).

[29] *Dobbs*, 142 S. Ct. at 2301 (Thomas, J., concurring).

individuals. In Hong Kong, though the government has been ordered to provide legal recognition to same-sex couples, it is not certain whether and to what degree it will comply with this order. Recall that the CFA asked the government in 2013 to conduct a comprehensive review of the legal framework on gender recognition. As of 2024, no recommendations have been made in this regard, nor has legislation been adopted to address the needs of gender-diverse people.

As for liberal constitutionalism, its fate seems clearer in some jurisdictions than others. Progressive LGBTQ+ rights judgments appear to be the last surviving strand of liberal constitutionalism in Hong Kong. This status quo may persist, or authoritarianism may become fully entrenched, but the possibility of a more liberal Hong Kong (outside the economic sphere) is remote.

In India, the Modi regime's systematic weakening of independent checks on its authority does not bode well for the future of liberal constitutionalism. The SCI is an institution in crisis along many dimensions and appears unlikely to be the fulcrum of any major progressive constitutional change. But there is room for optimism. The 2024 general election, in which the opposition rebounded from its poor showings in the two past elections, forced Modi and the BJP to form a coalition government to remain in power. This may lead to a revival of a more robust constitutional democracy in India and perhaps even untether the SCI and its justices from the government's influence.

In the United States, despite public support for Supreme Court reform, there is unlikely to be any major change to the Court's operation or personnel. For now, the liberal justices remain in the minority. They can hope, at best, to defend the few remaining progressive constitutional precedents from the conservative supermajority. But while the U.S. Supreme Court has facilitated democratic backsliding more than its counterparts in India and Hong Kong, its structural independence and immense power in the American constitutional system could be used to undo that regression. That would require Democrats to win presidential elections and to have the opportunity to replace sitting conservative justices with more progressive jurists. With national elections so closely contested, and the possibility of unexpected retirements or deaths of Supreme Court justices, it is difficult to predict the direction in which the Court (and the country) will proceed. Trump regained the presidency in 2024, but it is possible that a liberal majority emerges on the Court over the next two decades, which would significantly shift the constitutional landscape from its present, far-right orientation.

In sum, whether authoritarianism prevails, liberal constitutionalism rebounds, or some other paradigm takes hold in these societies, the book's analytical framework and findings should serve as a valuable point of departure in understanding what comes next for courts and for LGBTQ+ rights.

Selected Bibliography

Books and Journal Articles

Abeyratne, Rehan, *More Structure, More Deference: Proportionality in Hong Kong*, *in* Proportionality in Asia 25 (Po Jen Yap ed., 2020).

Abeyratne, Rehan, *Socioeconomic Rights in the Indian Constitution: Toward a Broader Conception of Legitimacy*, 39 Brook. J. Int'l L. 1 (2014).

Abeyratne, Rehan, *Upholding Judicial Supremacy: The NJAC Judgment in Comparative Perspective*, 49 Geo. Wash. Int'l L. Rev. 569 (2017).

Abeyratne, Rehan & Nilesh Sinha, *Insular and Inconsistent: India's Naz Foundation Judgment in Comparative Perspective*, 39 Yale J. Int'l L. Online 74 (2014).

Abeyratne, Rehan & Surbhi Karwa, *The Institutional Failings of India's Chief Justice in the Age of Modi*, Int'l J. Const. L. (forthcoming).

After Cosmopolitanism (Rosi Braidotti et al. eds., 2012).

Agarwal, Akshat, *Marriage Equality in India: Thinking Beyond Judicial Challenges to Secular Marriage Law*, 6(2) Indian L. Rev. 170 (2022).

Agnes, Flavia, *Personal Laws*, *in* Oxford Handbook of the Indian Constitution 903 (Sujit Choudhry et al. eds., 2016).

Ahmed, Farrah, Religious Freedom Under the Personal Law System (2016).

Alarie, Benjamin & Andrew J. Green, Commitment and Cooperation on High Courts: A Cross-Country Examination of Institutional Constraints on Judges (2017).

Albert, Richard, *The World's Most Difficult Constitution to Amend?*, 110 Cal. L. Rev. 2005 (2022).

Alford, Roger P., *In Search of a Theory for Constitutional Comparativism*, 52 U.C.L.A. L. Rev. 639 (2005).

Alford, Roger P., *Lower Courts and Constitutional Comparativism*, 77 Fordham L. Rev. 647 (2008).

Alford, Roger P., *Misusing International Sources to Interpret the Constitution*, 98 Am. J. Int'l L. 57 (2004).

Andhyarujina, T.R., *A Committed Judiciary: Indira Gandhi and Judicial Appointments*, *in* Appointment of Judges to the Supreme Court of India: Transparency, Accountability and Independence 18 (Arghya Sengupta & Ritwika Sharma eds., 2018).

Aney, Madhav S., et al., *Jobs for Justice(S): Institutional Corruption in the Supreme Court of India*, 64 J. L. & Econ. 479 (2021).

Aney, Madhav S. & Shubhankar Dam, *Decree Power in Parliamentary Systems: Theory and Evidence from India*, 84 J. Pol. 1432 (2021).

Atrey, Shreya, *Feminist Constitutionalism: Mapping a Discourse in Contestation*, 20(2) Int'l J. Const. L. 611 (2022).

Atrey, Shreya & Gautam Bhatia, *New Beginnings: Indian Rights Jurisprudence After Puttuswamy*, 3(2) U. Oxford Hum. Rts. Hub 1 (2020).

Austin, Granville, The Indian Constitution: Cornerstone of a Nation (2nd ed. 1999).

Austin, Granville, Working a Democratic Constitution (1999).

Balkin, Jack M., *Constitutional Crisis and Constitutional Rot*, *in* Constitutional Democracy in Crisis? 13 (Mark A. Graber et al. eds., 2018).

Balkin, Jack M., The Cycles of Constitutional Time (2020).

Balkin, Jack M., *The Long and Winding Road to Marriage Equality*, *in* What Obergefell v. Hodges Should Have Said 3 (Jack M. Balkin ed., 2020).

Balkin, Jack M., *We Are All Cafeteria Originalists Now (and We Always Have Been)*, Wm. & Mary Bill Rts. J. (forthcoming).

Barnett, Randy E., *Scalia's Infidelity: A Critique of "Faint-Hearted" Originalism*, 75 U. CIN. L. REV. 7 (2006).

Barrett, Amy Coney, *Originalism and Stare Decisis*, 92 NOTRE DAME L. REV. 1921 (2017).

Barrett, Amy Coney & John Copeland Nagle, *Congressional Originalism*, 19 J. CONST. L. 1 (2016).

Barrow, Amy, *Sexual Orientation, Gender Identity, and Equality in Hong Kong: Rights, Resistance, and Possibilities for Reform*, 15 ASIAN J. COMP. L. 126 (2020).

Baude, William & Michael Stokes Paulsen, *The Sweep and Force of Section Three*, 172 U. PENN. L. REV. 605 (2024).

BAUM, LAWRENCE, JUDGES AND THEIR AUDIENCES: A PERSPECTIVE ON JUDICIAL BEHAVIOR (2006).

Baxi, Upendra, *Taking Suffering Seriously*, 4 THIRD WORLD L. STUD. 107 (1985).

Begara, Mario et al., *Modeling Supreme Court Strategic Decision Making: The Congressional Constraint*, 28 LEGIS. STUD. Q. 247 (2003).

Berman, Mitchell N. & Guha Krishnamurthi, Bostock *Was Bogus: Textualism, Pluralism, and Title VII*, 97 NOTRE DAME L. REV. 67 (2021).

Bermeo, Nancy, *On Democratic Backsliding*, 27 J. DEMOCRACY 5 (2016).

Bhagwati, P.N., *Judicial Activism and Public Interest Litigation*, 23 COLUM. J. TRANSNAT'L L. 561 (1984–85).

Bhagwati, P.N., *The Role of the Judiciary in the Democratic Process: Balancing Activism and Judicial Restraint*, 18 COMMONW. LAW BULL. 1262 (1992).

Bhat, M. Mohsin Alam, *The Parliament and State Legislatures of India*, *in* ROUTLEDGE HANDBOOK OF ASIAN PARLIAMENTS 178 (Po Jen Yap & Rehan Abeyratne eds., 2023).

BHATIA, GAUTAM, THE TRANSFORMATIVE CONSTITUTION: A RADICAL BIOGRAPHY IN NINE ACTS (2019).

BHATIA, GAUTAM, UNSEALED COVERS: A DECADE OF THE CONSTITUTION, THE COURTS AND THE STATE (2023).

BHUWANIA, ANUJ, COURTING THE PEOPLE: PUBLIC INTEREST LITIGATION IN POST-EMERGENCY INDIA (2017).

Bjarnegård, Elin & Daniela Donno, *Window-Dressing or Window of Opportunity? Assessing the Advancement of Gender Equality in Autocracies*, 20(1) POL. & GENDER 229 (2023).

Black, Ryan C. et al., *Upending Global Debate: An Empirical Analysis of the U.S. Supreme Court's Use of Transnational Law to Interpret Domestic Doctrine*, 103 GEO. L.J. 1 (2014).

Black, Ryan C. et al., *We Are* the *World: The U.S. Supreme Court's Use of Foreign Sources of Law*, 46 BRITISH J. POL. SCI. 891 (2014).

Blackhawk, Maggie, *The Supreme Court, 2022 Term—Foreword: The Constitution of American Colonialism*, 137 HARV. L. REV. 1 (2023).

BREYER, STEPHEN, ACTIVE LIBERTY: INTERPRETING OUR DEMOCRATIC CONSTITUTION (2006).

BROWN, GARRETT WALLACE, GROUNDING COSMOPOLITANISM: FROM KANT TO THE IDEA OF A COSMOPOLITAN CONSTITUTION (2009).

Brown, Rebecca L., *Liberty, the New Equality*, 77 N.Y.U. L. REV. 1491 (2002).

Bugarič, Bojan & Tom Ginsburg, *The Assault on Postcommunist Courts*, 27 J. DEMOCRACY 69 (2016).

Calabresi, Steven G. & Gary Lawson, *The Depravity of the 1930s and the Modern Administrative State*, 94 NOTRE DAME L. REV. 821 (2019).

Calabresi, Steven G. & James Lindgren, *Term Limits for the Supreme Court: Life Tenure Reconsidered*, 29 HARV. J. L. & PUB. POL'Y 769 (2006).

Caldeira, Gregory A. et al., *Sophisticated Voting and Gate-Keeping in the Supreme Court*, 15 J. L. ECON. & ORG. 549 (1999).

Campante, Filipe & Daniel Hojman, *Media and Polarization: Evidence from the Introduction of Broadcast TV in the United States*, 100 J. PUB. ECON. 79 (2013).

Carbado, Devon W., *Black Rights, Gay Rights, Civil Rights*, 47 U.C.L.A. L. REV. 1467 (2000).

Carpenter, Leonore F., *The Next Phase: Positioning the Post-*Obergefell *LGBT Rights Movement to Bridge the Gap Between Formal and Lived Equality*, 13 STAN. J. C.R. & C.L. 255 (2017).

Chafetz, Josh & David Pozen, *How Constitutional Norms Break Down*, 65 U.C.L.A. L. REV. 1430 (2018).

Chan, Cora, *Demise of "One Country Two Systems"? Reflections on the Hong Kong Rendition Saga*, 49 HONG KONG L. J. 447 (2019).

Chan, Cora, *From Legal Pluralism to Dual State: Evolution of the Relationship Between the Chinese and Hong Kong Legal Orders*, 16(1) L. & ETHICS HUM. RTS. 99 (2022).

Chan, Cora, *Thirty Years from Tiananmen: China, Hong Kong, and the Ongoing Experiment to Preserve Liberal Values in an Authoritarian State*, 17 INT'L J. CONST. L. 439 (2017).

Chan, Eric, *The Legislative Council of Hong Kong*, *in* ROUTLEDGE HANDBOOK OF ASIAN PARLIAMENTS 158 (Po Jen Yap & Rehan Abeyratne eds., 2023).

Chan, Johannes, *A Storm of Unprecedented Ferocity: The Shrinking Space of the Right to Political Participation, Peaceful Demonstration, and Judicial Independence in Hong Kong*, 16 INT'L J. CONST. L. 373 (2018).

Chan, Johannes M.M., *A Shrinking Space: A Dynamic Relationship Between the Judiciary in a Liberal Society of Hong Kong and a Socialist-Leninist Sovereign State*, 72 CURRENT L. PROBLEMS 85 (2019).

CHAN, JUN, ERIC YAN-HO LAI & THOMAS E. KELLOGG, THE HONG KONG 2019 PROTEST MOVEMENT: A DATA ANALYSIS OF ARRESTS AND PROSECUTIONS (2023).

Chandra, Aparna, *Proportionality in India: A Bridge to Nowhere?*, 3 U. OXFORD. HUM. RTS. HUB J. 55 (2020).

CHANDRA, APARNA ET AL., COURT ON TRIAL: A DATA DRIVEN ACCOUNT OF THE SUPREME COURT OF INDIA (2023).

Chandra, Aparna et al., *The Supreme Court of India: A People's Court?*, 1(2) INDIAN L. REV. 146 (2017).

Chang, Stewart, *Made in Taiwan: Alternative Global Models for Marriage Equality*, 34 CONN. J. INT'L L. 143 (2019).

Chen, Albert H.Y., *Constitutional Adjudication in Post-1997 Hong Kong*, 15 PAC. RIM L. & POL'Y J. 627 (2006).

CHEN, ALBERT HUNG-YEE & PO JEN YAP, THE CONSTITUTIONAL SYSTEM OF THE HKSAR: A CONTEXTUAL ANALYSIS (2023).

Chenoweth, Erica & Zoe Marks, *Revenge of the Patriarchs: Why Autocrats Fear Women*, 101 FOREIGN AFF. 103 (2022).

CHILTON, ADAM S. & MILA VERSTEEG, HOW CONSTITUTIONAL RIGHTS MATTER (2020).

Chopra, Surabhi & Eva Pils, The *Hong Kong National Security Law and the Struggle over Rule of Law and Democracy in Hong Kong*, 50(3) FED. L. REV. 292 (2022).

Choudhry, Sujit, *Globalization in Search of Justification: Toward a Theory of Comparative Constitutional Interpretation* 74 IND. L.J. 819 (1999).

Choudhry, Sujit, *How to Do Comparative Constitutional Law in India: Naz Foundation, Same-Sex Rights, and Dialogical Interpretation*, *in* COMPARATIVE CONSTITUTIONALISM IN SOUTH ASIA 45 (Sunil Khilnani et al. eds., 2010).

Choudhry, Sujit, *Postcolonial Proportionality: Johar, Transformative Constitutionalism and Same-Sex Rights in India*, *in* THE GLOBAL SOUTH AND COMPARATIVE CONSTITUTIONAL LAW (Philip Dann et al. eds., 2020).

Choudhry, Sujit et al., *Locating Indian Constitutionalism*, *in* OXFORD HANDBOOK OF THE INDIAN CONSTITUTION 1 (Sujit Choudhry et al. eds., 2016).

Chowdhury, Rishad Ahmed, *Missing* the *Wood for the Trees: The Unseen Crisis in the Supreme Court*, 5 NUJS L. REV. 351 (2012).

Cinelli, Matteo et al., *The Echo Chamber Effect on Social Media*, PROC. NATL ACAD. SCI. 118 (2021).

Cleveland, Sarah H., *Our International Constitution*, 31 YALE J. INT'L L. 1 (2006).

Cohen, Susannah, *Redefining What It Means to Discriminate Because of Sex:* Bostock's *Equal Protection Implications*, 122 COLUM. L. REV. 407 (2022).

COHEN-ELIYA, MOSHE & IDDO PORAT, PROPORTIONALITY AND CONSTITUTIONAL CULTURE (2013).

Cossman, Brenda & Ratna Kapur, *Secularism's Last Sigh? The Hindu Right, the Courts, and India's Struggle for Democracy*, 38 HARV. INT'L L.J. 113 (1997).

Cottrell, Jill, *Fair Comment, Judges and Politics in Hong Kong*, 27 MELBOURNE U. L. REV. 33, 62 (2003).

Cox, Adam B. & Emma Kauffman, *The Adjudicative State*, 132 YALE L.J. 1769 (2023).

Craig, P.P. & S.L. Deshpande, *Rights, Autonomy and Process: Public Interest Litigation in India*, 9 OXFORD J. LEGAL STUD. 356 (1989).

Dahl, Robert A., *Decision-Making in a Democracy: The Supreme Court as a National Policymaker*, 6 J. PUB. L. 279 (1957).

DALY, TOM, THE ALCHEMISTS: QUESTIONING OUR FAITH IN COURTS AS DEMOCRACY-BUILDERS (2017).

Dam, Shubhankar, *Active After Sunset: The Politics of Judicial Retirement in India*, 51 FED. L. REV. 31 (2023).

DAM, SHUBHANKAR, PRESIDENTIAL LEGISLATION IN INDIA (2014).

DE, ROHIT, A PEOPLE'S CONSTITUTION: THE EVERYDAY LIFE OF LAW IN THE INDIAN REPUBLIC (2018).

Delaney, Erin, *Analyzing Avoidance: Judicial Strategy in Comparative Perspective*, 66 DUKE L.J. 1 (2016).

Devins, Neal, *Explaining* Grutter v. Bollinger, 152 U. PA. L. REV. 347 (2003).

DEVINS, NEAL & LAWRENCE BAUM, THE COMPANY THEY KEEP: HOW PARTISAN DIVISIONS CAME TO THE SUPREME COURT (2019).

Devins, Neal & Lawrence Baum, *Split Definitive: How Party Polarization Turned the Supreme Court into a Partisan* Court, 2016 SUP. CT. REV. 301 (2016).

Dhavan, Rajeev, *Law as Struggle: Public Interest Law in India*, 36 J. INDIAN L. INST. 302 (1994).

DIAMOND, LARRY, ILL WINDS: SAVING DEMOCRACY FROM RUSSIAN RAGE, CHINESE AMBITION, AND AMERICAN COMPLACENCY (2019).

Dixon, Rosalind, Abusive Feminism (draft on file with author).

DIXON, ROSALIND, RESPONSIVE JUDICIAL REVIEW: DEMOCRACY AND DYSFUNCTION IN THE MODERN AGE (2023).

DIXON, ROSALIND & DAVID LANDAU, ABUSIVE CONSTITUTIONAL BORROWING AND THE SUBVERSION OF LIBERAL DEMOCRACY (2021).

Dixon, Rosalind & Julie Suk, *Liberal Constitutionalism and Economic Inequality*, 85 U. CHI. L. REV. 369 (2018).

Dixon, Rosalind & Samuel Issacharoff, *Living to Fight Another Day: Judicial Deferral in Defense of Democracy*, 2016 WIS. L. REV. 683 (2016).

Dixon, Rosalind & Vicki Jackson, *Hybrid Constitutional Courts: Foreign Judges on National Constitutional Courts*, 57 COLUM. J. TRANSNAT'L L. 283 (2019).

Doerfler, Ryan & Samuel Moyn, *Democratizing the Supreme Court*, 109 CAL. L. REV. 1703 (2021).

Doerfler, Ryan & Samuel Moyn, *The Ghost of John Hart Ely*, 75 VAND. L. REV. 769 (2022).

Dorsen, Norman, *The Relevance of Foreign Legal Materials in U.S. Constitutional Cases: A Conversation Between Justice Antonin Scalia and Justice Stephen Breyer*, 3 INT'L J. CONST. L. 519 (2005).

Duca, John V. & Jason L. Saving, *Income Inequality, Media Fragmentation, and Increased Political Polarization*, 35 CONTEMP. ECON. POL'Y 392 (2016).

Duggan, Lisa, *The New Homonormativity: The Sexual Politics of Neoliberalism*, *in* MATERIALIZING DEMOCRACY: TOWARD A REVITALIZED CULTURAL POLITICS 175 (Russ Castronovo & Dana D. Nelson eds., 2002).

Dutta, Aniruddha, *Contradictory Tendencies: The Supreme Court's NALSA Judgment on Transgender Recognition and Rights*, 5 J. INDIAN L. & SOC. 225 (2014).

DWORKIN, RONALD, LAW'S EMPIRE (1986).

Elkins, Zachary, *Is the Sky Falling? Constitutional Crises in Historical Perspective*, *in* CONSTITUTIONAL DEMOCRACY IN CRISIS? 49 (Mark A. Graber et al. eds., 2018).

ELY, JOHN HART, DEMOCRACY AND DISTRUST: A THEORY OF JUDICIAL REVIEW (1980).

EPP, CHARLES R., THE RIGHTS REVOLUTION: LAWYERS, ACTIVISTS, AND SUPREME COURTS IN COMPARATIVE PERSPECTIVE (1998).

Epps, Daniel & Ganesh Sitaraman, *How to Save the Supreme Court*, 129 YALE L.J. 148 (2019).

Epstein, Lee, *Partisanship "All the Way Down" on the U.S. Supreme Court*, 51 PEPP. L. REV. 489 (2024).
Epstein, Lee & Andrew D. Martin, *Does Public Opinion Influence the Supreme Court? Possibly Yes (But We're Not Sure Why)*, 13(2) J. CONST. L. 263 (2010).
EPSTEIN, LEE & JACK KNIGHT, THE CHOICES JUSTICES MAKE (1998).
Epstein, Lee et al., *The Supreme Court as a Strategic National Policymaker*, 50 EMORY L.J. 583 (2001).
ESKRIDGE, WILLIAM N. JR. & CHRISTOPHER R. RIANO, MARRIAGE EQUALITY: FROM OUTLAWS TO IN-LAWS (2020).
Fallon, Richard H. Jr., *Legitimacy and the Constitution*, 118 HARV. L. REV. 1789 (2005).
Fallon, Richard H. Jr., *Selective Originalism and Judicial Role Morality*, 102 TEX. L. REV. 221 (2023).
Fishkin, Joseph & David Pozen, *Asymmetric Constitutional Hardball*, 118 COLUM. L. REV. 915 (2018).
Fok, Joseph, *Judges from Other Common Law Jurisdictions on the Hong Kong Court of Final Appeal*, *in* CAMBRIDGE HANDBOOK OF FOREIGN JUDGES ON DOMESTIC COURTS 41 (Anna Dziedzic & Simon N.M. Young eds., 2023).
FRANKS, MARY ANNE, THE CULT OF THE CONSTITUTION (2019).
FRIEDMAN, BARRY, THE WILL OF THE PEOPLE: HOW PUBLIC OPINION HAS INFLUENCED THE SUPREME COURT AND SHAPED THE MEANING OF THE CONSTITUTION (2009).
Fukuyama, Francis, *The End of History?*, 16 NAT'L INTEREST 3 (Summer 1989).
GADBOIS, GEORGE H. JR., JUDGES OF THE SUPREME COURT OF INDIA 1950–89 (2011).
Galanter, Marc & Nick Robinson, *India's Grand Advocates: A Legal Elite Flourishing in the Era of Globalization*, 20 INT'L J. LEGAL PROFESSION 241 (2013).
Ganguly, Sumit, *Autocratization in Kashmir*, *in* ROUTLEDGE HANDBOOK OF AUTOCRATIZATION IN SOUTH ASIA 49 (Sten Widmalm ed., 2021).
Ganguly, Sumit, *Modi's Undeclared Emergency*, 34(3) J. DEMOCRACY 144 (2023).
Ganguly, Sumit, *Threats to Pluralism*, 30(1) J. DEMOCRACY 83 (2019).
Gann Hall, Melinda & Paul Brace, *State Supreme Courts and Their Environments: Avenues to General Theories of Judicial Choice*, *in* SUPREME COURT DECISION-MAKING: NEW INSTITUTIONALIST PERSPECTIVES 281 (Cornell Clayton & Howard Gillman eds., 1999).
Gardbaum, Stephen, *Courts and Democratic Backsliding: A Comparative Perspective on the United States*, 2024 L. & POL'Y 1 (2024).
Garoupa, Nuno & Tom Ginsburg, *Judicial Audiences and Reputation: Perspectives from Comparative Law*, 47 COLUM. J. TRANSNAT'L L. 452 (2009).
Gauri, Varun, *Fundamental Rights and Public Interest Litigation in India: Overreaching or Underachieving?*, *in* THE SHIFTING SCALES OF JUSTICE: THE SUPREME COURT IN NEO-LIBERAL INDIA 89 (Mayur Suresh & Siddharth Narrain eds., 2014).
GELMAN, ANDREW, RED STATE, BLUE STATE, RICH STATE, POOR STATE: WHY AMERICANS VOTE THE WAY THEY DO (2010).
Gerken, Heather K., *Windsor's Mad Genius: The Interlocking Gears of Rights and Structure*, 95 B.U. L. REV. 587 (2015).
GERSTLE, GARY, THE RISE AND FALL OF THE NEOLIBERAL ORDER (2022).
GHAI, YASH, HONG KONG'S NEW CONSTITUTIONAL ORDER: THE RESUMPTION OF CHINESE SOVEREIGNTY AND THE BASIC LAW (1997).
Ginsburg, Ruth Bader, *"A Decent Respect to the Opinions of [Human]Kind": The Value of a Comparative Perspective in Constitutional Adjudication*, 64 CAMBRIDGE L.J. 575 (2005).
Ginsburg, Ruth Bader, *Looking Beyond Our Borders: The Value of a Comparative Perspective in Constitutional Adjudication*, 22 YALE L. & POL'Y REV. 329 (2004).
GINSBURG, TOM & AZIZ Z. HUQ, HOW TO SAVE A CONSTITUTIONAL DEMOCRACY (2018).
Ginsburg, Tom et al., *The Coming Demise of Liberal Constitutionalism?*, 85 U. CHI. L. REV. 239 (2019).
GLOBAL PERSPECTIVES ON SAME-SEX MARRIAGE: A NEO-INSTITUTIONAL APPROACH (Bronwyn Winter et al. eds., 2018).

GOLDSMITH, JACK, THE TERROR PRESIDENCY: LAW AND JUDGMENT INSIDE THE BUSH ADMINISTRATION (2007).

Graber, Mark, *Section Three of the Fourteenth Amendment: Insurrection*, WM. & MARY BILL RTS. J. (forthcoming).

Graff, Agnieszka et al., *Introduction: Gender and the Rise of the Global Right*, 44 SIGNS: J. WOMEN IN CULTURE & SOC. 541 (2019).

Green, Andrew & Albert H. Yoon, *Triaging the Law: Developing the Common Law on the Supreme Court of India*, 14 J. EMPIRICAL LEGAL STUD. 683 (2017).

Greenberg, Allison, *Lessons from* Bostock*: Analysis of the Jurisprudential (Mis)Treatment of "Sex" in Title VII Cases*, 13 U.C. IRVINE L. REV. 317 (2022).

GREENE, JAMAL, HOW RIGHTS WENT WRONG: WHY OUR OBSESSION WITH RIGHTS IS TEARING AMERICA APART (2021).

Greene, Jamal, *The Supreme Court, 2017 Term—Foreword: Rights as Trumps?*, 132 HARV. L. REV. 28 (2018).

Gross, Aeyal, *The Politics of LGBT Rights in Israel and Beyond: Nationality, Normativity, and Queer Politics*, 46 COLUM. HUM. RTS. L. REV. 81 (2015).

Gross, Aeyal, *Post/Colonial Queer Globalisation and International Human Rights: Images of LGBT Rights*, 4 JINDAL GLOBAL L. REV. 99 (2013).

Grove, Tara Leigh, *Which Textualism?*, 134 HARV. L. REV. 265 (2020).

GRUMBACH, JACOB M., LABORATORIES AGAINST DEMOCRACY: HOW NATIONAL PARTIES TRANSFORMED STATE POLITICS (2022).

Gupta, Alok, *Section 377 and the Dignity of Indian Homosexuals*, 41 ECON. & POL. WKLY. 4815 (Nov. 18, 2006).

HAMBURGER, PHILIP, THE ADMINISTRATIVE THREAT (2017).

Hargreaves, Stuart, *Canaries or Colonials? The Reduced Prominence of "Overseas Judges" on Hong Kong's Court of Final Appeal*, 16 ASIAN J. COMP. L. 187 (2021).

Hargreaves, Stuart, *Hong Kong's Overseas Judges Under the National Security Law*, *in* ROUTLEDGE HANDBOOK OF CONSTITUTIONAL LAW IN GREATER CHINA 356 (Ngoc Son Bui et al. eds., 2023).

Hasen, Richard L., *Polarization and the Judiciary*, 22 ANN. REV. POL. SCI. 261 (2019).

Hasen, Richard L., *The Supreme Court's Pro-Partisanship Turn*, 51 GEO. L.J. ONLINE 108 (2020).

Hazeldean, Susan, *Illegitimate Parents*, 55 U.C. DAVIS L. REV. 1583 (2022).

Hettinger, Virginia A. et al., *Comparing Attitudinal and Strategic Accounts of Dissenting Behavior on the U.S. Courts of Appeals*, 48 AM. J. POL. SCI. 123 (2004).

HIRSCHL, RAN, COMPARATIVE MATTERS: THE RENAISSANCE OF COMPARATIVE CONSTITUTIONAL LAW (2014).

Hirschl, Ran, *Opting Out of "Global Constitutionalism"*, 12(1) L. & ETHICS HUM. RTS. 1 (2018).

Hirschl, Ran, *The Question of Case Selection in Comparative Constitutional Law*, 53 AM. J. COMP. L. 125 (2005).

HIRSCHL, RAN, TOWARDS JURISTOCRACY: THE ORIGINS AND CONSEQUENCES OF THE NEW CONSTITUTIONALISM (2004).

HOCHSCHILD, ARLIE RUSSELL, STRANGERS IN THEIR OWN LAND: ANGER AND MOURNING ON THE AMERICAN RIGHT (2016).

HOLLIS-BRUSKY, AMANDA, IDEAS WITH CONSEQUENCES: THE FEDERALIST SOCIETY AND THE CONSERVATIVE COUNTERREVOLUTION (2014).

HUNTER, JAMES DAVISON, CULTURE WARS: THE STRUGGLE TO DEFINE AMERICA (1991).

HUNTINGTON, SAMUEL P., THE THIRD WAVE: DEMOCRATIZATION IN THE LATE TWENTIETH CENTURY (1991).

Huq, Aziz Z., *The Supreme Court and the Dynamics of Democratic Backsliding*, 699 ANNALS AM. ACAD. POL. & SOC. SCI. 50 (2024).

Hutchinson, Darren Lenard, *Gay Rights for Gay Whites? Race, Sexual Identity, and Equal Protection Discourse*, 85 CORNELL L. REV. 1358 (2000).

Hutchinson, Darryl Lenard, *Thinly Rooted: Tradition, and Reproductive Justice*, 65 ARIZ. L. REV. 385 (2023).

IP, ERIC C., HYBRID CONSTITUTIONALISM: THE POLITICS OF CONSTITUTIONAL REVIEW IN THE CHINESE SPECIAL ADMINISTRATIVE REGIONS (2019).

Ip, Eric C., *The Constitution of Economic Liberty in Hong Kong*, 26 CONST. POL. ECON. 307 (2015).

Ip, Eric C., *The Democratic Foundations of Judicial Review Under Authoritarianism: Theory and Evidence from Hong Kong*, 12 INT'L J. CONST. L. 330 (2014).

ISSACHAROFF, SAMUEL, DEMOCRACY UNMOORED: POPULISM AND THE CORRUPTION OF POPULAR SOVEREIGNTY (2023).

Jackson, Vicki C., *Constitutional Comparison: Convergence, Resistance, Engagement*, 119 HARV. L. REV. 109 (2005).

Jackson, Vicki C., *Constitutional Law in an Age of Proportionality*, 124 YALE L.J. 3094 (2015).

JAFFRELOT, CHRISTOPHE, MODI'S INDIA: HINDU NATIONALISM AND THE RISE OF ETHNIC DEMOCRACY (Cynthia Scoch trans., 2021).

Jain, Dipika, *Gendered Silences? The Lack of Women Chief Justices in India*, *in* JUDICIAL HEROINES? FEMALE CHIEF JUSTICES IN COMPARATIVE PERSPECTIVE (Erin Delaney & Rosalind Dixon eds., forthcoming).

Jain, Dipika, *Law-Making By and For the People: A Case for Pre-Legislative Processes in India*, 20 STATUTE L. REV. 1 (2019).

Jain, Dipika, *Shifting Subjects of State Legibility: Gender Minorities and the Law in India*, 32 BERKELEY J. GENDER L. & JUST. 39 (2017).

Jain, Dipika & Debanuj Dasgupta, *Law, Gender Identity, and the Uses of Human Rights: The Paradox of Recognition in South Asia*, 20(1) J. HUM. RTS. 110 (2021).

Jeffreys, Elaine & Pan Wang, *Pathways to Legalizing Same-Sex Marriage in China and Taiwan: Globalization and "Chinese Values," in* GLOBAL PERSPECTIVES ON SAME-SEX MARRIAGE: A NEO-INSTITUTIONAL APPROACH 198 (Bronwyn Winter et al. eds., 2018).

Jessee, Stephen et al., *A Decade-Long Longitudinal Survey Shows That the Supreme Court Is Now Much More Conservative Than the Public*, 119 PROC. NATL ACAD. SCI. e2120284119 (2022).

Jhaveri, Swati, *Reconstitutionalizing Politics in the Hong Kong Special Administrative Region of China*, 13 ASIAN J. COMP. L. 27 (2018).

JOHN, MATHEW, INDIA'S COMMUNAL CONSTITUTION: LAW, RELIGION, AND THE MAKING OF A PEOPLE (2023).

Kapur, Ratna. *The (Im)possibility of Queering International Human Rights Law*, *in* QUEERING INTERNATIONAL LAW 131 (Diane Otto ed., 2018).

Karlan, Pamela S., *The Supreme Court, 2011 Term—Foreword: Democracy and Disdain*, 126 HARV. L. REV. 1 (2012).

Karst, Kenneth L., *The Liberties of Equal Citizens: Groups and the Due Process Clause*, 55 UCLA L. REV. 99 (2007).

Keck, Thomas M., *The Reagan Revolution to the Present*, *in* OXFORD HANDBOOK OF THE U.S. CONSTITUTION 113 (Mark Tushnet et al. eds., 2015).

KENNEDY, RANDALL, THE PERSISTENCE OF THE COLOR LINE: RACIAL POLITICS AND THE OBAMA PRESIDENCY (2011).

Kersch, Ken I., *The New Legal Transnationalism, The Globalized Judiciary, and the Rule of Law*, 4 WASH. U. GLOBAL STUD. L. REV. 345 (2005).

Khaitan, Tarunabh, *Equality: Legislative Review Under Article 14*, *in* OXFORD HANDBOOK OF THE INDIAN CONSTITUTION 699 (Sujit Choudhry et al. eds., 2016).

Khaitan, Tarunabh, *Executive Aggrandizement in Established Democracies: A Crisis of Liberal Democratic Constitutionalism*, 17(1) INT'L J. CONST. L. 342 (2019).

Khaitan, Tarunabh, *Killing a Constitution with a Thousand Cuts: Executive Aggrandizement and Party-State Fusion in India*, 14 L. & ETHICS HUM. RTS. 39 (2020).

Khaitan, Tarunabh, Koushal v. Naz*: Judges Vote to Recriminalise Homosexuality*, 78 MODERN L. REV. 672 (2015).

Khaitan, Tarunabh, *The Indian Supreme Court's Identity Crisis: A Constitutional Court or Court of Appeals*, 4 INDIAN L. REV. 1 (2020).

KHOSLA, MADHAV, INDIA'S FOUNDING MOMENT: THE CONSTITUTION OF A MOST SURPRISING DEMOCRACY (2020).

Klarman, Michael J., From the Closet to the Altar: Courts, Backlash, and the Struggle for Same- Sex Marriage (2014).

Klarman, Michael J., The Framers' Coup: The Making of the United States Constitution (2016).

Klarman, Michael J., *The Supreme Court, 2019 Term—Foreword: The Degradation of American Democracy—And the Court*, 134 Harv. L. Rev. 1 (2020).

Klug, Heinz, *Model and Anti-Model: The United States Constitution and the "Rise of World Constitutionalism"*, 2000 Wis. L. Rev. 597 (2000).

Koh, Harold Hongju, *International Law as Part of Our Law*, 98 Am. J. Int'l L. 43 (2004).

Koh, Harold Hongju, *Transnational Legal Process*, 75 Neb. L. Rev. 181 (1996).

Koppelman, Andrew, Bostock, *LGBT Discrimination, and the Subtractive Moves*, 105 Minn. L. Rev. Headnotes 1 (2020).

Koppelman, Andrew, Gay Rights vs. Religious Liberty?: The Unnecessary Conflict (2020).

Koppelman, Andrew M., *Why Discrimination Against Lesbians and Gay Men Is Sex Discrimination*, 69 N.Y.U. L. Rev. 197 (1994).

Kosař, David, The Perils of Judicial Self-Government in Transitional Societies (2016).

Kumar Bharti, Nitin et al., *Income and Wealth Inequality in India 1922–2023: The Rise of the Billionaire Raj*, World Inequality Lab Working Paper No. 2024/09.

L'Heureux-Dubé, Claire, *The Importance of Dialogue: Globalization and the International Impact of the Rehnquist Court*, 34 Tulsa L.J. 15 (1998).

Landau, David, *Abusive Constitutionalism*, 47 U.C. Davis L. Rev. 189 (2013).

Landau, David & Rosalind Dixon, *Abusive Judicial Review: Courts Against Democracy*, 53 U.C. Davis L. Rev 1313 (2020).

Landau, David & Rosalind Dixon, Dobbs, *Democracy, and Dysfunction*, 2023 Wis. L. Rev. 1569 (2023).

Lau, Holning, *Comparative Perspectives on Strategic Remedial Delays*, 91 Tul. L. Rev. 259 (2016).

Lau, Holning, *Decriminalizing Same-Sex Activity: Jurisprudence from the Global South*, 22 Int'l J. Const. L. __ (forthcoming).

Lau, Holning, Sexual Orientation and Gender Identity Discrimination (2018).

Lau, Holning et al., Support in Hong Kong for Same-Sex Couples' Rights Grew over Four Years (2013–2017): Over Half of People in Hong Kong Now Support Same-Sex Marriage (2017).

Lau, Holning et al., Support in Hong Kong for Same-Sex Couples' Rights Grew over Ten Years (2013–2023): 60 Percent Now Support Same-Sex Marriage (2023).

Lau, Holning & Mara Malagodi, *Legal Gender Recognition in Comparative Context*, 45(2) U. Pa. J. Int'l L. 269 (2024).

Lau, Holning & Xavier Dyer, *Comparative Law and Freedom to Marry in Hong Kong*, 53 Hong Kong L.J. 51 (2023).

Law, David S., *Alternatives to Liberal Constitutional Democracy*, 77 Md. L. Rev. 223 (2017).

Law, David S., *Generic Constitutional Law*, 89 Minn. L. Rev. 652 (2005).

Law, David S., *Judicial Comparativism and Judicial Diplomacy*, 163 U. Penn. L. Rev. 927 (2015).

Law, David S. & Mila Versteeg, *The Declining Influence of the United States Constitution*, 87 N.Y.U. L. Rev. 762 (2012).

Law, David S. & Mila Versteeg, *The Evolution and Ideology of Global Constitutionalism*, 99 Cal. L. Rev. 1163 (2011).

Law, David S. & Wen-Chen Chang, *The Limits of Global Judicial Dialogue*, 86 Wash. L. Rev. 523 (2011).

Law & Globalization from Below: Towards a Cosmopolitan Legality (Bonaventura De Sousa Santos & Cesar A. Rodrigo-Garavito eds., 2009).

Laycock, Douglas, et al., *The Respect for Marriage Act: Living Together Despite Our Deepest Differences*, 2024 U. Ill. L. Rev. 511 (2024).

Lee, Eliza W.Y. et al., Public Policymaking in Hong Kong: Civic Engagement and State-Society Relations in a Semi-Democracy (2013).

Lerman, Kristina et al., *Affective Polarization and Dynamics of Information Spread in Online Networks*, 1(8) NPJ COMPLEXITY (2024).

Levendusky, Mathew et al., *Has the Supreme Court Become Just Another Political Branch? Public Perceptions of Approval and Legitimacy in a Post-*Dobbs *World*, 10(10) SCI. ADVANCES eadk9590 (2024).

LEVINSON, SANFORD, OUR UNDEMOCRATIC CONSTITUTION (2006).

LEVINSON, SANFORD & JACK M. BALKIN, DEMOCRACY AND DYSFUNCTION (2019).

LEVITSKY, STEVEN & DANIEL ZIBLATT, HOW DEMOCRACIES DIE: WHAT HISTORY REVEALS ABOUT OUR FUTURE (2018).

LEVITSKY, STEVEN & DANIEL ZIBLATT, TYRANNY OF THE MINORITY: WHY AMERICAN DEMOCRACY REACHED THE BREAKING POINT (2023).

LIM, C.L., TREATY FOR A LOST CITY (2022).

Lo, P.Y. & Albert H.Y. Chen, *The Judicial Perspective of "Separation of Powers" in the Hong Kong Special Administrative Region of China*, 5(2) J. INT'L COMP. L. 337 (2018).

Loh, Jennifer Ung, *Transgender Identity, Sexual Versus Gender "Rights" and the Tools of the Indian State*, 119 FEMINIST REV. 39 (2018).

Lombardo, Emanuela et al., *De-Democratization and Opposition to Gender Equality Politics in Europe*, 28(3) SOCIAL POL. 521 (2021).

Loper, Kelley, *Equality, Dignity and Same-Sex Marriage: Reflections on Developments in Hong Kong*, 53 HONG KONG L.J. 38 (2023).

Loper, Kelley, *The Courts, Public Opinion and the Rights of Lesbian, Gay, Bisexual and Transgender Persons: A Hong Kong Study*, 20 AUSTRALIAN J. ASIAN L. 4(1) (2019).

LOPER, KELLEY ET AL., PUBLIC ATTITUDES TOWARDS TRANSGENDER PEOPLE AND ANTIDISCRIMINATION LEGISLATION (2018).

Lund, Nelson, *Unleashed and Unbound: Living Textualism in* Bostock v. Clayton County, 21 FEDERALISM SOC'Y REV. 158 (2020).

LVOVSKY, ANNA, VICE PATROL: COPS, COURTS, AND THE STRUGGLE FOR URBAN GAY LIFE BEFORE STONEWALL (2021).

MALTZMAN, FORREST ET AL., CRAFTING LAW ON THE SUPREME COURT: THE COLLEGIAL GAME (2000).

Mandal, Saptarshi, *The Supreme Court's Marriage Equality Verdict*, 43 ECON. & POL. WKLY. 8 (Oct. 28, 2023).

MANN, THOMAS E. & NORMAN J. ORNSTEIN, IT'S EVEN WORSE THAN IT LOOKS: HOW THE AMERICAN CONSTITUTIONAL SYSTEM COLLIDED WITH THE NEW POLITICS OF EXTREMISM (2012).

Martin, Andrew D. et al., *The Median Justice on the United States Supreme Court*, 83 N.C. L. REV. 1275 (2005).

Mate, Manoj, *Globalization, Rights, and Judicial Review in the Supreme Court of India*, 25 WASH. INT'L L. J. 649 (2016).

McCaffrey, Stephen C., *There's a Whole Word Out There: Justice Kennedy's Use of International Sources*, 44 MCGEORGE L. REV. 201 (2013).

McClain, Linda C., *The Rhetoric of Bigotry and Conscience in Battles over "Religious Liberty v. LGBT Rights," in* RELIGIOUS FREEDOM, LGBT RIGHTS, AND THE PROSPECTS FOR COMMON GROUND 212 (William N. Eskridge Jr. & Robin Fretwell Wilson eds., 2018).

McGinnis, John O. & Michael B. Rappaport, *A Pragmatic Defense of Originalism*, 100 NW. U. L. REV. 383 (2006).

McGuire, Kevin T. & James A. Stimson, *The Least Dangerous Branch Revisited: New Evidence on Supreme Court Responsiveness to Public Preferences*, 66 J. POL. 1018 (2004).

Mehta, Pratap Bhanu, *Hindu Nationalism: From Ethnic Identity to Authoritarian Repression*, 10(1) STUD. INDIAN POL. 31 (2022).

Metzger, Gillian E., *The Supreme Court, 2016 Term—Foreword: 1930s Redux: The Administrative State Under Siege*, 131 HARV. L. REV. 1 (2017).

MEYER, JANE, DARK MONEY: THE HIDDEN HISTORY OF THE BILLIONAIRES BEHIND THE RISE OF THE RADICAL RIGHT (2017).

Mignot, Jean-François, *Decriminalizing Homosexuality: A Global Overview Since the 18th Century*, ANNALES DE DÉMOGRAPHIE HISTORIQUE (2022).

MOUNK, YASCHA, THE PEOPLE VS. DEMOCRACY: WHY OUR FREEDOM IS IN DANGER & HOW TO SAVE IT (2018).

Moustafa, Tamir & Tom Ginsburg, *Introduction: The Functions of Courts in Authoritarian Politics*, *in* RULE BY LAW: THE POLITICS OF COURTS IN AUTHORITARIAN REGIMES 1 (Tom Ginsburg & Tamir Moustafa eds., 2012).

Mukherjee, Gaurav, *The Supreme Court and Executive Law-Making: The Afterlife of Failed Ordinances in Krishna Kumar Singh II*, 1 INDIAN L.R. 312 (2017).

Murray, Melissa, Obergefell v. Hodges *and Nonmarriage Inequality*, 104 CAL. L. REV. 1207 (2016).

Murray, Melissa & Kate Shaw, Dobbs *and Democracy*, 137 HARV. L. REV. 728 (2024).

Nagar, Ila & Debanuj Dasgupta, *Transgender Rights and Religiosities in India: NALSA Judgment and Beyond*, 29(3) GLQ: J. LESBIAN & GAY STUD. 329 (2023).

NAIK, YESHWANT, HOMOSEXUALITY IN THE JURISPRUDENCE OF THE SUPREME COURT OF INDIA (2017).

Narayan, Vikram Aditya & Jahnavi Sindhu, *A Historical Argument for Proportionality Under the Indian Constitution*, 2(1) INDIAN L. REV. 51 (2018).

Narrain, Arvind, *Vacillating Between Empathy and Contempt: The Indian Judiciary and LBGT Rights*, *in* ENVISIONING GLOBAL LBGT HUMAN RIGHTS: (NEO)COLONIALISM, NEOLIBERALISM, RESISTANCE AND HOPE (Nancy Nicol et al. eds., 2018).

Narrain, Arvind & Arun Thiruvengadam, *Social Justice Lawyering and the Meaning of Indian Constitutionalism: A Case Study of the Alternative Law Forum*, 31 WIS. INT'L L. J. 525 (2013).

NG, MICHAEL, POLITICAL CENSORSHIP IN BRITISH HONG KONG: FREEDOM OF EXPRESSION AND THE LAW (1842–1997) (2022).

NORRIS, PIPPA & RONALD INGLEHART, CULTURAL BACKLASH: TRUMP, BREXIT, AND AUTHORITARIAN POPULISM (2019).

Novkov, Julie, *Equality*, *in* OXFORD HANDBOOK OF THE U.S. CONSTITUTION 455 (Mark Tushnet et al. eds., 2015).

O'Brien, David M., *More Smoke Than Fire: The Rehnquist Court's Use of Comparative Judicial Opinions and Law in the Construction of Constitutional Rights*, 22 J. L. & POL. 83 (2006).

O'Connor, Sandra Day, *Broadening Our Horizons: Why American Lawyers Must Learn About Foreign Law*, 45 FED. LAW. 20 (1998).

O'Scannlain, Diarmuid F., *What Role Should Foreign Practice and Precedent Play in the Interpretation of Domestic Law?*, 80 NOTRE DAME L. REV. 1893 (2005).

Osella, Stefano & Ruth Rubio-Marin, *Gender Recognition at the Crossroads: Four Models and the Compass of Comparative Law*, 21(2) INT'L J. CONST. L. 574 (2023).

Otto, Diane, *Gender and Sexual Diversity: A Question of Humanity?*, 17 MELBOURNE J. INT'L L. 1 (2016).

Panditaratne, Dinusha & Rehan Abeyratne, *Basic Law, Hong Kong Bill of Rights and the ICCPR*, *in* LAW OF THE HONG KONG CONSTITUTION (3rd ed., Johannes Chan & C.L. Lim eds., 2021).

Parrish, Austin, *Storm in a Teacup: The U.S. Supreme Court's Use of Foreign Law*, 2007 ILL. L. REV. 637 (2007).

Perju, Vlad, *Cosmopolitanism and Constitutional Self-Government*, 8 INT'L J. CONST. L. 326 (2010).

Peters, Anne, *A Plea for Proportionality: A Reply to Yun-Chien Chang and Xin Dai*, 19(3) INT'L J. CONST. L. 1135 (2021).

Petersen, Carole J., *Values in Transition: The Development of the Gay and Lesbian Rights Movement in Hong Kong*, 19 LOY. L.A. INT'L & COMP. L. REV. 337 (1997).

Porat, Iddo, *Court Polarization: A Comparative Perspective*, 46 HASTINGS INT'L & COMP. L. REV. 1 (2023).

Porat, Iddo, *Towering Judges and Global Constitutionalism*, *in* TOWERING JUDGES: A COMPARATIVE STUDY OF CONSTITUTIONAL JUDGES 21 (Rehan Abeyratne & Iddo Porat eds., 2021).

Posner, Eric, *Transnational Legal Process and the Supreme Court's 2003–2004 Term: Some Skeptical Observations*, 12 TULSA J. COMP. & INT'L L. 23 (2004).

Posner, Richard, *No Thanks, We Already Have Our Own Laws*, LEGAL AFF. July–Aug. 2004.

Post, Robert & Reva Siegel, Roe *Rage: Democratic Constitutionalism and Backlash*, 42 HARV. C.R.-C.L. L. REV. 373 (2007).

Pozen, David et al., *A Computational Analysis of Constitutional Polarization*, 105 CORNELL L. REV. 1 (2019).

Prasanna Kumar, Alok, *"More Executive Minded Than the Executive": The Supreme Court's Role in the Implementation of the NRC*, 31 NLSI REV. 203 (2019).

Puar, Jasbir, *Rethinking Homonationalism*, 45 INT'L J. MIDDLE EAST STUD. 336 (2013).

PUAR, JASBIR K., TERRORIST ASSEMBLAGES: HOMONATIONALISM IN QUEER TIMES (2007).

PUIG, GONZALO VILLALTA & ERIC C. IP, THE FREEST MARKET IN THE WORLD: THE CONSTITUTIONAL LOGIC OF ECONOMIC LIBERTY IN CHINA'S HONG KONG (2023).

Purbrick, Martin, *A Report of the 2019 Hong Kong Protests*, 50(4) ASIAN AFF. 465 (2019).

QUEERING INDIA: SAME-SEX LOVE AND EROTICISM IN INDIAN CULTURE AND SOCIETY (Ruth Vanita ed., 2001).

Raghavan, Vikram, *Navigating the Noteworthy and Nebulous in Naz Foundation*, 2(3) NUJS L. REV. 397 (2009).

Ramsden, Michael & Luke Marsh, *Same-Sex Marriage in Hong Kong: The Case for a Constitutional Right*, 19 INT'L J. HUM. RTS. 90 (2015).

RAO, RAHUL, OUT OF TIME: THE QUEER POLITICS OF POSTCOLONIALITY (2020).

Re, Richard M., *Does the Discourse on* 303 Creative *Portend a Standing Realignment?*, 99 NOTRE DAME L. REV. REFLECTION 67 (2023).

Rehnquist, William, *Constitutional Courts—Comparative Remarks*, *in* GERMANY AND ITS BASIC LAW: PAST, PRESENT AND FUTURE—A GERMAN–AMERICAN SYMPOSIUM 411 (Paul Kirchhof & Donald P. Kommers eds., 1993).

Roach, Kent, *Echoes Enhanced to a Cacophony: Hong Kong's Security Law Compared to Illiberal Elements of the Security Laws of Liberal Democracies*, *in* THE NATIONAL SECURITY LAW OF HONG KONG: RESTORATION AND TRANSFORMATION 306 (Hualing Fu & Michael Hor eds., 2022).

Robinson, Nick, *A Quantitative Analysis of the Indian Supreme Court's Workload*, 10 J. EMPIRICAL LEGAL STUD. 570 (2013).

Robinson, Nick, *Expanding Judiciaries: India and the Rise of the Good Governance Court*, 8 WASH. U. GLOBAL STUD. L. REV. 1 (2009).

Robinson, Nick, *Structure Matters: The Impact of Court Structure on the Indian and U.S. Supreme Courts*, 61 AM. J. COMP. L. 173 (2013).

Robinson, Russell K., *Unequal Protection*, 68 STAN. L. REV. 151 (2016).

Robinson, Russell K. & David M. Frost, *Marriage Equality and Intersectionality*, 23 ANALYSES SOC. ISSUES IN PUB. POL'Y 2019 (2023).

ROSENBERG, GERALD N., THE HOLLOW HOPE: CAN COURTS BRING ABOUT SOCIAL CHANGE? (2d ed. 2008).

Rosenfeld, Michel, *Is Global Constitutionalism Meaningful or Desirable?*, 25 EUR. J. INT'L L. 177 (2014).

Roux, Theunis, *American Ideas Abroad: Comparative Implications of US Supreme Court Decision-Making Models*, 13 INT'L J. CONST. L. 90 (2015).

ROUX, THEUNIS, THE POLITICO-LEGAL DYNAMICS OF JUDICIAL REVIEW: A COMPARATIVE ANALYSIS (2018).

SADURSKI, WOJCIECH, POLAND'S CONSTITUTIONAL BREAKDOWN (2019).

Scala, Dante J. & Kenneth M. Johnson, *Political Polarization Along the Rural- Urban Continuum? The Geography of the Presidential Vote, 2000–2016*, 672 ANNALS AM. ACAD. POL. & SOC. SCI. 162 (2017).

Scalia, Antonin, *Originalism: The Lesser Evil*, 57 U. CIN. L. REV. 849 (1988–89).

Scheppele, Kim Lane, *Aspirational and Aversive Constitutionalism: The Case for Studying Cross-Constitutional Influence Through Negative Models*, 1 INT'L J. CONST. L. 296 (2003).

SEGAL, JEFFREY A. & HAROLD J. SPAETH, THE SUPREME COURT AND THE ATTITUDINAL MODEL REVISITED (2002).

Segall, Eric J., Originalism as Faith (2018).

Shankar, Shylashri, Scaling Justice: India's Supreme Court, Social Rights, and Civil Liberties (2009).

Shapiro, Martin, *Stability and Change in Judicial Decision-Making: Incrementalism or Stare Decisis?*, 2 L. Transition Q. 134 (1965).

Sharma, Maya, Loving Women: Being Lesbian in Unprivileged India (2006).

Sheikh, Danish, *A Tale of Two Judgments: The Afterlives of a Defeat and a Victory for Queer Rights in India*, 8 LGBTQ + Pol'y J. 57 (2018).

Shiva Rao, B., The Framing of India's Constitution: A Study 307 (Subhash C. Kashyap ed., 1968).

Shukla, Surabhi, *Why the Clarification Petition Filed by the Union of India in the Transgender Case Is Incorrect in Law and Bad Faith on the Question of Reservation*, 22 Wm. & Mary J. Women & L. 585 (2016).

Siddique, Abu Bakar, *Job Market Polarization and American Poverty*, 57(30) J. Lab. Mkt. Rsch. (2023).

Siegel, Neil S., *The Wages of Crying Roe: Some Realism About* Dobbs v. Jackson Women's Health Organization, 2 J. Am. Const. Hist. 101 (2024).

Siegel, Reva B., *Memory Games:* Dobbs's *Originalism as Anti-Democratic Living Constitutionalism—and Some Pathways for Resistance*, 101 Tex. L. Rev. 1127 (2023).

Siegel, Reva et al., *Equal Protection in Dobbs and Beyond: How States Protect Life Inside and Outside the Abortion Context*, 43 Colum. J. Gender & L. 67 (2023).

Siems, Mathias, Comparative Law (3rd ed. 2022).

Silander, Daniel, *Contemporary Challenges to South African Democracy*, *in* South Africa's Democracy at the Crossroads 187 (Daniel Silander et al. eds., 2022).

Silverstein, Gordon, *Singapore: The Exception That Proves Rules Matter*, *in* Rule by Law: The Politics of Courts in Authoritarian Regimes 73 (Tom Ginsburg & Tamir Moustafa eds., 2012).

Singh, Parmanand, *Human Rights Protection Through Public Interest Litigation*, 45 Indian J. Pub. Admin. 731 (1999).

Singh, Pawan, *Complicating Privacy Further in the* Naz *Aftermath: Homonormativity and Queer Politics in India*, *in* Desire and Its Discontents: Queer Politics in Contemporary India 142 (Dipika Jain & Oishik Sircar eds., 2024).

Sircar, Neelanjan, *Religion-As-Ethnicity and the Emerging Hindu Vote in India*, 10 Stud. Indian Pol. 79 (2022).

Sitapati, Vinay, *Reservations*, *in* Oxford Handbook of the Indian Constitution 720 (Sujit Choudhry et al. eds., 2016).

Sitaraman, Ganesh, The Crisis of the Middle-Class Constitution: Why Economic Inequality Threatens Our Republic (2017).

Slaughter, Anne-Marie, *A Global Community of Courts*, 44 Harv. Int'l L.J. 191 (2003).

Slaughter, Anne-Marie, *A Typology of Transjudicial Communication*, 29 U. Richmond L. Rev. 99 (1994).

Slobodian, Quinn, Crack-Up Capitalism: Market Radicals and the Dream of a World Without Democracy (2023).

Solum, Lawrence B., *Incorporation and Originalist Theory*, 18 J. Contemp. L. Issues 409 (2009).

Solum, Lawrence B., *Originalism v. Living Constitutionalism: The Conceptual Structure of the Great Debate*, 113 Nw. U. L. Rev. 1243 (2019).

Solum, Lawrence B., *What Is Originalism? The Evolution of Contemporary Originalist Theory*, *in* The Challenge of Originalism: Theories of Constitutional Interpretation 12 (Grant Huscroft & Bradley W. Miller eds., 2011).

Songer, Donald R., *The Dog That Did Not Bark: Debunking the Myths Surrounding the Attitudinal Model of Supreme Court Decision Making*, 33 Just. Sys. J. 340 (2012).

Sperti, Angioletta, *United States of America: First Cautious Attempts of Judicial Use of Foreign Precedents in the Supreme Court's Jurisprudence*, *in* The Use of Foreign Precedents by Constitutional Judges 406 (Tania Groppi & Marie-Claire Ponthoreau eds., 2013).

STEIN, MARC, RETHINKING THE GAY AND LESBIAN MOVEMENT (2nd ed., 2023).
Stone Sweet, Alec, *Constitutional Courts*, *in* OXFORD HANDBOOK OF COMPARATIVE CONSTITUTIONAL LAW 816 (Michel Rosenfeld & Andras Sajo eds., 2012).
Stone Sweet, Alec, *The Necessity of Balancing: Hong Kong's Flawed Approach to Proportionality, and Why It Matters*, 50 HONG KONG L.J. 541 (2020).
Stone Sweet, Alec, *Why Europe Rejected American Judicial Review—and Why It May Not Matter*, 101 MICH. L. REV. 2744 (2003).
Stone Sweet, Alec & Jud Mathews, *Proportionality and Rights Projection in Asia: Hong Kong, Malaysia, South Korea, Taiwan—Whither Singapore?*, 29 SINGAPORE ACAD. L. J. 774 (2017).
STRAUSS, DAVID A., THE LIVING CONSTITUTION (2010).
Suen, Ying Tung & Miu Yin Wong, *Male Homosexual in Hong Kong: A 20-Year Review of Public Attitudes Towards Homosexuality and Experiences of Discrimination Self-Reported by Gay Men*, *in* EAST ASIAN MEN: MASCULINITY, SEXUALITY AND DESIRE 69 (Lin Xiaodong et al. eds., 2017).
SUTTNER, RAYMOND, RECOVERING DEMOCRACY IN SOUTH AFRICA (2015).
Swede, Richard, *One Territory–Three Systems? The Hong Kong Bill of Rights*, 44 I.C.L.Q. 358 (1995).
THE FRAMING OF INDIA'S CONSTITUTION: SELECT DOCUMENTS (B. Shiva Rao ed., Vol. 4, 1967).
THE GLOBAL EXPANSION OF JUDICIAL POWER (C. Neal Tate & Torbjorn Vallinder eds., 1997).
THE HONG KONG BILL OF RIGHTS: A COMPARATIVE APPROACH (Johannes Chan & Yash Ghai eds., 1993).
THE LESBIAN AND GAY MOVEMENT AND THE STATE: COMPARATIVE INSIGHTS INTO A TRANSFORMED RELATIONSHIP (David Paternotte & Manon Tremblay eds., 2011).
THE SHIFTING SCALES OF JUSTICE: THE SUPREME COURT IN NEO-LIBERAL INDIA (Mayur Suresh & Siddharth Narrain eds., 2014).
TOWERING JUDGES: A COMPARATIVE STUDY OF CONSTITUTIONAL JUDGES (Rehan Abeyratne & Iddo Porat eds., 2021).
Tribe, Laurence H., Lawrence v. Texas*: The "Fundamental Right" That Dare Not Speak Its Name*, 117 HARV. L. REV. 1893 (2004).
Tripathy, Rangin Pallav, *Supreme Court Collegium and Transparency: An Empirical Inquiry*, 56 ECON. & POL. WKLY. 33 (May 29, 2021).
TSANG, STEVE, A MODERN HISTORY OF HONG KONG (2015).
TULLY, JAMES, STRANGE MULTIPLICITY: CONSTITUTIONALISM IN AN AGE OF DIVERSITY (1995).
Tushnet, Mark, *Constitutional Hardball*, 37 J. MARSHALL. L. REV. 523 (2004).
TUSHNET, MARK, TAKING BACK THE CONSTITUTION: ACTIVIST JUDGES AND THE NEXT AGE OF AMERICAN LAW 101 (2020).
Tushnet, Mark, *The Inevitable Globalization of Constitutional Law*, 49 VA. J. INT'L L. 985 (2009).
Tushnet, Mark, *Transnational/Domestic Constitutional Law*, 37 LOY. L.A. L. REV. 239 (2003).
TUSHNET, MARK, WEAK COURTS, STRONG RIGHTS: JUDICIAL REVIEW AND SOCIAL WELFARE RIGHTS IN COMPARATIVE CONSTITUTIONAL LAW (2009).
TUSHNET, MARK & BOJAN BUGARIČ, POWER TO THE PEOPLE: CONSTITUTIONALISM IN THE AGE OF POPULISM (2022).
VAISHNAV, MILAN & JAMIE HINTSON, THE DAWN OF INDIA'S FOURTH PARTY SYSTEM (2019).
VANITA, RUTH, LOVE'S RITE: SAME-SEX MARRIAGE IN INDIA AND THE WEST (2005).
Varshney, Ashutosh, *How India's Ruling Party Erodes Democracy*, 33(4) J. DEMOCRACY 104 (2022).
VOGEL, EZRA F., THE FOUR LITTLE DRAGONS: THE SPREAD OF INDUSTRIALIZATION IN EAST ASIA (1993).
Waldman, Ari Ezra, *Policing Queer Sexuality*, 121 MICH. L. REV. 985 (2023).
Wan, Marco, *The Invention of Tradition; Same-Sex Marriage and Its Discontents in Hong Kong*, 18 INT'L J. COMP. L. 539 (2020).
WARNER, MICHAEL, THE TROUBLE WITH NORMAL: SEX, POLITICS, AND THE ETHICS OF QUEER LIFE (2000).

WHAT *Obergefell V. Hodges* SHOULD HAVE SAID: THE NATION'S TOP LEGAL EXPERTS REWRITE AMERICA'S SAME-SEX MARRIAGE DECISION (Jack M. Balkin ed., 2020).

WHITTINGTON, KEITH, POLITICAL FOUNDATIONS OF JUDICIAL SUPREMACY (2009).

Wiener, Antje et al., *Global Constitutionalism: Human Rights, Democracy and the Rule of Law*, 1 GLOBAL CONSTITUTIONALISM 1 (2012).

WEINRIB, LAURA, THE TAMING OF FREE SPEECH (2016).

WHITTINGTON, KEITH, POLITICAL FOUNDATIONS OF JUDICIAL SUPREMACY (2009).

Wilkinson, J. Harvie III, *The Use of International Law in Judicial Decisions*, 27 HARV. J.L. & PUB. POL'Y 423 (2004).

Wintemute, Robert, *Lesbian, Gay, Bisexual and Transgender Human Rights in India: From Naz Foundation to Navtej Singh Johar and Beyond*, *in* HUMAN RIGHTS IN INDIA 152 (Satvinder Juss ed., 2019).

Wong, Matthew Y.H., *Party Models in a Hybrid Regime: Hong Kong 2007–2012*, 15 CHINA REV. 67 (2015).

Yam, Julius, *Approaching the Legitimacy Paradox in Hong Kong: Lessons for Hybrid Regime Courts*, 46 L. & SOC. INQUIRY 153 (2021).

Yam, Julius, *Judging Under Authoritarianism*, 87 MODERN L. REV. 894 (2023).

Yam, Julius & Cora Chan, *Oratory Leadership of Chief Justices in Post-Handover Hong Kong*, INT'L J. CONST. L. (forthcoming).

Yap, Po Jen, *10 Years of the Basic Law: The Rise, Retreat, and Resurgence of Judicial Power in Hong Kong*, 36 COMMON L. WORLD REV. 166 (2007).

YAP, PO JEN, COURTS AND DEMOCRACIES IN ASIA (2017).

Yap, Po Jen, *Spouses Without Benefits: "Ring-Fencing" Marriage After W and QT Have Unbolted Its Gates*, 48 HONG KONG L.J. 365 (2018).

Yap, Po Jen, *Twenty Years of the Basic Law: Continuity and Changes in the Geoffrey Ma Court*, 49 HONG KONG L.J. 209 (2019).

Yap, Po Jen & Eric Chan, *Legislative Oaths and Judicial Intervention in Hong Kong*, 47 HONG KONG L.J. 1 (2017).

Yap, Po Jen & Julius Yam, *Legalism and Strategic Judicial Decision-Making in Hong Kong*, 53 HONG KONG. L.J. 207 (2023).

YOO, JOHN, DEFENDER IN CHIEF: DONALD TRUMP'S FIGHT FOR PRESIDENTIAL POWER (2020).

YOSHINO, KENJI, SPEAK NOW: MARRIAGE EQUALITY ON TRIAL, THE STORY OF HOLLINGSWORTH V. PERRY (2015).

Yoshino, Kenji, *The New Equal Protection*, 124 HARV. L. REV. 747 (2011).

Young, Simon N.M., *Domestic Criticisms of Foreign Judges: The Case of Hong Kong*, *in* CAMBRIDGE HANDBOOK OF FOREIGN JUDGES ON DOMESTIC COURTS 284 (Anna Dziedzic & Simon N.M. Young eds., 2023).

Young, Simon N.M., *Introductory Note to the Decision of the National People's Congress on Improving the Election System of the Hong Kong Special Administrative Region*, 60 INT'L L. MATERIALS 1 (2021).

Young, Simon N.M., *Judicial Review of Elections in Hong Kong: Resolving A Contradiction*, *in* JUDICIAL REVIEW OF ELECTIONS IN ASIA 11 (Po Jen Yap ed., 2016).

Young, Simon N.M. & Antonio Da Roza, *The Judges*, *in* HONG KONG'S COURT OF FINAL APPEAL (Simon N.M. Young & Yash Ghai eds., 2013).

Zaring, David, *The Use of Foreign Decisions by Federal Courts: An Empirical Analysis*, 3 J. EMPIRICAL L. STUD. 297 (2006).

Zelizer, Julian E., *The Conservative Embrace of Presidential Power*, 88 B.U. L. REV. 499 (2008).

Ziegler, Mary, Dobbs *and the Jurisprudence of Exclusion*, 55 POLITY 419 (2023).

Zumbansen, Peer, *Comparative, Global and Transnational Constitutionalism: The Emergence of a Transnational Legal-Pluralist Order*, 1 GLOBAL CONSTITUTIONALISM 16 (2012).

ZWEIGERT, KONRAD & HEIN KÖTZ, INTRODUCTION TO COMPARATIVE LAW (Tony Weir trans., 3rd ed. 1998).

Reports and Speeches

Altrata, World Ultra Wealth Report 2023 (September 2023), https://info.altrata.com/world-ultra-wealth-report-2023-pdf.

Bokhary, Kemal, *Keynote Address at the Towering Judges Conference Held at the Chinese University of Hong Kong* (Jan. 25, 2019).

Breyer, Stephen, *The Supreme Court and the New International Law, Address to the 97th Annual Meeting of the American Society of International Law* (Apr. 4, 2003), http://www.supremecourtus.gov/publicinfo/speeches/sp_04-04-03.html.

Buchanan, Patrick Joseph, *Culture War Speech: Address to the Republican National Convention* (Aug. 17, 1992), https://voicesofdemocracy.umd.edu/buchanan-culture-war-speech-speech-text/.

Coalition for Sex Workers and Sexuality Minority Rights (CSMR), Dignity First: One Year of Resistance to Re-Criminalisation of LGBT Lives (2014), http://feministlawarchives.pldindia.org/wp-content/uploads/report-on-11dec-anniversary.pdf.

Congressional-Executive Commission on China, One City, Two Legal Systems: Hong Kong Judges' Role in Rights Violations Under the National Security Law (May 2023), https://www.cecc.gov/sites/evo-subsites/cecc.house.gov/files/documents/CECC%20Staff%20Report%20May%202023-NSL%20Judges.pdf.

"Court Packing": Legislative Control over the Size of the Supreme Court, Cong. Rsch. Serv. (Dec. 14, 2020), https://crsreports.congress.gov/product/pdf/LSB/LSB10562.

Fraser Institute, Economic Freedom of the World: 2023 Annual Report (2023), https://www.fraserinstitute.org/studies/economic-freedom-of-the-world-21023-annual-report.

Global Reconfigurations, Constitutional Obligations, and Everyday Life (Judith Resnik & Clare Ryan eds., 2018), https://documents.law.yale.edu/sites/default/files/gcs2018.pdf.

Gorokhovskaia, Yana et al., Freedom in the World 2023: Marking 50 Years in the Struggle for Democracy (2023), https://freedomhouse.org/sites/default/files/2023-03/FIW_World_2023_DigtalPDF.pdf.

Interdepartmental Working Group on Gender Recognition, *Consultation Paper 1: Gender Recognition,* June 2017, https://www.iwggr.gov.hk/eng/pdf/esummary.pdf.

Jain, Dipika, Impact of the Naz Foundation Judgment on the Gay, Bisexual and Transgender People in Delhi: An Empirical Investigation (2012), https://pure.jgu.edu.in/id/eprint/2063/1/Report_Impact%20of%20the%20Naz%20Foundation.pdf.

National Defense Research Institute, Sexual Orientation and U.S. Military Personnel Policy: An Update of RAND's 1993 Study (2010), https://www.rand.org/pubs/monographs/MG1056.html.

Patel, Faiza et al., Foreign Law Bans: Legal Uncertainties and Practical Problems (2013), https://www.brennancenter.org/our-work/research-reports/foreign-law-bans-legal-uncertainties-and-practical-problems.

Presidential Commission on the Supreme Court of the United States: Final Report (2021), https://www.whitehouse.gov/wp-content/uploads/2021/12/SCOTUS-Report-Final-12.8.21-1.pdf.

Repucci, Sarah & Amy Slipowitz, Freedom in the World 2021: Democracy Under Siege (2021), https://freedomhouse.org/sites/default/files/2021-02/FIW2021_World_02252021_FINAL-web-upload.pdf.

The Wolfenden Report: Report of the Committee on Homosexual Offenses and Prostitution (1963), https://www.humandignitytrust.org/wp-content/uploads/resources/Wolfenden_Report_1957.pdf.

United States Senate, Examining the U.S. Capital Attack: A Review of the Security, Planning, and Response Failures on January 6 (2022), https://www.hsgac.senate.gov/wp-content/uploads/imo/media/doc/HSGAC&RulesFullReport_ExaminingU.S.CapitolAttack.pdf.

V-Dem Institute, Defiance in the Face of Autocratization (2023), https://www.v-dem.net/documents/29/V-dem_democracyreport2023_lowres.pdf.

Xiaoping, Deng, *Speech at a Meeting with the Members of the Committee for Drafting the Basic Law of The Hong Kong Special Administrative Region* (Apr. 16, 1987).

Index

For the benefit of digital users, indexed terms that span two pages (e.g., 52–53) may, on occasion, appear on only one of those pages.

Aadhaar 128
abortion 27–28, 29–30, 38, 73–74
adoption 21, 91, 160
African Americans 33–34, 64
age of consent 190
AIDS 104, 133
Alford, Roger P. 54
Alito Jr., Samuel A. 28, 58, 63–64, 70, 78, 79, 85, 97, 236
anal sex 25
anti-discrimination laws 86, 89–90, 91, 92
anti-discrimination scholarship 132–33
anti-sodomy laws 37–38, 39, 132–33
apex courts 13, 16–17, 18–20, 101
attitudinal model of judicial decision-making 29
authoritarian politics 2, 3, 11–12, 18, 25, 233
avoidance 123

backlash 11–12, 17, 19, 31, 33, 38
Barrett, Amy Coney 76, 80–81
Baude, William 72–73
Baum, Lawrence 70, 236
Bhatia, Gautam 124–26
Bhopal chemical disaster 108–9
Bhuwania, Anuj 105
Biden, Joe 46, 78, 80–81, 97
biometric identification systems 125, 128
Bokhary, Kemal 220
Borah, Rituparna 153–54
Bostock, Gerald 83
Boy Scouts 86–87
Breyer, Stephen 56
Buchanan, Pat 40
Bush, George H.W. 71
Bush, George W. 44, 70–71, 75
business interests 63–64
"but-for test" 83–84

Carter, Jimmy 37–38
case studies 22–25
Catholic Social Services (CSS) 91, 92
Chakraborty, Supriya 152
Chan, Cora 182
Chandra, Aparna 106–7
Chandrachud, Dhananjaya Yeshwant 139–40, 141–42, 143–44, 154–57, 158–59, 160–61, 163–64, 167, 168–69, 234–35
Chang, Teresa 224–25
Chang, Wen-Chen 56, 61–62
Cheung, Andrew 181, 182, 203, 212
China
  Hong Kong SAR 171–72, 174, 177, 179–80, 203, 219, 220–21
    judicial deference to the HKSAR government 182–87, 237–38
    oath of allegiance 180–81
  National People's Congress Standing Committee (NPCSC) 173, 174, 177, 197–99, 200, 201–2
    judicial deference to 179–82
    threat of intervention 216
Chowdhury, Rishad 107
Christian conservatism 74
citizenship 124, 125
Clinton, Bill 40, 66–67, 70
Clinton, Hillary 65–66
colonial legislation 18–19, 102, 146
colonialism 178–79, 219–20
common law jurisdictions 7, 22–23, 173, 214, 220–21
  incrementalism 59
competing rights 85–86
concept formation through multiple description 22
conservatism 73–76
constitutional change 12
constitutional courts 11–12
constitutional cross-fertilization 56
constitutional rights 2, 16–17
cosmopolitanism 9–11, 12, 21, 31, 48, 50–51, 54–55, 63, 113, 134, 168–69
COVID-19 pandemic 201
Craig, Charlie 88–89
credible threat 93
critical race scholarship 82
cultural backlash 11–12

cultural hegemony 12
culture wars 38–42, 49–65
  Bowers to *Lawrence* 49–51
  engagement with foreign materials 51–59, 61–63
  judicial, scholarly, and political divide 51–56
  originalism 59–61

Dahl, Robert 28–29
Dale, James 86
Dalmia, Ritu 130, 168
Dang, Abhay 152
Delaney, Erin 123
democratic backsliding 242
Deng Xiaoping 224
discrimination 83–85, 94
Dixon, Rosalind 3–4, 227–28
Doerfler, Ryan 77–78
Duggan, Lisa 81, 230
Dworkin, Ronald 10–11

elites 2, 11–12, 19
  Hong Kong 171–72, 173, 226, 230, 238–39
  India 151, 152–53, 167, 168, 169, 170
  United States 65, 69, 70
elitism 41–42, 50–51, 54–55
Ely, John Hart 35
Epps, Daniel 77–78
equal treatment 92
ethnonationalistic politics 3–4
European Court of Human Rights (ECtHR) 7, 50, 111, 115–16, 174, 186–87, 189, 192–93, 205, 211–12, 213, 221–22, 235–36, 238
evangelical Christians 38
exceptionalism 233
expressive associational rights 86–87
extramarital sex 25

family values 38
feminist scholarship 129, 132–33
Finnis, John 70–71
Fiss, Owen 55
Fok, Joseph 212, 213–14, 215–17, 220
foster care agencies 91, 92
Fraser Institute 226
free exercise of religion 21, 32, 67, 82, 90, 91–92
free expression 63–64, 90, 183–84
free speech 32, 82, 94, 95, 183–84
freedom of assembly 185–86
freedom of conscience 159
Friedman, Milton 172
fundamental rights 173–74
fundraising events 1

Gandhi, Indira 117, 125–26, 138–39
Gandhi, Mohandas (Mahatma) 119
Gandhi, Rahul 118
Gauri, Varun 105–6
gay rights organizations 37
gender-affirming healthcare 96
gender-neutral facilities 154–55
gender reassignment surgery 189, 192, 193
gender recognition 206
Gingrich, Newt 66–67
Ginsburg, Ruth Bader 5, 32, 47, 53–54, 57, 59, 76, 236
Ginsburg, Tom 228
global constitutionalism 2, 3, 9, 21, 54–55, 63, 168–69, 170, 235–36
Global South 178–79
globalization 12
Gogoi, Ranjan 124–25, 137, 142–43
Gowri, Victoria 139–40
Graber, Mark 72–73
Greene, Jamal 85–86
Greenhouse, Linda 70
Greenhouse Effect 70, 236

Hale, Brenda, Baroness Hale of Richmond 217
Hargreaves, Stuart 221
Hijra communities 114–15, 116, 146–47
Hirschl, Ran 22
historical context 4
HIV/AIDS 104, 133
homonormativity 81
homosexuality 12–13
Hong Kong 3, 4, 7–8
  age of consent 188–89, 190
  Basic Law 171–72, 176–78, 197–98, 199
    freedom of speech and expression 183–84
    fundamental rights claims 183, 184–85
    judicial deference to the NPCSC 179–82
    right to equality 211
    right to marry 211–12, 216
    separation of powers 224
  Bill of Rights Ordinance (BORO) 173, 178, 183
    freedom of speech and expression 183–84
    right to equality 211
    right to marry 211–12
    right to privacy 212–14, 216
  British precedents and principles 177
  Chief Executive (CE) 177
  common law legal system 173, 214, 220–21
  constitutional changes 174–75
  Court of Final Appeal *see* Hong Kong Court of Final Appeal
  COVID-19 pandemic 201
  criminalization of "buggery" 188–89, 190
  currency 171

declining economic freedom and rule of law rankings 226–27
economic importance 226
end of British colonial rule 171–72
flags 183, 184–85
freedom of assembly 185
freedom of speech and expression 183–84, 185
fundamental rights 173–74
government sensitivity to criticism 226–28
Housing Authority (HA) 207–9, 210
from hybrid to authoritarian (2019–21) 197–203, 224–25, 230
  electoral changes 201–3
  National Security Law (NSL) 198–202, 203
hybrid constitutional framework 171–72
Identity Cards (HKIDs) 204–5
immigration system 171, 194–97
income and wealth inequality 172
independence of courts 174
judicial review 173–74, 210, 211, 230–31
lack of housing and social services 172
laissez-faire economic system 171–73, 175–76, 226
Legislative Council (LegCo) 177, 197–98, 201–2
LGBTQ+ rights 174–76, 238–39
  authoritarianism 203–26, 237–38
  changing official gender markers 204–7
Occupy Movement 197–98
"One Country, Two Systems" (1997–2019)
  judicial appointments 220–21
  judicial deference and the HKSAR government 182–87
  judicial deference to the NPCSC 179–82
  Sino-British Joint Declaration and the Basic Law 176–79
prisoner voting rights 182–83
progressive LGBTQ+ rights jurisprudence (2006–19) 187–88, 242
  legal recognition of same-sex couples 241–42
  same-sex conduct and "intense" scrutiny 188–90
  status discrimination cases 191–97
proportionality analysis 173–74, 183, 184, 185, 186–87, 188, 194, 206
proposed Extradition Bill 197–98
prosperity and stability 226, 227
public order 185–86
public protests 175, 197–98, 201–2, 235
Public Rental Housing (PRH) 207–8
reliance on foreign sources and judgments 173–74
right to travel 182–83
robust constitutional rights jurisprudence (1997–2019) 182–83
social attitudes 17–18
social welfare rights 182–83
Special Administrative Region (SAR) of the PRC 171–72, 174, 177, 179–80, 203, 219, 220–21
  judicial deference to the HKSAR government 182–87, 237–38
  oath of allegiance 180–81
undemocratic government 172–73
Hong Kong Court of Final Appeal (CFA) 7–8, 13, 14–15, 18, 19, 175, 177
criticism and reputational damage 217–19, 238–39
freedom of assembly cases 185–86
freedom of expression cases 184–85
Hysan Development Co Ltd v. Town Planning Board 186–87
independence questioned 217–19
interpretation of NSL 230, 237–38
  HKSAR v. Lai Chee Ying 200–2, 221, 223, 230–31
judicial deference to the NPCSC 179–82
judicial independence 222–25
judicial patriotism 220–21
LGBTQ+ jurisprudence
  changing official gender markers 204–7, 214
  external legitimacy 238
  housing and estate benefits for same-sex couples 207–10, 214
  judicial self-preservation 214–22
  Leung (William Roy) v. Secretary of Justice 188, 190, 203
  Leung Chun Kwong v. Secretary of Civil Service 195, 197, 203, 207, 210, 213, 214, 215
  pinkwashing 240, 241
  Q v. Commissioner of Registration, 204–5, 206–7
  QT v. Director of Immigration 194–95, 197, 203, 210, 211–12, 213, 214, 215, 228–30, 231
  same-sex unions 211–14, 215, 222–23, 241–42
  Secretary for Justice v. Yau Yuk Lung 189, 190
  Sham Tsz Kit v. Secretary for Justice 7–8, 20, 21, 211, 212, 215, 216–17, 218, 222, 223, 228–30, 231, 235
  W v. Registrar of Marriages 21, 191
overseas non-permanent judges 178–79, 214, 219–22
progressive judgments and "Western" values 178–79
shift towards self-preservation 235
socioeconomic rights cases 186–87

Hong Kong Court of Final Appeal (CFA) (*cont.*)
  status discrimination 192–93, 194–95, 196–97
  threats to independence 20
Hosabale, Dattatreya 127
housing and estate benefits 207–10
Hubbard, William 106–7

identity cards 204–5, 206–7
illiberal politics 2, 3, 11–12, 18, 25
immigration status 194–97
India 3, 4, 5–7
  Adani Group 119–20
  Assam 124, 142–43, 153
  Bharatiya Janata Party (BJP) 5–6, 101, 102–3, 117, 118–20, 124, 125, 139, 146, 149–50, 151, 165–66, 169–70, 234–35, 242
  Bhopal chemical disaster 108–9
  biometric identification (Aadhaar) 125, 128
  Christian minorities 139–40
  citizenship 124, 142–44
  Constitution 99–100
  Hijra communities 114–15, 116, 146–47
  Hindu nationalism 117, 142–43, 146, 149–50, 170
  HIV/AIDS 104, 133
  Indian Penal Code 102, 234–35
  intercaste and interreligious marriage 165–66
  Kashmir 125–26, 143
  LGBTQ+ jurisprudence
    Delhi High Court: *Naz Foundation v. Gov't of NCT* 102, 103, 104–17, 124–25, 126–27, 128, 133–34, 141, 146, 169, 170, 234–35
    oscillation between judicial poles 108–17
    Supreme Court *see* Supreme Court of India
  "Love-Jihad" conspiracy theory 119, 165–66
  money bills 120–21
  Muslim community 118–19, 124, 139–40, 142–43, 146
  Narmada dam 105, 108–9
  National Judicial Appointments Committee (NJAC) 139
  National Register of Citizens 124, 142–43
  neoliberalism 104–8
  ordinance mechanism 121–22
  partition 99
  political donations 125
  Rashtriya Swayamsevak Sangh (RSS) 118–19, 146, 149–50
  religions 99
  separation of powers 164–65
  shift in constitutionalism under Modi (2014–19) 117–26
  socioeconomic inequality 102–3, 119–20
  structural inequalities 123
  Supreme Court *see* Supreme Court of India
  transgender rights 144–50
Infinger, Nick 207, 208, 214
institutional context 4
intense scrutiny 189, 190
international human rights instruments 115–16
intersectional analysis 82
Ip, Regina 222

Jackson, Vicki 227–28
Jain, Dipika 149
Jaitley, Arun 127
Johar, Navtej 130
judge-led constitutionalism 3
judicial dialogue 131–32
judicial independence 16–17, 20, 174, 217–19, 222–26
judicial polarization 69–71
judicial reputations 16–17, 19–20, 90–91, 170, 217–19
judicial review 3–4, 22, 23
  Hong Kong 173–74, 210, 211, 230–31

Kagan, Elena 65
Kalantry, Sital 106–7
Keane, Patrick 214, 215–17, 228
Kennedy, Anthony 4, 5, 31, 32, 41–42, 43–44, 46–48, 50–51, 52, 53–54, 57, 58, 64–65, 70, 234, 235–36
Kersch, Ken 54–55
Khaitan, Tarunabh 118, 123
Khosla, Madhav, 99
Koh, Harold 61–62
Koppelman, Andrew 84, 88–89
Koushal, Suresh Kumar 112
Kumar, Alok Prasanna 124–25
Kureshi, Akil 141

labor unions 63–64
Lai, Jimmy (Lai Chee Ying) 200–2, 221, 223, 230–31
Lam, Carrie 222, 224–25
Lam, Edgar 207–8, 209, 210, 214
Law, David 56, 61–62
law and political science 28
Lee, John 225
legitimacy 19, 20
Leung, Sixtus 180–81
LGBTQ+ jurisprudence 2
  Hong Kong 7–8 *see also* Hong Kong Court of Final Appeal
  India 5–7 *see also* Supreme Court of India
  United States 4–5 *see also* United States Supreme Court

LGBTQ+ rights
  changing audiences for LGBTQ+ rights judgments 235–39
  culture wars *see* culture wars
  exceptionalism 233
  future of LGBTQ+ rights and liberal constitutionalism 241–42
  Hong Kong *see* Hong Kong
  India *see* India
  judicial commitments to 2, 3
  liberal values and 1–2
  pinkwashing 239–41
  United States *see* United States
LGBTQ+ scholarship 15–22
Li, Andrew 224
Li Yik Ho (Henry Li) 207–8, 210
liberal constitutionalism 3, 4, 9–10, 22–24, 169
  decline 11–12, 24, 233
  future of LGBTQ+ rights 241–42
liberal values 1–2, 10–11, 151
living constitutionalism 59, 65

Ma, Geoffrey 203, 224
Mandal, Saptarshi 21–22, 168
marriage
  definitions 41
  historical roots 61, 64–65
  traditional values 81
  see also same-sex marriage; transgender marriage
McConnell, Mitch 65–66
men who have sex with men (MSM) 4.18
methodology 22–25
military service 40
misogyny 25
Misra, Dipak 131, 134–35, 137–38, 140, 169
Modi, Narendra 5–6, 101–3, 108–9, 117, 126–27, 128, 130, 234–35, 237, 242
  constitutional violations 165, 167–68
  institutional crises (2019–23) 135, 136, 139, 141, 142–43, 144
    same-sex marriage 150–51
    transgender rights 72–76, 169–70
  shift in constitutionalism (2014–19) 117–26
Moustafa, Tamir 228
Moyn, Samuel 77–78
Mullins, Dave 88–89
Muralidhar, S. 141

Narmada dam 105, 108–9
Naz Foundation 104–17
Nehru, Jawaharlal 117
neoliberalism 11–12
  Hong Kong 171–73
  India 104–8
  UK 172
  US 172
Netherlands 12–13
Newsom, Gavin 44
non-binary status 12–13

oaths of allegiance 180–81
Obama, Barack 45–46, 65–66, 71
O'Connor, Sandra Day 57, 58–60, 86, 233–34
official gender markers 204–7
opinion polls 37, 38, 42, 62–63
originalism 59–61, 65, 70–71, 72–73

parental rights 81
partisan decision-making 19–20
patriarchal narratives 25
Paulsen, Michael Stokes 72–73
Phillips, Jack 88–89, 93
pinkwashing 239–41
polarization 31, 32
  judicial 69–71
  political 5, 66–69
populism 9
prisoner voting rights 182–83
privacy 27–28, 31, 110–12, 113, 125, 126–35, 205, 206–7, 212–14, 216–17
pro-life positions 38
progressive judgments 18
progressive politics 1–2, 3, 16–17, 19, 26
proportionality analysis
  Hong Kong jurisprudence 173–74, 183, 184, 185, 186–87, 188, 194, 206
  US jurisprudence 85–87
public accommodation laws 85, 87, 88, 91–92, 94, 95–96
public interest legislation (PIL) 101, 105–6
public opinion 16–17, 28, 29–30, 31
public opinion polls
  India 151
  US 37, 38, 42, 62–63
public order 185–86
public referenda 23

racial minorities 35, 64, 82
Radhakrishnan, Thottathil Bhaskaran Nair 114–16, 145, 146–47
Rao, P.V. Narasimha 104
Rashtriya Swayamsevak Sangh (RSS) 118–19, 127
reactionary politics 25
Reagan, Ronald 38, 66
Rehnquist, William 31, 50, 51–52, 57–58, 64–65, 86–87, 90

religious conservatism 74
religious freedom 21, 82, 90, 91–92, 95
reputational challenge 19–20
right to citizenship 125
right to life 110
right to personal dignity 110
right to privacy 110–12, 113, 125, 126–35, 205, 206–7
Rijiju, Kiren 142
Robinson, Nick 108

same-sex marriage 12–13, 18–19, 21–22, 23, 25, 27–28
  Hong Kong 193–97, 211–14, 215–16, 222–23
    Sham Tsz Kit 211, 212, 215, 216–17, 218, 222, 223, 228–30, 231, 235
  housing and estate benefits 207–10
  India 150–65
    Supriyo 150–51, 152, 154–60, 161–62, 163, 164, 165–67, 168, 169, 170, 234–35, 237, 241
  United States
    Obergefell 27–28, 29–30, 31–32, 47, 48–49, 61–65, 81–82, 96–97, 150, 162–63, 235–36, 240–42
    parental rights 81
    public approval 29–30, 31
    public opinion polls 37, 38, 42, 62–63
Scalia, Antonin 32, 41–42, 50–53, 54–55, 57–60, 65–66, 70, 76, 236
Semmalar, Gee Imaan 146
separation of powers 224, 225–26
sex discrimination 83–85, 132–33
sexual privacy *see* privacy
sexual reassignment surgery (SRS) 115–16, 189, 192, 193
Shah, A.P. 108–9
Shankar, Shylashri 106
Siegel, Neil 28, 29–30
Sikri, Arjan Kumar 145, 147
Sitaraman, Ganesh 77–78
Siva, Tiruchi 147–48
Slaughter, Anne-Marie 55, 56
slavery 33–34
Smith, Lorie 93–95
social mobilization 37
social movements 17–18
socioeconomic inequality 102–3, 119–20
socioeconomic rights 186–87
Sotomayor, Sonia 47, 60–61, 71, 95, 96
Souter, David 70
South Africa 150, 162–65
Spigelman, James 216–17
status discrimination cases 191–97
Stephens, Aimee 83
stereotypes 132–33
Stonewall Bar raid 37
strategic avoidance 123
strategic model of judicial decision-making 29, 30
Supreme Court of India (SCI) 5–7, 13, 14–15, 19
  bias against less advantaged groups 105–6, 123
  caution under Modi government (2014–19) 120
    fundamental rights 122–26
    money bills and ordinances 120–22
  contradictory jurisprudence 102, 108
  history of expansive fundamental rights jurisprudence 113
  institutional and reputational self-preservation 164–70, 234–35
  institutional crisis (2019–23) 135, 136, 242
    judicial appointments 138–40
    master of roster authority 136–38, 143–44
    transgender rights under Modi 144–50
    undue influence 141–44, 165
  institutional legitimacy 123–24
  jurisdiction 100–1, 102, 103
  LGBTQ+ jurisprudence 101–3, 170
    constitutional right to privacy 128–35
    Koushal 112, 113, 114–17, 126–27, 129–32, 146, 154, 161, 162, 163, 166, 167–68
    NALSA 114–17, 127, 130, 131, 144–48, 149, 161–62, 169–70, 237
    Navtej Johar 130, 131–35, 150–51, 154, 158, 161, 163, 164, 167–69, 170, 234–35, 237, 241
    oscillation between judicial poles 113–17
    pinkwashing 240, 241
    privacy and the decriminalization of same-sex relations 126–35
    Puttuswamy v. Union of India 128–30, 131, 132–33, 134, 135, 154, 158, 161, 163, 241
  same-sex marriage 150–65
    Supriyo 150–51, 152, 154–60, 161–62, 163, 164, 165–67, 168, 169, 170, 234–35, 237, 241
  National Register of Citizens (NRC) process 124
  neoliberalism and 105–8
  overburdened docket 106–8
  polyvocal ideology 108
  populist turn 101
  public interest litigation (PIL) 101, 105–6
  refusal to hear constitutional challenges to the notice and objections regime 165–66
  reputation 165, 170

retirement benefits 142
sealed covers 124–25
self-preservation and reputational concerns 164–70, 234–35
Special Leave Petitions (SLPs) 100–1, 102, 122–23
strategic avoidance 123, 125
threats to independence 20
use of precedent 108
vulnerable appellants 123
Suri, Keshar 130

third-gender status 12–13
Thomas, Clarence 27–28, 50–51, 59–60, 70–71, 78, 79, 85, 97, 236, 241
traditional values 81
transgender community 25, 114–16, 169–70
transgender marriage 160, 191–93
transgender rights
changing official gender markers 204–7
India 144–50
transgender students 96
Trump, Donald 5, 32, 65–66, 67–68, 71, 72–73, 76, 83, 97, 242
immunity from criminal prosecution 74–75
Tse, Henry 204–5, 206–7

United Kingdom: Wolfenden Report 50, 235–36
United States 3, 4
Bill of Rights 34
civil and political rights 35
Civil War (1861–65) 34, 72
Constitution 33–34, 36
Fifth Amendment 85–91, 94, 95–96, 97
Fourteenth Amendment 72–73
culture wars 49–65
engagement with foreign materials 51–59, 61–63
judicial, scholarly, and political divide 51–56
originalism 59–61
Electoral College 67–68
gradual recognition (1986–2015) of LGBTQ+ rights
Bowers and "cultural war" 38–40
divided legal and cultural landscape 40–42
early years 36–38
rise of federal judicial supremacy 33–36
toward legalization and same-sex marriage 42–48
immigration 68–69
judicial polarization 69–71
media 69
political polarization 66–69
progressive change and conservative backlash 31
slavery 33–34
wealthy donors 68–69
United States Supreme Court 4–5, 13–15
303 Creative LLC v. Elenis 5, 32, 91, 93, 95–96, 97, 234, 236–37
accusations of partisanship 19–20
attitudinal model of judicial decision-making 29
Bostock 84–85, 96, 98, 151, 234
Bowers v Hardwick 38–40, 43–44, 49–51
citation of foreign sources 31, 51–59
conservative judicial appointments 32, 33, 242
conservative rulings 73–76
credibility 79
Dale v. Boy Scouts of America 32, 86–89, 90, 91, 94, 95–96
dignity claims 95–96
Dobbs v. Jackson Women's Health Organization 27–28, 30, 240–41
Fulton v. City of Philadelphia 5, 21, 32, 91, 92, 95, 97, 234, 236–37
hostility to precedent 80, 81
hybrid liberty/equality claims 95–96
institutional and reputational self-preservation 76–81, 96–98
judicial supremacy 36
justices' individual ideologies 233–34
Lawrence v. Texas 27–28, 31, 32, 42–44, 47–49, 96, 97, 150, 235–36, 240–41
LGBTQ+ rights in the second Roberts Court (2018–23) 81–96
expanding federal statutory protection 83–85
incrementally broadening exemptions 91–96
privileging the First Amendment 85–91
Masterpiece Cakeshop, Ltd. v. Colo. Civil Rights Comm'n 32, 87–88, 89–92, 93, 94, 95
Obergefell v. Hodges 27–28, 29–30, 31–32, 47, 48–49, 61–65, 81–82, 96–97, 150, 162–63, 235–36, 240–42
partisanship 72–76, 78, 79, 80, 81, 96–98
pinkwashing 240–41
Planned Parenthood v. Casey 27, 28, 29–30, 43–44, 53, 57–58, 70
power and accountability 36
presidential immunity 74–75
public opinion 16–17, 28, 29–30
reform proposals 77–79, 80–81
Roe v Wade 27–28, 35, 97

United States Supreme Court (*cont.*)
Romer v. Evans 4, 41–42, 43–44, 46–47, 48, 90–91, 95–96
shift towards institutional self-preservation 233–34
sociological legitimacy 80–81
strategic model of judicial decision-making 29, 30
structural independence 242
undermining the administrative state 75–76
unethical conduct of justices 78–79
United States v. Windsor 46–48, 96

Vajpayee, Atal Bihari 117, 119
Vidler, Michael 203

Washington Consensus 104
wedding cakes 88–89, 91
wedding websites 93, 94–95
Wolfenden Report 50, 235–36
World Health Organization 134
World Inequality Lab 119–20
World Values Survey 126–27

Xi Jinping 227

Yau Wai-Ching 180–81
Yogyakarta Principles 111, 115–16, 134
Yoshino, Kenji 95–96

Zarda, Donald 83

The manufacturer's authorised representative in the EU for product safety is Oxford University Press España S.A. of el Parque Empresarial San Fernando de Henares, Avenida de Castilla, 2 – 28830 Madrid (www.oup.es/en or product.safety@oup.com). OUP España S.A. also acts as importer into Spain of products made by the manufacturer.

www.ingramcontent.com/pod-product-compliance
Lightning Source LLC
LaVergne TN
LVHW011752200926
848484LV00003B/680

* 9 7 8 0 1 9 8 8 8 2 7 7 *